MODERN AMERICAN CENTERFIRE HANDGUNS

MODERN AMERICAN

Stanley W. Trzoniec

CENTERFIRE HANDGUNS

WINCHESTER PRESS • *Tulsa, Oklahoma*

Library of Congress Cataloging in Publication Data

Trzoniec, Stanley W.
Modern American centerfire handguns.

1. Pistols, American. I. Title
TS537.T79 683.4'3 81-10395
ISBN 0-87691-341-9 AACR2

Published by Winchester Press
1421 South Sheridan Road, P.O. Box 1260
Tulsa, Oklahoma 74101

A Talisman/Winchester Book

Book design by The Etheredges

Printed in the United States of America
1 2 3 4 5 85 84 83 82 81

Contents

To Inge
my wife . . .
        my best friend

Preface

Some of my best friends are gun writers. I enjoy their company and am comfortable with them. While part of this is undoubtedly based on a common interest in the finer points of firearms, their function, and uses, there is more.

I also admire competence and knowledge—and I have found that many gun writers demonstrate a comparatively high degree of these assets in their chosen subject matter.

Nevertheless, gun writers as a group are sometimes misunderstood and even unappreciated by their writing peers in other fields. A few years back, I was asked by the editors of an anthology of American outdoor writing to add a commentary on the contributions to this field by gun writers. The point I tried to make was simple. Over the years the American gun writer has done an outstanding job of serving the single, most basic function of the printed word: that function is to *inform*, to pass along to others useful and accurate information. My advice was to seek from the gun writer no more than ability in this primary function, and to treat anything else provided as a bonus.

Stanley Trzoniec, author of *Modern American Centerfire Handguns*, is a writer who gives you both. His coverage of the subject is broad, detailed, and accurate. If there is some aspect of centerfire handguns that Stan has omitted, I can't find it. The book shows ample evidence not only of his thorough familiarity with the subject but also of a lot of hard work to provide such comprehensive treatment.

The bonus that Stan Trzoniec bestows on us is his photography. It is superb. For the reader, this is more than an artistic bonus. It allows him to view the subject involved with a clarity of detail little removed from seeing the object first-hand. The fact that Stan Trzoniec is a photographer by profession is only part of the reason. I have seen some otherwise talented professional photographers come to grief trying to light and photograph correctly the frustrating combination of wood and multi-angled shiny metal surfaces of which guns are comprised. Gun photography is an art in itself, and Stan Trzoniec is one of a relatively small group that has mastered the art.

Since a good part of my work is to know and work with gun writers and to serve as their link to some forms of information, it was inevitable that Stan and I would meet. When we did, I was seeking him as much as he was seeking me, for I had already seen samples of his work. Since then we have shared services, to our mutual benefit and enjoyment.

Stan Trzoniec is a dedicated, enthusiastic, and knowledgeable gun man. There are, in the firearms field, those who appear on the scene for a time and then drift away to other areas. There are others who, one can often sense after a meeting or two, have come to stay.

I think Stan Trzoniec will be with us for a long time.

Richard F. Dietz

Foreword

Those who do not dwell in the world of firearms find it difficult to understand the fascination these instruments hold for many of us. There's nothing dark or Freudian about it; rather, a fine gun casts its spell in the same way as a Patek Philippe wristwach, a piece of fine Tiffany silver, or a Mercedes 250 SL.

The guns about which Stan Trzoniec writes are such things. They follow the uniquely American dictum of Frank Lloyd Wright: "Form follows function." They embody American craftsmanship, as typified by an engraved Smith & Wesson or the action of a Colt Custom Shop Python. Gingerly holding the first, you can feel your sensibilities getting lost in the intricate patterns of gold-inlaid steel, carved out particle by minute particle with the patient skill of masterly fingers. Squeeze the trigger of the second and metal rolls effortlessly on glass-polished metal, with a sensation like running your fingertip across Waterford crystal.

Within these pages, you'll also see a tribute to both American ingenuity and the Calvinist ethic. You'll see Ruger revolvers whose frames and internal parts are cast by lost-wax systems in one of the world's most modern plants, designed specifically for scientific production flow. Yet Rugers are not only smooth and graceful, but also marvels of rugged reliability, the equivalent of automobiles that can run a million miles.

You will see Dan Wesson revolvers, created in the 1960's by the scion of Smith & Wesson's founder. Saved from bankruptcy by new principles of both management and manufacturing, the Dan Wesson gun now equals the finest revolvers in finish, accuracy, and durability, sometimes at half the price. The difference is in new-wave sintered metal technology, in a heavily female labor force that has shattered myths about male dominance in handfitting of precision parts, and in brilliant engineering that finds less expensive ways to do the job better.

These things are the essence of Stan's book. The text is a valuable overview of today's U.S. centerfire handguns. There are guns Stan likes that I do not care for, but this means little; if we all agreed on everything, progress would be stifled. Indeed, fundamental disagreements between experts and engineers have richly benefitted the market with meaningful choices: the stainless steel forgings of the Smith & Wesson 600 series, versus the cast stainless mechanisms of the Ruger revolvers, versus the friction-free, corrosion-resistant electroless nickel finish on the new breed of Colts.

Like many in the field, I have enjoyed reading Stan Trzoniec's work. Guns are Stan's avocation, but fine industrial photography is his profession, and he has combined these two pursuits in a series of images taken with loving care and the highest degree of skill.

Novice or Master, the reader will be absorbed in these pages. Trzoniec's cameras have captured the clean lines, the painstaking polishing, and the user-oriented human engineering of America's finest handguns. Soft lighting and face powder do not work on cold polished steel. The beauty must be there intrinsically for the lens to capture. But this is only the first requirement. For those unfamiliar with firearms, a gun can be an ugly thing, its silhouette symbolic of the bad press it has received in a world where some minds link firearms with violence. It takes both a master photographer and a man who thoroughly understands handguns to bring out the beauty of their form and their function. Seen through the viewfinder of a tourist's Instamatic, Wright's magnificent Bannerstone House may look like a Chinese restaurant. Yet an architect with the proper Nikon lens can capture its enthralling sweep of line and open space in a way that takes the breath away.

Thus has Trzoniec captured the beauty of the American centerfire handgun, as you shall see when you browse through these pages. He rushes you in for close-ups that scrupulously probe the fine workmanship of these precision instruments, then he pans you back to full frames that show the guns sometimes in dynamic action, sometimes in a poised yet dignified repose that reminds you of a sleeping champion Alsatian.

He involves the reader. I see his shot of the Python laid out in stark simplicity next to the shooting paraphernalia, and I remember my first combat match with that gun in my hand, tension coursing through my fingers as I waited for the target to turn. His perfectly composed shot of the Gold Cup with snapshots of shooters running a Practical event transports me to the many moments I have vaulted such barricades with such a gun in my hand, my heart pounding with the exertion as I locked in on the target.

I thank Stan for rekindling these memories, and many more evoked as I read his galley proofs. I think you, the readers will have many such moments as you leisurely explore these pages.

For the newcomer to the handgun world, *Modern American Centerfire Handguns* is a very functional introduction to a complex spectrum of instrumentation. For the Master, it is a treat for the senses, coupled with the pervasive feeling that this writer/photographer *understands*.

And even for the non-shooter, or the person approaching firearms on the impetus of logic and against an ingrained fear of pistols and revolvers, it is a reassuring affirmation that guns are but the tools of man, like timepieces and serving trays and automobiles. They are tools that embody the finest traditions of engineering and workmanship for a user sophisticated and responsible enough to understand their parameters, use them wisely, and take pride and pleasure in owning them.

It is for all of these reasons, and especially the last, that Stanley W. Trzoniec's *Modern American Centerfire Handguns* is destined to occupy a permanent spot on my coffee table.

Massad F. Ayoob
Handgun Editor, *GUNS* magazine
Associate Editor, *HANDGUNNER* magazine

Introduction

It may seem strange that the beginning of a book is the place where one reflects on the closing few moments of over a year's work. During that year, dozens of phone calls were made, hundreds of photographs taken, and thousands upon thousands of words written. Then the whole ball of wax was typed, once in a rough draft, then once again in its final form for the publisher. If it sounds like a lot of work, it was!

In spite of the work involved, I cannot help but be saddened by the fact that all those sleepless nights thinking about how to start this paragraph or finish that chapter are now behind me. It's like losing a friend. MACH, as it was affectionately known around the house, is now being put to rest, which is one way of looking at it, but maybe coming alive is a better word. For in its printed form, it not only contains my observations, but literally hundreds of ideas and opinions of people all across the country.

Therefore, to say this book is mine alone would be simply untrue. While researching this book, I met so many super people in the industry who unselfishly gave their time, their knowledge, and their expertise. It is these people who give an author substance, and make him whole. Until the next project, I will miss the contact with them all. They are friends in the truest sense, and they deserve the title without reservation.

Webster defines a preface as "an introduction to a book which explains its scope, intention or background." In short, the scope of this book is American centerfire handguns. The intention was to compile a reference book with illustrations, comments, and specifications on all handguns now in production in the United States. By going through the book, I think you'll agree that most of this intention was realized. I know there may be some models or companies missing, but this is in no way a reflection on the quality or durability of the product. In most cases it can be justified because a particular model was not available when I needed it. Then again, this could lead to a revision at a later date.

Now that makes me happy! A revision. Another project. More friends. What more could a fellow ask for!

MACH, live on forever.

SWT
1980

Acknowledgments

A well-deserved and hard-earned thanks goes out to all the firearm, accessory, reloading and component manufacturers that you will see mentioned or illustrated in this book. They were all unfailing in their efforts to supply equipment (even under some really tight chapter deadlines) for evaluation or photography. During the writing of this book I have never worked with a more understanding group of people. Thanks fellows!

Because of the very nature of their jobs, a few must be given extra consideration for their efforts on my behalf!

Roy Jinks, Smith & Wesson
Bill Clede, in association with Smith & Wesson
Judy Burham, Colt's Firearm Division
Richard Dietz, Remington Arms
John Falk, Winchester Arms
Howard French, *Guns and Ammo* magazine
Lee Jurras, Jurras Associates
Public relations staff at Sturm, Ruger and Company.

For graphic illustrations, my thanks goes to *Guns and Ammo*, Sierra Bullets, and DBI Books for their kind permission to reproduce certain line drawings and photographs.

My deep appreciation and heart-felt thanks go to Peter and Beth Barnard for all their work in producing the fine line drawings in the reloading chapter. My thanks also to John MacAdams and Steve Clews, my friendly neighborhood gun dealers, who helped me round up numerous products for photographic purposes.

And finally, I am deeply indebted to Bob Elman at Winchester Press for helping me to fulfill a lifelong dream.

SMITH & WESSON
PYTHON 357

ONE

The American Handgun

Since the beginning of the fourteenth century, man has conducted a love affair with the handgun. The ability to carry a small and powerful sidearm has intrigued many from the days of old on through colonial times and up into the present.

And this is where we will begin; the present. The modern American centerfire handgun of today is both a marvel of engineering and dependability. It carries with it a heritage of craftsmanship unsurpassed by any other country in the world. But perhaps most of all, American handguns display a certain pride and workmanship that one is hard pressed to find in many of today's products. Superlative steel, good walnut, and hard work are combined to bring the American handgunner one of the finest products ever made.

The pleasures of owning a finely crafted, well-balanced handgun can be expressed in a number of ways. To the spirited hunter who perhaps has traveled hundreds of miles, a humane kill on a superb trophy after a long and trying stalk is truly thrilling. Perhaps he has used a Colt Python with a fine single- or double-action pull to place the shot exactly where he envisioned before the trigger was pulled. By combining his skills and tailoring his handloads to the gun and to his type of shooting, the hunter now has the complete confidence needed to do the job right the very first time.

Most combat-type shooting requires the inherent speed and agility of a semiautomatic pistol, such as the Colt .45 Auto. Now don't get me wrong, combat shooting in no way requires that you *must* use an auto, for many fellows use revolvers. The original intent was to show that the much fabled auto can be used effectively and lethally in any combat situation. Along with this new sport comes a myriad of accessories such as new sights, grips, ambidextrous safeties, holsters, and other gear which you shall read about later on.

To the gun buff, the game of silhouette shooting has grown rapidly over the last

A modern and efficient Colt Python is the choice of many who may choose the sport of handgun hunting.

Equipped with a .45 Auto, the hardened combat shooter must rely on concentration, speed and accuracy to ensure good solid hits downrange.

High energy cartridges and bolt action guns like this Remington XP-100 are just the ticket for the long-range silhouette fans.

couple of years. Using pistols with barrel lengths up to 10¾ inches in the production-grade series, you try your luck at iron chickens at 50 meters, javelina at 100 meters, turkeys at 150, and finally, for the real sharp-eyed troops, the rams out at the 200-meter mark. Only iron sights are used, and two grades are allowed, production and unlimited classes. In the production class, you are limited to a factory-run gun, special barrel length, and 4 pounds of weight. The unlimited class is for the daring and innovative. Fancy stocks, longer barrels, rifle actions with rifle cartridges are turning these guns into "handgun rifles" to hit those 52-pound targets. If you love to experiment, this may be the sport for you.

Target shooters, or "paper punchers" as they are known throughout shooting circles, use the precision shooting instrument, the target revolver or semiautomatic pistol. A handgun made to a stringent requirement of 2-inch groups at 50 yards narrows the field considerably. The S&W Model 52 and the Colt Gold Cup are semiautomatics well suited to the task, as are the K-38 single action and Model 25 .45 ACP in the revolver class. Add to this the fact that there are literally dozens of fine men around the country who specialize in tuning guns for the aspiring competitive shooter, and you now have a field of fellows with good eyes, steady nerves and a strong desire to win by placing all their shots in that small X ring at regional, state, and national shoots.

To the collector, a special tribute must be paid. For he is the man who can take us back into history, show us details of a Colt .44-40 revolver we never had seen before, and preserve for future generations the guns that made this country famous. There is also the serious gun buff who will buy a gun for its beauty or possibly because it is a rare find. Some

Bullseye target shooting, perhaps the oldest form of handgun competition, is alive and well thanks to precision pistols such as the Smith and Wesson Model 52 shown here.

also decide to collect the various commemorative series now on the market in greater numbers and at even greater prices. For a hedge against inflation, it's worth your while to investigate this field.

After reading the above brief summaries of the various gun-related activities, it should come as no surprise to anyone breaking into the shooting game, that there is an almost unlimited supply as far as gun models go. Let's look at the basic actions available, some of the design differences, and let's touch on a few options available. More on any particular model will be found in the catalog sections of the book, under the various manufacturers.

A revolver, so stated, is a gun with a cylinder revolving around a central axis holding five or six shots in a centerfire handgun. When the hammer is cocked, a lever pushes up on the hand, rotating the cylinder to a fresh round. As the round is brought up to the firing position, the cylinder stop then takes over, stopping the cylinder, holding it in place until the round is fired. The dropping of the hammer completes the cycle and fires the round. This is the single action mode of ignition.

With double-action revolvers, the shooter pulls on the trigger (although the trigger arch would be much longer than single action) thereby operating the hammer by mechanic leverage in the gun's mechanism. This is used to get the gun into action quickly, as would be the case of drawing from a holster and facing a frenzied or armed opponent.

The semiautomatic pistol is another type of action and can, like the revolver, be fired single- or double-action, depending on the sidearm used. Using a Colt .45 in the cocked and locked mode, all one has to do is draw his weapon, flip off the safety and fire. Using a S&W Model 39 or 59, all he has to do is draw and squeeze the trigger. The hammer will come back and strike the primer as soon as it has reached its limit of its rearward travel. Of course all this will happen only if one has the foresight to load the auto via the clip and pull back the slide to charge the weapon.

Herein lies the makings of a great debate. Many police departments frown on the idea of their men walking around with a loaded cartridge lying just under that firing pin. They are afraid that a blow on the hammer, even in the cocked and locked position, will set the gun off. I see no point in their argument as a police officer walking around all day with a revolver faces the same problem unless he carries only five rounds. Any blow severe enough to set off a semiautomatic will, in my opinion, do likewise for the revolver. No doubt the debate will go on, for wherever there is a choice (auto versus revolver) there is going to be a difference of opinion.

Another popular action is the single-shot. Here the T/C Contender and Jurras-type pistols shine. In a single shot there is no cylinder gap to hinder the performance of high powered loads like the bigger magnums. There is no gap in the automatics either, but they only handle loads in the range of .380-.45 ACP. The Auto-Mag and Wildey are exceptions of course, but both deal in their own specialized and stylized ammunition.

The single shots lend themselves to the experimenter. The Contender will digest loads in the rifle category, as in the case of chambering the .35 Remington and .30-30 Winchester. Chambered for one of these cartridges, scoped with a bright 2× scope and hung on the body with a shoulder holster, it comes darn close to an ideal weapon for the eastern whitetail deer hunter.

When it comes to design, hardly any two companies are alike. For example, Smith & Wesson cylinders turn left, their rifling goes right. Colt's cylinders go right and their rifling goes in the opposite direction, left. Smith's cylinder release goes forward, Colt's pulls back and Ruger's pushes in. The safeties on the S&W automatics go off when pushed up, Colt's famed .45 goes off when pushed down. Now you can see how important it is to know your

In single action shooting, the gun is cocked by merely pulling back the hammer.

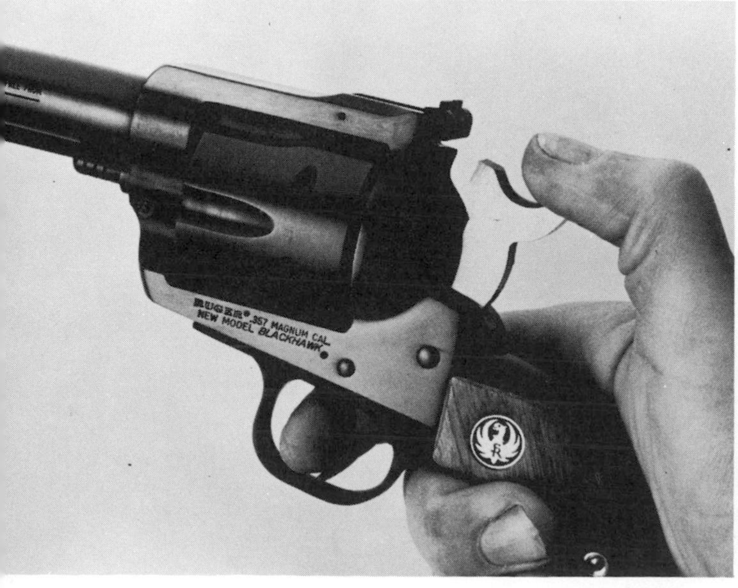

DA (or double action) revolvers require the user to pull the trigger back in one swift motion to cock and fire the weapon.

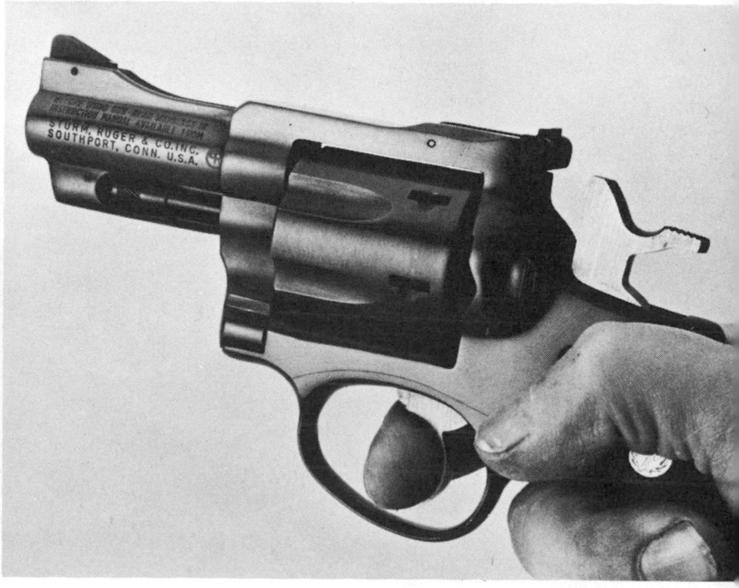

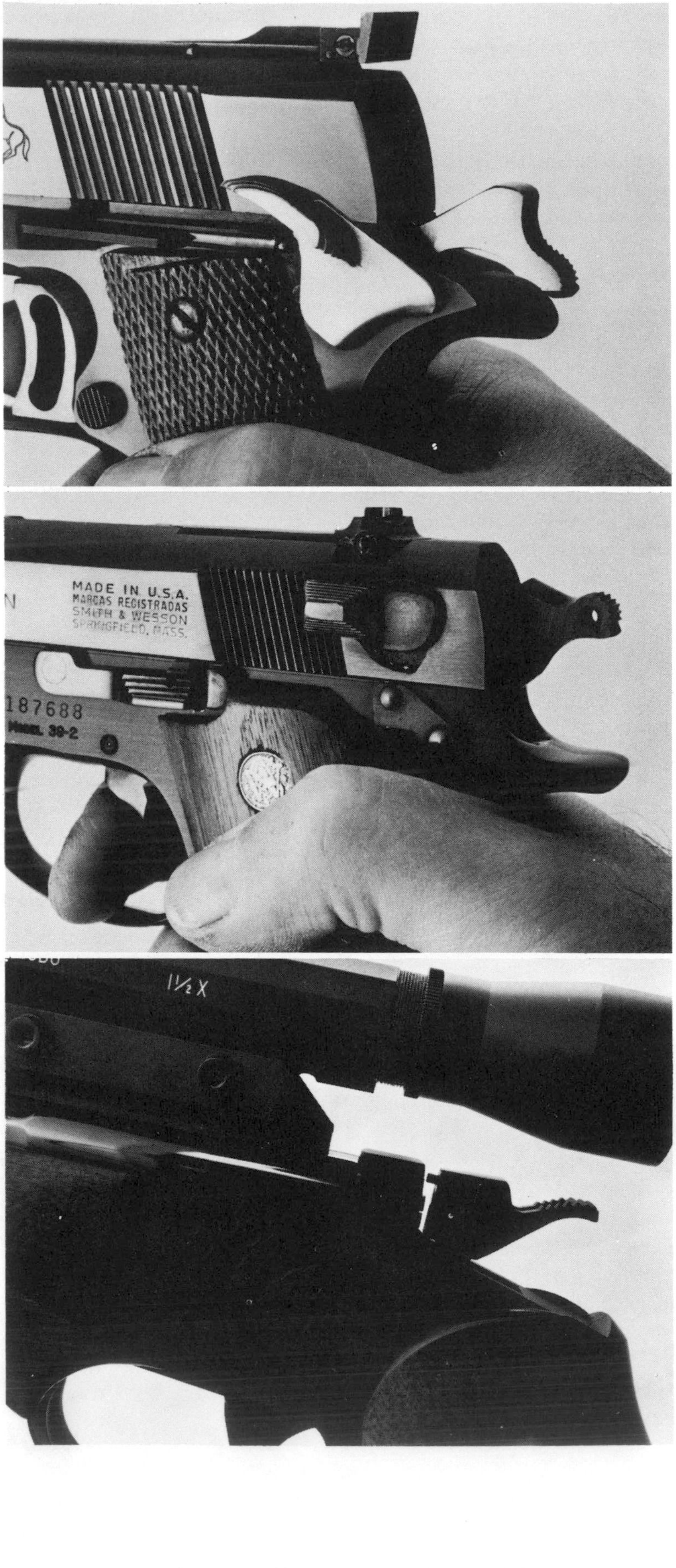

A

B

C

Safety interlocks come in many configurations such as the Colt type (A), Smith & Wesson (B), and a novel approach by Thompson/Center (C).

particular sidearm when the chips are down, whether in a heated competition or up against an unfriendly attacker.

Rate of twist is also different in various sidearms. Besides going right or left, they also turn in different degrees. Taking the popular .357 caliber as one example we find that in the Colts, it makes one complete turn every 14 inches, in the Rugers every 16 inches, in the Contenders every 18 inches and finally in the Smiths every 18¾ inches. Looking at the above we can say that Colt has a fast twist, the Smiths a much slower rate.

Which is better? There have been tests recently pitting the Colt against the Smith. The Colt with its faster rate of twist seemed to stabilize bullets better, especially the wadcutters. But in this field, unlike others, there are so many variables—such as depth of rifling, outside diameter of the bullet, weighing of the powder charge, primer mixture—that it is really hard to pin anything down, and I am certainly not going to do it here.

For the record, and your curiosity, the Colt Python did better then the Smith, but not by much. My final word here is that it is up to the shooter. Pick a gun you like, reload for it, run it through the mill, tune it, balance it, but the point I want to stress is, make the gun work for you.

For variety in your firearms, the American arms makers have rallied to the cause. I'll be going into greater detail in Chapter Seven, dealing with factory and specialized accessories, but here I'd like to touch on a few of the more popular items that are available on direct order factory guns.

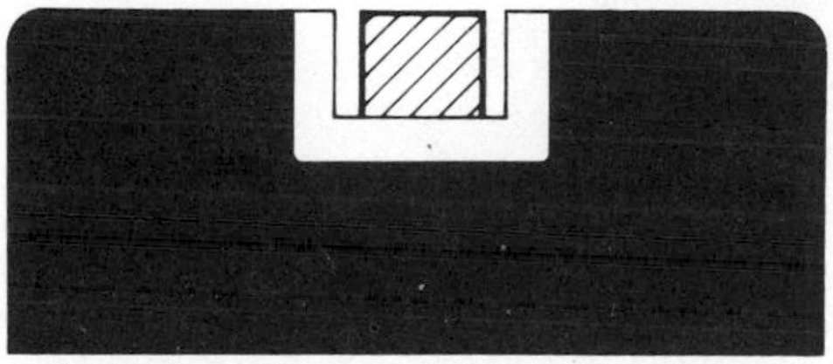

The perfect sight picture is shown here. The front sight (crosshatch) is perfectly centered and leveled with the rear sight blade.

SIGHTS

Since the sights are the first item you see when you pick up and point a handgun, we'll start there. Depending on that model and caliber you choose, your sights will be one of two types; either fixed or moveable.

Fixed sights consist of nothing more than a ramp front sight and a grooved channel (U or V type) cut into the frame to serve as a rear sight. They are *simplicity* themselves and are usually the first choice of working professionals; the cop on the beat, private detectives and full-time working soldiers. Detailed sighting is accomplished by filing down front sight for elevation or using a brass drift for rear windage.

Movable, or target sights are available on most American centerfire guns. They consist of a blade that will move, by way of adjustment screws, either horizontally or vertically, to compensate for windage and elevation. To center a group on the target you must move the rear sight in the direction in which you want the group to move. Hence if the group is to be higher, elevate the sight. If to the right, move the sight to the right. Depending on your gun, each click will average out to about ⅜ inches in elevation or about ¼ inch for windage at a 50 meter distance. On a home defense gun they are known for not getting the piece snagged on a nearby curtain or worse yet, your robe, and these are worries you don't need in the middle of the night.

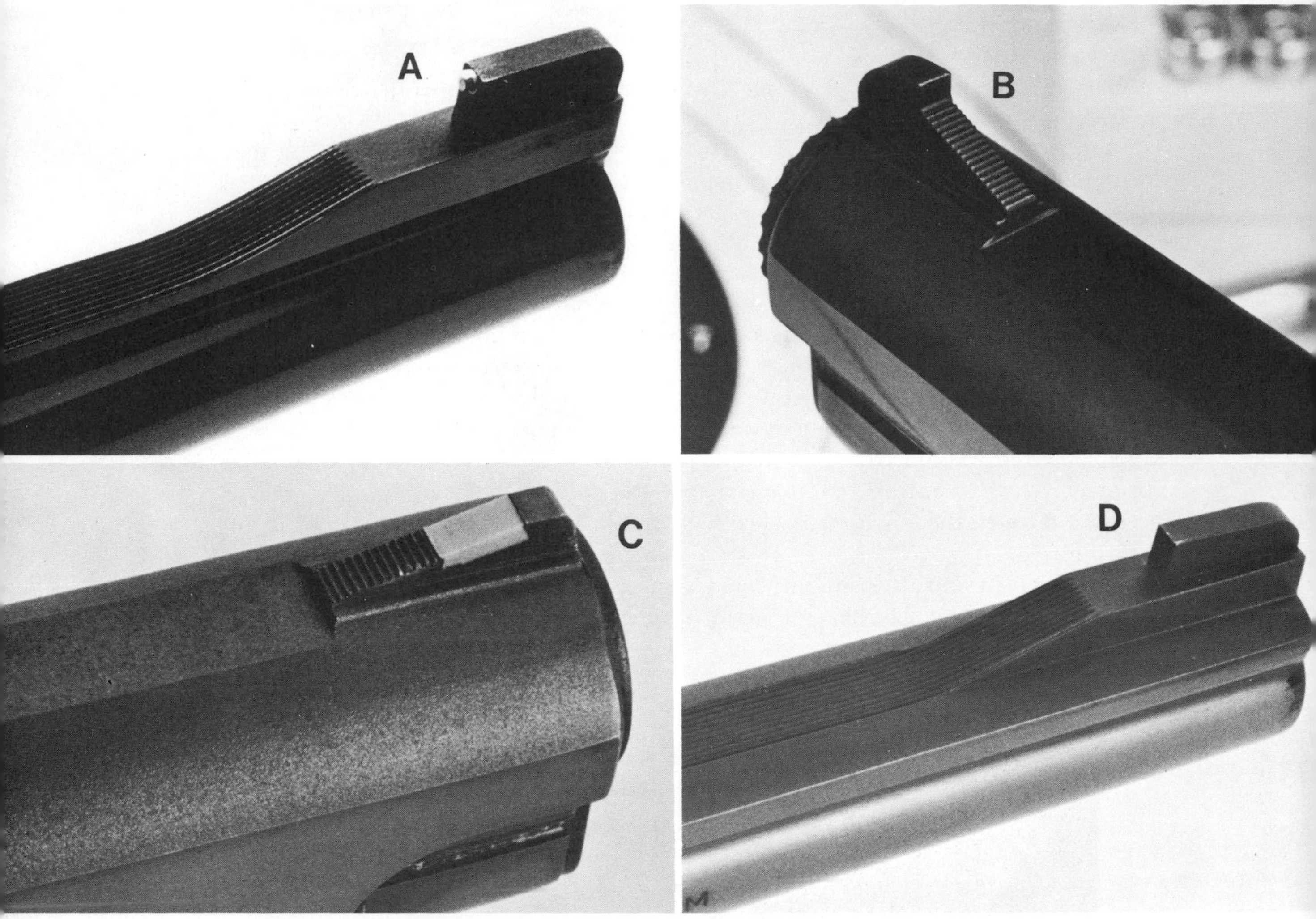

Depending on the use, front sight blades come in (A) Gold bead on a Patridge blade, (B) Target Patridge (C) ramp with a red insert and (D) plain Patridge blade.

On the front sight, Smith & Wesson has one of the most complete selections of front sight options. Depending on the model, some can be factory ordered and others must be installed after purchase because of the type of installation required. Consult the most recent catalog for advice on any and all options.

As of this printing I can count no less than six different front ramp styles with eight possibilities of installing your favorite on a ramp base or blade. This selection consists of the following target sights and comes in a width of ⅛ inch only. You can choose from a Patridge, Baughman, S&W Red Ramps, S&W Red Post, McGivern Gold Bead, and a Call Gold Bead front sight insert. Bear in mind here, the above are only available in large (N) and medium (K) frame models that carry a full length barrel rib.

The field narrows when you approach the rear sight. Here your choice is limited to either a plain black or a white outline rear slide.

For owners of the Model 39 and Model 59 semiautomatic pistols, S&W has just recently brought out a fine, fully-adjustable rear sight. This is available only as an accessory item and is furnished complete with simple instructions for installation. Versatility is the byword as this item is adjustable for both windage and elevation, whereas the original equipment is good only for windage.

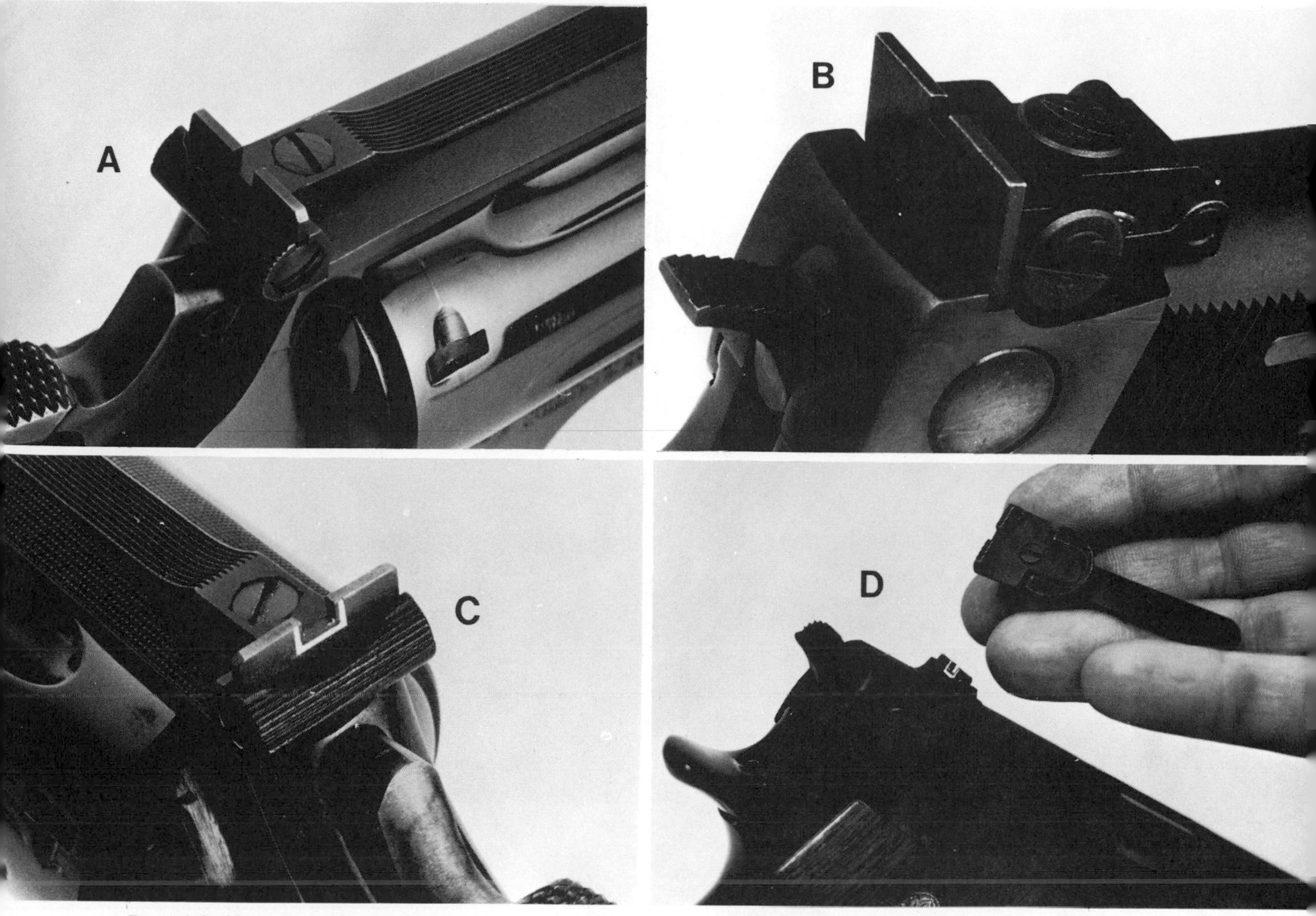

Rear sight blades are offered in many varieties and include (A) plain, (B) coin adjustable target (C) white outline, and (D) replaceable assembly for factory equipment needing both windage and elevation as in the Smith & Wesson Model 39.

Colt also has a choice of sights—not as extensive as S&W, but enough to satisfy most users. Fixed sights come standard on their Single Action Army, Detective Special, and Lawman Mark III Series, as well as the Government Model autos.

Fully adjustable rear sights (with a ramped front blade) are standard equipment on their premium guns which include the New Frontier, Trooper Series, and Pythons. The .45

Examples of some Colt front sights include the basic smooth ramp for easy draw on a Detective Special and a no-nonsense front blade on the famous "Peacemaker."

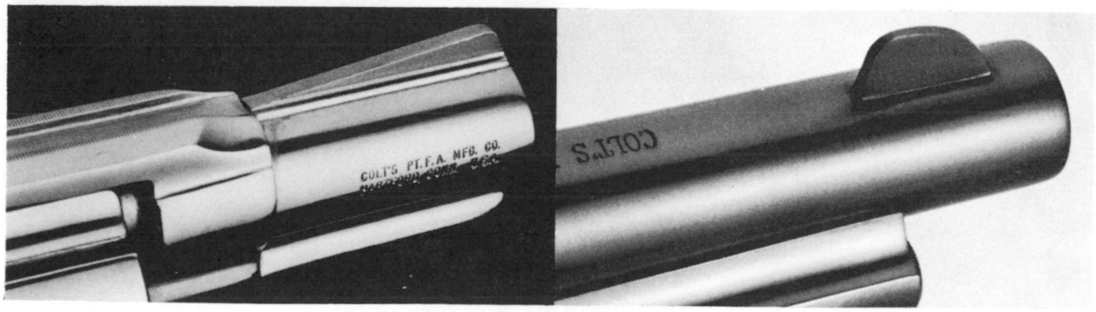

Gold Cup carries the Elliason target sights, and these may be special ordered on the Python for that "family appearance" in your firearms.

The Ruger family of handguns carry either fixed or Micro rear sights depending on the model and caliber. This is par for all of the independents that make up the rest of the firearms industry.

An exception to the above would be the Ruger and Dan Wesson front sights. The new Ruger .44 Magnum Redhawk will offer removeable front blades with different colors to suit any shooter. Dan Wesson has had this for years with your choice of red, yellow and white, plus a Patridge blade that slips in and out of a milled slot on the barrel rib. An Allen screw keeps it there even with the tremendous recoil of the bigger calibers.

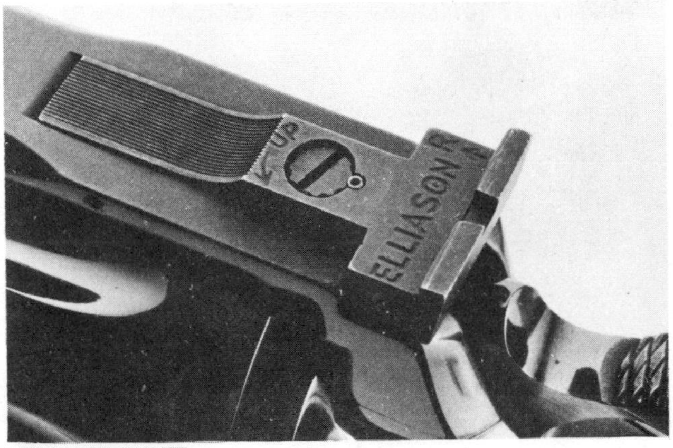

For the purist, the Colt Elliason rear sight assembly mounted on a Python is a rugged and trouble-free piece of equipment.

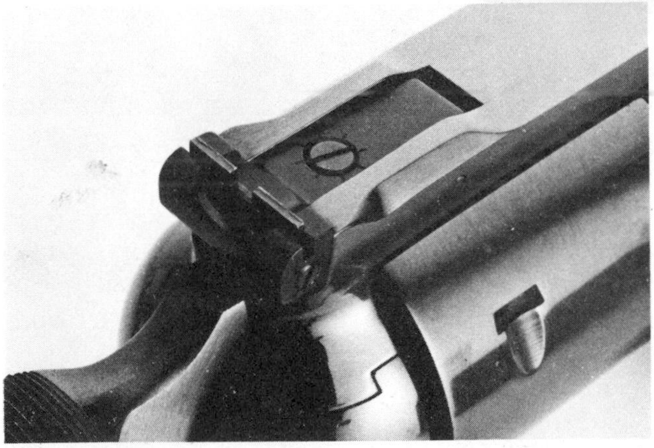

For guns capable of generating severe recoil, such as the Ruger .44 Magnum, small, streamlined sights are the answer.

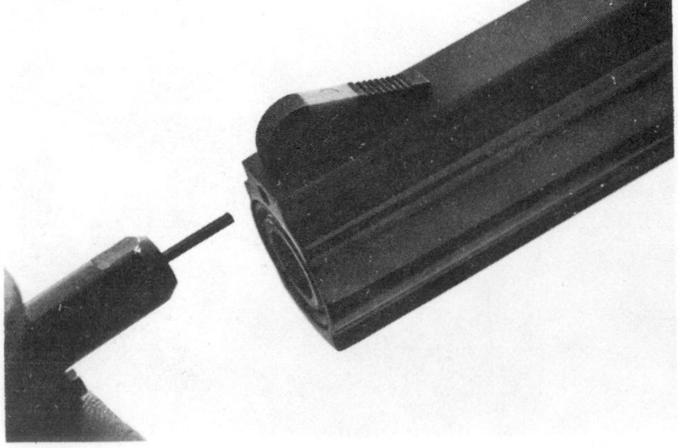

Dan Wesson Arms was the first maker to offer interchangeable front sights in colors on their top of the line .357 Magnum revolvers.

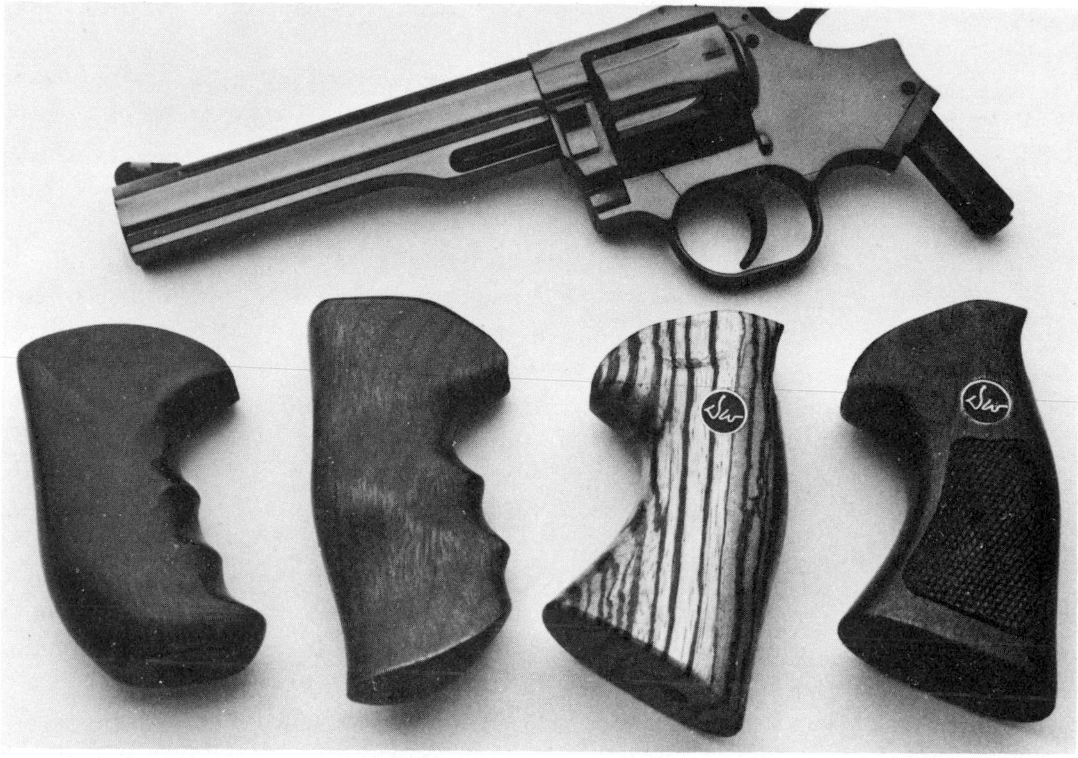

With Dan Wesson's neat way of attaching grips, anything is possible from combat (left) to target style (right) in fancy or walnut-grained woods.

From Goncalo Alves to walnut, these S&W grips will add a certain amount of "class" to any of their guns.

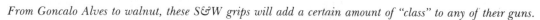

GRIPS

As grips are a very personal item, I am only going to touch on them briefly here.

The great American firearms machine has been very receptive to the wants and needs of the average shooter. You can get grips that are checkered or smooth, with or without a "combat cut" for speedloaders, plain or fancy woods, and grips to fit just about every hand from magna (small) to target-style configurations (large).

With the exception on my Ruger single action guns, all of my big bore handguns carry grips of checkered wood. For me the checkering works in many ways. First, when I grip the piece I know it will stay there when fired, and two, the checkering helps me to keep that same position after the weapon has been fired. This is very important on a string of double-action shooting in a match. During a timed phase, any time taken to reposition the hand will undoubtedly lead to points lost in the heat.

Walnut is the traditional wood for grips and has been for many years. This is the wood that goes on 75 percent of the factory guns made. Well, what about the other 25 percent?

If you special order a gun from S&W with different sights or trigger, for example, you can specify that they equip your new handgun with Rosewood or Goncalo Alves fancy wood, which is available smooth or checkered. A word to Dan Wesson Arms will get either fancy walnut or striking zebra wood. They also offer in their "Quickshift" series a block of walnut for the aspiring stockmaker to whittle out a grip that suits him perfectly.

Ruger offers its "Bib Grip" as an option on its Security Six DA revolvers. Colt offers a multitude of shapes and styles and the custom shop can fix you up with a pair of fancy Rosewood, Cocobolo or even pewter for its Model O-frame autoloaders. If your tastes run to the super fancy, they can outfit you to a pair of ivory grips for your favorite Colt product.

The list is, of course, endless, and will get even more staggering when you reach the chapter on accessories. To round out the spectrum we will also go into custom grips that some stockmakers will shape to fit your hand.

FINISH

Like grips, the outside finish on any handgun is a very personal preference. The most common type is blue in color and most naturally is called "bluing". Your work guns carry the satin finish while factory premium guns will carry a brilliant high gloss bluing that could almost pass for black chrome. Smith calls theirs bright blue; Colt has named their finish royal blue. Either way, a lot of polishing is required on the piece before it is applied. Only skilled craftsmen with many years at the plant get to do this job.

Against the popular bluing, durability is poor compared to other finishes. With constant use, it will wear on the tip of the muzzle, cylinder sides and trigger guards. To the policeman it is a poor choice, but to the collector who will purchase a gun to look at, the choice is excellent. It is a handsome finish and will last if proper care is exercised through the life of the firearm.

Nickel plating probably comes next in popularity, as many factory guns are available in this finish. The old wives' tale that a nickel gun will spook game is just that, an old wives' tale. When hiking through the woods, the gun is holstered until the last minute and by then it is too late for the quarry to get a bead on your gun. Considering you are under cover, the chances are very small indeed that a reflection will send the game bounding over hill and

Because of popular demand, some Ruger guns are available with a "Bib Grip" for fuller control of the gun during double action shooting.

Colt Firearms is one manufacturer who offers various grip styles in a wide assortment of woods, metal designs, and natural ivory.

dale before you get your shot in. And if it still bothers you, some factory guns come with a satin nickel finish. Durability is excellent, although in years you may experience some flaking or cracking of the finish. Application to the gun is cold, and I rate it as the best plating for handguns.

The new kid on the block is stainless steel. As it is not an outside finish, but a structural material. Durability is by far the best, for no matter how much you wear the outside of the piece down, you're not going through the finish. Resistance to corrosion is excellent and most manufacturers offer it in one style, brushed.

As with nickel-plated guns, the factories have blessed us with blue sights on their stainless guns as well, a definite aid in sighting on a bright day.

Exterior finishes available on today's handguns include royal blue, stainless, nickel, and non-glare satin-finished blue.

BARRELS

Gun barrels for American production handguns range in length from the 2-inch "snubbie," favored by police detectives, to 15 inches in the Dan Wesson series. Actually anything above 8 inches has little value except in specialized areas like silhouette or long range varmint shooting. Practical use dictates the 6-inch as the best for all around general use. The handy 4-inch length gets the nod from our uniform officers who must, because of their profession, wear a gun all day long. It is easy to draw, and for getting in and out of police cruisers it can't be beat, unless you wear a swivel rig.

In a shoulder holster, the handgun hunter can carry the 8-inch size through the heaviest of blowdowns or tallest of mountains and still keep both hands free for climbing and keeping his balance.

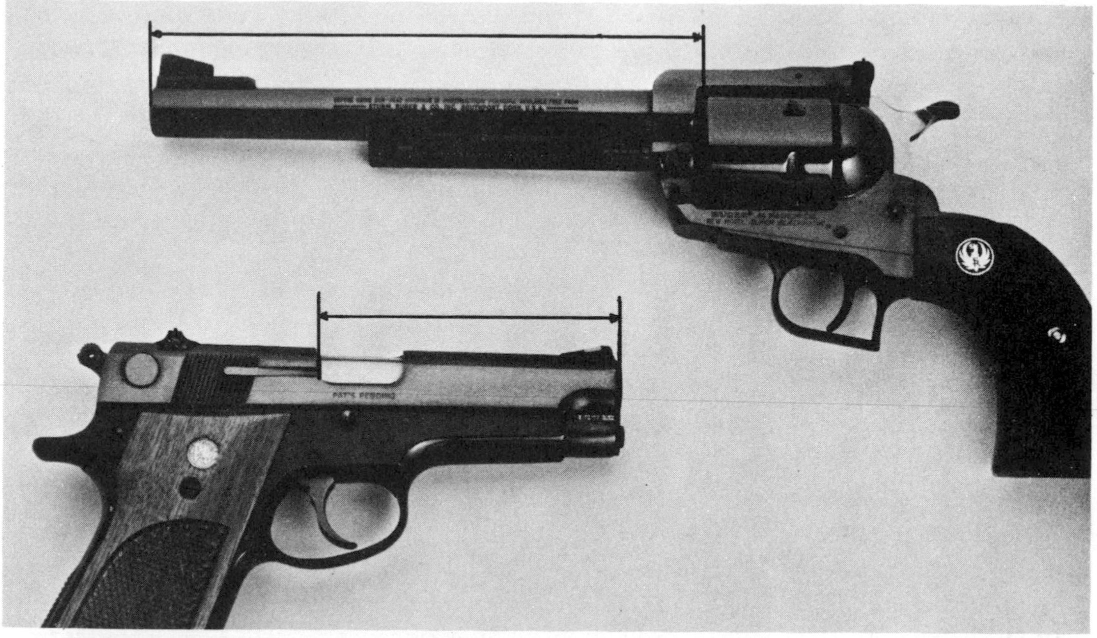

Barrel length is measured on revolvers from the face of the cylinder to the muzzle, and on semiautomatics, from the rear part of the ejection port to the muzzle.

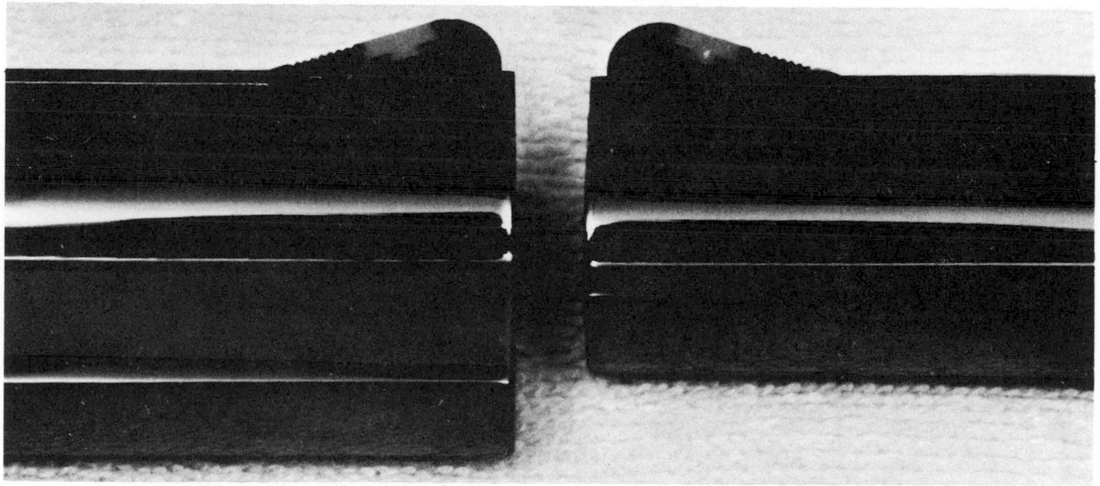

Since some shooters like their handguns "muzzle heavy," Dan Wesson offers a choice of heavy (left) or regular (right) barrel weights.

Today's modern handgun barrels are made from SAE 4140 steel. It is extremely high in tensile strength and, unlike stainless steel, machines easy. SAE 4140 is an alloy, consisting of chromium and molybdenum, and it makes for a very tough steel blend. Commonly called chrome-moly in the trade, it serves the needs of the manufacturers well.

Revolver barrels are measured from the face of the cylinder to the end (or muzzle) of the barrel. Semiautomatic pistols are measured from the back portion of the ejection port, or the face of the slide, to the end of the barrel. Besides using this yardstick to help figure out which holster you'll need, you can also use this information to calculate bullet velocity loss in any given barrel length when computing the difference, for example, between a 6- or 8-inch tube, but only in a general sort of way. The barrel itself is not exactly the determining factor for calculations. What you need to make very exact computations is what ballistics experts call the expansion ratio. This includes the barrel length and chamber (or cartridge case) volume. But, for the amateurs that we are, if you figure roughly 65-75 feet per second per inch in magnum handguns, you can come pretty close to the right velocity.

In conclusion, you have the final word in what you want and what you need. Consider the job the gun has to fill (target, hunting, etc.), what barrel length is handy for the job and then go from there.

To make matters even worse for your decision making, most manufacturers give you a choice of a standard, heavy or bull-type barrel. In the S&W family, their Model 19 carries a barrel diameter of roughly .685 inches, while the Model 29 .44 Magnum carries a diameter of .890 inches. Rugers Super Blackhawk (old model) has a 7½-inch barrel and a diameter averaging .725 inches. No one follows a pattern. Each maker tries to put on a barrel that will be best for the weight or balance of the piece.

When considering balance, handle the gun or guns that you are seriously contemplating. For instance, if you desire the weight out front, choose a Colt Python. The Python's muzzle heaviness is due to its ventilated rib and barrel underlug. It makes for a rock-steady handgun for punching paper or chucks. On automatics, one can get an extended slide to push the balance of the piece forward, but since this is custom work, the cost will be higher.

For those of you who like the balance "in the hand", most American handguns will fit the need. But bear in mind, the longer the barrel the more muzzle-heavy the piece will be.

On modern revolvers with swing-out cylinders, the ejector rod will fall under the barrel. The design of the piece will dictate how the rod is placed. There are basically three different positions. It will either hang there in mid-air, be attached at the end to form a lock, or be completely enclosed. This is the way most firearm makers have chosen for their near magnum or magnum handguns. On single action guns, the ejector rod is housed under the barrel and is used to literally punch the fired cases out of the cylinder.

The 6-inch barrel, as shown on this Colt Python, is the most popular length among handgunners.

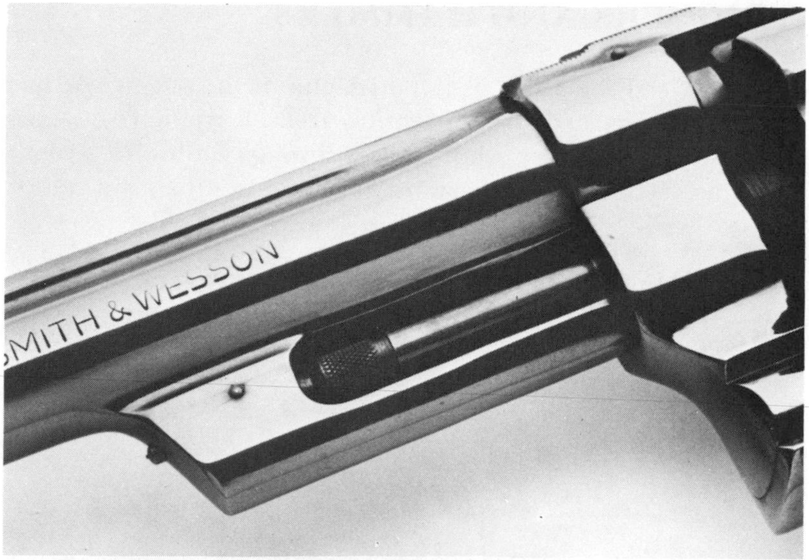

All revolvers, especially police models, should have a fully protected ejector rod. A damaged rod could mean the difference between life and death in a tense situation.

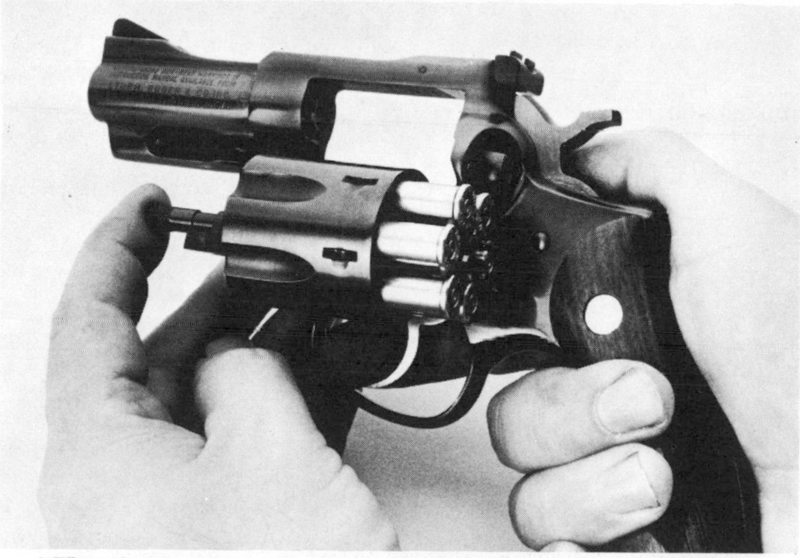

Cases are ejected all at once in double action revolvers; one at a time in single action guns.

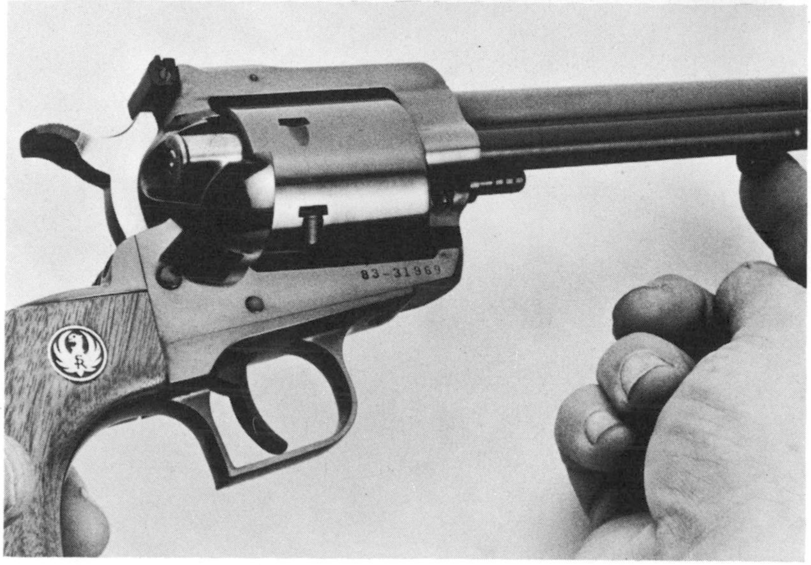

TRIGGERS AND HAMMERS

Often termed the heart of any handgun, both trigger and hammer work in unison to deliver the force necessary for positive, reliable ignition of the primer. The hammer is the spring-driven member which moves through an arc to strike the primer and fire the cartridge. When moved rearward, it compresses the main spring and is held cocked by a

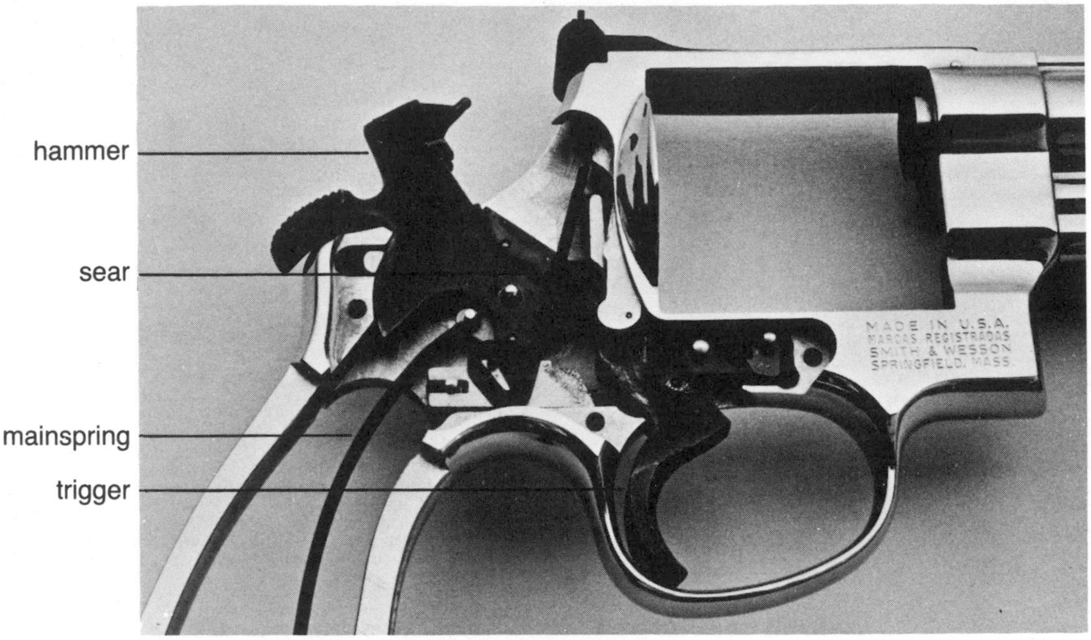

Smith & Wesson's time-tested and proven lockwork designs are dependable in all situations. The illustration shows the gun in the full-cock mode.

There is a wide variety of trigger styles to choose from. Shown are: (A) wide target type on a S&W M27; (B) standard service width on the Ruger Security Six; (C) smooth combat on the S&W M49; and (D) a Colt Gold Cup with a wide adjustable trigger.

A

B

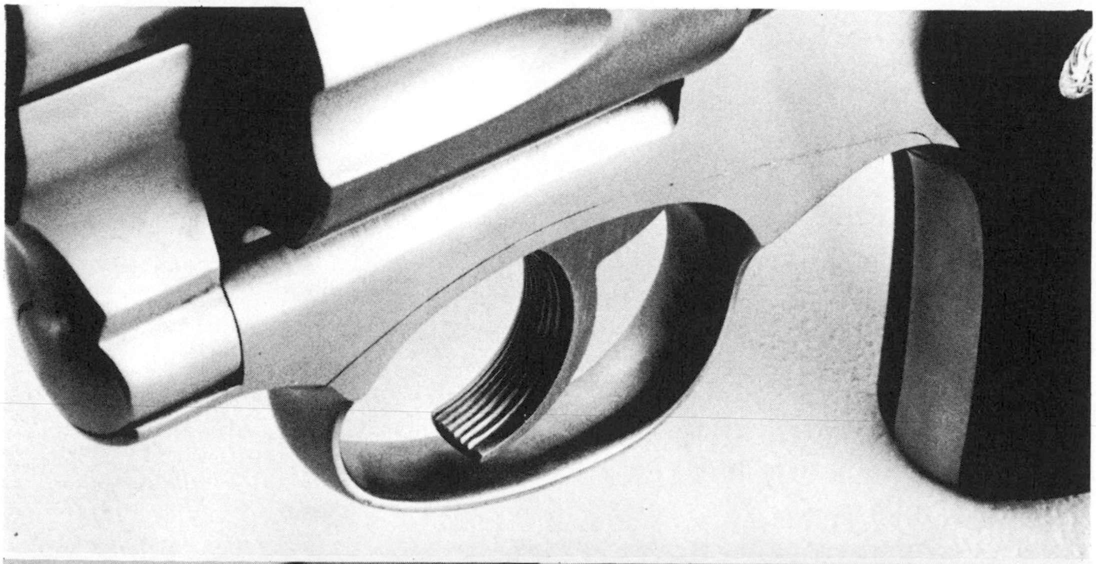

C

D

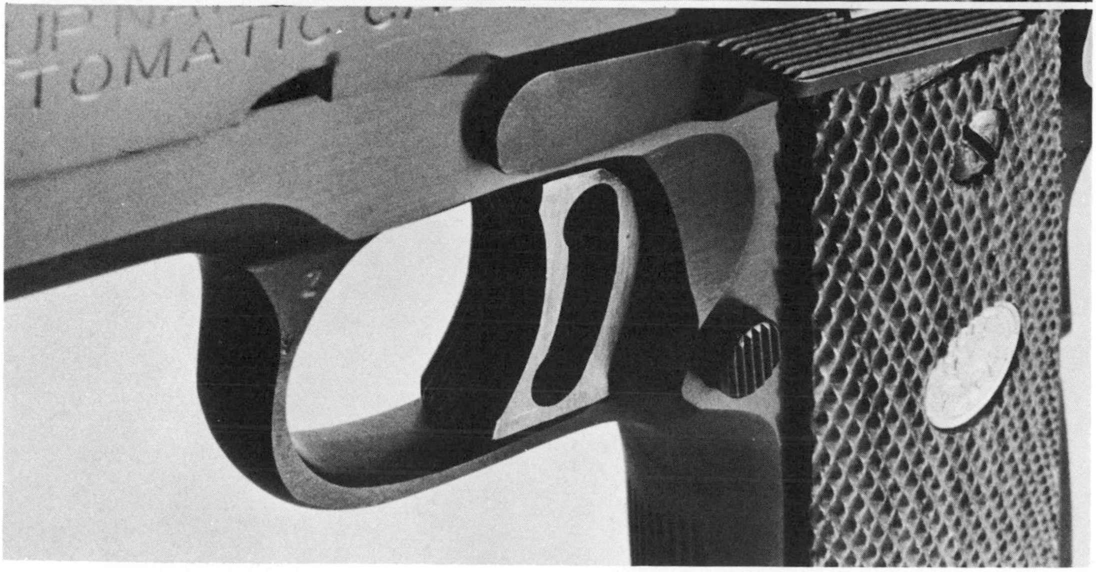

sear. Trigger pressure will disengage the sear, allowing the hammer to fall against the primer.

Again, like many of the other parts on the handgun, you have a choice here. One can order either standard or target widths in triggers, with smooth (combat) or serrated (target) finishes as additional options. Personal requirements will dictate your choice here. If you do a lot of single-action target shooting, the serrated will fit you well. If, on the other hand, your forte is double-action combat shooting, a smooth trigger will allow better control of your finger by allowing it to actually "roll" on the trigger.

The trigger pull of any piece is a topic of conversation that often rises above taxes, religion and the country. A person who will shoot extremely well with his personal pistol will more often than not do poorly with another gun. This has been proven to me more than once, and if you should disagree, try it with another fellow. Take two identical guns, making sure both have different trigger pulls (in pounds). Shoot yours first. Then shoot your friend's and you undoubtedly will pull your shots to one side or the other. This is why

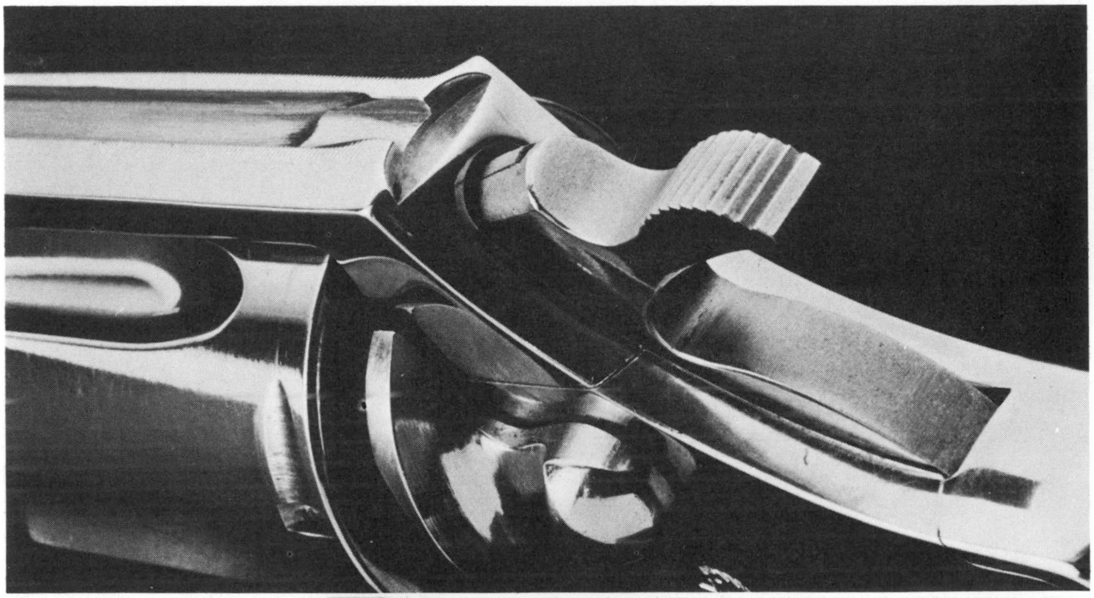

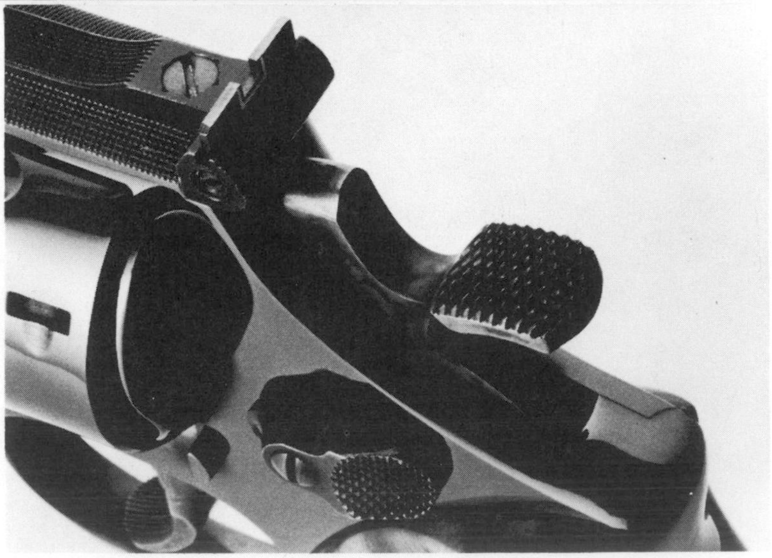

Hammers vary from the service type (A) on a Colt Detective Special to the wider target type as installed on a S&W M27 (B).

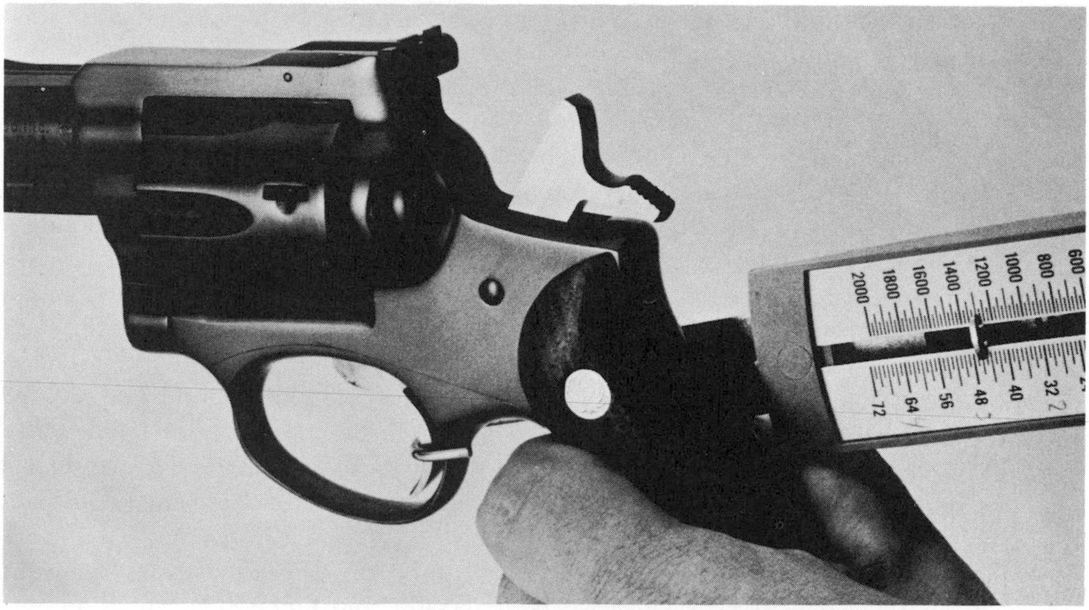

For serious target shooting or hunting, make sure your trigger releases at around 3 pounds single action, and breaks clean like a "glass rod." Don't guess; use the proper trigger pull gauge.

so many target or combat shooters will have a backup gun which will be matched as closely as possible to the primary piece in all respects, and closer than you thought possible in trigger pulls.

For single action, I like mine to break at about $2\frac{3}{4}$ to $3\frac{1}{2}$ pounds. Double action should go around 9 to 11 pounds for smooth fluid shooting. My smooth-as-silk Colt Python tops the double action mode at $7\frac{3}{4}$ pounds. We'll cover a little more of this later along with some dos and don'ts on maintaining your handgun.

CARTRIDGES

Since I am devoting a whole chapter to cartridges, I will cover them only briefly here. They run the gamut from the small .25 caliber ACP round (73 foot-pounds), to the big, brawny and thunderous .44 magnums (741 foot pounds). We have specialized calibers like the .22 Remington Jet and .221 Remington Fireball for the XP-100 pistol, but these are in the bottleneck category.

We are also fortunate in that as time goes on, we see the development of new and exciting handgun rounds. We now have the flat shooting Herrett series of so called "wildcat" rounds, the new 9mm and .45 caliber Winchester-Western rounds and more recently Lee Jurras has introduced some really big calibers like the .375, .416, .460, .475 and .500. Although these are very costly, and feel like a stick of dynamite going off in your hand, they do have their place for the man who wants something really big for any and all big game he may choose to pursue.

The American shooter also has a choice either to reload his own cartridge cases, or buy factory-loaded ammo. Factory ammunition does have its place in the shooting fraternity and offers excellent accuracy, wide choice and convenience. The only strike against it is cost. At the thought of spending up to three times the price per shot, wise shooters have turned to reloading not only to shoot more, but for the sheer challenge of working up a load that will be the most accurate in a particular gun—in effect, the one load that is tuned to a particular handgun.

Getting back to calibers, and starting at the low end of the scale, the .380 ACP is a popular round suitable for a back-up piece. When mated with the AMT "380 Back-Up" pistol, and hidden under the shirt or in a night table, this diminutive little gun could get you out of a jam. Developing only 192 foot-pounds, this round is not suitable for hunting because the guns made for it are not sufficiently accurate for any kind of distance shooting.

The 9mm Parabellum, or 9mm Luger as it is commonly known here in the U.S., is a popular cartridge. Chambered in many American centerfire handguns, this round is accurate, easy to shoot, and can be loaded to the tune of fourteen rounds in guns like the S&W Model 59. Growing steadily as the years pass, the 9mm is gaining as an important tool on the law enforcement front. In urban areas an officer with a Model 59 and three clips (52 rounds) has a better chance of holding his own in a tough situation than the fellow with a loaded revolver and two speed loaders (18 rounds). For hunting, the 9mm is marginal at best. For small varmints, the use of a fast, light bullet (90 grain) driven about 1,450 fps is the answer.

Next is the .38 Special, the most popular round in America. Besides being the standard for policemen, the .38 Special is both versatile and highly accurate as a target round. It is often the very first round that a handloader cuts his teeth on. The 148-grain wadcutter seated flush with the top of the case and fired from a S&W Model 52 .38 Master semiautomatic has no competition on the production front.

For defense, a snubbie in the bedroom is extremely handy. Mine has the first chamber loaded with a Speer .38 shotshell to scare and intimidate any intruder. If after feeling those pellets, he doesn't turn tail and run, I have more potent JHP's behind that. Another favorite trick of mine is to load hollow-base wadcutters backwards for immediate expansion at short distances. Going on to lead Keith-type bullets makes for a fine hunting load, as do jacketed hollow or soft point bullets to around 950 feet per second. The .38 Special is fine for small game or varmints at distances of 100 meters or less when using a good semi-target arm like the Colt Python or Dan Wesson heavy barreled VH series.

Of all the magnum cartridges, the .357 is not only one of the first, it also ranks as the reigning "king of the magnums." Developed and introduced in 1935, the .357 uses the same bullet diameter (.357) as the .38 Special. Since the inventors were concerned with shooters trying the new round in guns too weak to withstand the pressures, they made the case longer by 1/10 of an inch, so it couldn't be chambered in such arms. Since leading is a problem here, jacketed bullets from 110 to 158 grains go hand in hand with high velocity and accuracy.

Every major firearms maker in the country chambers this round for its guns. It goes without saying that when buying a .38 caliber gun, consider buying the .357 model. In that way you can use both the .38 Special and .357 loads in one gun. The reverse is impossible; you cannot fire a .357 in a .38 Special revolver. By using a stainless steel handgun (S&W, Ruger) chambered for the .357 and a potent load of about 1,200 fps, you are well equipped for hunting anything up to medium-size game in any kind of weather. A truly great caliber!

The .41 Magnum ranks as one of my favorites. Introduced in 1964 and chambered now in S&W, Ruger and Contender guns, this round was to be the replacement for the .38 now in service at many police departments. It is a darn good cartridge, and ranks just under the .44 Magnum in power. It's easy on recoil, has a flat trajectory and groups tight at all ranges. Checking my records with handloads and Remington, Sierra, Hornady, and Speer bullets, I had no trouble keeping all shots within 2 inches or less at 25 yards. The .41 is a worthy cartridge for anyone's handgun battery.

The Remington .44 Magnum is the epitome of a hunting cartridge. With its diameter of .429 inches and high velocity of 1,400 fps, it has taken big game animals up to the big bears and moose. Being ranked as the most powerful commercial handgun cartridge in the world has helped it gain the fame it now has. Chambered by many firearm manufacturers, this round is both hard hitting and accurate. For those of us who use the guns and don't need full-power loads every day, loads can be reduced to the .44 Special level, and may be used in any .44 Magnum handgun. Here again the story is the same as with the .357; the .44 Magnum cartridge was made longer so it could not be chambered in .44 Special weapons of vintage age and questionable quality.

The "official round of the cowboys," the .45 Colt is regaining its popularity. This caliber now approaches reasonable velocity levels when used in such firearms as the Ruger Blackhawk and Smith 25-5 models. Loads can be made to approach 1,000 fps very easily in Ruger and T/C guns, but a steady diet of these will eventually result in a loosening up of the pieces. For any shooter, it is best to shoot this round at moderate velocities. If you desire more, go to the magnums.

The .45 ACP has come a long way in recent years and has been grossly underrated by the factories. Recently, the use of lighter bullets (185 grain) at higher velocities (900 fps) and the introduction of hollow-pointed bullets have allowed the .45 to come into its own. As a combat weapon it is tops. I use a Colt Gold Cup in combat matches and it has never failed me. The police could take notice and change to the .45 for superior knockdown power and the easy accessibility to guns and parts via the federal government. Loading is quick via clips and with Colt's newly designed barrel bushing introduced in the 1970's, accuracy has increased by almost 200 percent.

For hunting, the .45 can be used on animals about the size of wild boar or deer, but do not forget that any handgun is marginal on very big and dangerous game. Plenty of time must be allowed for proper placement of the bullet.

Now that we have an overview of the modern American centerfire handgun, let's see exactly what is available on today's market.

FEDERAL
50 CENTER FIRE
PISTOL CARTRIDGES
FEDERAL
357 MAGNUM
HIGH VELOCITY
158 GRAIN HOLLOW
POINT JACKETED BULLET
NO. 357E
Remington
Remington
41 Rem. Mag.
PISTOL TARGET
SMITH & WESSON
WASHINGTON, D.C.

TWO

The Smith & Wesson Company

The mere mention of the name Smith & Wesson to any handgun buff will certainly get you into a conversation regarding their quality, dependability, and consistent reliability.

Of the two founders of Smith & Wesson, Horace Smith was the more reserved. With his knowledge and experience in designing machinery and tooling, he had a great deal to offer. Daniel Wesson, on the other hand, was the outgoing member of the team. Wesson had a more formal education, and with his many years of practical experience relating to cost problems, licensing and patent rights, he provided the business savvy needed to launch the new enterprise.

Like many young companies, they had their problems. From a small start in 1852, the company went into a second partnership in 1854 due to a lack of product sales. J.W. Post had approached the men with financial aid and the desire to purchase the S&W line. Not happy at all with the situation, Smith had left the parent company to go to work in Springfield, Massachusetts.

In the meantime, Wesson had gotten involved with a ex-Colt employee named Rollin White who had a patent on a revolver which used a bored-through cylinder. This would enable the use of a newly-invented item called a "cartridge." White was given a royalty of twenty-five cents per gun, and after all the paperwork was finalized, Wesson contacted Horace Smith and began production on this firearm.

The year of 1857 was actually the real and earnest beginning of the Smith & Wesson Company. From that year, S&W moved onward and upward, starting with the early Model 1 tip-ups, top-breaks, hand ejector models, and then into the modern J, K, N and semi-automatic framed handguns.

The present line of J-frame guns consists mainly of police-type guns such as the

Chief's Special (Model 36) and the Bodyguard Airweight (Model 38). These are five-shot pistols and were designed for comfort and concealability. Models are available blued, nickel-plated or in stainless steel, and offer a choice of both stock and trigger styles.

The famed Model 10 (Military and Police) and popular Model 19 guns fall into the K-frame line. These medium-framed guns have proved extremely popular among police officers and sportsmen not only because of their ideal size and weight factor, but also because of the availability of a wide number of grips, sights, triggers and hammer options.

Smith & Wesson's series of big bore guns are supplied on their time-tested N-frame. Largest of all, they have the extra heft and weight needed for calibers with heavy recoil. Included in this series would be the Models 27 (.357 Magnum), 29 (.44 Magnum), and 57 (.41 Magnum). Again, like its smaller brothers, the N-frame guns offer versatility in different stocks, triggers and hammers.

The centerfire autoloading pistol lineup at the present time consists of three models in two chamberings. The double action group, known presently as Model 39 and Model 59, will be replaced with Models 439 and 459. These latter two, incorporating an improved firing pin lock and fully protected and adjustable rear sights (for windage and elevation), are scheduled for production sometime in 1980-81.

Chambered for 9mm Luger (Parabellum), the newer guns will keep the eight-round capability of the M39 and the staggered fourteen-round magazine capacity of the M59. Outward appearances of these handguns have not been altered (except for the sights) thus retaining the classic lines, good pointability and ease of handling that have made them popular with law enforcement agencies across the country.

Still in the centerfire semiautomatic series, the .38 Master, or Model 52, is a excellent choice for serious target shooters. Manufactured with a steel frame, as opposed to the alloy frame on the M39 and M59, the 52 has all the ingredients that make it one of the most accurate out-of-the-box centerfire target pistols in the world today.

Now over 125 years old, the Smith & Wesson Company has grown into a corporation which has diversified itself into many fields. Not only do they make some of the most sought-after handguns in the world today, they have also branched out into police equipment and ammunition.

SMITH & WESSON HANDGUNS

MILITARY AND POLICE—MODEL 10

Frame	K	**Sights**	**Front**	Serrated ramp
Caliber	.38 Special		**Rear**	Square notch
Capacity	Six rounds	**Stocks**		Service walnut
Barrel Lengths	2, 4, 5, and 6 in.	**Hammer**		Standard factory
Weight	32 oz. with 6-in. barrel	**Trigger**		Standard factory
Finish	Blue or nickel	**Options**		—

Model 10

Thoughout the years, the Model 10, or Military and Police, has served as the "bread and butter" gun of the line. Carried by thousands of police officers around the world, it is the perfect no-nonsense tool of the working professionals whose departments have standardized the use of .38 Special amunition.

MILITARY AND POLICE—MODEL 10 (Heavy Barrel)

Frame	K	**Sights**	**Front**	Serrated ramp
Caliber	.38 Special		**Rear**	Square notch
Capacity	Six rounds	**Stocks**		Service walnut
Barrel Lengths	4 in.	**Hammer**		Standard factory
Weight	34 oz.	**Trigger**		Standard factory
Finish	Blue or nickel	**Options**		—

Model 10 HB

Almost a carbon copy of the Model 10, the Model 10 HB (Heavy Barrel) is only available with the heavy 4-inch barrel. It was designed for the man who wants the weight of the gun out front and is offered either blued or nickel-plated in .38 Special.

MILITARY AND POLICE AIRWEIGHT—MODEL 12

Frame	KA	**Sights**	**Front**	Ramp ⅛ in.
Caliber	.38 Special		**Rear**	Square notch
Capacity	Six rounds	**Stocks**		Service walnut
Barrel Lengths	2 and 4 in.	**Hammer**		Standard factory
Weight	18 oz. with 2-in. barrel	**Trigger**		Standard factory
Finish	Blue or nickel	**Options**		—

Model 12

Designated as the Model 12, .38 Military and Police Airweight, this gun could fall into yet a third version of the Model 10. Weighing in at 18 ounces with a 2-inch barrel, it too was designed for police officers with comfort in mind.

MILITARY AND POLICE—MODEL 13 (Heavy Barrel)

Frame	K	**Sights**	**Front**	Serrated ramp
Caliber	.357 Magnum		**Rear**	Square notch
Capacity	Six rounds	**Stocks**		Service walnut
Barrel Lengths	4 in.	**Hammer**		Standard factory
Weight	34 oz.	**Trigger**		Standard factory
Finish	Blue or nickel	**Options**		—

Model 13

Originally manufactured for the New York State Police, the Model 13 has all the time-tested qualities of the Model 10, yet offers the heavy barrel and the more powerful .357 Magnum cartridge. A "must" gun when departments allow this high-velocity round.

MASTERPIECE—MODEL 14

Frame	K	**Sights**	**Front**	Patridge
Caliber	.38 Special		**Rear**	Micrometer
Capacity	Six rounds	**Stocks**		Service walnut
Barrel Lengths	6 and 8⅜ in.	**Hammer**		Target
Weight	38½ oz. with 6-in. barrel	**Trigger**		Target
Finish	Blue	**Options**		—

Model 14

Introduced in 1947, the K-38 was brought out to satisfy shooters who wanted a pistol that matched the weight and feel of the K-22 Masterpiece in .22 rimfire for all target events. After starting out about 2½ ounces under the K-22, a heavier barrel was marketed in 1949 to bring it up to 38½ ounces, equal now to the K-22 fully-loaded with six rounds. A classic in the true sense of the word, the K-38 can still be seen on the target circuit.

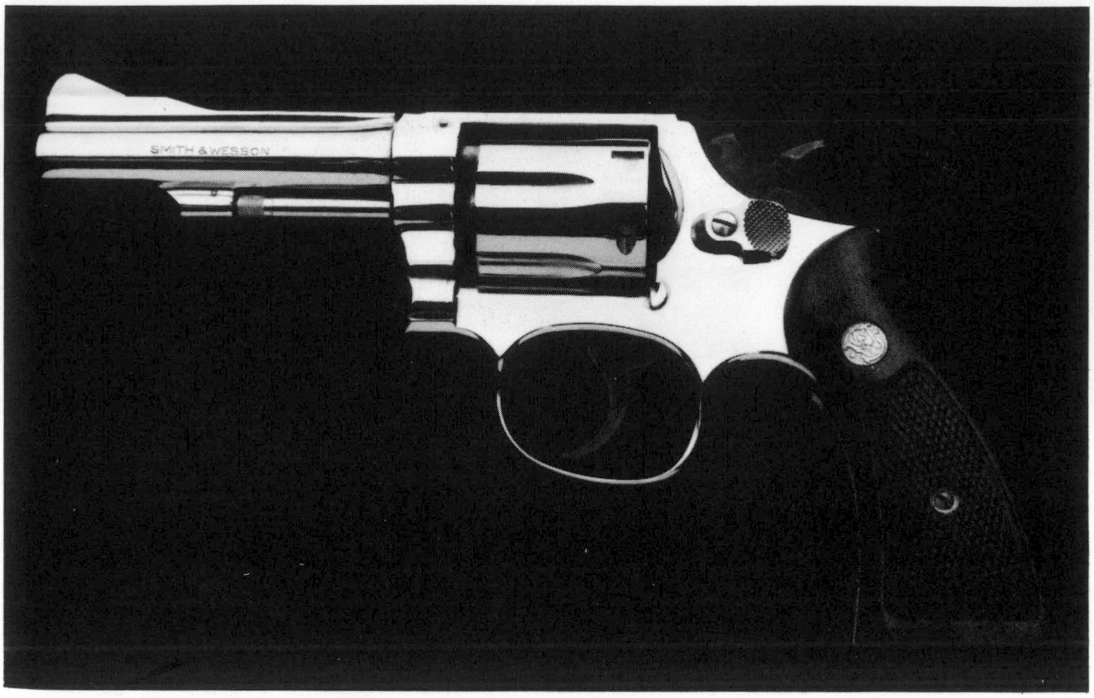

COMBAT MASTERPIECE—MODEL 15

Frame	K	**Sights**	**Front**	Baughman Quick Draw
Caliber	.38 Special		**Rear**	Micrometer Click
Capacity	Six rounds	**Stocks**		Service walnut
Barrel Lengths	2 and 4 in.	**Hammer**		Standard factory
Weight	34 oz. with 4-in. barrel	**Trigger**		Standard factory
Finish	Blue or nickel	**Options**		—

Model 15

Available only with a 2- or 4-inch barrel, the Combat Masterpiece is for the police department that might allow a lighter gun with adjustable rear sights. As an added feature, Baughman Quick Draw front sights add to the ease of drawing the weapon without any fear of the sight hanging up on the inside of a holster or shirt. For sportsmen, its an ideal gun to carry afield, especially in the stainless model.

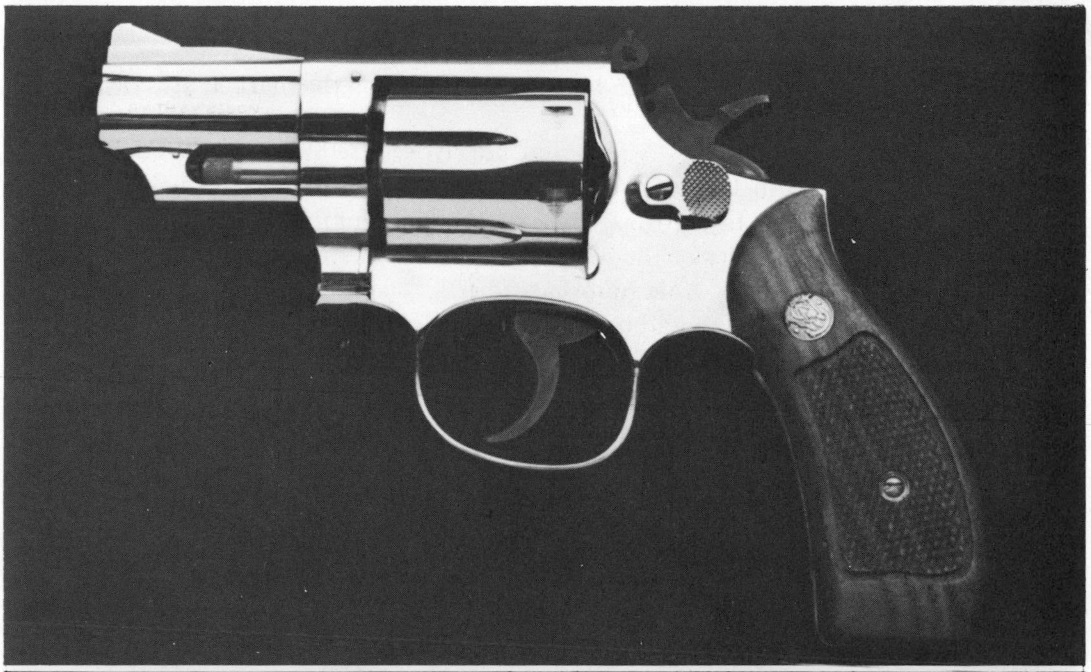

COMBAT MAGNUM—MODEL 19

Frame	K	**Sights**	**Front**	Baughman Quick Draw
Caliber	.357 Magnum		**Rear**	Micrometer Click
Capacity	Six rounds	**Stocks**		Target type (4 and 6 in. sizes)
Barrel Lengths	2½, 4, and 6 in.	**Hammer**		Standard factory
Weight	40 oz. with 6-in. barrel	**Trigger**		Standard factory
Finish	Bright blue or nickel	**Options**		Sights, hammers, and triggers

Model 19

Hailed as the most popular gun of the entire Smith & Wesson line, the Model 19, or .357

Combat Magnum, was first introduced in 1956. This gun originally was issued with a 4-inch barrel, but as its popularity increased, a 6-inch barrel and fancy target stocks were offered in 1963. In 1968, a round-butt, 2½-inch-barrel model came on the market, thus completing the full circle of barrel lengths.

The Model 19 as made today is a first rate police/defense/hunting weapon. Weighing in at 35 ounces with a 4-inch tube, this gun finds favor with many state police agencies nationwide. It is considered by many as "the" law enforcement tool, not only because of its weight, but also the availability of the weapon, its handy medium-sized K frame, and its ability to handle the potent .357 Magnum cartridge.

One other feature that should be considered by all agencies is the shrouded extractor rod. To me this is a vital necessity in any service revolver. To be put out of service because of a bent extractor rod during some rough play could be fatal in many instances.

For hunters, the Model 19 is a welcome companion on dark nights in the wilds. For men shooting the PPC course, a Model 19 with its smooth action is a winner in many timed events.

Offered in a bright blue, nickel or stainless steel (as the Model 66) the Combat Magnum comes pretty close to being an all-around handgun.

1955 TARGET—MODEL 25

Frame	N	**Sights**	**Front**	Patridge
Caliber	.45 ACP		**Rear**	Micrometer Click
Capacity	Six rounds	**Stocks**		Oversize target
Barrel Lengths	6 in.	**Hammer**		Target
Weight	45 oz.	**Trigger**		Target
Finish	Blue	**Options**		Sights, grips

Model 25

Chambered for the .45 ACP this is the gun for the man who prefers a revolver to an automatic in target competition. Made originally with a 6½-inch barrel, Smith & Wesson now makes this gun with a 6-inch heavy barrel. Equipped with Patridge front sights for ease of sight pickup, this fine gun also comes with a low hammer, target trigger and checkered Goncalo Alves grips.

MODEL 25-5

Frame	N	**Sights**	**Front**	Red ramp
Caliber	.45 Colt		**Rear**	Micrometer with white outline
Capacity	Six rounds	**Stocks**		Oversize target
Barrel Lengths	4, 6, and 8⅜ in.	**Hammer**		Target
Weight	46 oz. with 6-in. barrel	**Trigger**		Target
Finish	Bright blue or nickel	**Options**		Various sights

Model 25-5

The S&W Model 25-5 started out as the 125th Anniversary Commemorative Gun. Smith & Wesson has now tooled up to produce this model on a regular basis.

Chambering the .45 Colt, this new entry is destined to be a hit. Whenever the word ".45 Colt" is mentioned among shooters, people seem to perk up and take notice. For the boys who like a big bore in a smooth double-action revolver, this is the one.

Exactly like the firm's Model 29, the 25-5 is a handsome piece. Outfitted in bright blue, this gun carries all the target features of the other N-frame models. Shooting impressions are favorable, since this big gun rides the recoil arc with ease. One word of caution here for the handloaders. Please do not try to "Magnumize" this caliber. The cartridge is fine as is, and any attempt to increase any one factor in any direction would be looking for trouble, as the metal is thin from machining at the cylinder stop notches. Use all reloading data supplied and listed under "Colt Models and Replica's." Remember the .45 slug is almost ½-inch in diameter. Big, heavy bullets do not need to expand to do their job if the placement is correct in the first place.

The .45 Colt cartridge is now 100-plus years old, and guns like the Smith & Wesson Model 25-5 will keep it around for a long time.

MODEL 27

Frame	N	**Sights**	**Front**	Choice of any S&W sight
Caliber	.357 Magnum		**Rear**	Micrometer Click
Capacity	Six rounds	**Stocks**		Oversize target
Barrel Lengths	4, 6, and 8⅜ in.	**Hammer**		Target
Weight	44 oz. with 6-in. barrel	**Trigger**		Target
Finish	Bright blue or nickel	**Options**		Various sights and grips

Model 27

This is the gun that started it all! Introduced to the market in 1935, the 27 was the first of the big N-frame magnums. Since it was at first a special order handgun, one could have any barrel length from 3½ to 8¾ inches. In addition the owner received a registration certificate listing all the options of "his" gun on it. Today it still reigns as one of the most prestigious .357's on the market.

Sporting a finely-checkered top strap and rib, this gun is still a favorite of many gun buffs. Furnished in either bright blue or nickel, the Model 27 can still be ordered with any Smith & Wesson front sight. It's the only gun in the entire line where this service is still available, which adds a nice custom touch for the owner.

One other feature should be offered on this model. Talking to many shooters in the course of writing this book, I have found that quite a few would like to see this gun available with a 6-inch heavy barrel similar to those on the 25, 29 or 57 magnums. I know the traditionalists are against it, but this would, in the opinion of many, including the writer, make a fine gun even better.

HIGHWAY PATROLMAN—MODEL 28

Frame	N	**Sights**	**Front**	Baughman Quick Draw
Caliber	.357 Magnum		**Rear**	Micrometer Click
Capacity	Six rounds	**Stocks**		Service walnut
Barrel Lengths	4 and 6 in.	**Hammer**		Standard factory
Weight	44 oz. with 6-in. barrel	**Trigger**		Standard factory
Finish	Satin blue	**Options**		Target stocks

Model 28

Since the Model 27 was a super deluxe pistol and not readily available to police officers who wanted a truly rugged handgun, plans were made under the supervision of C.R. Hellstrom to bring down the cost of this gun. Enter the Model 28, or Highway Patrolman, which carried the same fine lockwork and big frame of its brother, the 27. Even though S&W deleted such fancy frills as the checkered top strap and the bright blue finish, this is still one of the best .357's made for law enforcement work. A bit heavy, but one tough gun.

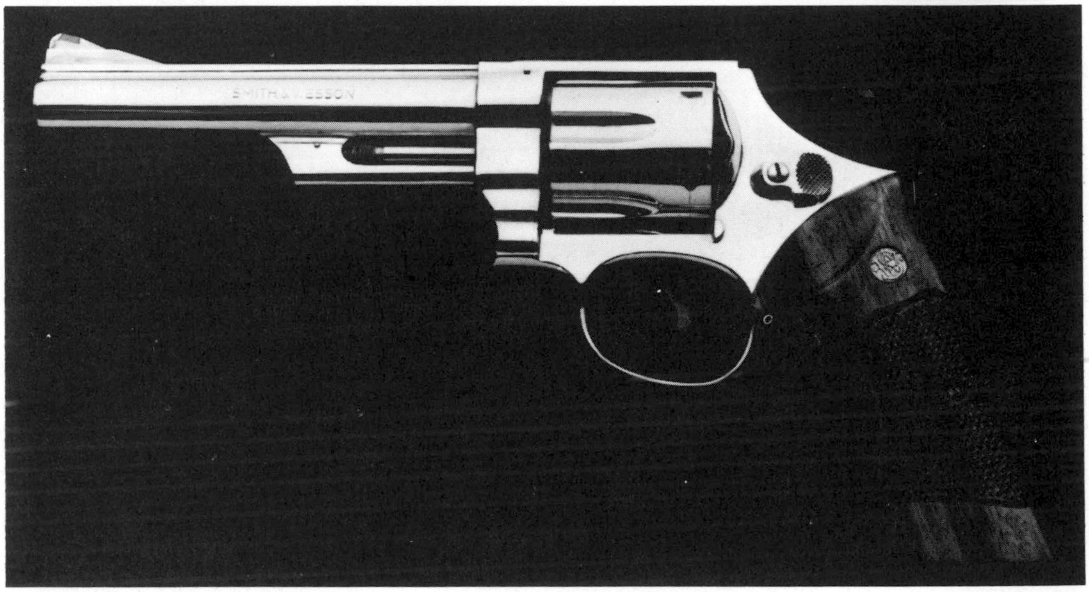

MODEL 29

Frame	N	**Sights**	**Front**	Red ramp
Caliber	.44 Magnum		**Rear**	Micrometer with white outline
Capacity	Six rounds	**Stocks**		Oversize target
Barrel Lengths	4, 6 and 8⅜ in.	**Hammer**		Target
Weight	46 oz. with 6-in. barrel	**Trigger**		Target
Finish	Bright blue or nickel	**Options**		Various sights and grips

Model 29

The brainchild of Elmer Keith, together with Mr. Hellstrom of Smith & Wesson, and Remington executive R.H. Coleman, the S&W .44 Magnum has reached a popularity never before seen in a big bore hand weapon.

This gun is limited in use for law enforcement work because of severe recoil and barrel whip. Nevertheless it has found plenty of favor with hunting enthusiasts, silhouette shooters and collectors.

S&W has built one of the best double-action .44 revolvers around today. As noted in the specs, three barrel lengths are available. The 29 comes from the factory with all the target extras (target hammer, target trigger, and target grips) and a choice of outside finishes.

Using factory or handloaded ammunition, the American shooter can tailor his loads to take anything from antelope to zebra. In fact this gun and cartridge have done just that, as one can see in many hunting journals.

Since any modern gun chambered for the hot .44 Magnum can also shoot the mild .44 Special (but not conversely), the Model 29 is an excellent field gun in the hands of competent hunters or sportsmen. Launching a 240-grain projectile at 1,500 feet per second, this weapon will never leave you feeling "undergunned" stalking most North American big game.

REGULATION POLICE—MODEL 31

Frame	J	**Sights**	**Front**	Serrated ramp
Caliber	.32 S&W Long		**Rear**	Square notch
Capacity	Six rounds	**Stocks**		Service walnut
Barrel Lengths	2 and 3 in.	**Hammer**		Standard factory
Weight	20 oz. with 2-in. barrel	**Trigger**		Standard factory
Finish	Blue or nickel	**Options**		—

Model 31

Manufactured today on the J-frame, the .32 Regulation Police is not as much in demand now by police departments as it was in the early twentieth century. Chambered for the .32 S&W Long round, which upon firing only generated around 115 foot-pounds of energy, the Model 31 quickly lost its appeal, especially after the .38 Special came on the scene. In the hands of a trained officer, it still beats the little .32 by between 300 and 400% in a Plus-P loading.

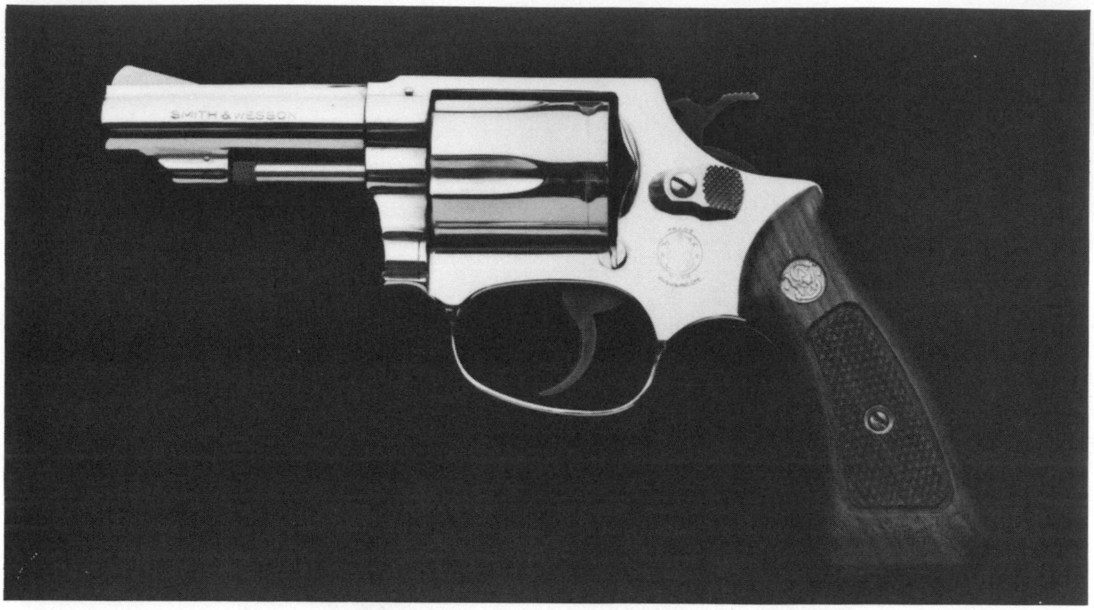

CHIEF'S SPECIAL—MODEL 36

Frame	J	**Sights**	**Front**	Fixed 1/10 in.
Caliber	.38 Special		**Rear**	Square notch
Capacity	Five rounds	**Stocks**		Service walnut
Barrel Lengths	2 and 3 in.	**Hammer**		Standard factory
Weight	19 oz. with 2-in. barrel	**Trigger**		Standard factory
Finish	Blue or nickel	**Options**		—

Model 36

Holding only five rounds of .38 Special ammo, the Model 36 gun is excellent for concealment purposes by plainclothesmen or off-duty officers. Available in 2- or 3-inch barrels, the Chief's Special is a very popular piece for all branches of law enforcement work.

MODEL 37

Frame	JA	**Sights**	**Front**	Fixed 1/10 in.
Caliber	.38 Special		**Rear**	Square notch
Capacity	Five rounds	**Stocks**		Service walnut
Barrel Lengths	2 and 3 in.	**Hammer**		Standard factory
Weight	14 oz. with 2-in. barrel	**Trigger**		Standard factory
Finish	Blue or nickel	**Options**		—

Model 37

With the same specifications as the Model 36, this model is made on the JA frame and only weighs 14 ounces. Using a special alloy frame helps to hold the weight down without losing the capability of shooting the .38 Special cartridge. This gun is sought by many who don't wish to carry the extra weight of the 36 on their belts. The 37 is a hard gun to find in the shops because of its popularity.

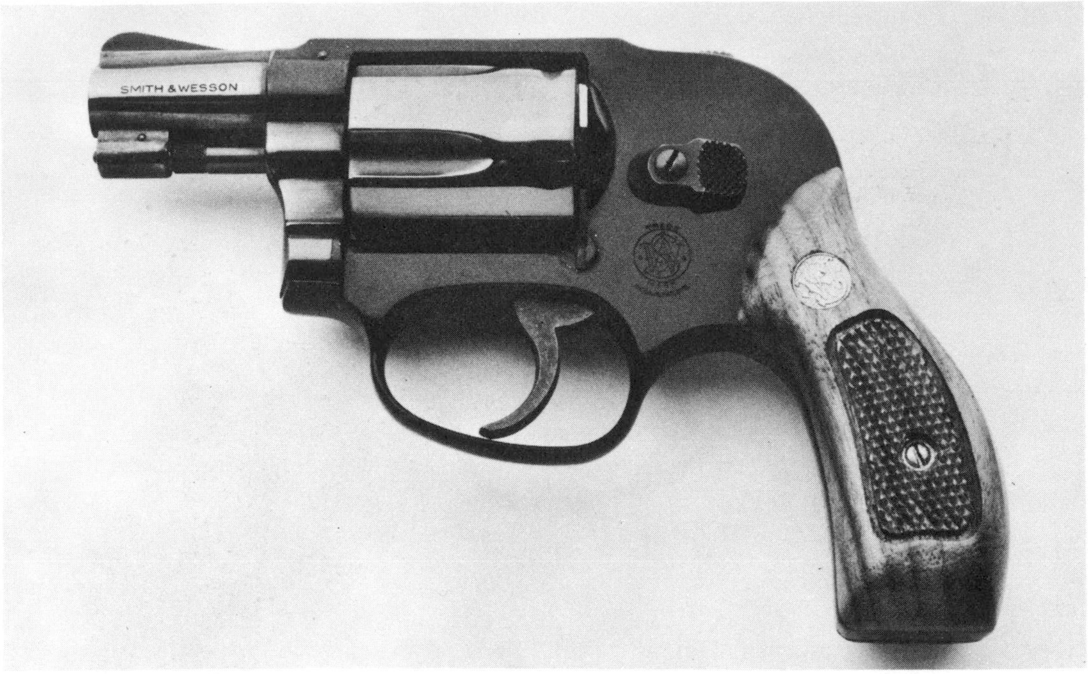

BODYGUARD AIRWEIGHT—MODEL 38

Frame	JA	**Sights**	**Front**	Fixed 1/10 in.
Caliber	.38 Special		**Rear**	Square notch
Capacity	Five rounds	**Stocks**		Service walnut
Barrel Lengths	2 in.	**Hammer**		Protected
Weight	14½ oz.	**Trigger**		Standard factory
Finish	Blue or nickel	**Options**		—

Model 38

Officially designated as the .38 Bodyguard Airweight, this model is easily identifiable by the lack of the familiar hammer. A protected hammer configuration is offered for professional people who need the utmost in streamlining in order to prevent an exposed hammer from getting caught on anything during a tense situation. Made on the J-frame, this piece operates in either the single- or double-action mode, and can be obtained in either blue or nickel, but with only a 2-inch barrel.

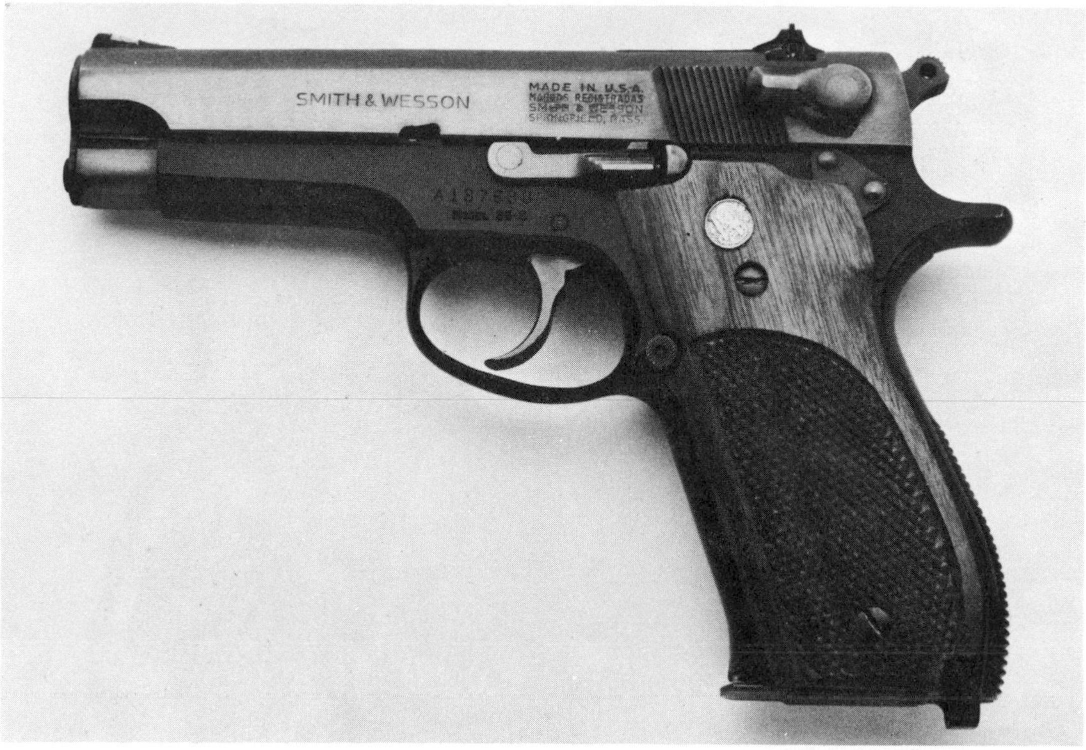

MODEL 39

Frame	Semiautomatic	**Sights**	**Front**	Ramp
Caliber	9mm Luger		**Rear**	Micrometer, adjustable for windage only
Capacity	Eight rounds	**Stocks**		Walnut
Barrel Lengths	4 in.	**Hammer**		Combat
Weight	26½ oz.	**Trigger**		Smooth
Finish	Blue or nickel	**Options**		Accessory rear sight

Model 39

Brought out in its original form on a steel frame, current models of this famous 9mm semiautomatic pistol now have an aluminum alloy handle. The Model 39 holds eight rounds in the magazine; it can be loaded with nine rounds by simply charging the weapon with one in the "tube," then adding the extra one to the clip when the first one is seated home. A truly versatile gun, it can be fired in either the single- or double-action mode. New optional rear sights will add elevation to an already fine sight picture, but these are only available as a separate item from the S&W parts department.

MODEL 439

Frame	Semiautomatic	**Sights**	**Front**	Ramp
Caliber	9mm Luger		**Rear**	Adjustable for windage and elevation
Capacity	Eight rounds	**Stocks**		Walnut
Barrel Lengths	4 in.	**Hammer**		Combat
Weight	27 oz.	**Trigger**		Smooth
Finish	Blue or nickel	**Options**		—

Model 439

As stated in the introduction to this chapter, the 439 will replace the Model 39. A check with the factory in Springfield confirms that production began in late 1980.

Three improvements or modifications have been made with the gun, and in order not to cause confusion in relation to parts, Smith & Wesson has elected to renumber the gun to the 439 designation.

The sights have been improved. Winged side panels have been added to protect the sights from damage due to dropping the gun. S&W designers should be congratulated for this, for it's the first step in making a service arm fully reliable under any condition. The sights are adjustable for both windage and elevation, something the Model 39 lacked.

The second modification consists of a new firing pin lock which locks the pin and allows it to operate only when the trigger is pulled to its rearmost position. This is in addition to the regular safety, which by the way, has been greatly improved structurally through the use of a high-strength casting.

The Model 439 also has redesigned extractors that will exert a heavier positive force against the cartridge case for faultless ejection.

Other than the above features, the 439 will in most respects be the same fine semiautomatic we've been used to.

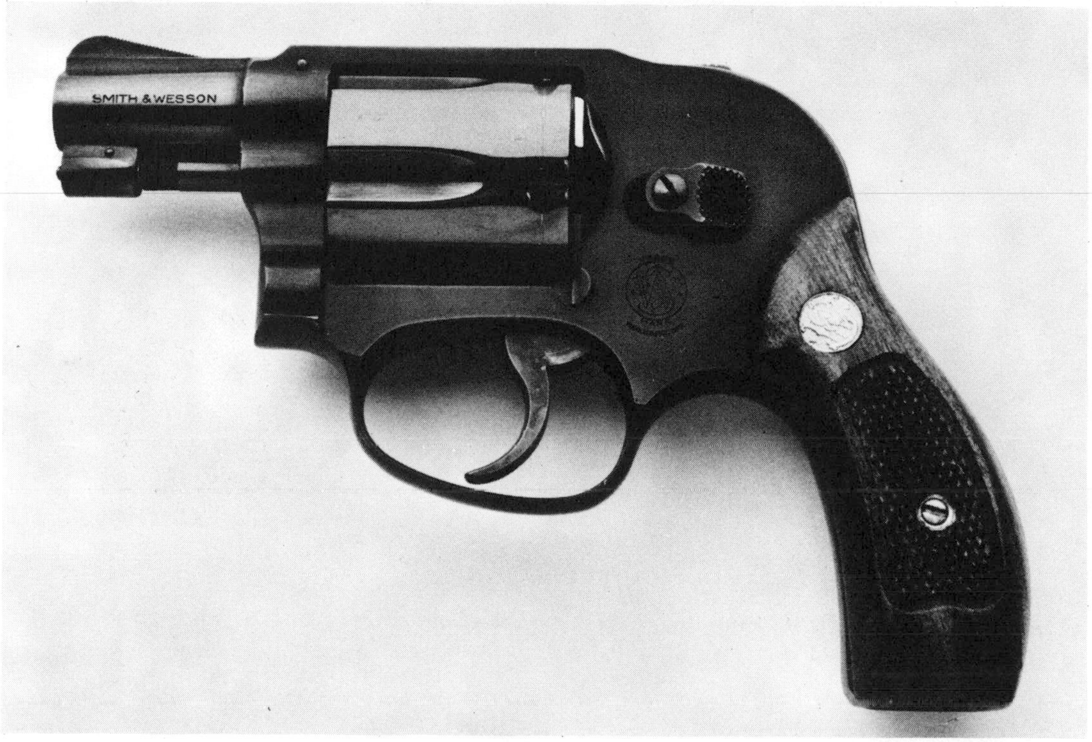

BODYGUARD—MODEL 49

Frame	J	**Sights**	**Front**	Fixed 1/10 in.
Caliber	.38 Special		**Rear**	Square notch
Capacity	Five rounds	**Stocks**		Service walnut
Barrel Lengths	2 in.	**Hammer**		Protected
Weight	20½ oz.	**Trigger**		Standard factory
Finish	Blue or nickel	**Options**		—

Model 49

A steel-framed copy of the Model 38, the 49 is heavier by about 6 ounces. Fixed sights, checkered stocks and availability in either blue or nickel make for an attractive defensegun.

MASTER—MODEL 52

Frame	Semiautomatic	**Sights**	**Front**	Patridge on ramp
Caliber	.38 Special		**Rear**	New S&W Micrometer with wide blade
Capacity	Five rounds	**Stocks**		Walnut
Barrel Lengths	5 in.	**Hammer**		Target
Weight	41 oz.	**Trigger**		3/8 in. wide
Finish	Bright blue	**Options**		—

Model 52

The Smith & Wesson Model 52, or .38 Master, is a semiautomatic specially designed for the serious target shooter. This gun is chambered for the .38 Special Wadcutter (flush-seated in the case) and equipped with excellent sights, longer barrel, and a crisp trigger pull. It's obvious that Smith & Wesson spared no expense to give the competition shooter the best that could be made. As with most guns of this high pedigree, the workmanship is first class and accuracy is individually checked at the factory for ten ring groups or better at 50 yards.

Since some semiautomatic target guns using the .38 Special are not especially noted for smooth functioning, extra care should be taken to prevent malfunctions while shooting. Cases should be trimmed to factory specs, the right powder and charge should be used and a moderate roll or taper crimp should be employed to allow the flush-seated wadcutters to chamber freely. Patience on your part with reference to careful reloading and testing will go a long way in to insure that this gun will shoot as good as it looks.

Bill Blankenship won the 1966 World's Championship with an unmodified, out-of-the-box Model 52. For the match shooter who enjoys shooting three calibers (.22, .38 and .45) the 52 has no equal in a factory-produced handgun.

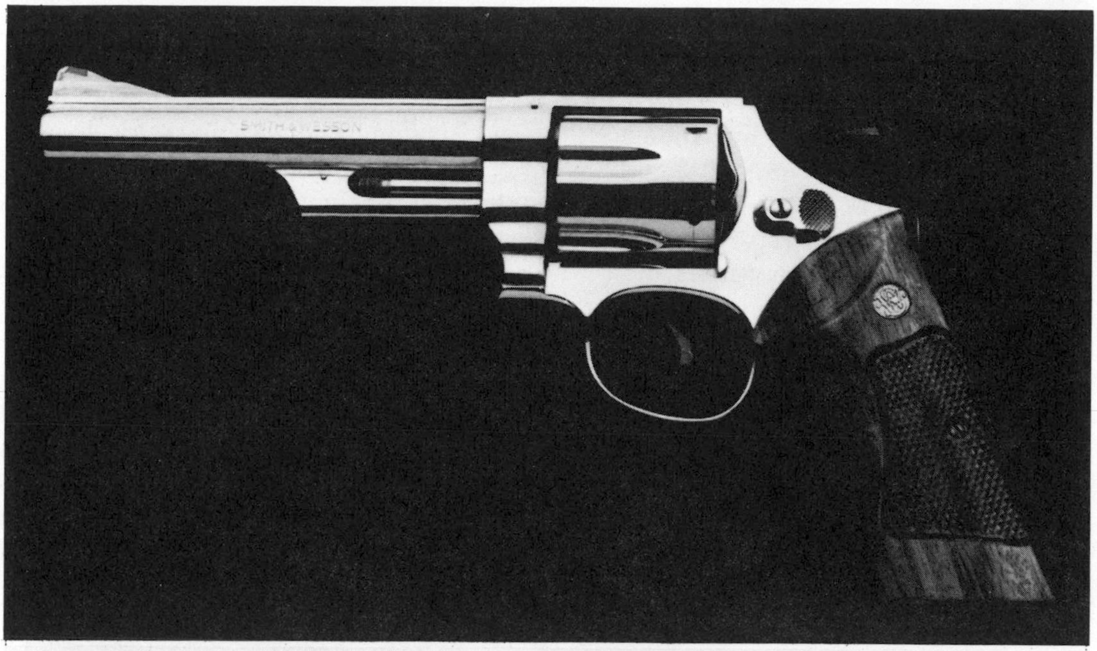

MODEL 57

Frame	N	**Sights**	**Front**	Red ramp
Caliber	.41 Magnum		**Rear**	Micrometer Click with white outline
Capacity	Six rounds	**Stocks**		Oversize target
Barrel Lengths	4, 6, and 8⅜ in.	**Hammer**		Target
Weight	48 oz. with 6-in. barrel	**Trigger**		Target
Finish	Blue or nickel	**Options**		Various sights

Model 57

I generally try not to force my feelings or opinions on anyone, but I feel I must in regards to the S&W Model 57 and particularly the cartridge to be used with this gun. Brought out in 1964 in cooperation with Remington, this .41 Magnum is deserving of much more recognition than it is now getting.

More powerful than the .357, but less so than the .44 Magnum, the .41 nevertheless makes for an ideal hunting round. Keeping a low recoil profile plus a taut string trajectory, the .41 is gaining steadily among those who are tired of the blast and shake of the .44 Magnum. I will have more to say about the cartridge later on in the book.

Regarding the gun itself, S&W has marketed a fine revolver. Built on the big N-frame, this gun comes with the standard three T's (target hammer, target trigger, and target grips) and in two finishes. Trigger pull is crisp at 3½ pounds on my own 57. With groups running 2 to 2½ inches at 25 yards, I have nothing to complain about when shooting this handgun.

Most handgunners seem to prefer the 6-inch barrel length, but the 4-inch comes in handy for fishermen or back-country folks. For silhouette shooters, the 8⅜-inch barrel is a blessing and adds another 50 feet per second in velocity for even better downrange knock-down power.

The S&W .41 Magnum is a sleeper worthy of your consideration when purchasing that next magnum handgun.

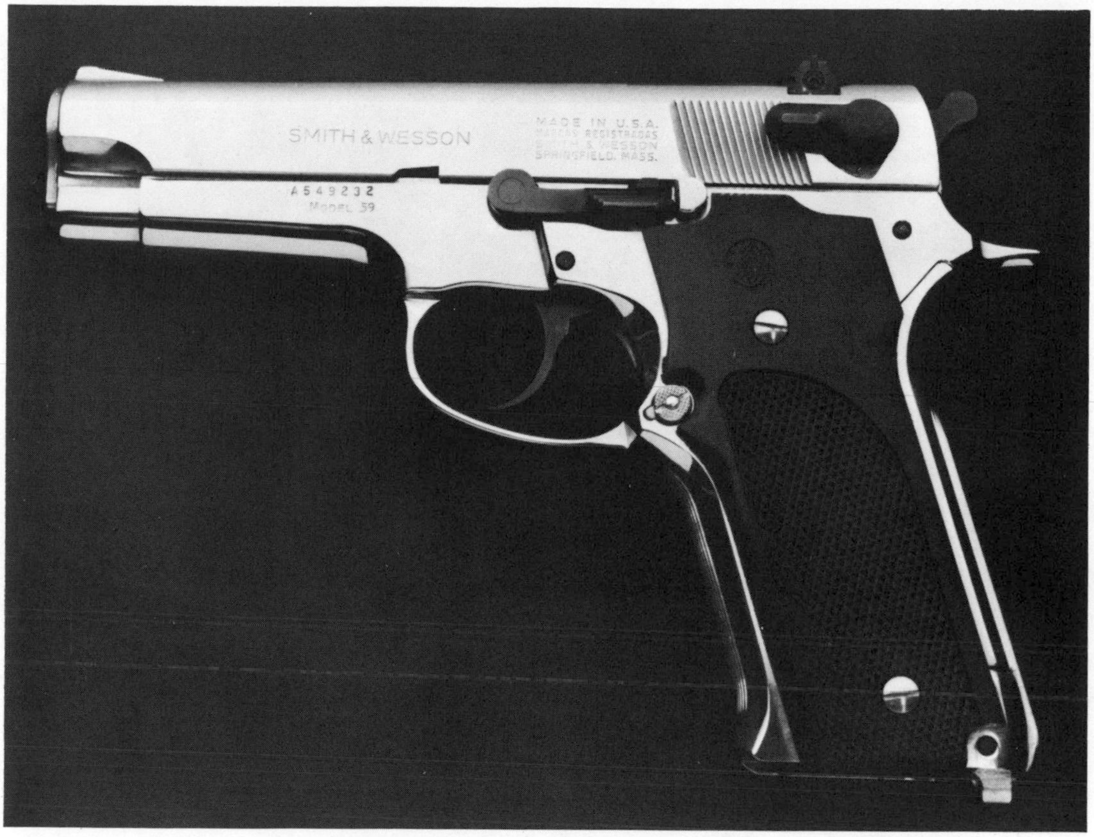

MODEL 59

Frame	Semiautomatic	**Sights**	**Front**	Ramp
Caliber	9mm		**Rear**	Micrometer, adjustable for windage
Capacity	Fourteen rounds	**Stocks**		Molded nylon
Barrel Lengths	4 in.	**Hammer**		Combat
Weight	27½ oz.	**Trigger**		Smooth
Finish	Blue or nickel	**Options**		—

Model 59

In July of 1971 the first of the Model 59s were introduced. Basically the same gun as the aforementioned 39, this piece carries extra firepower by holding fourteen rounds in a staggered magazine. Also incorporated are grips made of high impact plastic to prevent breakage in rough encounters, and the availability of a nickel finish for all-weather use.

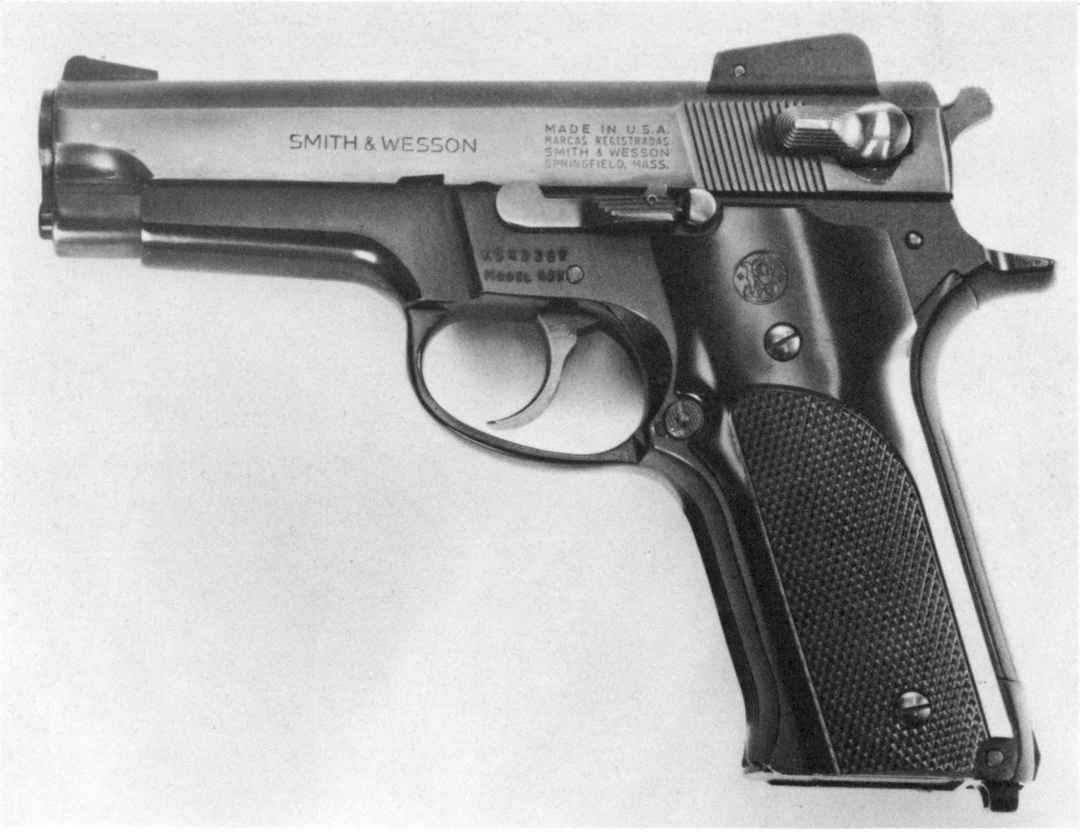

MODEL 459

Frame	Semiautomatic	**Sights**	**Front**	Ramp
Caliber	9mm		**Rear**	Adjustable for windage and elevation
Capacity	Fourteen rounds	**Stocks**		Molded nylon
Barrel Lengths	4 in.	**Hammer**		Combat
Weight	28 oz.	**Trigger**		Smooth
Finish	Blue or nickel	**Options**		—

Model 459

Identical to the Model 59 which it will be replacing in the near future, the 459 will carry all the improvements and modifications already mentioned with the new 439.

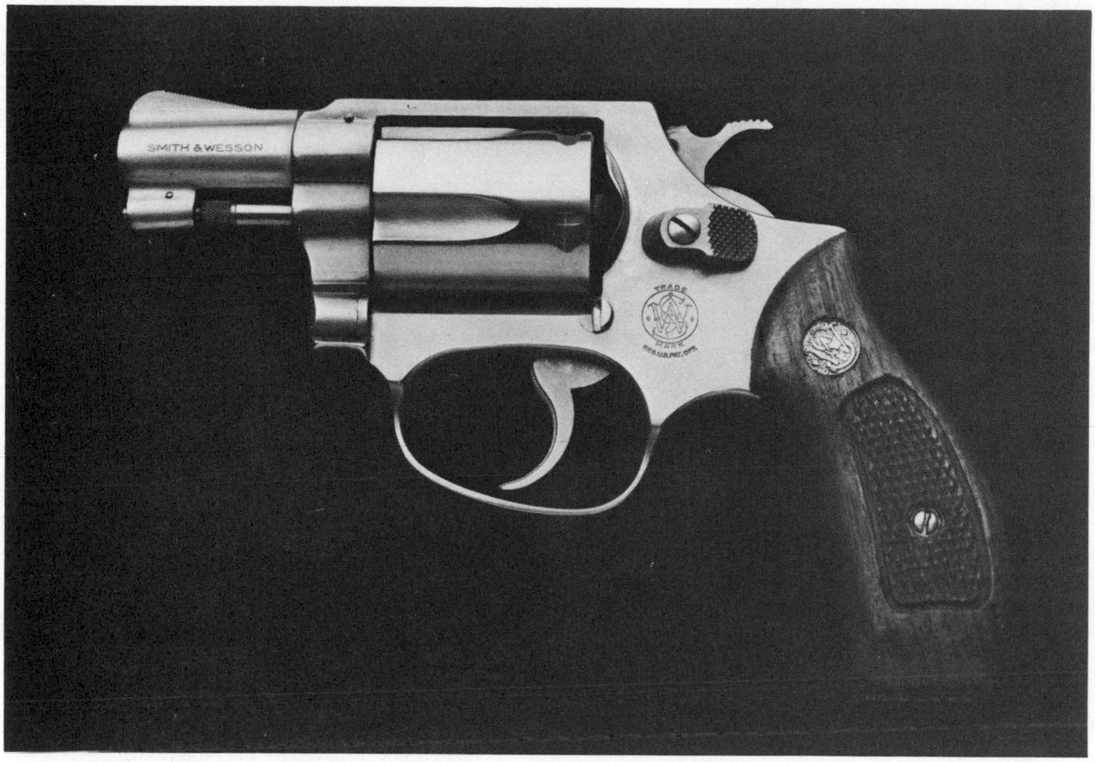

CHIEF'S SPECIAL—MODEL 60

Frame	J	**Sights**	**Front**	Fixed 1/10 in.
Caliber	.38 Special		**Rear**	Square notch
Capacity	Five rounds	**Stocks**		Service walnut
Barrel Lengths	2 in.	**Hammer**		Standard factory
Weight	19 oz.	**Trigger**		Standard factory
Finish	Stainless steel	**Options**		—

Model 60 (Stainless)

This .38 Chief's Special is the cornerstone of Smith & Wesson's stainless pistols. The initial response to this weapon was overwhelming to say the least. Still a very popular item with the law enforcement crowd, the Model 60 is a short, light, and easy to maintain handgun.

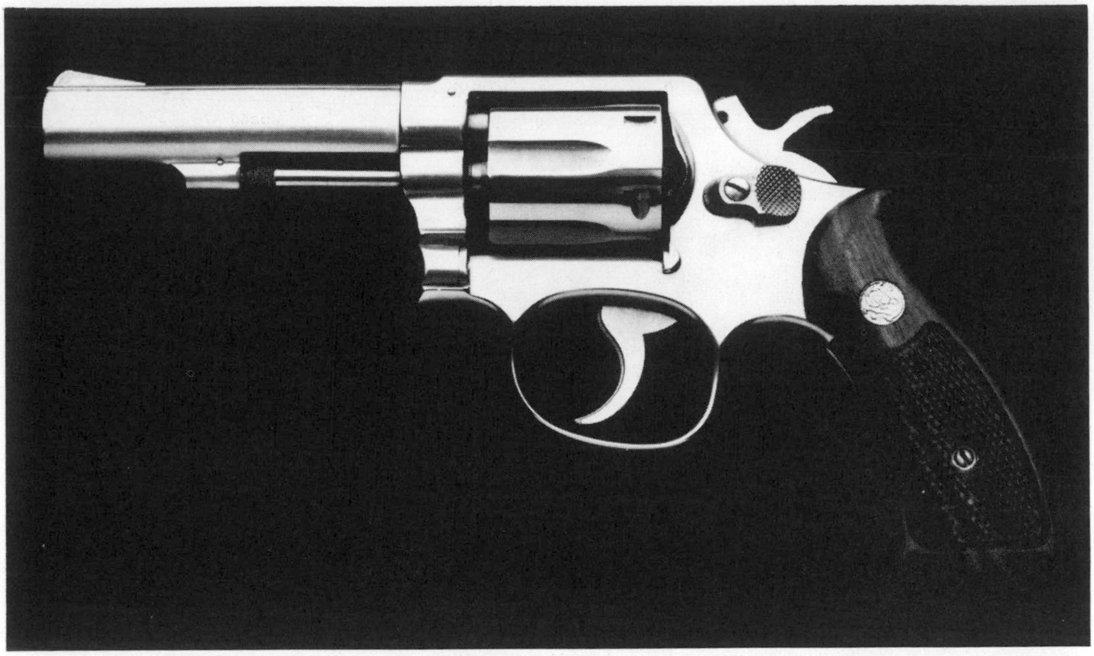

MILITARY AND POLICE—MODEL 64 (Heavy Barrel)

Frame	K	**Sights**	**Front**	Fixed 1/8 in.
Caliber	.38 Special		**Rear**	Square notch
Capacity	Six rounds	**Stocks**		Service walnut
Barrel Lengths	2 and 4 in.	**Hammer**		Standard factory
Weight	34 oz. with 4-in. barrel	**Trigger**		Standard factory
Finish	Stainless steel	**Options**		—

Model 64 (Stainless)

A duplicate of the steel version Model 10 Heavy Barrel, this gun offers good pointability, easy maintenance and a satin finish to minimize reflections. Loaded with .38 Special Plus-P loads, this pistol is becoming a favorite in many police departments as it is made in both the round or square butt models with availability of barrels running in 2- or 4-inch lengths.

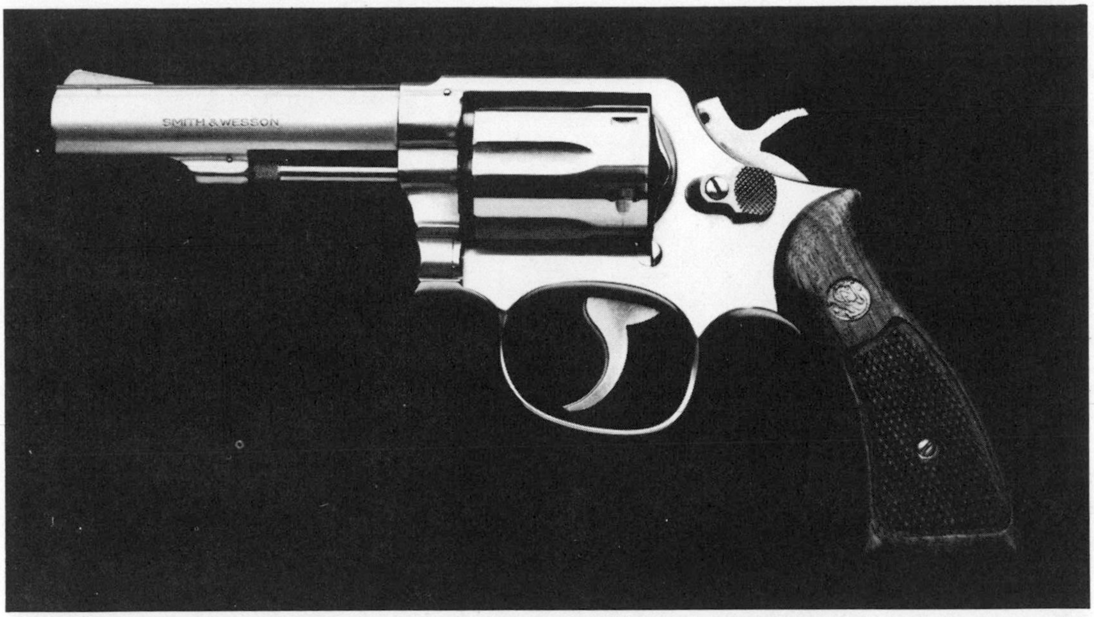

MILITARY AND POLICE—MODEL 65 (Heavy Barrel)

Frame	K	**Sights**	**Front**	Fixed 1/8 in.
Caliber	.357 Magnum		**Rear**	Square notch
Capacity	Six rounds	**Stocks**		Service walnut
Barrel Lengths	4 in.	**Hammer**		Standard factory
Weight	34 oz.	**Trigger**		Standard factory
Finish	Stainless steel	**Options**		—

Model 65 (Stainless)

This stainless steel version of the Model 13 is available only with the 4-inch Heavy Barrel and fixed sights. It is chambered for the high-stepping .357 Magnum loads. This model is increasingly popular with outdoorsmen as well as the police establishment.

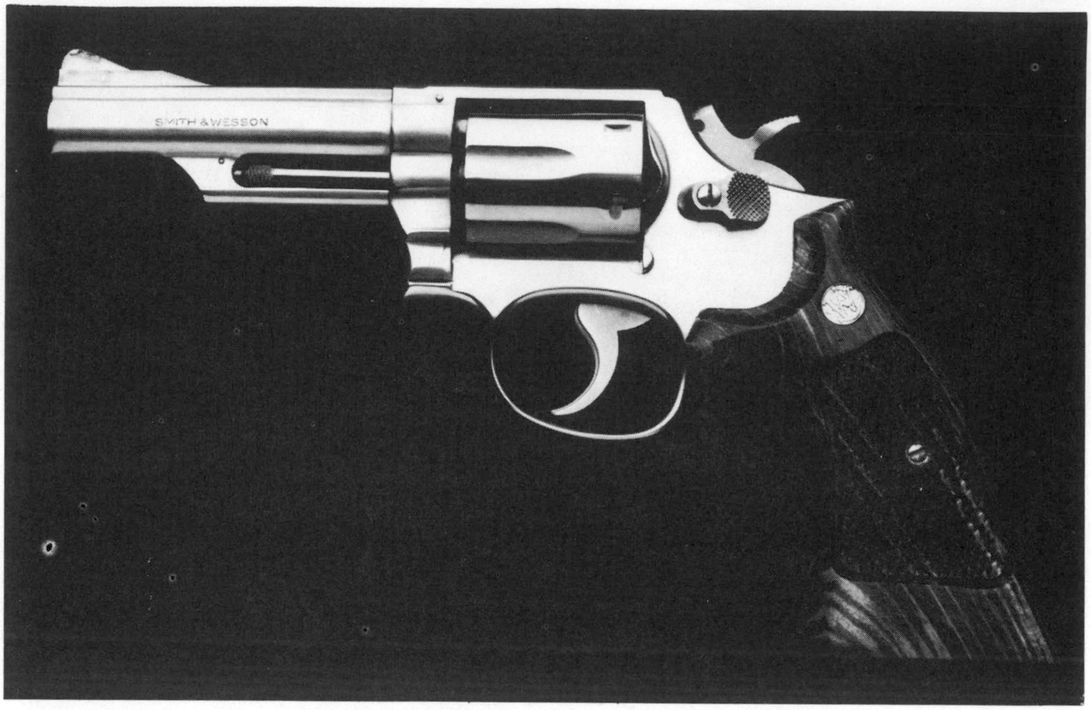

COMBAT MAGNUM—MODEL 66

Frame	K	**Sights**	**Front**	Red ramp
Caliber	.357 Magnum		**Rear**	Micrometer Click
Capacity	Six rounds	**Stocks**		Oversize target
Barrel Lengths	2½, 4, and 6 in.	**Hammer**		Standard factory
Weight	40 oz. with 6-in. barrel	**Trigger**		Standard factory
Finish	Stainless steel	**Options**		Sights and grips

Model 66 (Stainless)

The Model 66 .357 Combat Magnum has all the makings of an extremely fine handgun. A cousin of the famed Model 19, this revolver comes equipped with a shrouded extractor rod, target sights and grips, and is destined to be one of the greats in handgun history. Already getting "black market" prices at twice the retail price, this piece will be in heavy demand for years to come.

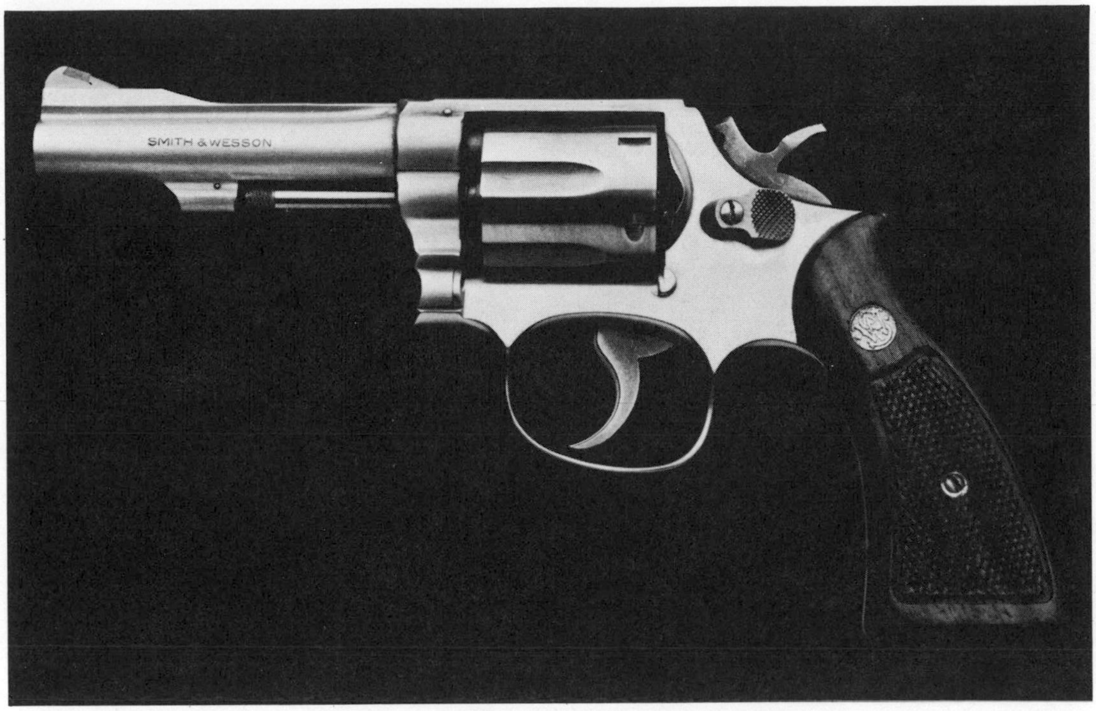

COMBAT MASTERPIECE—MODEL 67

Frame	K	**Sights**	**Front**	Red ramp
Caliber	.38 Special		**Rear**	Micrometer Click
Capacity	Six rounds	**Stocks**		Service walnut
Barrel Lengths	4 in.	**Hammer**		Standard factory
Weight	34 oz.	**Trigger**		Standard factory
Finish	Stainless steel	**Options**		—

Model 67 (Stainless)

As with the rest of the stainless models, Smith & Wesson has taken a well-known steel gun, the Model 15, and has transformed it into an object of beauty. Equipped with service grips, black stainless target sights, and a handy 4-inch barrel, this model is fast becoming a favorite of both the cop on the beat and the outdoorsman.

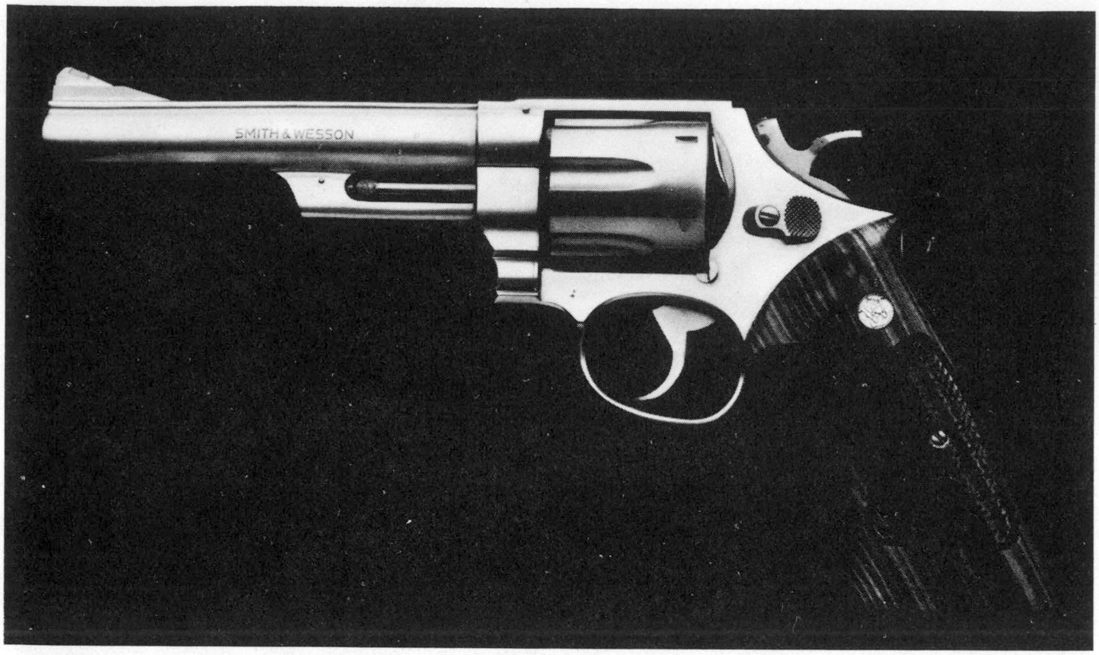

MODEL 629

Frame	N	**Sights**	**Front**	Red ramp
Caliber	.44 Magnum		**Rear**	Micrometer with white outline
Capacity	Six rounds	**Stocks**		Oversize target
Barrel Lengths	4, 6, and 8⅜ in.	**Hammer**		Target
Weight	47 oz. with 6-in. barrel	**Trigger**		Target
Finish	Stainless steel	**Options**		Sights and grips

Model 629 (Stainless)

The "6" designation in an S&W model number denotes the use of stainless steel, thus we have a stainless Model 29 .44 Magnum revolver. This gun is perfect for the hunter who wants a big bore .44, which will be equally at home in the jungles of South America or the cold of the Arctic. With a choice of 4-, 6-, or 8⅜-inch barrels, this model will make a handsome addition to anyone's collection of fine handguns.

SMITH & WESSON COMMEMORATIVES

Although Smith & Wesson puts out fewer commemorative models than its Hartford neighbor, they produce them in larger numbers. Most notable of the S&W special editions are the Texas Ranger and the S&W Anniversary issues. All were run at 10,000 copies each and were sold out in no time.

The Texas Ranger was a specially modified Model 19 .357 Magnum brought out in 1973. Features included a red ramp front with a white outline rear sight. Smooth Goncalo Alves grips and a narrowed trigger guard completed the picture. Most of the sets included a special Bowie knife, although some of the guns were sold separately.

In 1977 Smith & Wesson came out with a special edition to celebrate their 125th anniversary. This time the commemorative was an N-framed Model 25 chambered for the .45 Colt cartridge. It too has special sights, smooth grips, and a seal stamped in gold on the side plate to commemorate the occasion.

Smith & Wesson commemoratives will continue to hold high collector appeal especially in the special engraved models put out with each series.

FACTORY ENGRAVING/CUSTOM SERVICES

Smith & Wesson offers factory engraving in four different and distinct styles. Custom engraving is in a class by itself and is only limited by the imagination of the client. One may order any design and include such items as seals, crests and inlays of precious metals. Descending grades from the Custom are Class A (full coverage), Class B (two-thirds coverage) and Class C (one-third coverage). More details and prices are available from the Smith & Wesson Engraving Department.

Custom Services

Aside from the addition of wide hammers, triggers and fancy wood on handgun grips, no special Custom services are available at this time. However, plans are being formulated for a Custom Shop with complete facilities to handle any special work on S&W products.

Fine examples of Custom Class engraving are these specimens made for Bill Jordan by Smith & Wesson. Seals, gold inlays and bank note portraits are small details that go a long way to ensure high collector value.

44 MAGNUM
1965-1976

SMITH & WESSON

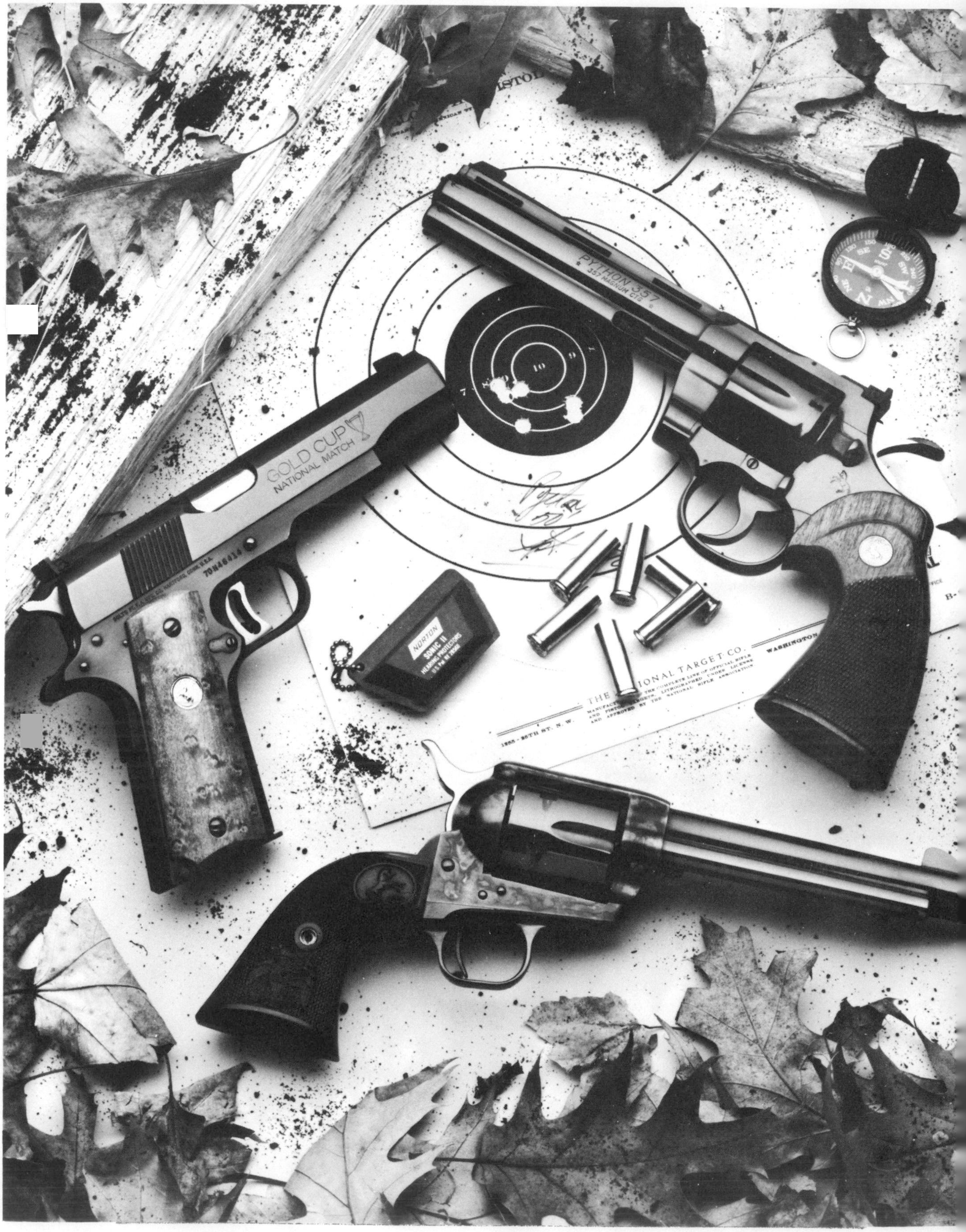
PYTHON 357
357 MAGNUM CTG
GOLD CUP
NATIONAL MATCH
NORTON
SONIC II
HEARING PROTECTORS
TARGET CO.

THREE

Colt Firearms

Colt Firearms dates back to 1836, but even before that, Colonel Sam Colt conceived the idea of a revolving handgun while at sea. The long days lent themselves to hours of thinking, and being the type of man he was, Sam Colt just could not let this time go to waste.

So carving his first model from wood, young Sam soon realized that in his hand was the model for a weapon that would change the destiny of more than one man, or possibly even a country or two. With the introduction of his first model, the Paterson, Colt was on his way. From fine fit to beautiful finish, the Paterson Colts were a joy to behold. The Patersons looked like something was missing on the piece—it had no trigger guard. The trigger itself dropped down when the hammer was cocked. Because it was the first model, there were shortcomings to overcome in design and function. Because of this and lack of government orders, Colt Firearms—then called Patent Arms Manufacturing—would cease operations in 1842.

Undaunted, Colt continued in the munitions field and came up with ideas for waterproofing ammunition and harbor mines. This kept him busy until 1846 when the pressures and demands of the Mexican war revived his interest in firearms.

The next step was the Dragoon revolver which was brought to light with the endorsement of Captain Samuel Walker. He mentioned in a letter how fifteen men with Patersons had fought over eighty Indians, killing or wounding about half that number. With major improvements in design, a new gun called the Walker Dragoon emerged. It was to prove very reliable and perfect for the horse soldier of the time. From 1847 until around 1873, more models and variations of cap and ball revolvers were made than you could count on both hands. From that era on, Colt Firearms gained great respect for its products and was on the road to financial success.

Samuel Colt died on January 10, 1862, much too early for a man of his brilliance and inventiveness. In 1864, fire destroyed a large portion of the factory. But through the efforts of his wife, who used his personal fortune of $15,000,000.00, the factory was rebuilt.

Today, Colt Firearms continues to produce fine guns for both the military and sportsmen. From the period of the famous "Peacemaker," which incidentally was the first successful mass production Colt to use the metallic cartridge, up through the 1911 .45 Automatic pistol, through modern firearms, Colt has been a leader in the field.

As of this writing, Colt handguns are made on five different frame sizes perfectly tailored to the type of piece involved. The D frame is for the small and lightweight guns such as the Detective Special and .38 Special Diamondback. Examples of I-frame guns are the .38 and .357 Python series. For police use, the rugged Lawman and Trooper models are mounted on what Colt calls their J frame. The O-frame designation goes to the semiautomatic guns; the Government, Commander and the Gold Cup models. Finally, the P series is used for the excellent Single Action Army and New Frontier .45 Colt revolvers.

For almost 145 years the Colt tradition of fine firearms has flourished beyond the good Colonel's wildest dreams. Colt will continue to supply fine American made firearms to sportsmen, collectors and law enforcement agencies worldwide. You can bet your last bullet that Sam Colt wouldn't want it any other way!

D-FRAME HANDGUNS

DETECTIVE SPECIAL

Frame	D	**Sights**	**Front**	Ramp
Caliber	.38 Special		**Rear**	Square notch
Capacity	Six rounds	**Stocks**		Checkered walnut
Barrel Lengths	2 in.	**Hammer**		Standard serrated
Weight	21½ oz.	**Trigger**		Smooth
Finish	Blue or nickel	**Options**		—

Detective Special

Dating back to 1927, the Detective Special is one of the best six-shot hideaway guns on the market today. With a 2-inch barrel, this piece weighs 21½ ounces empty. It is available in blue or nickeled finishes, and features checkered walnut target grips. The Detective Special is chambered for the .38 Special, but it should be noted that the newer Plus-P high-performance loads should not be used except in an extreme emergency. Such loads can easily damage light-framed guns and can injure the shooter with continued use. This gun is built on an all-steel frame, has excellent balance, and fixed sights. The small size makes the Detective Special a favorite of plainclothesmen and it is well-suited for use as a personal protection firearm in the home.

DIAMONDBACK

Frame	D	**Sights**	**Front**	Ramp
Caliber	.38 Special		**Rear**	Adjustable
Capacity	Six rounds	**Stocks**		Checkered walnut
Barrel Lengths	4 and 6 in.	**Hammer**		Target
Weight	27½ oz. with 4-in. barrel	**Trigger**		Smooth
Finish	Colt blue	**Options**		—

Diamondback

A scaled-down version of the Colt Python, the Diamondback was brought on the scene in 1966. Featuring a full-length ventilated rib and ejector rod shroud, this light weight model is a good choice for sportsmen who desire a compact gun for hunting small game. There is a choice of either a 4- or 6-inch barrel length, with blue the only outside finish now catalogued. Complete with wraparound grips, target hammer and adjustable sights, the Diamondback is a welcome addition to anyone's handgun battery.

I-FRAME HANDGUNS

PYTHON

Frame	I	**Sights**	**Front**	Ramp
Caliber	.357 Magnum		**Rear**	Adjustable
Capacity	Six rounds	**Stocks**		Checkered walnut
Barrel Lengths	2½, 4, 6, and 8 in.	**Hammer**		Target
Weight	43½ oz. with 6-in. barrel	**Trigger**		Target
Finish	Blue or nickel	**Options**		Elliason Target sights

Python

This particular gun represents the top of the line in Colt revolvers and is considered by many as the world's finest .357 Magnum revolver. The Python features a hand-honed and hand-fitted action. The Custom Shop will provide two additional action tune-ups to satisfy everyone from target shooters to hunters. The Python is an extremely accurate revolver, partially because of its long one turn in 14 inches barrel-twist. With the addition of a full-length ventilated rib, and a choice of four barrel lengths (2½, 4, 6, and 8 inches), and two finishes (blue and nickel) Colt sure makes it hard for the prospective buyer to choose his options.

One other option I would strongly recommend is the Elliason front and rear sight package for a greatly improved sight picture. The Python is an expensive revolver to be sure, but one that will outlast the shooter.

J-FRAME HANDGUNS

LAWMAN MARK III

Frame	J	**Sights**	**Front**	Fixed blade
Caliber	.357 Magnum		**Rear**	Square notch
Capacity	Six rounds	**Stocks**		Checkered walnut
Barrel Lengths	2 and 4 in.	**Hammer**		Standard
Weight	35 oz. with 4-in. barrel	**Trigger**		Service
Finish	Blue or nickel	**Options**		—

Lawman

The Lawman series is aimed primarily at the law enforcement field. A well made and rugged .357 revolver, this gun is all business. In the 4-inch model, the Lawman carries a semi-bull barrel of hefty proportions. Even though this gun has fixed sights, they are easy to pick up thanks to a wide front sight blade. A feature worth noting here is the enlarged trigger guard to accommodate a gloved hand. The 2-inch version has a shrouded ejector rod. I only wish the 4-inch carried one too. This should be standard on every law enforcement gun. The Lawman is a fine gun, equally matched to the .357 cartridge it fires.

TROOPER MARK III

Frame	J	**Sights**	**Front**	Quick draw ramp
Caliber	.357 Magnum		**Rear**	Adjustable
Capacity	Six rounds	**Stocks**		Checkered walnut
Barrel Lengths	4, 6, and 8 in.	**Hammer**		Standard serrated
Weight	42 oz. with 6-in. barrel	**Trigger**		Smooth
Finish	Blue and nickel	**Options**		—

Trooper Mark III

Next in the J-frame lineup is Colt's Trooper Mark III. Available in 4-, 6-, or 8-inch barrel lengths, this handgun is a good all around piece for the police or the sportsman. To me it would be an ideal choice for law enforcement in either the 4- or 6-inch tubes. I am prone to the 6-incher; to me the balance is superb. With a barrel diameter of .750 inches, this gun has been built to take rough use. It is available in blue or nickel finishes, with adjustable rear sights, and target grips, and it sports a wide hammer spur. The Mark III has a smooth action to help in double-action shooting. The Colt Trooper, in my opinion, is a sleeper, one that has not yet reached its peak in popularity.

O-FRAME AUTOMATICS

COMBAT COMMANDER

Frame	O	**Sights**	**Front**	Fixed blade
Caliber	9mm, .38 Super, .45 ACP		**Rear**	Square notch
Capacity	Seven rounds (.45 ACP)	**Stocks**		Checkered walnut
Barrel Lengths	4¼ in.	**Hammer**		Lanyard
Weight	36 oz. with .45 ACP	**Trigger**		Standard
Finish	Blue or satin nickel	**Options**		—

Commander Series—Combat and Lightweight

A recent addition to the Colt line, the steel-framed Combat Commander comes in three chamberings (9mm, .38 super and .45 ACP) and two finishes; blue or satin chrome. Of the two, the latter would get the nod for a gun in constant use. It is a beautiful and durable finish and I would personally encourage Colt to offer it as an option on all of its semiautomatic pistols. In .45 ACP, it rates as a superior defense gun.

The Lightweight Commander is identical to the Combat Commander except for its weight, and the fact that it is only chambered for the .45 ACP cartridge. Also, it is available only in the blue finish. Toying with the idea of a lighter weapon than the standard government-issue model, Colt engineers found a high-tensile-strength aluminum alloy. By going to aluminum, Colt managed to decrease weight by 11 ounces. To a man on the beat this can mean a lot by the time the day is over. As with the other O-frame autos, magazine capacity is seven rounds.

The Big Three. From left to right: Ruger Super Blackhawk, single action, .44 Magnum; Colt Python .357 Magnum; Smith & Wesson Model 29, .44 Magnum.

Left to right: Smith & Wesson Model 52, .38 Special; Model 27, .357 Magnum, 6-inch barrel; Model 57, .41 Magnum, 6-inch barrel.

Colt Firearms. Clockwise from left: Gold Cup National Match, .45 Caliber; Python .357 Magnum; Single Action Army, available in .357 Magnum, .45 Colt, and .44 Special.

Sturm, Ruger and Company. From left to right: Ruger Blackhawk, .357 Magnum, Security Six, .357 Magnum, 2¾ inch barrel, Security Six, .357 Magnum, 6-inch barrel.

GOVERNMENT MODEL MARK IV SERIES 70

Frame	O	**Sights**	**Front**	Ramp
Caliber	9mm, .38 Super, .45 ACP		**Rear**	Square notch
Capacity	Seven rounds (.45 ACP)	**Stocks**		Checkered walnut
Barrel Lengths	5 in.	**Hammer**		Wide target
Weight	38 oz. with .45 ACP	**Trigger**		Standard
Finish	Blue or nickel	**Options**		—

Government Model Mark IV Series 70

One of the most famous of all the pistols in the world is the Colt automatic built around the .45 ACP cartridge. Designed and produced in concert with John Browning, the Colt 1911 was born for the combat troops who needed a large caliber weapon in close encounter situations. Since then, the Government Model .45 has been the standard issue weapon of the services. It is dependable, finely finished and accurate. In 1970 Colt introduced a very small but highly significant improvement in the gun's performance. They designed a new barrel and spring-loaded bushing to grip the barrel as the slide returned to its normal position. Available in blue or nickel, this pistol comes in 9mm, .38 Super or the classic .45 ACP chamberings.

GOLD CUP NATIONAL MATCH MARK IV SERIES 70

Frame	O	**Sights**	**Front**	Undercut
Caliber	.45 ACP		**Rear**	Elliason
Capacity	Seven rounds	**Stocks**		Checkered walnut
Barrel Lengths	5 in.	**Hammer**		Wide target
Weight	38½ oz.	**Trigger**		Wide target
Finish	Blue	**Options**		—

Gold Cup National Match Mark IV Series 70

The "flagship" of the semiautos just has to be the Gold Cup National Match .45. This finely-tuned piece is the best large caliber handgun a dedicated target shooter could buy. Loaded up with semi-wadcutter bullets and a target load of Bullseye powder, X-ring accuracy is almost guaranteed with this gun. Equipped with Elliason target sights, full-length barrel rib, enlarged ejection port, super polishing and bluing, this automatic is rated as one of the best anywhere. Other features include an ajustable trigger stop, wide target trigger and walnut grip panels.

P-FRAME HANDGUNS

SINGLE ACTION ARMY

Frame	P	**Sights**	**Front**	Fixed blade
Caliber	.357 Magnum, .45 Colt, .44 Special		**Rear**	Square notch
Capacity	Six rounds	**Stocks**		Composite rubber
Barrel Lengths	4¾, 5½, and 7½ in.	**Hammer**		Standard
Weight	37 oz. with 5½-in. barrel in .45 Colt	**Trigger**		Standard
Finish	Blue or nickel	**Options**		—

Colt Single Action Army—Standard Model

The Colt Single Action Army, or "Peacemaker," as it is known, is one of the most popular, expensive, and finely crafted guns ever produced. In its 107-year existence, the Single Action Army has been chambered in thirty different cartridges, ranging from .22 rimfire to the .476 Eley. This is a superbly balanced gun, but it is not suited to hunting because of the fixed sights and long hammer throw. Nonetheless, it has become a favorite among many who value it for its romantic and nostalgic appeal.

Today the gun is available in .357 Magnum, .44 Special and .45 Colt, and comes in many barrel lengths, including 4¾, 5½ and 7½ inches. The 5½-inch is my favorite mainly because it puts the balance of the piece in the hand for a rock steady feeling of confidence. Add black composition grips (blued version) or walnut panels (nickeled finish) and you have a piece that deserves the title of "the gun that won the West."

Made for Ned Buntline by Colt, the Buntline Special version has the same features as the Single Action Army except for a 12-inch barrel. Not very practical in the field because of its barrel length, this Colt still offers the advantages of a longer sight radius and increased bullet velocity. Weighing 44 ounces empty and displaying a 17⅜-inch overall length, it is a big piece to carry around. It is available in blued steel or nickel finish and in .45 Colt only.

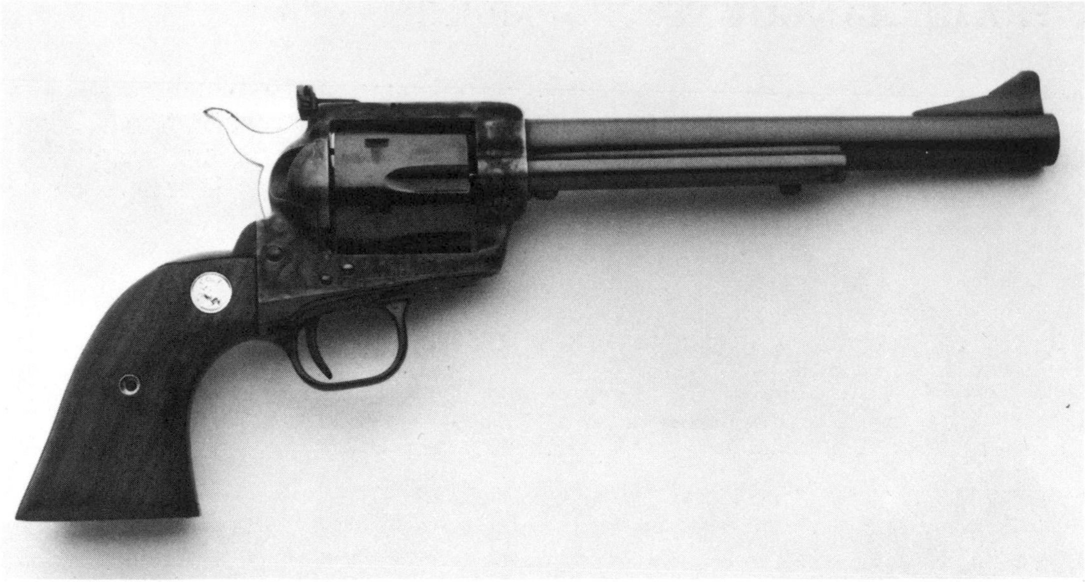

NEW FRONTIER—SINGLE ACTION ARMY

Frame	P	**Sights**	**Front**	Ramp
Caliber	.44 Special, .45 Colt, .44-40		**Rear**	Adjustable
Capacity	Six rounds	**Stocks**		Walnut
Barrel Lengths	4¾ and 7½ in.	**Hammer**		Standard
Weight	37½ oz. with 4¾-in. barrel in .45 Colt	**Trigger**		Standard
Finish	Blue	**Options**		—

Single Action Army—New Frontier Model

Brought on the market in 1961, the New Frontier is for the shooter who really loves the SAA and its calibers for hunting purposes. Better suited to the task than its fixed-sight brothers, the New Frontier carries fully adjustable rear and high-bladed front sights. Superlatively finished and furnished with walnut grips, you can order this model in .44 Special, .45 Colt, or for that pure western flair, .44-40. This gun may not be much in the way of ballistics, but it is fun to shoot. For outside finishes, you have a choice of either a blued or nickeled surface.

One word of caution: It is inadvisable to load any of the Colt Single Action Western-style revolvers with more than five rounds. The cylinder should be rotated so that the empty chamber is underneath the hammer in the safety-notch position. Colt Firearms has choosen to keep this authentic type of safety, and with a little common sense in its use, we can have our Single Actions the way they have been since 1873.

COLT COMMEMORATIVE MODELS

Hardly a year goes by without Colt introducing something special for the collector. Colt is the leader when it comes to commemoratives, having marketed about 132 different models and variations since 1961. In fact, in 1964 alone, Colt brought fourth twenty-six different commemoratives ranging from the Nevada Statehood to a Wyatt Earp Buntline Single Action model. For the dyed-in-the-wool collector, Colt Firearms is the place to turn to for plenty of variety in the Commemorative field.

FACTORY ENGRAVING AND CUSTOM SERVICES

The custom shop at Colt offers more services than anyone could possibly take advantage of. While other gun companies have engraving services, Colt's is the only one to have a full service shop capable of doing most anything to a Colt firearm.

You can order custom etching or engraving in six different styles and four different coverages from one-quarter to full coverage. You may order a gun with special serial numbers or special presentation cases. Grips are available in ivory, mother of pearl, or select rosewood. Custom gunsmithing is also done on factory order guns and includes such items as the Custom Tuned Actions, Elliason rear target sights, slide safeties and combat-style grip safeties. More information and a beautifully illustrated color catalog is available from Colt.

Here an artisan at Colt's Custom Shop works on the final details for a Single Action Army handgun.

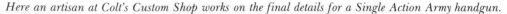

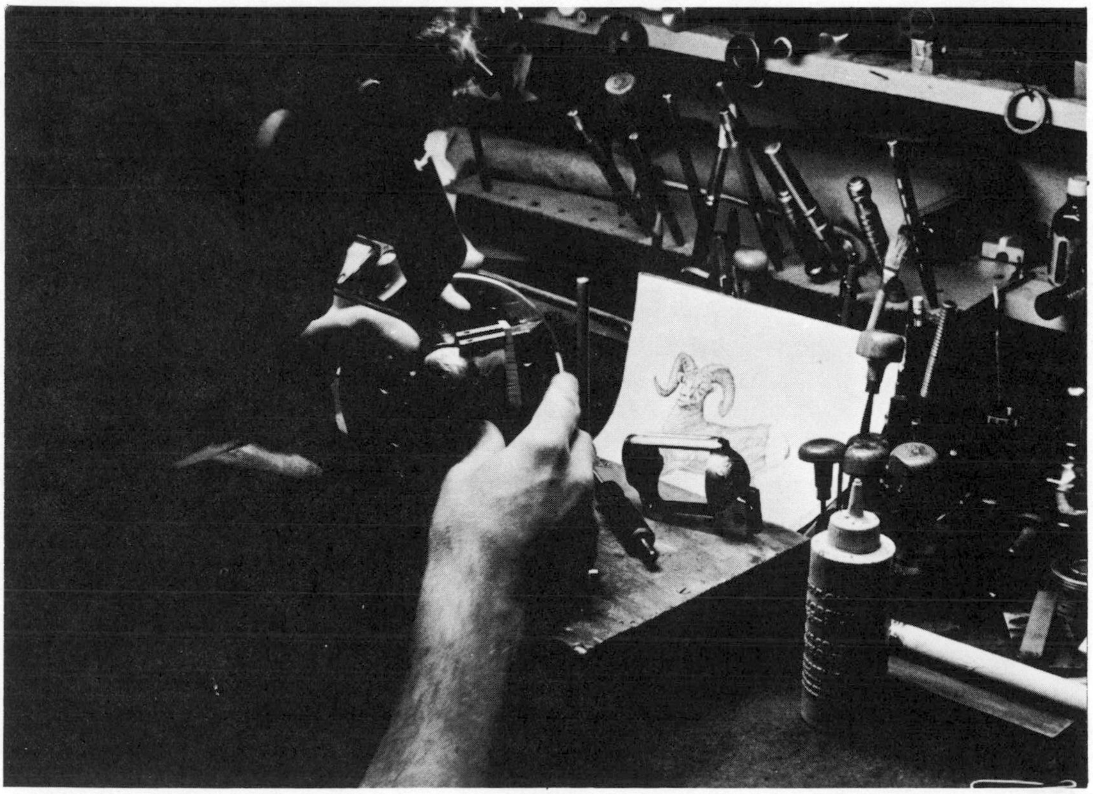

High Velocity
50 CENTER FIRE CARTRIDGES
WARNING: KEEP OUT OF REACH OF CHILDREN
Remington
7
8
9
LICENSE

FOUR

Sturm, Ruger and Company

Even though Sturm, Ruger and Company is only thirty years old, they have probably introduced and made more models in this short span than most of the other arms makers put together. The youngest company of the big three had its start in January, 1949. With an investment of $50,000.00, William B. Ruger and Alexander M. Sturm started with an initial production run of a .22 semiautomatic pistol. Sales were brisk, which completely took the two men by surprise. The word was out that they were giving a solid dollar's worth of value.

In 1951, Sturm, Ruger introduced its Mark I semiautomatic pistol with adjustable sights and various barrel lengths. It proved to be such a fine and durable pistol that it was adopted by the army and air force as a training arm for the men in uniform. This year was also going to put Bill Ruger into a new and unexpected position; he became president of the company, due to the untimely death of his partner at the age of 29.

It was now up to Bill Ruger to bring his young company up to the worldwide status he had often dreamed about. Since the Mark Is were on their way to establishing themselves as a durable piece, Bill was looking down the road for more variety in design and applications for the shooting public. In 1953, a successful design was finalized on a .22 rimfire called the Single-Six. After that came a lighter model and then the .22 Magnum Single-Six.

The big break for the centerfire fans came in 1955 when Sturm, Ruger introduced a model called the "Blackhawk" which was centered around the popular .357 cartridge. Built on a bigger and beefier frame, this gun was to be the cornerstone of a series of big-bore handguns.

In the years that followed, single action models were introduced in .41 and .44 Magnums, .30 Carbine and .45 Colt, plus a whole new concept in handguns to be known as the Ruger Convertibles. Packed with each single action in this line was an extra cylinder chambered in 9mm Luger (with the .357) and .45 ACP (with the .45 Colt). These would go a long way to insure the shooter the greatest possible versatility.

In 1963, Bill Ruger brought out the now legendary "Super Blackhawk." A big piece for sure, this model weighs in at 48 ounces, has a non-fluted cyclinder for extra strength and safety, and additional extras like a deeply serrated hammer spur and "Dragoon" style trigger guard designed to keep it (the trigger guard) away from your fingers during heavy recoil. Adjustable sights and a 7½-inch barrel complete this excellent hunter's rig.

Now on its way as a well-established firearms company, Sturm, Ruger ventured into the double action revolver market in the early seventies with their Security-Six series. Though this line was aimed primarily at the law enforcement field, it wasn't long before sportsmen would be using it in the field. Available in .38 and .357 Magnum, this rugged gun with its novel method of disassembly was soon on backorder in many parts of the country.

There seems to be no limit to the inventiveness of this company. The seventies brought about the introduction of a new patented "transfer-bar" ignition system and a brand new stainless steel .44 Magnum revolver called the Redhawk. In brief, the transfer-bar system allows the user to carry six rounds in the cylinder, against the five normally carried with one empty chamber under the hammer for safety. The Ruger Redhawk has all the ingredients necessary to make the piece very popular. Made totally from stainless steel, the new Redhawk incorporates a brand new trigger-hammer mechanism, interchangeable front colored sight blades, and the heft of about 52 ounces with a 7-inch barrel. More details on this gun can be found in the catalog section of this chapter.

RUGER SINGLE-ACTION HANDGUNS

BLACKHAWK—BN-31

Frame	SA	**Sights**	**Front**	Patridge
Caliber	.30 Carbine		**Rear**	Adjustable
Capacity	Six rounds	**Stocks**		Walnut
Barrel Lengths	7½ in.	**Hammer**		Serrated
Weight	44 oz.	**Trigger**		Standard
Finish	Satin blue	**Options**		—

Model BN-31—.30 Carbine

For the hunter or trapper this Ruger Blackhawk in .30 Carbine is an excellent choice. Using round nose, jacketed bullets at moderate velocities, this gun is just the ticket for the man who sells his furs on the market. This gun may also be used in conjunction with shoulder arms in the same caliber.

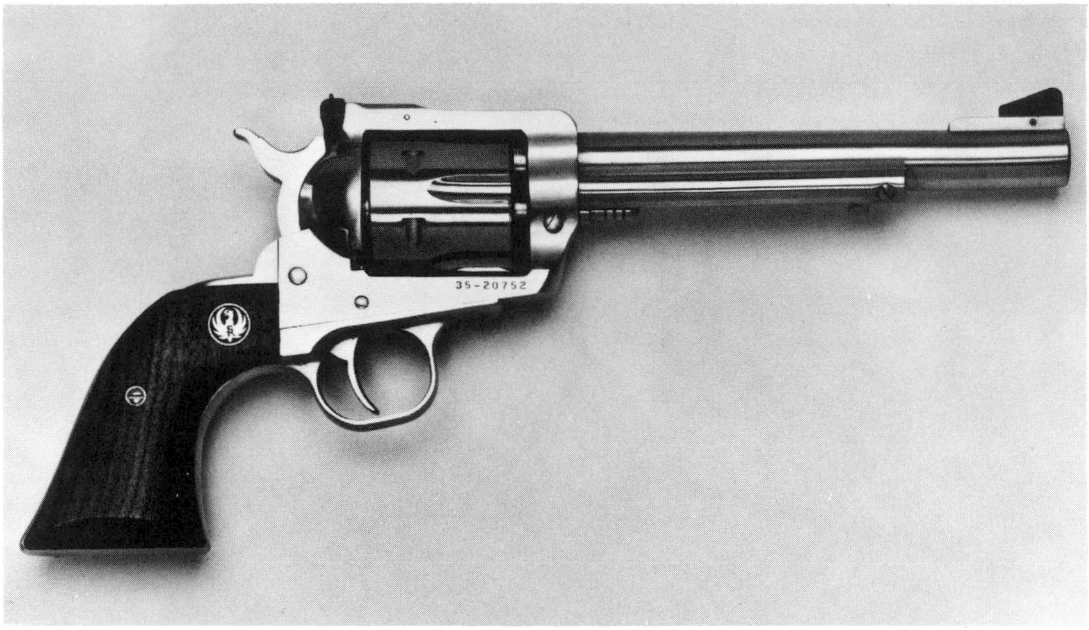

BLACKHAWK—KBN-36/BN-34/BN-36

Frame	SA	**Sights**	**Front**	Patridge
Caliber	.357 Magnum		**Rear**	Adjustable
Capacity	Six rounds	**Stocks**		Walnut
Barrel Lengths	4⅝ and 6½ in.	**Hammer**		Serrated
Weight	42 oz. with 6½-in. barrel	**Trigger**		Standard
Finish	Stainless steel or blue	**Options**		—

Model BN-34, BN-36 and KBN-36—.357 Magnum

By far the most popular gun in the single action line, this Blackhawk chambered for the high-stepping .357 Magnum will feel right at home on any game field. Available with a 4⅝-inch barrel (BN-34) or 6½-inch barrel (BN-36), this blued model weighs 40 and 42 ounces respectively. The stainless version (KBN-36) is sought after by knowledgeable hunters who hunt in all kinds of weather.

BLACKHAWK—BN-36X/BN-34X CONVERTIBLE

Frame	SA	**Sights**	**Front**	Patridge
Caliber	.357 Magnum/9mm Luger		**Rear**	Adjustable
Capacity	Six rounds	**Stocks**		Walnut
Barrel Lengths	4⅝ and 6½ in.	**Hammer**		Serrated
Weight	42 oz. with 6½-in. barrel	**Trigger**		Standard
Finish	Satin blue	**Options**		Comes with extra cylinder for 9mm Luger

Model BN-34X, BN-36X—.357/9mm Convertible Series

Introduced as a totally new concept in centerfire handguns, this Convertible series in a .357/9mm combination has proved to be both versatile and popular among Ruger followers. Since the 9mm Luger is a good all-around cartridge, putting it together in concert with the .357/.38 Special actually makes this gun a tri-combo piece.

BLACKHAWK—BN-41/BN-42

Frame	SA	**Sights**	**Front**	Patridge
Caliber	.41 Magnum		**Rear**	Adjustable
Capacity	Six rounds	**Stocks**		Walnut
Barrel Lengths	4⅝ and 6½ in.	**Hammer**		Serrated
Weight	40 oz. with 6½-in. barrel	**Trigger**		Standard
Finish	Satin blue	**Options**		—

Model BN-41, BN-42—.41 Magnum

Bill Ruger has seen fit to barrel this .41 Magnum with a handy 4⅝-inch tube. Carried on the hip in a high-ride holster, this gun has proven to be a hunter's delight on long hunts. This gun has good, adjustable sights, and the .41 caliber 170-grain bullet has a trajectory approaching a ruled line. This model has become a favorite of experienced deer and bear hunters nation-wide.

BLACKHAWK—BN-44/BN-45

Frame	SA	**Sights**	**Front**	Patridge
Caliber	.45 Colt		**Rear**	Adjustable
Capacity	Six rounds	**Stocks**		Walnut
Barrel Lengths	4⅝ and 7½ in.	**Hammer**		Serrated
Weight	40 oz. with 7½-in. barrel	**Trigger**		Standard
Finish	Satin blue	**Options**		—

Model BN-44, BN-45—.45 Colt

Because of the ability of the Ruger guns to hold and digest more pressure than their Smith & Wesson or .45 Colt counterparts, many gun buffs have tried to "magnumize" the .45 Colt with only modest success. The old warhorse .45 in the Ruger series is alive and well and at its full potential as a good, solid cartridge. This model Blackhawk is a handsome addition to any handgunner's battery.

BLACKHAWK—BN-44X/BN-45X

Frame	SA	**Sights**	**Front**	Patridge
Caliber	.45 Colt/.45 ACP		**Rear**	Adjustable
Capacity	Six rounds	**Stocks**		Walnut
Barrel Lengths	4⅝ and 7½ in.	**Hammer**		Serrated
Weight	40 oz. with 7½-in. barrel	**Trigger**		Standard
Finish	Satin blue	**Options**		Comes with extra cylinder for .45 ACP

Model BN-44X, BN-45X—Convertible Series .45 Colt/.45 ACP

To make the .45 Colt more desirable to shooters, Ruger brought the .45/.45 ACP line out in 1971. Serving the same purpose as the .357/9mm combo, this gun is for the fellow who likes his bores big and bullets heavy. Here the buyer again has a choice of barrel lengths (4⅝ and 7½ inches) but as before, I find the shorter barrel the best bet in the field.

SUPER BLACKHAWK—S47N

Frame	SA	**Sights**	**Front**	Patridge
Caliber	.44 Magnum		**Rear**	Adjustable
Capacity	Six rounds	**Stocks**		Walnut
Barrel Lengths	7½ and 10 in.	**Hammer**		Wide serrated
Weight	48 oz. with 7½-in. barrel	**Trigger**		Wide
Finish	Highly-polished blue	**Options**		—

Model S-47N—44 Magnum Super Blackhawk

Originally introduced as a plain Flat-Top Blackhawk in 1956, this gun was updated in 1959 to its present configuration. Truly one of America's great handguns, this Ruger has taken big game the world over. Chambered for the thunderous .44 Magnum, which in some cases can deliver twice the energy of the .357 (depending of course on who is doing the loading), this revolver can also fire the mild-mannered .44 Special with no problems. At 48 ounces, it is a heavy gun, but once the trigger is squeezed, one is more than happy with the additional weight engineered into the gun. The recently marketed 10½-inch version is for the silhouette fans, while the 7½-inch model is the most popular among field hunters.

RUGER DOUBLE-ACTION HANDGUNS

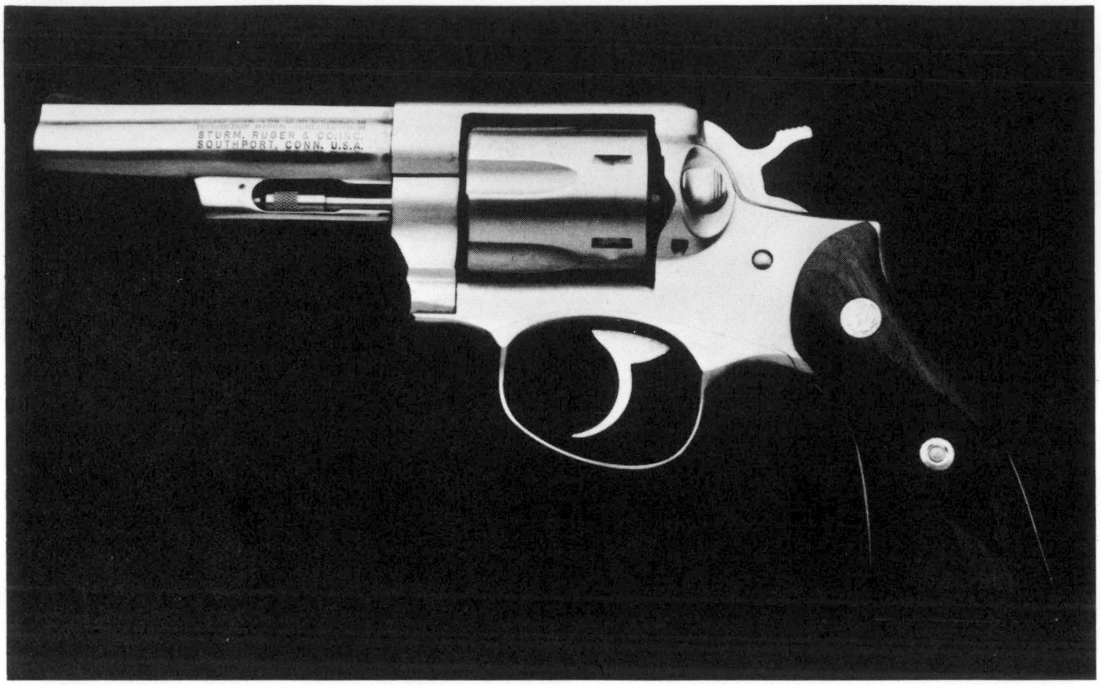

POLICE SERVICE SIX—GF-84

Frame	DA	**Sights**	**Front**	Ramp
Caliber	.38 Special		**Rear**	Notch
Capacity	Six rounds	**Stocks**		Walnut
Barrel Lengths	4 in.	**Hammer**		Serrated
Weight	33½ oz.	**Trigger**		Standard
Finish	Stainless steel	**Options**		—

Model GF-84—.38 Special Police Service-Six

Since the entire Ruger line of double-action revolvers shares most of the same features, we will delve into six different models of the Security/Service-Six series.

First on the list will be the GF-84 called the Police Service-Six, and crafted for our men in the law enforcement field. The main difference in the police series is non-adjustable sights and its availability in 2¾- or 4-inch barrels. Chambered in combinations of .38 Special and .38 Special/.357 Magnum, this gun is manufactured in both blue and stainless finishes.

SECURITY SIX—RDA-32

Frame	DA	**Sights**	**Front**	Ramp
Caliber	.357 Magnum		**Rear**	Adjustable
Capacity	Six rounds	**Stocks**		Walnut
Barrel Lengths	2¾, 4, and 6 in.	**Hammer**		Serrated
Weight	33½ oz. with 4-in. barrel	**Trigger**		Standard
Finish	Blue	**Options**		—

Model RDA-32—Security-Six

The RDA-32 is easily one of the best "snubbies" I have ever handled. It is chambered for the hot .357 Magnum. Though very uncomfortable in shooting, mainly because of the short barrel and rough muzzle blast, it is still a very handy gun for undercover work or backpacking. Adjustable sights and easy take-down make this a desirable gun in the Ruger lineup.

SPEED SIX—SS-32

Frame	DA	**Sights**	**Front**	Ramp
Caliber	.357 Magnum		**Rear**	Notch
Capacity	Six rounds	**Stocks**		Walnut
Barrel Lengths	2¾ and 4 in.	**Hammer**		Serrated
Weight	33½ oz. with 4-inch barrel	**Trigger**		Standard
Finish	Blue	**Options**		—

Model SS-32—Speed-Six

Whatever was mentioned above for the RDA series goes ditto for this model. Except for a few items like a round butt for hip-carrying and fixed sights, both models are basically the same. The SS-32 is a good choice when comfort and concealability are paramount considerations. Using high speed hollow-points in the .357 makes for a good man-stopper when and if the time comes.

SECURITY SIX—RDA-34HT

Frame	DA	**Sights**	**Front**	Ramp
Caliber	.357 Magnum		**Rear**	Adjustable
Capacity	Six rounds	**Stocks**		Target walnut
Barrel Lengths	4 in.	**Hammer**		Serrated
Weight	33½ oz.	**Trigger**		Standard
Finish	Blue	**Options**		—

Model RDA-34HT—Security-Six

The RDA-34HT Security-Six is a heavy-barreled model. Designed for men with big hands, this model comes equipped with what the Ruger company calls the "Big Grip." Essentially a target-style grip, this piece of walnut will help fill the bill for those in the need of such an accessory.

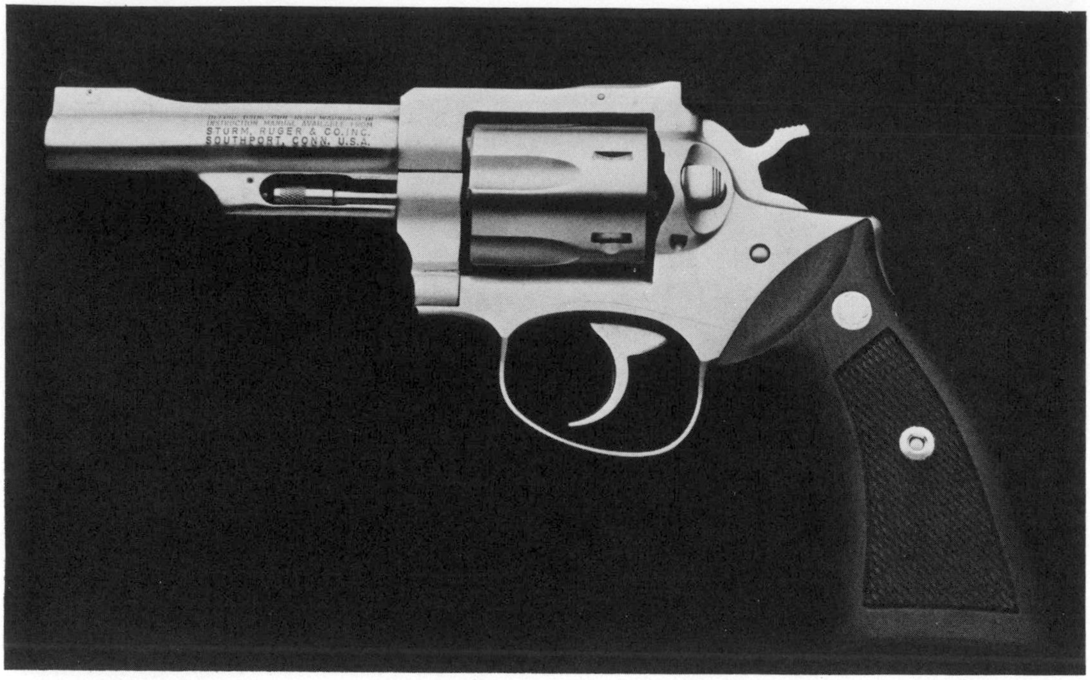

SECURITY SIX—GA-34HT

Frame	DA	**Sights**	**Front**	Ramp
Caliber	.357 Magnum		**Rear**	Adjustable
Capacity	Six rounds	**Stocks**		Target walnut
Barrel Lengths	4 in.	**Hammer**		Serrated
Weight	33½ oz.	**Trigger**		Standard
Finish	Stainless steel	**Options**		—

Model GA-34HT—Security-Six

A heavy-barreled, big grip model, this Security Six is available in stainless steel. The patrolman, whether assigned to a foot patrol or cruiser duty, will find this gun both handy and easy to maintain. Since it comes in the .357 Magnum chambering, police units still on the .38 Special can use this gun with the new Plus-P loading with ease.

SECURITY SIX—GA-36

Frame	DA	**Sights**	**Front**	Ramp
Caliber	.357 Magnum		**Rear**	Adjustable
Capacity	Six rounds	**Stocks**		Walnut
Barrel Lengths	6 in.	**Hammer**		Serrated
Weight	35 oz. (approximately)	**Trigger**		Standard
Finish	Stainless steel	**Options**		—

Model GA-36—Security-Six

Here is a super handgun for the all-weather hunter. The GA-36 is equipped with adjustable sights, checkered walnut grip panels, and stainless steel finish. With a little work on the trigger system this Ruger can be counted on for some pretty fancy groups at 100 meters.

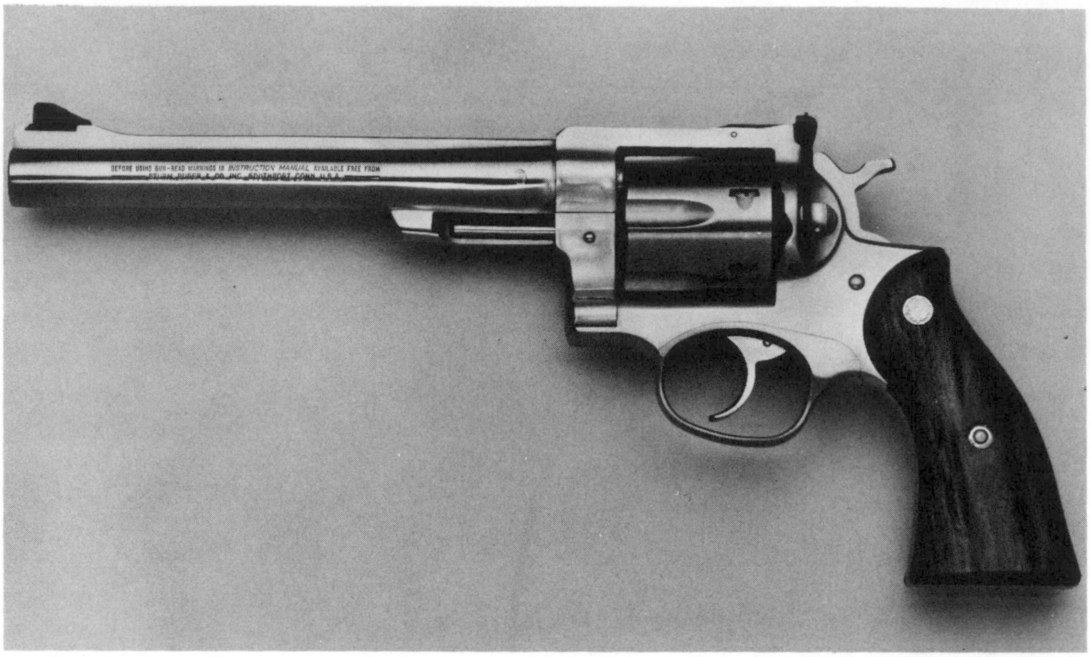

REDHAWK

Frame	Large	**Sights**	**Front**	Red ramp
Caliber	.44 Magnum		**Rear**	White outline
Capacity	Six rounds	**Stocks**		Smooth walnut
Barrel Lengths	7½ in.	**Hammer**		Serrated
Weight	52 oz.	**Trigger**		Smooth
Finish	Stainless steel	**Options**		Yellow ramp front sight blade

Redhawk .44 Magnum Revolver

Ruger's latest entry in the handgun field is the new Redhawk in stainless steel and chambered for the "big bore" .44. Hitting the scales at 52 ounces, this Ruger balances well in the hand. With cylinder wall dimensións greater than 25 per cent thicker than its nearest competitor, the Redhawk will digest all factory ammo and any reasonable handloads with ease and safety. Additional features—consisting of a smoother double-action pull, removable front sight blades of different colors, and a white-outline rear sight—all add to the versatility of this handsome revolver. The Redhawk will be available in greater numbers in 1980-81.

RUGER COMMEMORATIVE MODELS

As of this date, Ruger has not produced any commemorative centerfire models aimed at the general public. Most have been made for special occasions such as state centennial celebrations. We hope to see more Ruger commemoratives in the future.

50
Hornady's
FRONTIER
WITH
HORNADY BULLETS
FRONTIER CARTRIDGES
DETONICS
OFFICIAL
50
CENTER FIRE
PISTOL-
REVOLVER
CARTRIDGES
Western

FIVE

Other Major Manufacturers

Smith & Wesson, Colt, and Sturm-Ruger are considered to be the "Big Three" arms manufacturers in the United States, but there also are several smaller firms in the firearms business. These independents tend to produce firearms that may be similiar in appearance, but which are in reality quite different. These endeavors stir up the competition and provide consumers with a better choice and sometimes a better product than ever before.

In this particular chapter on the independents, we'll talk about different firms and individuals who have contributed to the growth and well-being of the firearms industry. Since new models are introduced all the time, every effort has been made to include everyone who could provide a gun for pictures and evaluation. If any particular piece is missing, in all probability it will be included in a revised edition at a later date.

From AMT to Wildey, and from the small .25 ACP to the big .44 Magnum, the American shooter now has more choice in firearms than ever before. Tough, durable steel and select natural walnut go hand-in-hand with mountains of pride to produce some of the finest handguns in the world today.

ARCADIA MACHINE AND TOOL (AMT)

AMT Auto-Mag Semiautomatic Pistol

Brought out in the sixties, the Auto-Mag has always had a certain mystique for a select group of handgunners who desire the extra power and bullet weights the big .44 Magnum cartridge delivers, but in a semiautomatic weapon.

Blasting out of a standard 6½-inch barrel, factory ammo will churn up roughly 1,350 fps at 975 foot-pounds of muzzle energy. The Auto-Mag will digest bullet weights from 180 to 240 grains.

AMT AUTO-MAG

Frame	Semiautomatic	**Sights**	**Front**	Ramp
Caliber	.44 Magnum, .357 Magnum		**Rear**	Adjustable
Capacity	Seven rounds	**Stocks**		Wood or plastic
Barrel Lengths	Varying	**Hammer**		Serrated
Weight	57 oz.	**Trigger**		Serrated
Finish	Stainless steel	**Options**		Various grips and barrels

The gun itself is massive, weighing 57 ounces empty. Made from stainless steel, it makes for a rugged handgun in any kind of weather. This piece can be loaded with seven rounds, and shoulder holsters are available, which in my estimation is the best way to carry this heavy auto.

Regrettably, the Auto-Mag is an on-again, off-again manufacturing proposition. Discontinued a few years back, the "B" model is now back in production, but only in a limited production run. Starting at $1,000.00 plus, this gun is for the dedicated aficionado for sure. Mint condition guns can still be found at prices which reflect supply and demand.

AMT .380 BACKUP

Frame	Small	**Sights**	**Front**	Fixed
Caliber	.380 Automatic		**Rear**	Fixed
Capacity	Five rounds	**Stocks**		Hardwood
Barrel Lengths	2½ in.	**Hammer**		Internal
Weight	19 oz.	**Trigger**		Standard
Finish	Stainless steel	**Options**		—

AMT .380 Backup

Made entirely from stainless steel (except for the grips), this gun was designed primarily as a backup piece. Chambered for the .380 ACP cartridge, this gun will do the job at close ranges with the help of hollow point bullets.

Holding five rounds (plus one up the tube), this little defensive pistol weighs 19 ounces. Adding a few more ounces for a loaded piece, this gun would make an ideal hideout gun in a pancake or ankle holster.

The gun was engineered with the following specifications in mind to hold down the weight and insure complete reliability. For one, there is no double-action mode, and no hold-open device to hold open the slide after the last shot is fired. The safety is located on the left side behind the trigger, and like other semiautomatics, there is a grip safety which prevents the gun from going off if it should fall.

Sights are milled in the top slide and are fixed, but they offer a decent sight picture considering the close distances at which this gun will be used.

The AMT Backup is well made, and deserves a place in today's small and portable defense handgun market.

AMT .45 ACP Series

Since combat shooting as a sport has mushroomed during the last few years, it was only a matter of time before AMT would bring out a .45 ACP weapon. They not only brought out one, but three different versions. All are stainless steel and follow the Colt/Browning design.

AMT HARDBALLER

Frame	Semiautomatic	**Sights**	**Front**	Patridge
Caliber	.45 ACP		**Rear**	Adjustable
Capacity	Seven rounds	**Stocks**		Checkered walnut
Barrel Lengths	5 in.	**Hammer**		Standard target
Weight	39 oz.	**Trigger**		Wide adjustable
Finish	Stainless steel	**Options**		—

AMT .45 Hardballer. The most popular of these is what the company calls the Hardballer. Seen at many a combat match, this model weighs 39 ounces, and incorporates a brush-finished frame with brightly polished slide flats.

Other features include adjustable sights, extended combat safety, wide adjustable trigger, beveled magazine well, and a loaded chamber indicator. These features plus the convenience of a semiautomatic weapon make for a gun now in demand in most parts of the country.

AMT .45 Combat Government. Similar in appearance to the Hardballer, the AMT Combat Government model was designed with law enforcement use in mind. Lacking adjustable sights, the combat model comes with high visability fixed sights for instant alignment. The only other feature that distinguishes this model from the Hardballer is the absence of a matte rib, *a la* Colt Gold Cup, running the length of the slide. As is the rest of the .45 ACP series, the Combat Government is chambered for the .45 ACP cartridge.

AMT HARDBALLER LONGSLIDE

Frame	Semiautomatic	**Sights**	**Front**	Patridge
Caliber	.45 ACP		**Rear**	Adjustable
Capacity	Seven rounds	**Stocks**		Checkered walnut
Barrel Lengths	7 in.	**Hammer**		Standard target
Weight	42 oz.	**Trigger**		Wide adjustable
Finish	Stainless steel	**Options**		—

AMT .45 Hardballer Longslide. Last on our list is the .45 ACP Hardballer Longslide. Designed for competition use, it is generally found to be too long in a standard holster unless the bottom plug is removed. This recoil-operated handgun has a slide and barrel a full 2 inches longer than the Hardballer. With a length of 10½ inches, this model puts the weight of the piece forward for better balance and increased sight radius. This alone is often a deciding factor in choosing a special competition rig. As a plus, the extra length and weight contribute to a lower recoil sensation. The same features are found on this piece as with other AMT .45 models, so the user gets good value without having to spend additional money on accessories or customizing.

Priced about $675.00, the Longslide is a good investment. Considering what a good pistolsmith will charge for converting your gun to a longslide, it indeed is money well spent.

AMT also offers slide fits in the Handballer and Longslide for those who demand particularly fine tuning. Write for details and prices.

BAUER CORPORATION

BAUER SEMIAUTOMATIC

Frame	Small	**Sights**	**Front**	Fixed
Caliber	.25 ACP		**Rear**	Fixed
Capacity	Six rounds	**Stocks**		Pearlite
Barrel Lengths	2⅛ in.	**Hammer**		Internal
Weight	10 oz.	**Trigger**		Standard
Finish	Stainless steel	**Options**		—

Bauer .25 Automatic

The Bauer .25 automatic is one of the smallest guns I handled in my research. Tipping the scales at 10 ounces, this little stainless steel piece is at its best in your pocket or purse.

Nicely finished and very attractive with its pearlite grips, this .25 caliber pistol is listed as a defense gun, although the small caliber limits its effectiveness for this purpose. With a cartridge an inch in length and developing 73 foot-pounds at the muzzle, the .25 ACP is hardly a man-stopper. To make matters worse, it seems to be a factory-loaded cartridge only, meaning reloaders tend to stay away from it.

Magazine capacity is six rounds and sights are fixed. When shooting this piece, one must be careful to practice proper holding technique. If not held right, the slide has a tendency to come back and catch the web of skin between the thumb and forefinger. But all things considered, for the purpose intended, the Bauer .25 does its job.

CHARTER ARMS

CHARTER ARMS UNDERCOVER

Frame	Medium	**Sights**	**Front**	Semi-patridge
Caliber	.38 Special		**Rear**	Fixed
Capacity	Five rounds	**Stocks**		Smooth walnut
Barrel Lengths	2 and 3 in.	**Hammer**		Serrated
Weight	16 oz.	**Trigger**		Serrated
Finish	Blue or nickel	**Options**		—

Charter Arms Undercover .38

Billed as the first model to leave the doors of the newly-founded Charter Arms Corporation in 1965, the .38 Undercover model is still a breadwinner for the company.

An all time favorite of law enforcement personnel, this .38 is advertised as the smallest steel framed snubbie on the market. It is very comfortable in the hand, but because of its light weight, you do feel it bite when firing. For the plainclothes officer on the street however, I'll wager he would rather feel that light weight on his hip all day then worry about the recoil sensation when and if he has to use it.

With a cylinder diameter of 1.295 inches, this Charter Arms model holds five rounds of .38 Special ammunition. Light weight and small frame size would preclude the use of high-speed Plus-P factory ammunition.

Nicely polished and blued, the Undercover makes no bones about being a workhorse. The only negative aspect of this piece (and some other Charter Arms products) is the lack of ejector rod protection. No gun, aimed at the law enforcement market should be without an ejector shroud. The reasons are self-evident.

CHARTER ARMS BULLDOG TRACKER

Frame	Medium	**Sights**	**Front**	Semi-patridge
Caliber	.357 Magnum		**Rear**	Adjustable
Capacity	Five rounds	**Stocks**		Checkered walnut
Barrel Lengths	6 in.	**Hammer**		Serrated
Weight	27 oz.	**Trigger**		Serrated
Finish	Blue	**Options**		—

Charter Arms Bulldog "Tracker" .357

A recent addition to the Charter Arms lineup is the heavy barreled .357 Tracker. Intended for use in the woods or fields, this model not only incorporates a heavy 6-inch barrel but uses the versatile .357 Magnum cartridge as well. Even with a larger cylinder (1.430 inches) than its Undercover brother, this revolver is only chambered for five rounds.

External features include adjustable sights and a nice set of hand-filling checkered grips. Good fit and finish rate high on this piece, but don't expect the bluing to match the quality of that used on premium guns. All Charter Arms products are made for hard work, and they perform admirably.

Weighing in at approximately 30 ounces loaded, the oversize barrel helps to steady the piece before firing during recovery. Reminiscent of the barrels used on PPC courses with the cut out on the bottom for the extractor rod, the 6-inch barrel measures .770 inches in average diameter.

For a man who spends time afield, the Tracker makes a good companion.

CHARTER ARMS TARGET BULLDOG

Frame	Medium	**Sights**	**Front**	Ramp
Caliber	.357 Magnum		**Rear**	Adjustable
Capacity	Five rounds	**Stocks**		Checkered walnut
Barrel Lengths	4 in.	**Hammer**		Serrated
Weight	20½ oz.	**Trigger**		Serrated
Finish	Blue	**Options**		—

Charter Arms .357 Target Bulldog

Staying in line with the other members of its five-round family, the Target Bulldog is Charter Arms' answer to the many requests for a rugged, lightweight and dependable handgun in a magnum chambering.

Carrying a weight of only 20½ ounces empty, this gun could very well be the answer to those hunters who desire a gun powerful enough for the final *coup de grace* on most big game animals if necessary. Equipped with a 4-inch barrel, the .357 Bulldog is easily carried afield in a pancake or high-ride holster with a minimum of discomfort.

Sighting equipment consists of a full length ramp-style front sight free of any sharp angles or burrs for ease of drawing. Rear sights are adjustable for windage and elevation and respond well to any adjustment. My only wish is that Charter Arms would consider using bigger adjustment screws on the windage movement. This may be of small consequence I know, but you do need a special small screwdriver to make any sight changes whether in the field or at the range.

Other features include a fully encased ejector rod, case-hardened hammer and man-sized walnut grips.

Whether you use this piece as a light field gun, in defense or police work, the Charter Arm .357 Target Bulldog will fill most duty requirements quite well.

CHARTER ARMS BULLDOG

Frame	Medium	**Sights**	**Front**	Semi-patridge
Caliber	.44 Special		**Rear**	Fixed
Capacity	Five rounds	**Stocks**		Checkered walnut
Barrel Lengths	3 in.	**Hammer**		Serrated
Weight	19 oz.	**Trigger**		Serrated
Finish	Blue	**Options**		—

Charter Arms .44 Special Bulldog

Over 60,000 guns and seven years have passed under the bridge since its introduction into the world of firearms, yet the .44 Special Bulldog continues to be a very popular item in the company lineup.

Made to order for big bore defense gun buffs, this piece should be a standard issue on police forces around the country—not as a duty gun mind you, but for a backup piece when the chips are down and you need plenty of punch for a frenzied intruder or assailant.

The Charter Arms Bulldog is finished in a good serviceable blue and sports checkered walnut grips. When you receive your Charter Arms Bulldog, before ripping off these grips and running around for what you think might be better, give these a fair shake. They fit my hand nicely and since this gun is a "hideaway," fancy grips are not desirable because of the extra bulk they would add.

Sights are fixed, the trigger is set for 3½ pounds single action pull. All in all, this is a fine gun worthy of your consideration.

One additional note: Charter Arms offers American Scroll engraving on all models for presentation purposes.

CROWN CITY ARMS

CROWN CITY CONDOR

Frame	Semiautomatic	**Sights**	**Front**	Fixed blade
Caliber	.45 ACP		**Rear**	Adjustable for windage
Capacity	Seven rounds	**Stocks**		Smooth rosewood
Barrel Lengths	5 in.	**Hammer**		Serrated
Weight	39 oz.	**Trigger**		Adjustable
Finish	Stainless steel	**Options**		(See text)

The .45 Series

The Crown City Company of Cortland, New York, has one of the most extensive lineups of .45 semiautomatics available from one source. As of this writing, there are five different models in three calibers, plus the added versatility of three very distinct combinations offered by few in the firearms field.

Since the big thing nowadays is stainless steel, Crown City has rallied to the cause with a .45 they call the Condor. Full size and with fancy smooth rosewood grips, the Condor jumps on the scales at a trim 39 ounces empty. For standard features, check the catalog, but a brief list would include adjustable sights and trigger, magazines with rounded followers, extended combat-type safety, and a tuned trigger set for around 4½ to 6 pounds pull.

The Falcon is stainless and is the Commander-size .45 in this group. Carrying a

4¼-inch barrel, it tips the scales at 36 ounces. Standard features are nearly identical to the Condor. For the collector or shooter who likes two-barrel sets in his shooting battery, you can purchase what is known as the Condor/Falcon Combo. This set is just what it says; the basic .45 frame, a 4¼- and 5-inch slide unit, barrels and all the parts necessary to put the two together.

The all-steel versions of the above are called the Eagle and Hawk, and have the same specs as the stainless series. For the combo lovers, order the Eagle/Hawk combination. This gives you the standard Government and Commander length barrel/slide parts.

Finally, there is the Swift. Chambered in .38 Super or 9mm Luger, this model is available in a Commander size only. It too is offered in combination, but the two barrels, chambered for 9mm and .38 Super, are both 4¼-inches long.

A multitude of parts is offered by this firm and all will fit your Government or Colt model .45s.

DETONICS CORPORATION

DETONICS MASTER

Frame	Small semiautomatic	**Sights**	**Front**	Ramp
Caliber	.45 ACP		**Rear**	Fixed
Capacity	Six rounds	**Stocks**		Checkered walnut
Barrel Lengths	3 in.	**Hammer**		Serrated
Weight	29 oz.	**Trigger**		Serrated
Finish	Satin blue	**Options**		Various finishes

Detonics .45 ACP Master

With all the full-size .45s around, it was a pleasure to inspect and hold something a little different! The Detonics, like the Charter Arms .44 Special Bulldog, is designed to be a good, reliable, big bore hideaway piece.

Expertly constructed from regular or stainless steel, these models exhibit fine fit, finish, and solid workmanship. Depending on what model you pick, you can have an arched or straight mainspring housing and adjustable sights. Your choice broadens with the availability of finishes in blue, polished blue, satin or hard chrome, as well as stainless steel.

The Combat Master 45 series is your basic, all-around, good-shooting defense piece. Chopped down to 6¾-inches long by 4½-inches high, this sidearm is easily hidden in a snug-fitting hip or anke holster. It feeds reliably with selected semi-wadcutters or military ball ammunition, and will even accept the longer (standard) .45 magazines. Sights are fixed and were designed for a quick pickup when brought up to the Weaver stance.

DETONICS PROFESSIONAL

Frame	Small semiautomatic	**Sights**	**Front**	Fixed
Caliber	.45 ACP		**Rear**	Adjustable
Capacity	Six rounds	**Stocks**		Checkered walnut
Barrel Lengths	3 in.	**Hammer**		Serrated
Weight	29 oz.	**Trigger**		Serrated
Finish	Stainless steel	**Options**		Various finishes

Detonics .45 ACP Professional

The newer Professional series stainless steel models are equipped with adjustable sights for even greater accuracy. But since this gun has one sole purpose, that of defense at close range, it is debatable that this feature is necessary. Be that as it may, if you feel comfortable with adjustable sights, by all means look into this series.

Other standard features of both series include a combat accuracy job, beveled magazine inlets, a full clip indicator, a crisply tuned trigger, and a relieved ejection port.

These guns are hard to fault, and I rate them as a best buy for a semiautomatic defense gun.

HARRINGTON AND RICHARDSON

Harrington and Richardson is an old and trusted company founded in the early 1870's that has made the transition into modern firearms production with continued success. Although their line in the centerfire group is limited and dominated by one caliber (.32 Smith & Wesson Long) the quality and dependability of these weapons are good.

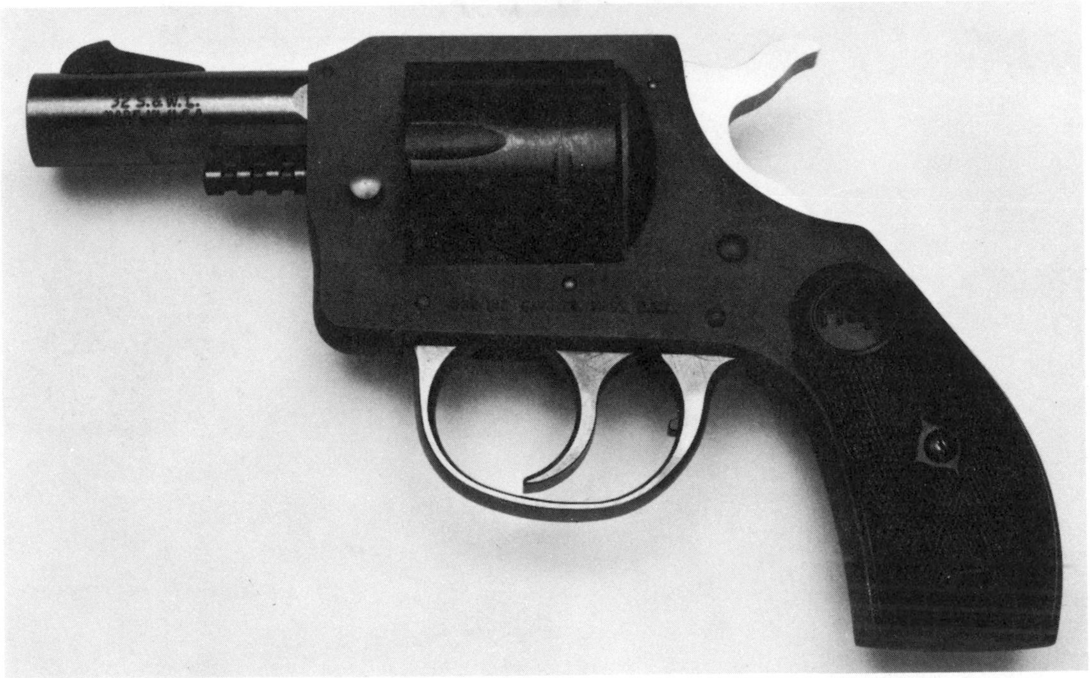

HARRINGTON AND RICHARDSON MODEL 632

Frame	Small	**Sights**	**Front**	Semi-ramp
Caliber	.32 S&W Long		**Rear**	Fixed
Capacity	Six rounds	**Stocks**		Black plastic
Barrel Lengths	2½ and 4 in.	**Hammer**		Serrated
Weight	20 oz.	**Trigger**		Smooth
Finish	Blue	**Options**		—

Model 632 and 633

Of the two major guns manufactured by H&R, the 632 and 633 are the smallest by virtue of barrel and grip length. Finished in Lustre Blue (632) or nickel (633), these guns lend themselves very easily to trail or camp use. Ruggedly constructed, nicely finished, and devoid of major tooling marks, they provide inexpensive protection. However, they do have two major and distinct drawbacks, one of which is a pull-pin cylinder. To load the weapon, you must pull out the cylinder base pin, charge the weapon and replace the pin.

Hardly a piece for a tense confrontation, but then again it wasn't designed for this job.

A second drawback is the cartridge, the 32 S&W Long. Buzzing out of the barrel at 705 fps (with 15 foot-pounds of muzzle energy), it falls far short on power, even when compared to the .380 ACP.

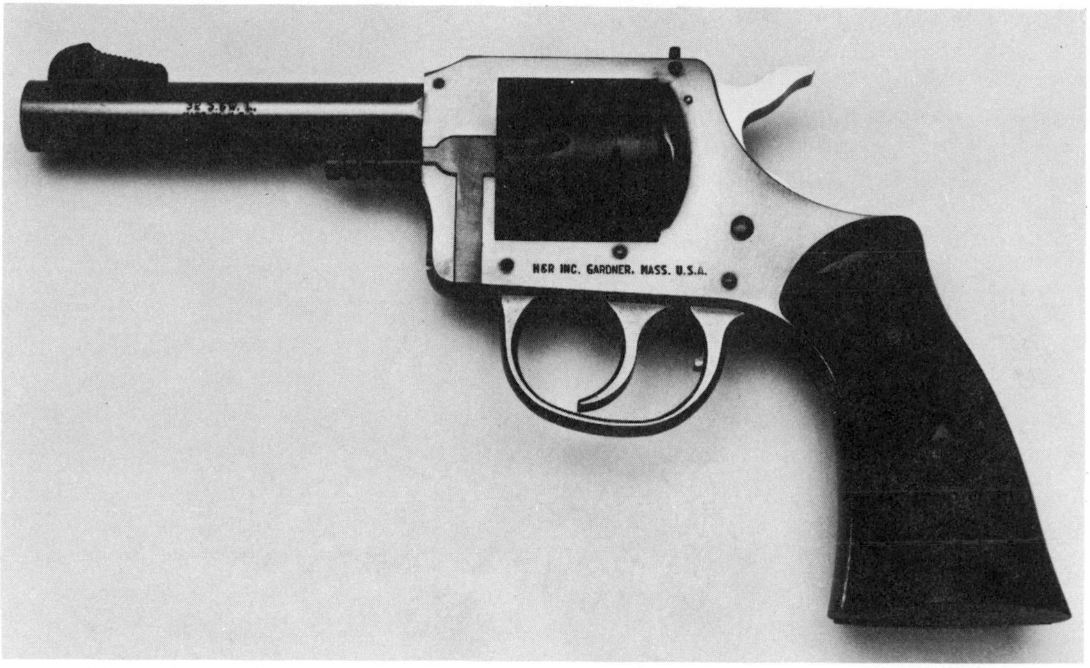

HARRINGTON AND RICHARDSON MODEL 732

Frame	Small	**Sights**	**Front**	Semi-ramp
Caliber	.32 S&W Long		**Rear**	Adjustable for windage
Capacity	Six rounds	**Stocks**		Checkered plastic
Barrel Lengths	2½ and 4 in.	**Hammer**		Serrated
Weight	24 oz.	**Trigger**		Smooth
Finish	Blue or nickel	**Options**		—

Model 732 and 733

The solid frame H&R 732/733 is next on the list of revolvers. Although chambered for the anemic .32 S&W cartridge it does register one step above the 632/633 series.

The 732 features a swing-out cylinder and excellent pointability thanks to the fine design of the grip/frame combination. Adjustable sights (windage only), safety interlock, and a cylinder that has very little lateral play after the trigger is pulled, make this a fine sidearm for the outdoorsman.

My only comment is that with all the years of experience and knowledge in the field, H&R, with its fine name and reputation, should consider bringing forth a gun of at least .38 Special caliber. In the same frame size as the 732/733—in stainless steel—the new addition would have no trouble finding owners.

INTERARMS

INTERARMS VIRGINIA DRAGOON

Frame	SA	**Sights**	**Front**	Ramp
Caliber	.357, .41, and .44 Magnum, and .45 Colt		**Rear**	Adjustable
Capacity	Six rounds	**Stocks**		Walnut
Barrel Lengths	5, 6, 7½, 8⅜, and 12 in.	**Hammer**		Serrated
Weight	56 oz. with .357 Magnum	**Trigger**		Serrated
Finish	Blue or stainless steel	**Options**		(See text)

Virginia Dragoon

Interarms' entry into the handgun field in the early seventies produced an American-made single-action Colt-type revolver. Made to withstand the pressures of magnum calibers, the designers chose to use tough 4140 steel which provides extra weight. In fact, picking up the Dragoon, one immediately notices the extra heft and size of this firearm. At 3½ pounds, it rates as the heaviest "hogleg" on the market today.

Chambered in four different calibers (.357, .41, .44 Magnums and .45 Colt), with five barrel lengths (5, 6, 7½, 8⅜ and 12 inches) and provided in two finishes (blue and stainless), it does offer numerous choices to the handgunner.

The sample I received showed good workmanship, polishing and attention to detail. Case hardening on my sample was dull and mottled, but this did not detract from the overall appearance of the piece. Grips are walnut, and are numbered to match that of the gun's serial number. Obviously they are fitted to one gun, for the fit was close and tight.

The safety on the Dragoon is the cylinder pin, and is activated by pushing it through the frame until it contacts the hammer in the half-cock position. Hardly made for speed, the intention here was probably for use in the home or camp.

Sights were clean, sharp and ajustable. The front sight carried an extra feature: a white dot to aid in aiming. Placed against dark objects, it did its job well. If you are prone to big, heavy guns, this may be the one for you.

SAFARI ARMS

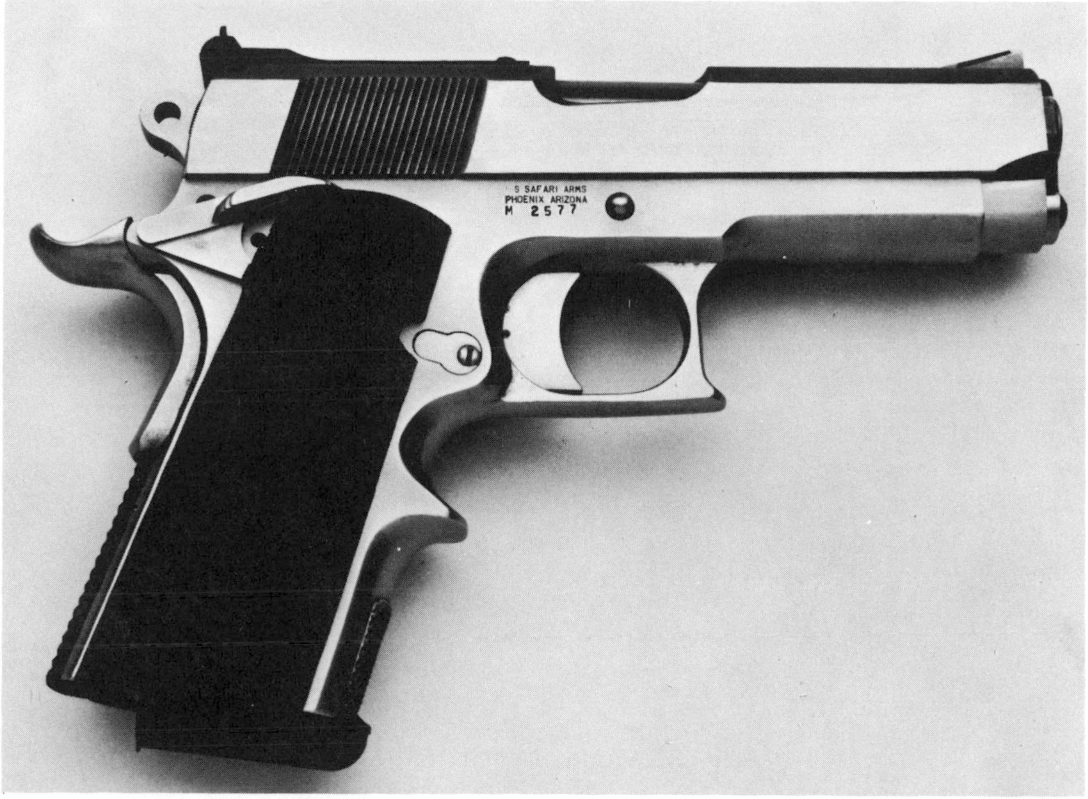

SAFARI ARMS ENFORCER

Frame	Semiautomatic	**Sights**	**Front**	Red ramp
Caliber	.45 ACP		**Rear**	Adjustable
Capacity	Six rounds	**Stocks**		Walnut or rubber
Barrel Lengths	3.8 in.	**Hammer**		Commander
Weight	35 oz.	**Trigger**		Service
Finish	(See text)	**Options**		(See text)

The Enforcer

Safari Arms' Enforcer model .45 semiautomatic has helped many shooters get into combat shooting with a gun so fully-equipped with extra features that any further investment is not needed. There are over seventeen custom additions which come as standard equipment, including S&W "K" sights, red ramp insert, a combat hammer, an ambidextrous safety, squared trigger guard, enlarged ejection port, and special magazines. The Enforcer comes with a 3.8-inch barrel and is available in weather-resistant Teflon, hard chrome, Armaloy, stainless steel, or the standard blue, most of which are available in either a high-luster or sandblasted finish.

SAFARI ARMS MATCHMASTER

Frame	Semiautomatic	**Sights**	**Front**	Red ramp
Caliber	.45 ACP		**Rear**	Adjustable
Capacity	Six rounds	**Stocks**		Walnut or rubber
Barrel Lengths	5 in.	**Hammer**		Commander
Weight	40 oz.	**Trigger**		Service
Finish	(See text)	**Options**		(See text)

The Matchmaster

This model is almost an exact duplicate of the Enforcer, except for a 5-inch barrel and an extra 5 ounces of weight. Like its little brother, the Matchmaster is available in Teflon, hard chrome, Armaloy, stainless steel, and blue. Both guns were built around the .45 ACP and were computer designed to provide maximum reliability in a wide variety of situations. Whether you use the high-stepping 185-grain jacketed hollow point or the slower 230-grain military hardball, rest assured that either weapon can handle either load with ease.

Fixed sight models are now available to law enforcement personnel, and as an added bonus, all Safari components can be ordered by shooters who want to add these custom additions to their present weapon. More on those in the accessory section.

STERLING ARMS

STERLING ARMS MODEL 300

Frame	Small semiautomatic	**Sights**	**Front**	Fixed
Caliber	.25 Auto		**Rear**	Fixed
Capacity	Six rounds	**Stocks**		Cycolac
Barrel Lengths	2¼ in.	**Hammer**		Internal
Weight	13 oz.	**Trigger**		Service
Finish	Stainless steel or blue	**Options**		—

Model 300

The Sterling Arms 300 is this firm's entry into the pocket defense handgun market. Made in .25 ACP, the 300 neatly fills not only your hand, but the need of those who feel it's better than nothing in today's sometimes hostile society.

Weighing only 13 ounces with a magazine capacity of six rounds, the Sterling can deliver 438 foot-pounds of energy toward the intended victim. I know it's only the energy of approximately two .38 Specials, but nevertheless, I for one would not enjoy being on the receiving end of this gun.

Features of the 300 include blued or stainless steel construction, fast lock time, and the feeling that you are holding something more than a .25 in your hand. This is due to the design, and the fact that this gun has a bit more metal in some spots then most pocket pistols. As with most miniature pistols, beware of the slide catching the web of skin between your thumb and forefinger. Small enough to be put in your shirt pocket, the Sterling 300 is not shy on overall performance.

STERLING ARMS MODEL 400

Frame	Semiautomatic	**Sights**	**Front**	Ramp
Caliber	.380 Auto		**Rear**	Adjustable
Capacity	Seven rounds	**Stocks**		Checkered walnut
Barrel Lengths	3½ in.	**Hammer**		Commander
Weight	18 oz.	**Trigger**		Standard
Finish	Stainless steel or blue	**Options**		—

Model 400

Aimed at the police and security fields, the 400 is a double-action semiautomatic chambered in that popular defense cartridge, the .380 Automatic. Built around a seven-shot magazine, this model is a popular seller for those looking for a good and dependable hideaway piece. Provided in blued or stainless finish, the weight wavers around the 26 ounce mark with a full magazine.

For the cartridge, this gun is a little larger than usual, but then the additional magazine capacity makes up for the difference. Notable features include adjustable sights for windage and elevation, low profile hammer, hand-checkered American walnut grip panels, and a rolling block safety. As for the safety, it is positioned on the left side for ease of use. Because of this gun's internal design, you may carry an eighth round in the chamber. When so carried, flipping the safety up with the thumb releases it and puts the 400 into the firing mode.

The slide remains open after the last shot and magazines are easy to eject thanks to the already familiar pushbutton release.

DAN WESSON ARMS

DAN WESSON MODEL 14-2

Frame	Medium	**Sights**	**Front**	Ramp
Caliber	.357 Magnum		**Rear**	Fixed
Capacity	Six rounds	**Stocks**		Walnut target
Barrel Lengths	2, 4, 6, and 8 in.	**Hammer**		Wide target
Weight	34 oz. with 4-in. barrel	**Trigger**		Standard
Finish	Satin blue	**Options**		Barrels and grips

Service Revolvers 14-2 Series

The Model 14-2 revolver is the basic weapon for everyday use. It consists of the Dan Wesson .357 revolver in satin blue, and comes with oversized target grips and interchangeable barrels in lenghts of 2½, 4, 6, or 8 inches. No fancy frills on this piece: ramp front sight and fixed rear sight are standard features. If you need a gun just to handle the .38 Special cartridge then you'll want the 8-2 sub-series of the 14-2. If you are looking for a gun to take a lot of abuse, this Dan Wesson may be what you're looking for.

DAN WESSON MODEL 15-2V

Frame	Medium	**Sights**	**Front**	1/8-in. colored blade
Caliber	.357 Magnum		**Rear**	White outline target
Capacity	Six rounds	**Stocks**		Seven styles available
Barrel Lengths	2½, 4, 6, 8, 10, 12, and 15 in.	**Hammer**		Wide target
Weight	39 oz. with 6-in. barrel	**Trigger**		Wide target
Finish	Blue	**Options**		Barrels and grips

Target Revolvers 15-2 Series

The 15-2 series has all the features a handgunner could want and then some. To start with, the 15 series has a smooth, glossy blue finish. The absence of polishing or tooling marks accounts for the superb finish as does what I am sure is a sharp-eyed quality control manager.

This target series is further broken down into four sub-series, each with its own different barrel shroud. Briefly they are the standard, the heavy barrel, the vent rib, and the vent rib heavy barrel. In each of these groups the owner of a Dan Wesson revolver can purchase barrel lengths from 2½ to 15 inches, for a total of seven in each group. No matter what the job is, be it hunting, police work, target, or silhouette shooting, you can find a barrel length and weight to do it right. For installation of any particular barrel, a spanner wrench and feeler gauge are supplied. Replacement of any barrel and shroud takes about two minutes to complete. Dan Wesson is to be congratulated on the foolproof system and the technique they have devised.

Sights too, are interchangeable and colored front sight blades come in red, yellow or white ramp styles. Plain Patridge blades are standard for the long 15-inch barrels. Rear sights on target models are outlined in white for quick pickup and visibility.

Moving on to the grips you have a choice of target, combat, Sacramento and even a inletted blank to carve your own. All the above grips are available in American walnut. The

Interchangeable barrels and sights are one way to add unlimited versatility to your handguns.

target grips come in your choice of walnut or colorfully-hued Zebrawood, checkered or smooth. Like the barrels and sight blades, these are fully interchangeable from one gun to the other.

As a added bonus, each Dan Wesson target-style revolver is offered in what the maker calls a Pistol-Pac. Choose any Dan Wesson 8-inch revolver, add the 2½, 4- and 6-inch barrels, extra grips, sight inserts and a shoulder patch, place them all in a handsome lined case and you are ready for any foray in the brush.

Starting from humble beginnings in August of 1970, Dan Wesson Arms has grown considerably in size and reputation over the years. Two distinct series, interchangeable barrels, grips and sight blades are just part of the story of the Dan Wesson .357 line of handguns. The other side of the coin is quality. Samples sent to me exhibit polishing and bluing a cut above anyone now in the market; in fact one is led to believe the finish is actually blued chrome! It's that good!

Since no innovative company stands still, plans are being made to bring out a similiar series of the target group in a .44 Magnum configuration. I saw this gun at a recent seminar and the design and features look good. The .44 will have interchangeable barrels and also a new type of barrel venting system to keep the gun down during recoil. A talk with a Dan Wesson spokesman indicated that the guns should start coming out of the factory in late 1980 or early 1981.

The Dan Wesson line of sporting arms is moderately priced for the quality, accuracy and versatility received. Check them out at your local dealer or write for an updated catalog.

Factory Engraving

Dan Wesson revolvers are available in a Class A (1/4 coverage), Class B (1/2 coverage), Class C (3/4 Coverage), or Class D (Full). These are standard engraved models, and in addition, special custom engraved models can be made upon a customer's request to include precious metal inlays or designs. Quotes will be given on any type of commission work. Please write for details.

WILDEY FIREARMS

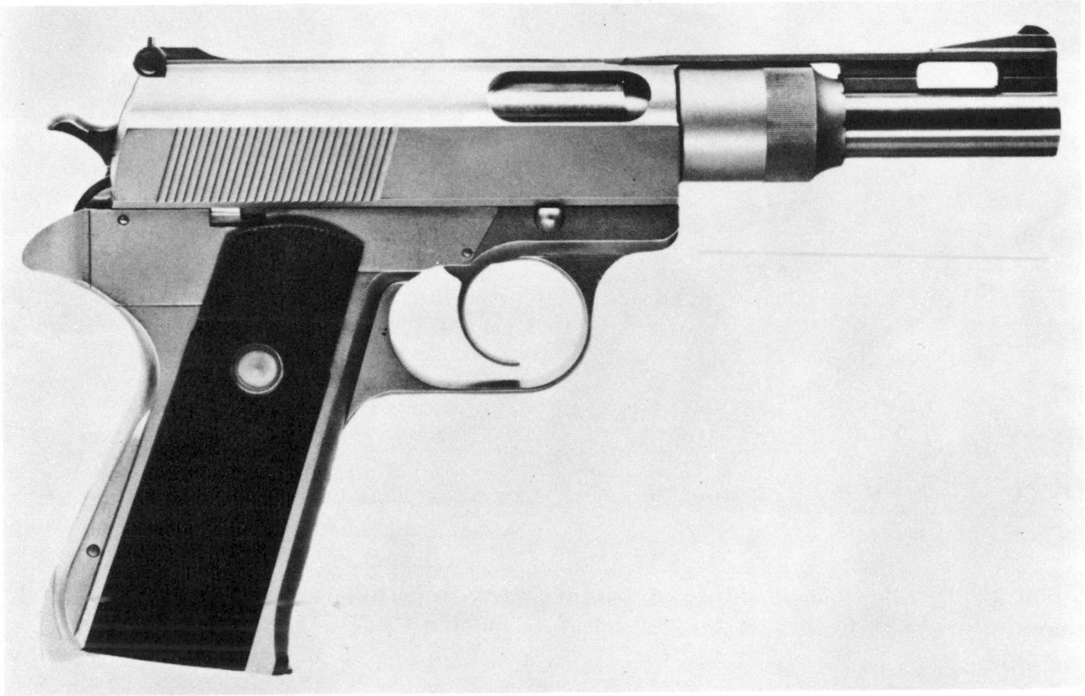

WILDEY SEMIAUTOMATIC

Frame	Semiautomatic	**Sights**	**Front**	Ramp
Caliber	9mm and .45 Winchester Magnum		**Rear**	Adjustable for windage and elevation
Capacity	Fourteen rounds (9mm) Eight rounds (.45)	**Stocks**		Select hardwood
Barrel Lengths	5, 6, 7, 8, and 10 in.	**Hammer**		Serrated
Weight	51 oz.	**Trigger**		Smooth
Finish	Stainless steel	**Options**		(See text)

Wildey Automatic

Every once in a while something comes along that is not only different in style but radically different in terms of performance. Such a firearm is the gas-operated semiautomatic pistol from Wildey that is chambered in 9mm and .45 Winchester Magnum.

For those of you who are asking the question, "why a gas operated pistol," let's look at a couple of reasons. The main one is that like the Auto-Mag, the Wildey allows the use of super high-powered magnum ammunition in a semiautomatic weapon. While all blowback autos work in the 30,000 c.u.p. range, the Wildey with its special ammo will dwell in the 60,000 c.u.p. area. For the serious handgunner/reloader, this may well be the auto he is looking for.

The second reason is ammunition. When building or designing specialized equipment like the Wildey, much of its success depends on the availability of factory ammunition or unprimed cases for it. To this end, Winchester-Western has tooled up to make factory loaded ammo even before the gun hit the market. The Wildey will be chambered for the two cartridges mentioned above.

The 9mm Winchester Magnum will leave the muzzle at a smart 1,475 fps (556 foot-pounds) versus the conventional 9mm at 1,155 fps. These figures were calculated using the standard 9mm 115-grain full metal jacketed bullet. Likewise when comparing the .45 Winchester Magnum against a .45 ACP, we arrive at 1,400 fps for the Winchester/Wildey against 810 fps for the government .45 round. Again, both rounds were using the 230-grain "hardball" jacketed bullet. Exciting to say the least!

But back to the Wildey. Specifications include a manageable 51 ounces of weight with a 6-inch barrel which is stable enough to quell the heavy recoil these rounds generate. Other features consist of selective or autoloading capability, tailoring the action for the load used by adjustable venting of the gas system, and a magazine capacity of up to 15 rounds for the 9mm version.

Barrel lengths of 5, 6, 7, 8 and 10 inches will be offered as well as various sight options. True to form with modern American guns, the Wildey will be constructed in stainless steel.

Since all new endeavors relate in time and money spent to achieve a certain goal, the Wildey should justify both once it is on the market. For the handloader a new challenge has arisen, for the silhouette shooter or hunter, a new tool to try.

Winchester-Western's newest entries in the field of high velocity rounds are the .45 Winchester Magnum (left) and the 9mm Winchester Magnum (third from left). Both were created for greater knockdown power downrange.

CCI
3940
WARNING
EAR PUFFF
LOBO

SIX

The Single Shots

Looking at our lead chapter photograph of single shot handguns one can sum up their success very easily with one word; versatility! And versatile they are, for if you counted up all of the combinations of barrel lengths, barrel types, calibers, guns available and manufacturers, you would see that any shooter could busy himself for virtually a lifetime. Since single shot handguns are a totally different field unto themselves, let's take a brief look at the types available and compare actions, designs, principles of operation and other aspects.

We'll begin at the heart of the gun; the action. Single shot pistols seem to be almost equally divided between the break open and bolt action models. The Jurras "Howdah" and Contender fall under the break open types, with the Remington XP-100 and Wichita following with the traditional bolting system of operation.

Break open actions on the Jurras and Thompson/Center Contender are of the same basic design. Thompson/Center makes both of them, and the difference is that one is a production gun (Contender) while the other is strictly custom-made (Jurras). The T/C receiver is very strong and can handle cartridge types from .22 to .500 caliber. It would seem that the only limit is practicability and how much the shooter can handle in terms of recoil. The design is simple, and in operation all one has to do is squeeze the trigger guard up and back to open the action. Load the weapon, close the action, and, when you are ready to fire, cock the hammer. Very straightforward, and this is one of the main reasons why the Contender is so very popular today.

Moving on to the bolt actions, again we find a production gun in the Remington XP-100 and a semi-custom gun in the Wichita series. The heart of the XP-100, the action, is based on the famous M600 and M700 rifle models. This right-handed bolt action carries a

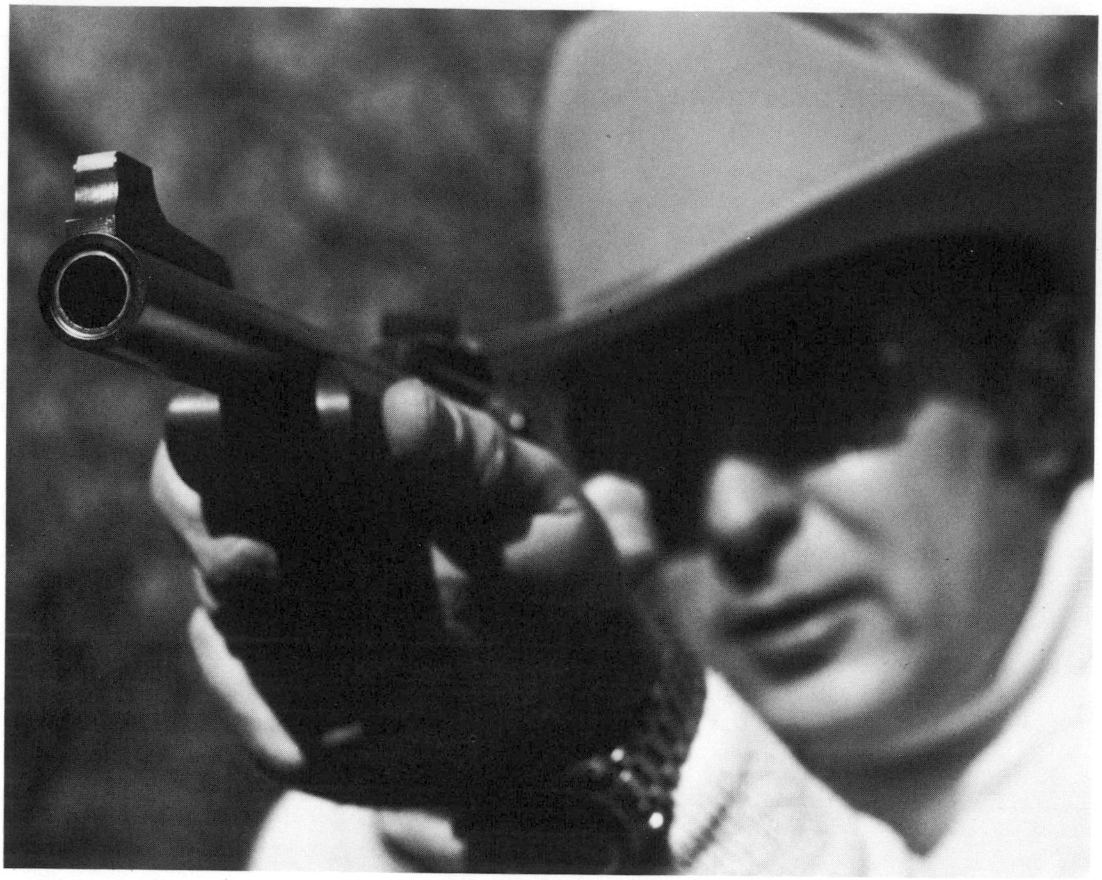

By combining strong break open actions with big, bone-crushing calibers, today's single shot handguns can take on the largest of North American game.

10½-inch ribbed barrel and is housed in a highly resistant nylon stock suitable for one-handed operation. The XP-100 has had a very strong following since its introduction and it is not very hard to find this rugged piece customized into various wood stock designs and exotic chamberings ranging into and sometimes above .30 caliber.

The Wichita pistol is a highly refined piece targeted at the advanced silhouette shooter. Beautifully finished and available either in right- or left-handed versions, this gun is made to extremely close tolerances. The bolt is ground to ensure a perfect fit and all lugs are hand-lapped for true alignment with the chamber. Although the cost is high—about three times that of the XP-100—one gets a good pistol for money spent.

Aside from the technical aspects of the guns, why have the single shots proved to be so popular over the years? Essentially, I believe the answer lies with their ability to change barrels and cartridges. For instance, in the Contender you have a choice of two different barrel lengths and four different styles, and in these four, caliber choices run the centerfire gamut from the .22 Hornet through the .35 Remington and upward to the .30 and .357 Herretts. In the T/C series we have over thirty-five different and distinct combinations.

The Jurras pistols start where the others leave off. These guns are for the big-bore enthusiast. Starting at the bottom and working upwards, we see the .375 thru .500 Jurras cartridges. Recoil is high, but this should be no problem once the shooter gets used to his particular gun and loads. Special grips, extra weight and a carbine version are available to deal with this problem.

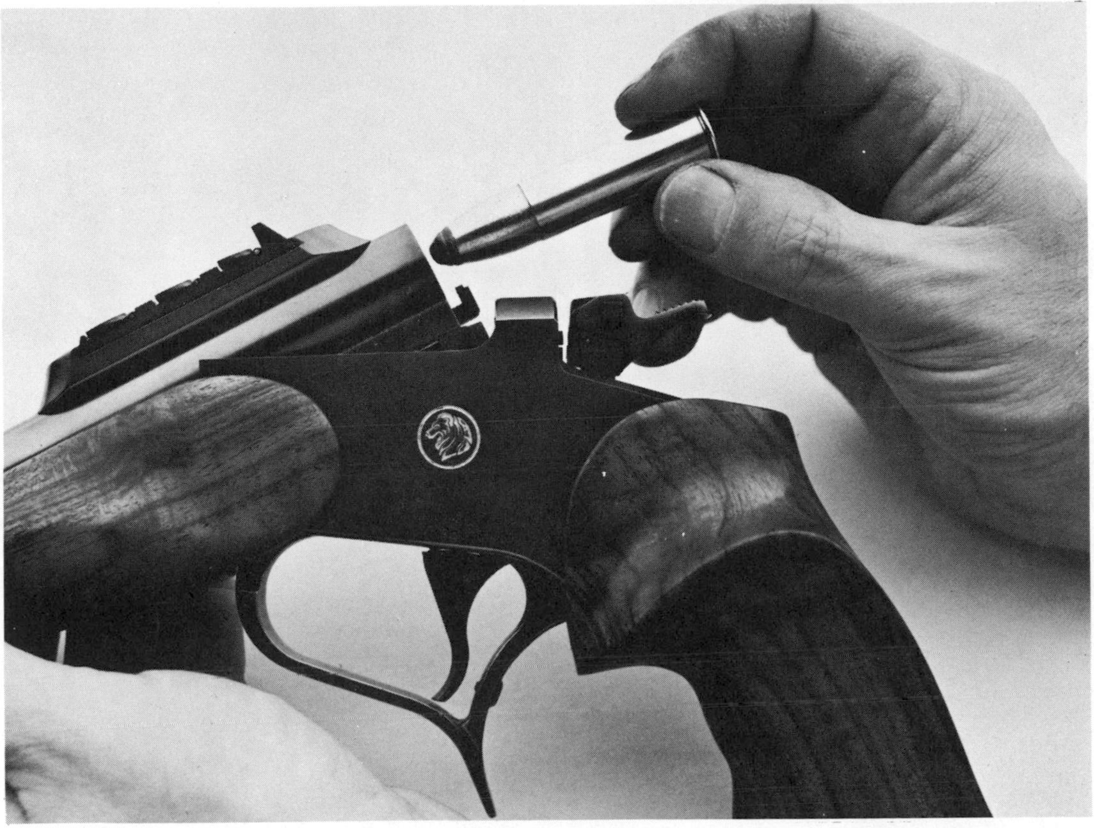

Simplicity of design makes all single shot pistols extremely reliable.

The takedown of the Thompson/Center Contender is easily accomplished by removing the fore end, drifting out the barrel pivot pin, then lifting the barrel assembly out of the frame.

Even without an optical sight, woodchucks have plenty to worry about if the hunter is equipped with this Remington XP-100 chambered for the .221 Fireball cartridge.

For the serious long-range shooter, single shot handguns can be equipped with carbine stocks and express sights as in the case of this Jurras gun.

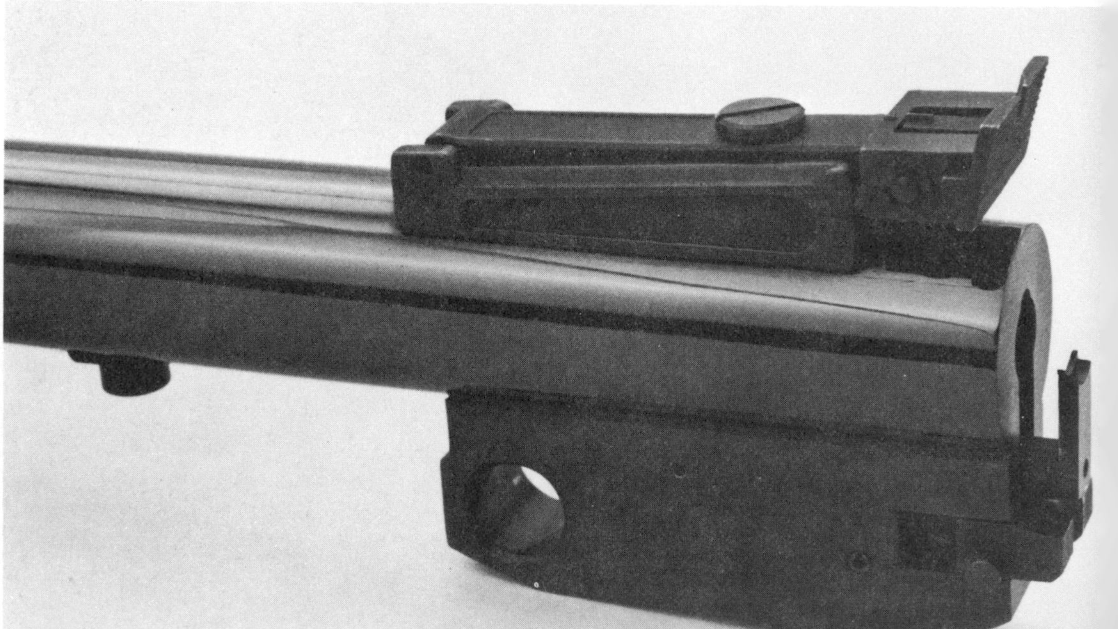

To take the heavy recoil, rear sights have to be rugged, yet fully adjustable. Note the fine fit and finish on this Contender barrel.

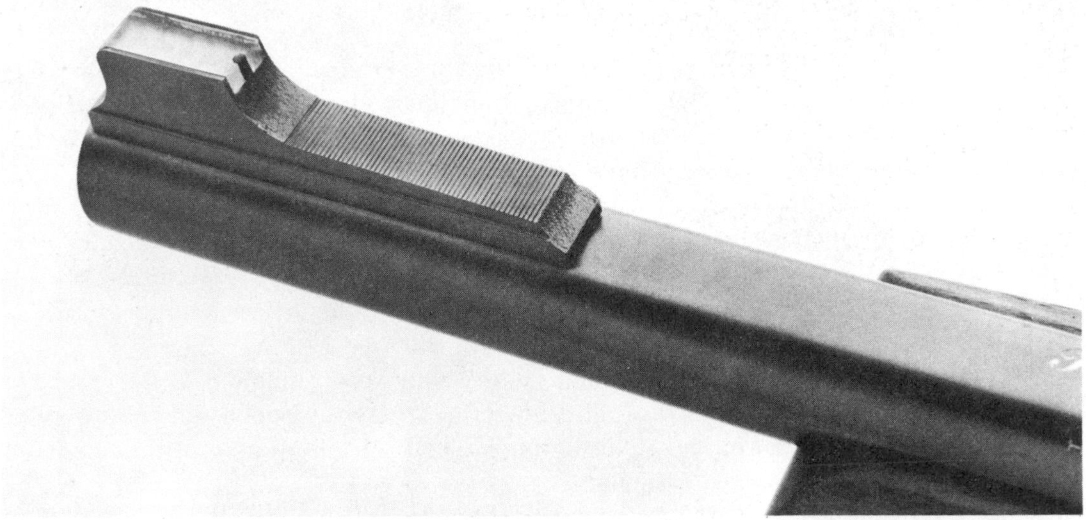

On this Jurras "Howdah," the front sight is completely filled with a luminous filler thus enabling the hunter to pick it up quickly.

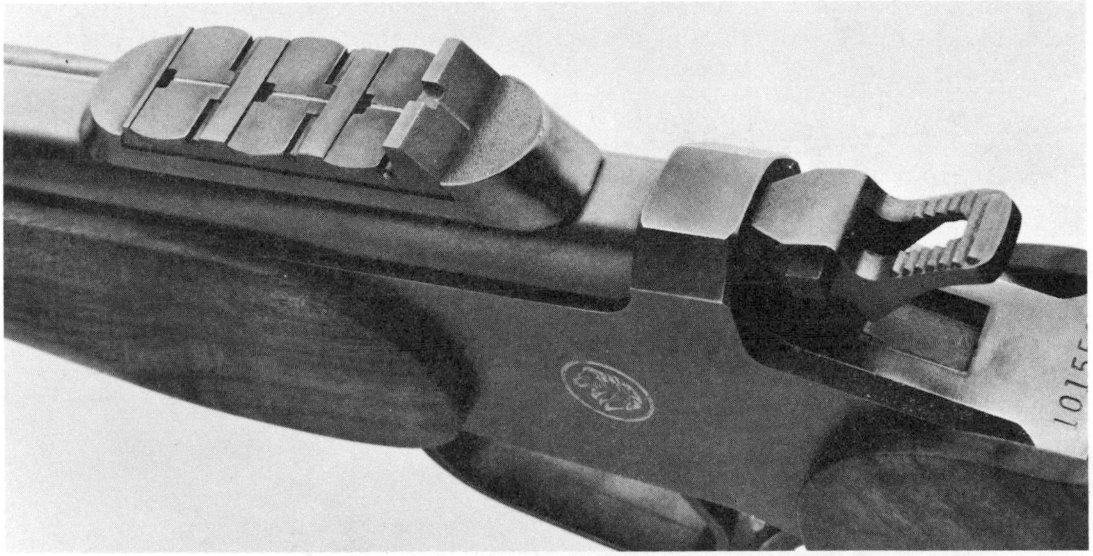

Finely-crafted rear "express sights" can be made to mark certain known distances. For example, the closest sight (standing) can be calibrated for 50 yards, the next 100, 150, and 200 yards.

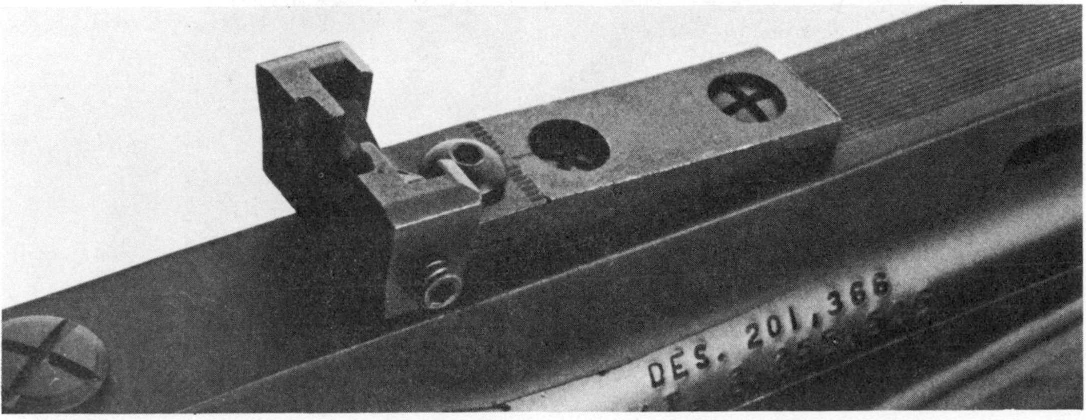

Easily removable, these XP-100 sights can be used in lieu of optical sights for closer distances.

Remington's XP-100 is chambered for the .221 Fireball, and when the pistol is scoped, it makes for a super varmint gun. Remington is now making a second model, chambered for the 7mm Bench Rest, a new variation for the silhouette crowd. This new XP-100 Silhouette has special sights and a longer barrel.

The Wichita is offered in one commercial and two special calibers. As you may have guessed, these three, plus the Remington entry are for the advanced handloader who enjoys experimenting for maximum range and accuracy in silhouette shooting. Most loading data can be found in recent editions of firearms journals or by writing to various manufacturers for the latest in up-to-the-minute information.

Choice of sights on any of the single shots is almost as unlimited as the cartridge choice. Thompson/Center comes through with refined, standard open sights on regular models and a beefed-up set of rear sights on the Super 14. In the Jurras group, one has a choice of several front and rear combinations.

Both the bolt actions feature good sights, although because of the very nature of the Wichita, I'd rate this as the better of the two. Remington's standard equipment is a set of open sights of which the rear sight is adjustable for windage and elevation. Open sights on the Wichita consist of a Lyman Front Globe with inserts and a Lyman Receiver sight with knurled knobs for ease of adjustment when the target distances change, as in silhouette shooting.

The new breed of single shot pistols was made to use clear, sharp scopes. Here the T/C Contender is equipped with a Redfield 2½ power scope and "Magnum" rings and base.

Scopes are another alternative when it comes to sighting equipment. To me the best of any single shot comes through when a scope is mounted. For some reason these guns lend themselves so naturally to a scope it is really a shame if you don't use one. Of course it depends on the caliber, but for varmints or small game hunting, nothing beats the combination of a fine single shot with scope, teamed with a flat-shooting cartridge. Around New England we use the .22 Hornet or .222 Remington on short distances, the Herrett series for longer ranges.

For 1-inch tubed scopes, Leupold and Redfield make some fine ones. All are clear, sharp, and sensitive to reticle changes at the bench. Those shooters who would walk a lot on a hunt might want to go with the Bushnell 1.3 or 2.5× scopes. The Bushnell scopes carry a ⅞-inch tube. Their system of mounting the scope to the pistol makes for smaller and lighter scopes than present competitors.

American single shot handguns are quality products which deserve your attention. No matter what model you decide on, you will not be disapponted. The following catalog section will help you in your quest for the right single shot handgun for your needs and applications.

JURRAS HOWDAH SINGLE SHOT

As the newest entry on the single shot scene, these Howdah pistols leave little to be desired for big bore fans. Named for the era in which the big bore was king in India, these guns are produced strictly on a custom basis.

They incorporate a special Thompson/Center action that has been heat-treated in specific areas to absorb the stress and recoil of the big calibers. All of the Howdah calibers are based on the big .500 Nitro Express case that is shortened and fire-formed to the respective cartridge. Right now you have a choice of .375, .416, .460, .475 and .500 caliber. To give you the idea of power, the .500 caliber cartridge generates almost five times the amount of energy in foot-pounds as does the .44 caliber!

For comparison of case sizes, please take note of the four cartridges on the lead chapter photograph under the Jurras Howdah in the upper right-hand corner. The case on the right is a .357, the other three to the left are Jurras Wildcats! By those examples alone, you can readily see these guns are made for the serious handgunner who is going after big game and needs what amounts to a small hand cannon.

Samples shipped to me for photographs and evaluation showed excellent workmanship and attention to detail. To me, these custom guns represent an investment and will surely appreciate in value as time goes on.

JURRAS HOWDAH PISTOL

Frame	S/S	**Sights**	**Front**	(See text)
Caliber	.375 to .500		**Rear**	(See text)
		Stocks		Rubber or wood
Barrel Lengths	12 in.	**Hammer**		Serrated
Weight	48 oz.	**Trigger**		Adjustable
Finish	Blue or hard-chromed	**Options**		(See text)

Howdah Handgun

The Howdah model is available in two grades and offers the following features. In the custom grade, you can order any caliber from .375 to .500. The gun comes equipped with a satin, hard-chrome finish and Pachmayr cushioned neoprene stocks. The presentation grade (shown in the above photograph) carries a rust blue finish, colored insert front sight, and stocks with a hand-rubbed oil finish on a "select grade" of walnut.

Since all of the guns are one-of-a-kind creations, the list of additional features seems almost to have no bounds. One can order his choice of sights, including a three-leaf express sight for the rear. If one is so inclined, the barrel can be Magna-Ported for recoil reduction. In fact, any accessory or modification that is reasonable may be incorporated into the final product added to the gun.

JURRAS HOWDAH CARBINE

Frame	S/S	**Sights**	**Front**	(Many different styles)
Caliber	Unlimited range		**Rear**	(Many different styles)
		Stocks		Select walnut
Barrel Lengths	16¼ in.	**Hammer**		Serrated
Weight	Approximately 4½ lbs.	**Trigger**		Adjustable
Finish	Blue	**Options**		(See text)

Howdah Carbine

Basically the same as the pistol, this model incorporates a shoulder stock to steady the weapon when perhaps a longer shot is needed. The stock is a thumbhole design and has an extra-wide cheek piece to channel recoil away from the face area. The combinations here are unlimited, and choice of caliber is up to the buyer. All guns in this category are strictly special order.

REMINGTON XP-100

REMINGTON XP-100

Frame	Short bolt type	**Sights**	**Front**	Open
Caliber	.221 and 7mm BR		**Rear**	Adjustable
		Stocks		Nylon
Barrel Lengths	10½ and 15 in.	**Hammer**		Internal
Weight	3¾ lbs.	**Trigger**		Target tuned
Finish	Blue	**Options**		—

The XP-100, or Bolt Action Pistol, as the specs read, is available in two models suitable to most tasks. The original model, introduced in 1963, is chambered for the high-stepping .221 Fireball cartridge. Blasting out of the 10½-inch barrel at a respectable 2,650 feet per second, this round is a favorite with varmint hunters across the land. Available in a factory loading, or handloaded, the .221 is an efficient and effective round out to 200 yards on a scoped XP-100.

The newest model, introduced in 1980, is aimed at the silhouette shooter. Termed model number 5471, this XP-100 carries a 15-inch barrel, special front sight and a brand new 7mm Bench Rest Remington round. Please note that this particular round is not available as a factory loading; it is strictly a handloading situation. The 7mm Bench Rest can also be necked-down for use in other guns, with calibers ranging from .224 to .243 in diameter.

The stock on the XP-100 is Dupont "Zytel" and is not prone to warping or breakage under normal conditions. Considering the excellent trigger, instant availability, and the various custom options made for this gun (stocks, cartridges, sights), it is easy to understand why this piece is so popular.

THOMPSON/CENTER CONTENDER

The ads call the Contender "the most versatile handgun available." To dispute that would be like trying to beat an audit on your tax return. Possible, but not very likely. The T/C Contender has been on the scene since the late sixties and has made quite an impression on American shooters. To date, the Contender is chambered for twenty different centerfire rounds from the .22 Hornet to the .45 Colt. In the Wildcat series we have the .22 K-Hornet, .30 and .357 Herrett rounds. In essence, if you get bored shooting one caliber, simply change barrels and go from there.

In 1980, the Contender took on a new look. New wood was added, designed to flow with the now classic lines of the gun. Made for T/C by Herrett, the pistol grip is contoured to fit the hand better during sighting and shooting. The fore ends are streamlined and longer, and on the Super 14's, they are even longer and fuller to suit the needs of the long-range shooter.

Tight quality control on the Contender is evident as all models show excellent workmanship. Deep rich blueing, good woodwork and generally fine appearance all add up to a gun worthy of its reputation.

Thompson/Center also supplies scopes, holsters, shot shell ammunition and various other accessories for its products. Their recent catalog is a must for your library.

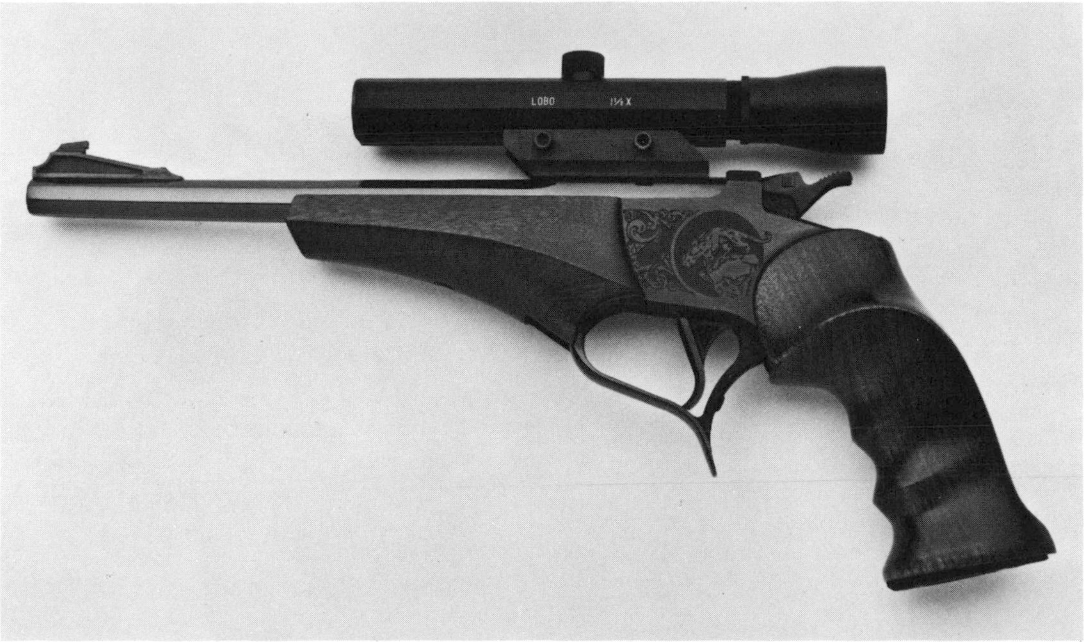

THOMPSON/CENTER CONTENDER STANDARD MODEL

Frame	S/S	**Sights**	**Front**	Ramp (blade type)
Caliber	(See text)		**Rear**	Adjustable
		Stocks		Walnut
Barrel Lengths	10 in.	**Hammer**		Serrated
Weight	41 oz.	**Trigger**		Adjustable
Finish	Blue	**Options**		—

Contender Standard Model

The Contender Standard model is supplied with a 10-inch octagonal barrel with open sights, and is chambered for fourteen different rounds. It's easy to see why this or any other of the Contenders are handloader's delights. Since no cylinder gap is employed, you are assured of top-notch performance from any round. The model shown above has an optional T/C Lobo scope and mounts. This model is chambered for the following centerfire rounds: .22 Hornet, .22 K-Hornet, .22 Remington Jet; .218 Bee, .221 Fireball, .222 Remington, .256 Winchester, .25-35, .30-30 Winchester, .38 Special/.357 Magnum, .44 Magnum, .45 ACP, .45 Colt, plus .357 and .44 Magnum shot shells.

THOMPSON/CENTER CONTENDER BULL BARREL

Frame	S/S	**Sights**	**Front**	Ramp (blade type)
Caliber	(See text)		**Rear**	Adjustable
		Stocks		Walnut
Barrel Lengths	10 in.	**Hammer**		Serrated
Weight	43 oz.	**Trigger**		Adjustable
Finish	Blue	**Options**		—

Contender Bull Barrel Model

Weighing in at only 3 ounces more than the standard barrel model, the bull or heavy series is finding increased popularity among the shooting fraternity. Standard calibers come equipped with open sights; wildcats either with or without sights. Nothing makes a better combination than a bull barrel mated to a scope of 1½ or 2½× power for long-range kills on small game.

The bull barreled model is offered in .22 Hornet, .221 Fireball, .222 and .223 Remington, .256 Winchester. .25-35, .30-30 Winchester, .30 and .357 Herrett, .38/.357 Magnum, .41 Magnum, .45 Colt and .45 Winchester Magnum.

THOMPSON/CENTER CONTENDER VENT RIB

Frame	S/S	**Sights**	**Front**	Blade
Caliber	.357 and .44 Magnum		**Rear**	Fold-down
		Stocks		Walnut
Barrel Lengths	10 in.	**Hammer**		Serrated
Weight	43 oz.	**Trigger**		Adjustable
Finish	Blue	**Options**		—

Contender Vent Rib Model

This single shot is the most novel of the bunch. Available in either .357 or .44 Magnum, it incorporates an internal choke for shotshell use. Since the T/C has no limitations as to the length of the shotshell (i.e. revolver cylinder), the plastic capsule can be better than three times as long as those made for your common revolver. This model would make a great all-around camp gun. It can take quail in the morning (shotshell) or deer in the afternoon (.357 or .44 Magnum).

THOMPSON/CENTER CONTENDER SUPER 14

Frame	S/S	**Sights**	**Front**	Rifle type
Caliber	(See text)		**Rear**	Fully adjustable
		Stocks		Walnut
Barrel Lengths	14 in.	**Hammer**		Serrated
Weight	56 oz.	**Trigger**		Adjustable
Finish	Blue	**Options**		—

Contender Super 14

The net result of years of experience is that you can apply all that expertise and understanding to a totally new and different concept and have it work out fine. The "Super 14" series seems to be just that. By taking the T/C frame and mechanism, and mounting a 14-inch barrel and longer foreend, you come up with a piece that has great appeal for a lot of shooters.

Chambered for the .222 or .223 Remington and scoped, this model is dynamite on "chucks." For the silhouette shooter, either of the two Herrett wildcats, .30-30 Winchester, or .35 Remington will knock down his targets. Holstered in a shoulder rig, the Super 14 is a steady and reliable game-getter. With its new wood design, this Contender is not only pleasing to the eye, but to the hand when firing any of the high-performance loads. Calibers include .222 and .223 Remington, .30-30 Winchester, .30 and .357 Herrett, .35 Remington, .41, .44 and .45 Winchester Magnums.

WICHITA SILHOUETTE PISTOL

WICHITA SILHOUETTE PISTOL

Frame	Short bolt type	**Sights**	**Front**	Lyman Globe
Caliber	(See text)		**Rear**	Lyman Receiver
		Stocks		Walnut or fiberglass
Barrel Lengths	$14^{15}/_{16}$ in.	**Hammer**		Internal
Weight	4½ lbs.	**Trigger**		Target tuned
Finish	Satin blue	**Options**		Stocks

Manufactured by Wichita Engineering and Supply, this particular pistol comes the closest to being the ultimate silhouette handgun. It is listed as a single shot bolt action pistol and for all purposes is in the same category as the XP-100.

But that is where the similarity ends. This gun is super finished inside and out. Chamberings available from the factory include the 7mm PPC, .308 × 1½-inch, and the .308 Winchester (full length). the trigger is of target configuration, and the firing pin fall is a mere .200 of an inch.

For stocks you have two options, walnut or fiberglass. The walnut stocks are oil-finished and glass bedded. The fiberglass handles are not prone to changes of humidity. They can be ordered in yellow or black epoxy. Other options include a normal grip (illustrated above) or a rear-grip model.

One design feature all shooters like is that the Wichita is available with either a right- or left-hand action. For example, if the shooter is right-handed and orders a left hand model, all he has to do during a match is load and unload with his left hand. The pistol is never released from the dominant hand, thereby making this option a real timesaver during those short relays. Although I thoroughly recommend this piece for the silhouette circuit, hunting is a different matter. The Wichita has NO safety, which could cause serious problems afield.

Poly-Choke
Hornady's

SEVEN

Accessories

Americans by their very nature are "gadgeteers." From car buffs to camera buffs to gun buffs, we all share that same natural instinct to customize, modify or improve on a product that has been designed and built for us in such a way as to be perfectly operational straight from the factory. Whether it be that new mirror for the car, a longer telephoto for the Nikon, or that new set of grips for the Colt, you can rest assured that the manufacturers will supply a steady stream of accessories. Of course, no one needs all the accessories listed in this chapter, but as you progress in a certain field of shooting, the need will arise for the product that lends itself to a particular job at hand.

In this day and age of mass production, the quality of grips, scopes, sights and countless other items must match that of the original equipment manufacturer. The American handgunner will not tolerate second class merchandise and he cannot afford to have accessories of inferior quality on his gun, especially if he is involved in police or defense work. Shoddy workmanship in fitting, weak metallurgy or just plain bad manufacturing practices have no place in firearm manufacturing.

Still, it's exciting to purchase a new gun, and one easy way to enhance that excitement is to add a set of adjustable micro-sights in lieu of the fixed sights that came with the gun, or possibly the grips are a little small, as in the case of certain Rugers or J- and K-frame Smiths. Then, a pair of hand-filling, custom production over-the-counter grips is called for. In short, accessories are problem-solvers, made with a solution in mind that will benefit both the shooter and his firearm.

Ninety-nine percent of all accessories in this chapter are of the simple add-on type and do not require the services of a gunsmith. These include grips, magazine rubber base pads, mainspring housings, slide releases and the like. They are specifically made for the home practitioner and can be installed with little or no trouble on his part. Others however, like BoMar sights, special scope mounts and bases, speed or ambidextrous safeties, do require professional attention. Not everyone can drill and tap a hole straight and true, and believe me, the couple of days delay combined with an investment of a few dollars is worth it in peace of mind alone.

Most accessories mentioned in this chapter are available through your local gun dealer; others like custom grips, special combat devices and related items can be purchased direct from the manufacturers.

Of all the accessories made for the handgunner today, the most popular are listed herein. But if you're in doubt whether a certain accessory will work on a particular handgun, a short note to the maker will get you detailed information on the product in question. Their names and addresses are listed in the appendix for your convenience. By all means contact them for specific advice on the use of their product.

BARREL BUSHING WRENCHES

Available from Colt, Safari Arms, and Smith & Wesson.

Often neglected but always needed, this useful little item was born when accurized .45s came on the scene. Used only on tight fitting automatics with barrel bushing installed, this wrench has a definite place in the competition shooter's tool box. As a footnote, for the man handy with tools, the broad-handled end can be filed down into a screwdriver to fit grip or sight screws.

CARTRIDGE BOXES

Available from Flambeau and MTM Products.

The variety of shooting-related accessories has grown over the years, especially when it comes to cartridge boxes. For convenience, protection and efficiency, they aid in our quest for accuracy. Plastic cartridge boxes should be on the list for any serious handloader.

The Flambeau series includes boxes for both handgun and silhouette shooters using rifle cartridges in serious competition. They are available in yellow or brown to aid in keeping brass and loads separate as may be the case of using one cartridge with two guns. Favorite loads may be kept in brown for your Smith M39, while yellow may be used for your Colt Government Model in the same 9mm chambering.

On the other hand, the MTM Company seems to be more diversified as their twelve page catalog will show. From cartridge boxes to ammo wallets, MTM includes such additional gems as moisture-proof magazine wallets or your choice of round or square holed storage containers. Like Flambeau, all products are made from drop- and break-resistant plastic.

EYE AND EAR PROTECTION

Available from American Optical, Bausch and Lomb, Bushnell, David Clark, J.B. Holden, Hudson Shooting Optics, Norton Company, Tasco, and Wilson Products.

Shooting glasses are perhaps the best investment you'll ever make. Besides protecting your valuable vision, shooting safety glasses help to relax your eyes and reduce fatigue.

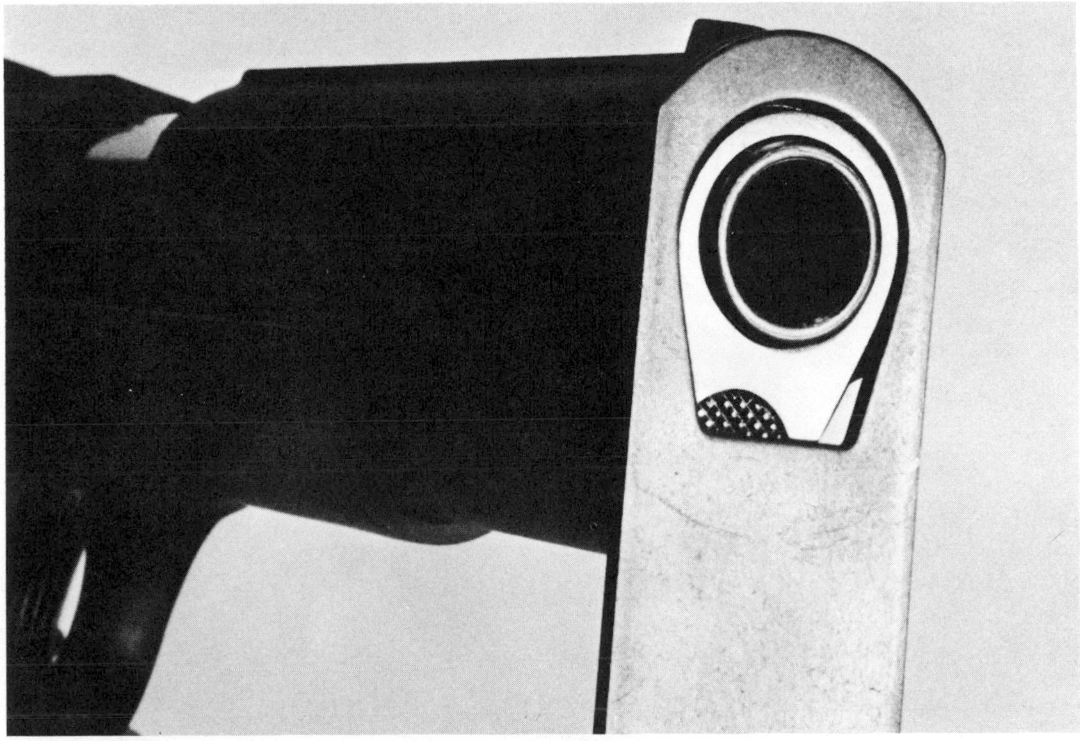

For accurized .45s, this special wrench is a must for removing tight fitting barrel bushings.

These Flambeau cartridge boxes offer identification and protection at a modest cost.

Eye and ear protection should never be treated lightly when firing modern centerfire ammunition. In this example, my wife Inge is wearing American Optical eyeglasses and hearing muffs.

This in turn promotes higher scores in the form of better accuracy because of high eye energy.

When looking for a pair of good glasses, one should be prepared to pay a fair price for value received. By this I mean, look for glass lenses, not plastic. Plastic will distort around the edges, but glass is ground to match the arc in which your eyeball actually turns in the socket.

Look for comfort. Better sets have adjustable nose pads and temples which will allow you to shape them to your face. On the subject of temples, most makers have two styles; flexible and semi-rigid or straight ear grips. The straight type is good for almost all shooting activities, but the flexible is the best choice for shooters on the run as in the fast moving combat shoots. They wrap around the ear to prevent the glasses from slipping or coming off during a match.

Another consideration is color. Over the years I have found that a neutral gray is best for all outdoor sports. It transmits roughly 30 percent of the available light and reduces glare. For hunting on hazy days or indoor shooting, yellow glasses rate extremely high with target shooters. While not noted for reducing much glare, these yellow lenses do transmit 80 percent of all available light.

As of September 1980, by order of the EPA, every hearing protector sold in this country must have a noise reduction label stating how much this particular model will reduce the amount of noise actually transferred to the wearer. Simply put, the higher the number, the greater reduction.

Hearing protectors are marketed in a number of styles for a number of reasons. First is wide availability of choice, and the various makers have seen fit to provide us with a good selection. There are over, behind, and under the head muffs, as well as spongy little puffs that fill your ear canal when released, and scientifically designed ear plugs that allow only normal sounds to get by. Other loud sounds are closed off by a minute valve built into these devices.

The second consideration is the job at hand. Pistol shooters can get away with wearing the usual banded-type muff with little or no problem. Shotgunners and riflemen, because of the gunstock, tend to go with the small inserts because there is less interference than with the common band type.

Comfort is also an important aspect. During a long practice session or match, the hearing protectors should fit correctly. They should not pinch, bind or bother you in any way. Every shooter owes it to himself to buy a pair that not only fits his requirements, but offers the greatest resistance to noise.

For the transportation of firearms to the range and/or matches, rigid gun cases made by MTM (left) or Pachmayr (right) fill the bill.

GUN CASES for Transportation

Available from Brauer Bros., Browning, Kolpin, MTM, Pachmayr, Protecto, and most leather makers.

For the man on the go, some form of transporting and protecting prized firearms should be considered. Soft pistol cases (or rugs) are used when one gun will be carried to a match. Although limited in such a way as to carry only the gun, soft flexible cases do have their place. Caution should be exercised when using a soft case. When returning from a match, the gun should be taken out of this particular case and returned to the gun rack. The reason is that most of the case and leather makers line their pistol cases with a soft material and this material can attract moisture and induce rust.

But like any other product on the face of this earth, there is an exception. Brauer Brothers of St. Louis, offers a pistol rug made from genuine Bark Tan Shearling which they claim is safe to store your guns in for extended periods of time. This may be the answer for people who want to store their guns but have limited space in which to do so.

Rigid or compartment cases are probably the best solution in the long run. Those offered by MTM and Pachmayr fill the bill very nicely. MTM's offering is a plastic case roughly 21 × 9 × 9 inches that fits any confined space. Because it is equipped with movable partitions, and a closed and compartmentalized top section, the user can literally customize this box to his own needs. Made from strong polypropylene plastic and incorporating hefty hinges with stainless steel hinge pins, this box will most likely outlast the shooter!

Next up is Pachmayr's popular Match Shooter's Handgun case. Designed years ago for the match shooter, this case is a classic in its field. Available in two grades and styles and holding up to five guns, this unit is made to exacting specifications. The Lok-Grip tray holds the guns without marring, thanks to padded gun slots. The slots themselves are grooved to accept a multitude of different guns which are held in by one large adjustable rack nut. Extra racks are available for those who need them or who think they can build a better case themselves. Accessories such as a carrying strap and spotting scope mount brackets help to keep this versatile shooter's box one of the most popular in its field.

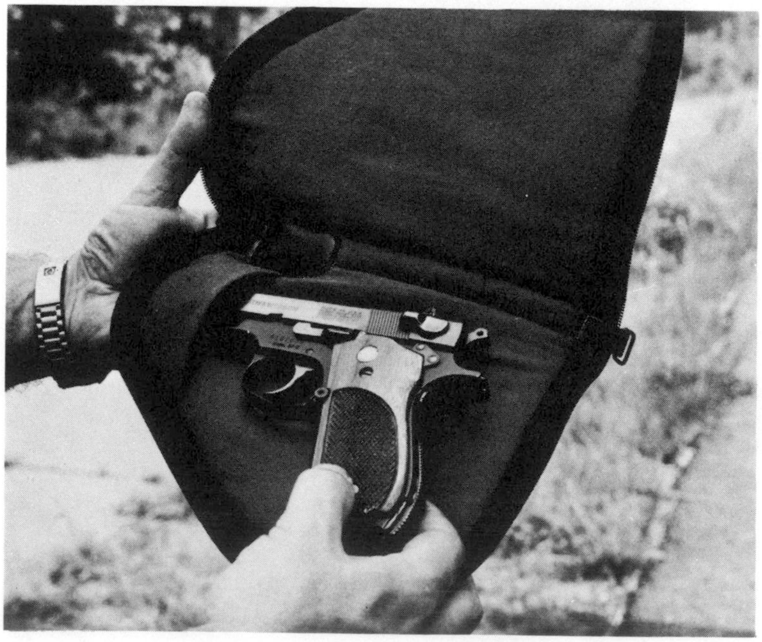

Single guns are easily carried in "pistol rugs" which are padded and lined to protect the gun. Prolonged storage in such a case should be discouraged however, as moisture can be trapped inside, thus accelerating the rusting process.

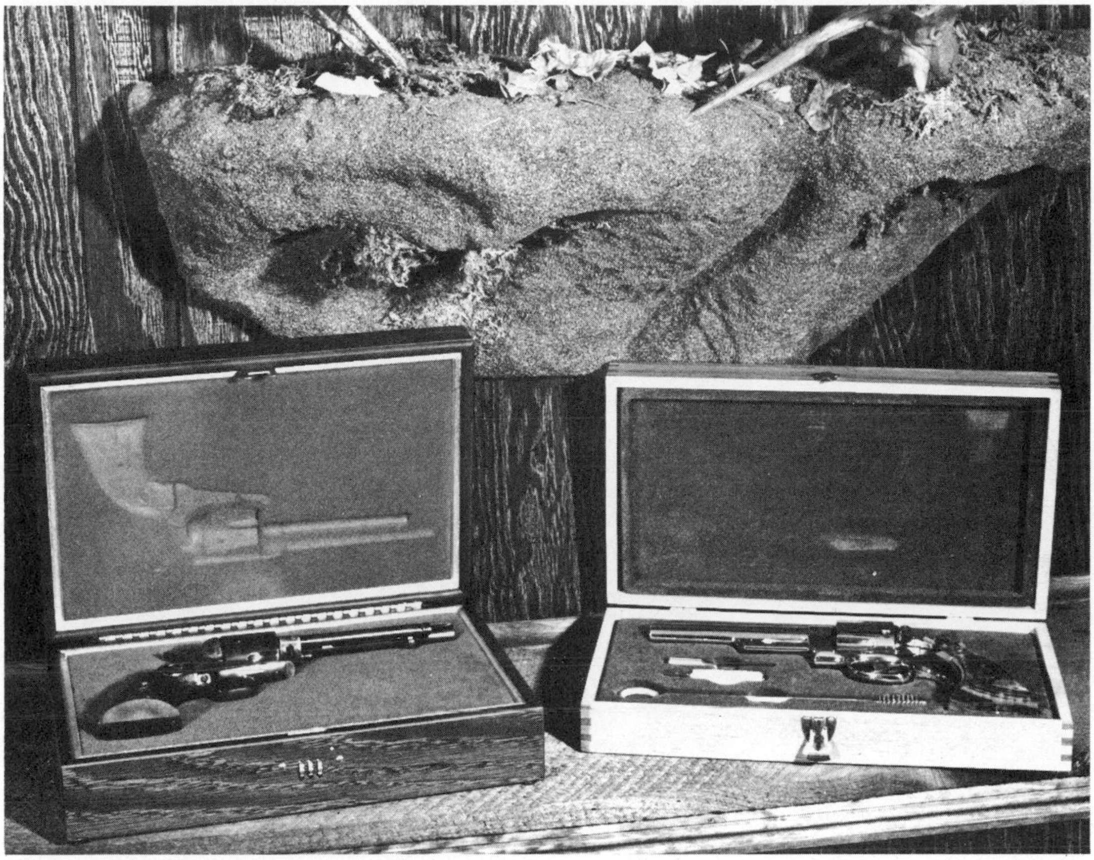

At home, guns can be protected and kept dust free through the use of especially designed hardwood cases.

GUN CASES for Home Storage

Available from Browning, Colt's Custom Shop, Griffin, and Smith & Wesson.

Gun cases for display purposes, whether custom-made or production grade, serve the discriminating handgunner in a number of ways. For just plain pride of ownership, there is no better way to show off a prized possession than in a beautifully lined presentation case. Protection also plays a big role in the ownership of handguns. Besides keeping dust and hand marks off your favorite gun, presentation cases keep it away from young hands. The saying "out of sight out of mind" surely applies here.

Production cases are available from Smith & Wesson in three sizes to accommodate all but the larger Buntline models. Up to about a year ago, S&W sold only molded inserts to fit a particular model. Now however, a spongy insert is coming around which will fit all guns, even awkward autoloaders.

Colt's Custom Shop puts out a beautiful series of cases which will handle one or two guns with barrel lengths from 2 to 7½ inches. French fit and compartment cases in rich rosewood or walnut come with genuine velvet interiors in a rainbow of colors to suit every taste and style.

Griffin Cases of Maine markets nicely-finished display cases in simulated Spanish oak which feature an internal corrosion inhibitor and interiors that mold to the exact shape of the gun. I've had mine for years, and it never seems to lose its shape. It still looks as good as the day I purchased it.

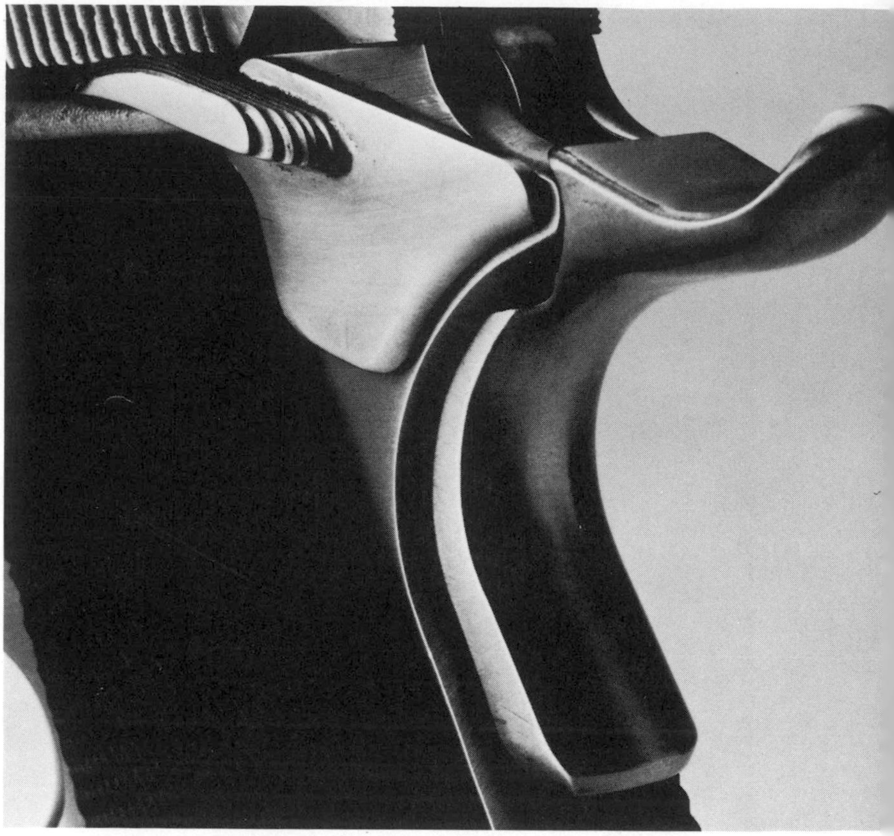

Besides eliminating hammer pinch, this widened and contoured grip safety by Safari Arms also helps the shooter control his weapon by spreading out the recoil effect of the big bore .45.

GRIP SAFETIES

Available from Colt's Custom Shop, H&D Products, and Safari Arms.

The world of combat shooting has brought about a raft of new ideas, designs and products not only related to the field, but also applicable in other facets of shooting. Undoubtedly one of the better accessories to come of age is the grip safety redesigned to an improved contour, thus taking the bite out of our famous "slabside" .45.

Machining or milling of the frame will be necessary on some makes, but others like the Colt model fit with little or no modification.

HANDGUN GRIPS Custom and Production

Available from Herrett's, Guy Hogue, Mustang, Pachmayr, Jay Scott, Sile, and Melvin Tyler (grip adapter).

The present lineup of handgun grips available to the modern handgunner has almost no bounds. From a wide selection of styles, materials, finishes, checkering patterns, and mounting systems, shooters often have a difficult and sometimes frustrating time picking out what is just right for them.

In this short essay on grips, I am not going to tell you what's best for you, or what to buy, since the choice in grips is highly subjective. What I am going to show is what to look for in a good set of grips, and what's available.

Handgun grips, to begin with, must be made to extremely close inletting tolerances. Any movement of the grip during shooting will not only affect accuracy because the shooter's hand position has changed, but will in due time start to split the wood at key stress points. Automatic machines that turn out grips on a production basis will wear from time to

The largest of all custom stockers, Herrett's also produces a fine line of standard hand-filling grips to fit all American handguns.

Guy Hogue's detailed custom grips are made from the finest rosewood and cocobolo imported woods. His son Aaron does all the fine line checkering.

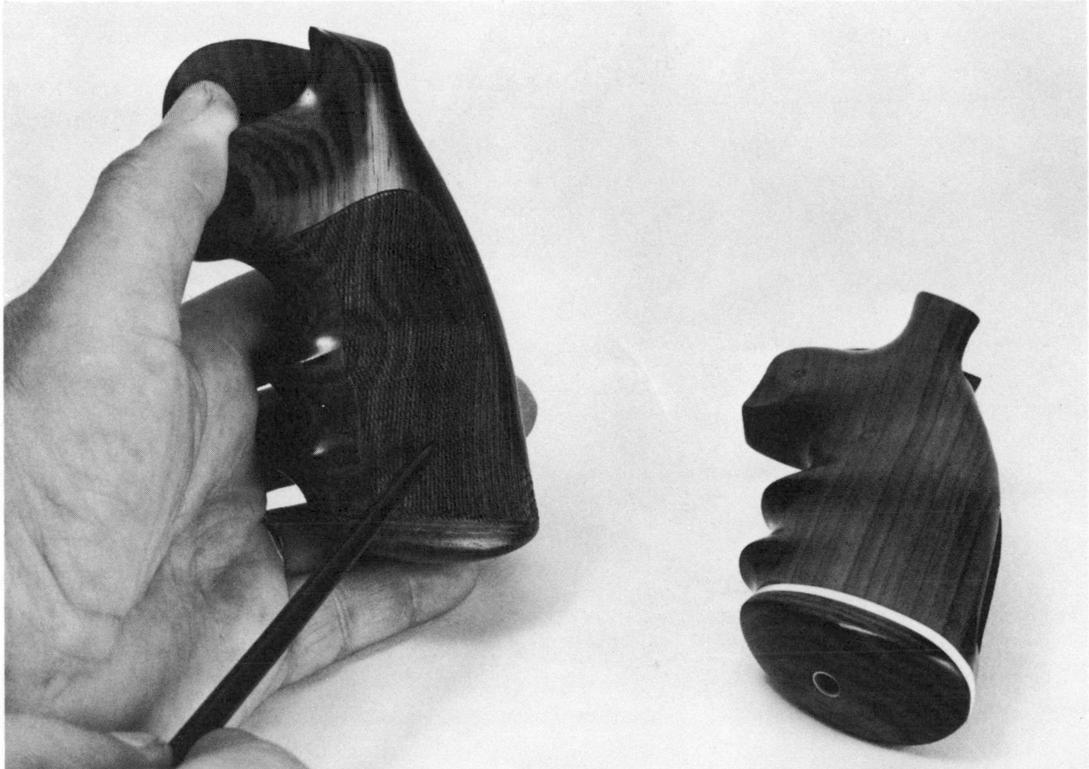

time, but this in itself is no excuse, as quality control should weed the bad ones out. Ill-fitting grips should be returned to the factory for replacement and/or correction. A grip tracing of the gun should be forwarded in the event of a design change that may have occurred years ago during a transition between certain models.

Pistol stocks, as they are sometimes called (although I think the word stocks should be reserved for rifles and shotguns) should be designed and manufactured with the shooter foremost in mind. They are essential for sight alignment and recoil control, especially in the brutal magnums. Production grips are middle-of-the-road solutions to the problem and are sufficient to a certain degree. In other words, if you're the average American with average hands, these will do the trick.

But what if your hands are bigger or smaller than the norm; how do you cope with that problem? Stockmakers have for years offered grips on a custom basis that will fit your personal hand physique to perfection. Along with the various catalogs, those who offer this service will have a blank page on which you trace your shooting hand. Then, by magical equations, the maker will tailor the depth, diameter and circumference to your hand size.

Mass-marketed and available for a vast array of guns, Mustang Grips are cut from walnut or colorfully grained Goncalo Alves, a South American wood. Shown on the Smith & Wesson Model 19, is their latest entry into the rubber grip field, the Rangefield.

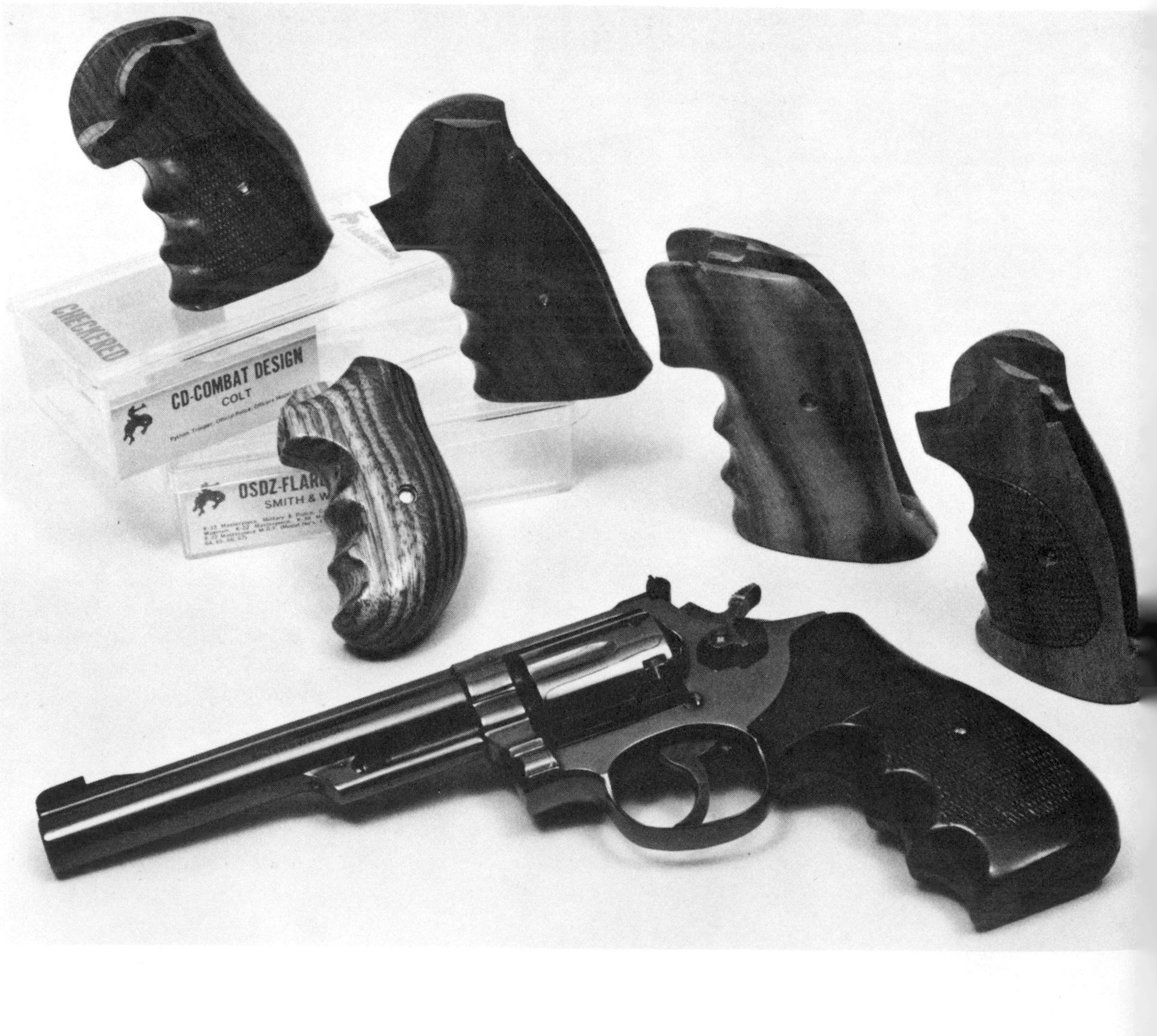

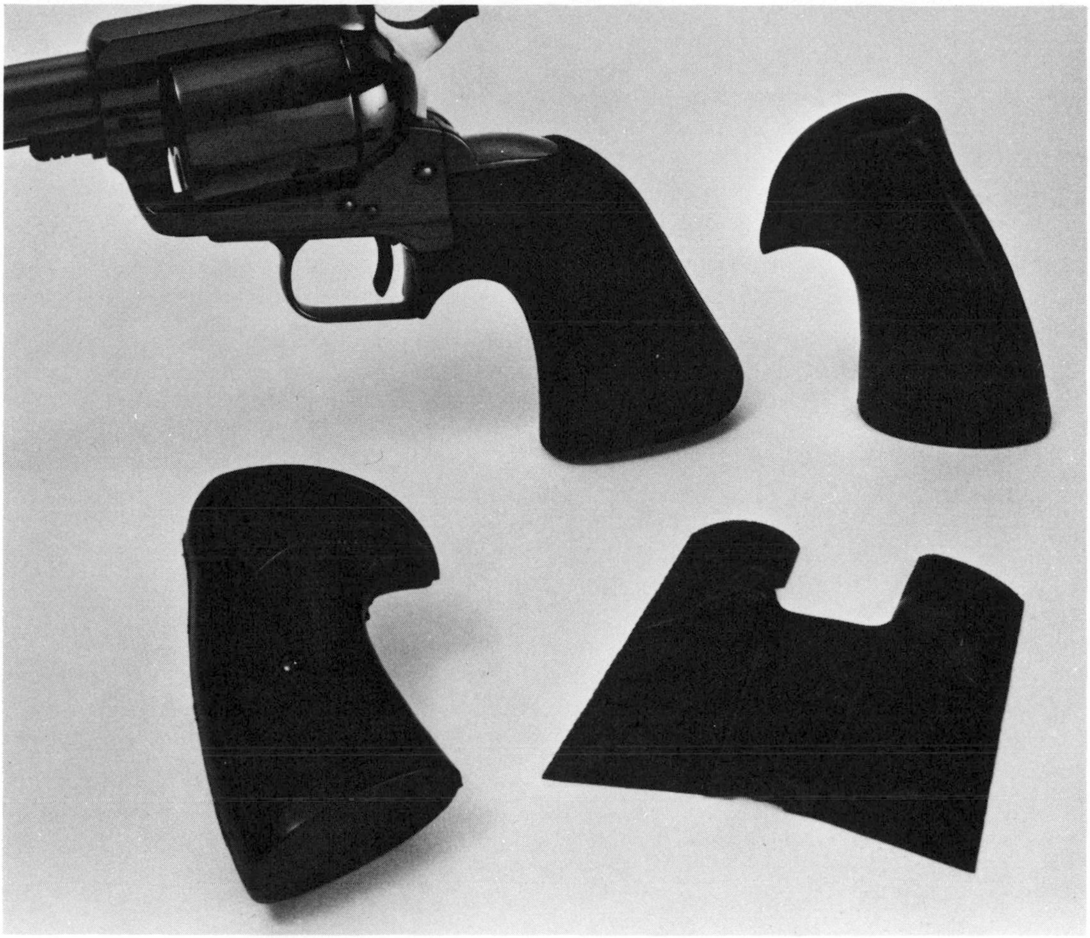

Pachmayr's neoprene grips fit over a hundred different guns. Called the Presentation series, these molded products are maintenance free and virtually indestructible.

Of course in this situation labor charges will raise the price, but the final result is worth the extra expense. Considering the comfort involved, the higher cost is justified.

Styles tend to range from the conservative or classic, to modern combat and specialized target handles. Herrett probably has the biggest selection as far as production and custom grips are concerned. They tailor their grips for competitors, police and those who desire a better fitting set of grips than those which came with the revolver. The two most popular styles, the Shooting Star and Shooting Ace, have been around for years, proving there is a need for finely crafted wood grips.

Newer to the scene is what Herrett calls the Shooting-Master. Looking at the illustration, you'll notice its clean lines and form. With a smooth semi-round butt section and finger grooves, it's bound to become a hit with men who wear the gun all day.

Guy Hogue's stylized grips lean toward the combat and PPC competition games. The nylon "Monogrip" shown has been a big seller because of certain design features incorporated in the product. A cut-out for speedloaders, proportioned finger grooves and palm swells all aid the shooter in his quest for additional points. His custom wood grips are second to none in quality, with checkering cut by his son Aaron.

Mustang Grips is a high-volume manufacturer who maintains high quality. With styles and woods to suit everyone, Mustang's production series has grips to fit most American handguns.

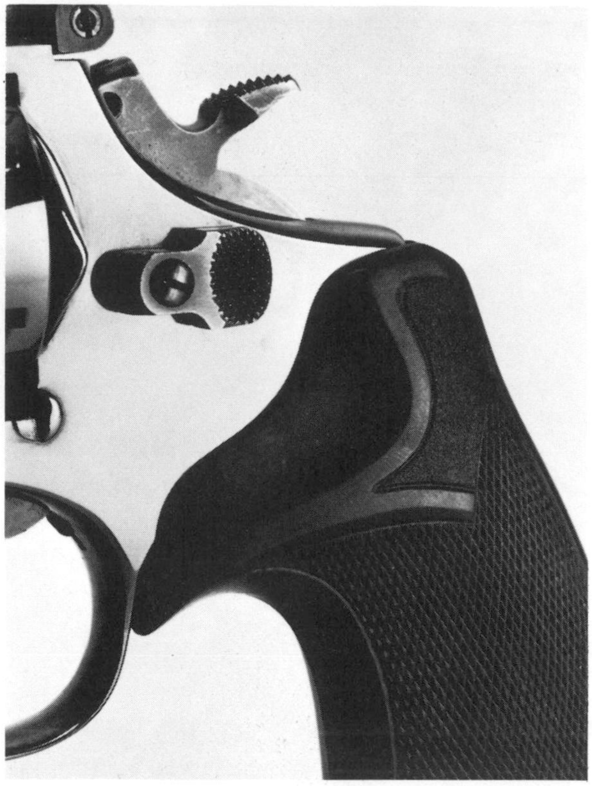

At the request of combat, police, and match shooters, Pachmayr has seen fit to include this cutout for speedloader use.

Laminated grips, such as those available from Jay Scott, offer finishes of ivory, stag, and simulated mahogany at very modest prices. Unfinished wood handles can be purchased by the hobbyist who enjoys molding them to his own hand or shooting need.

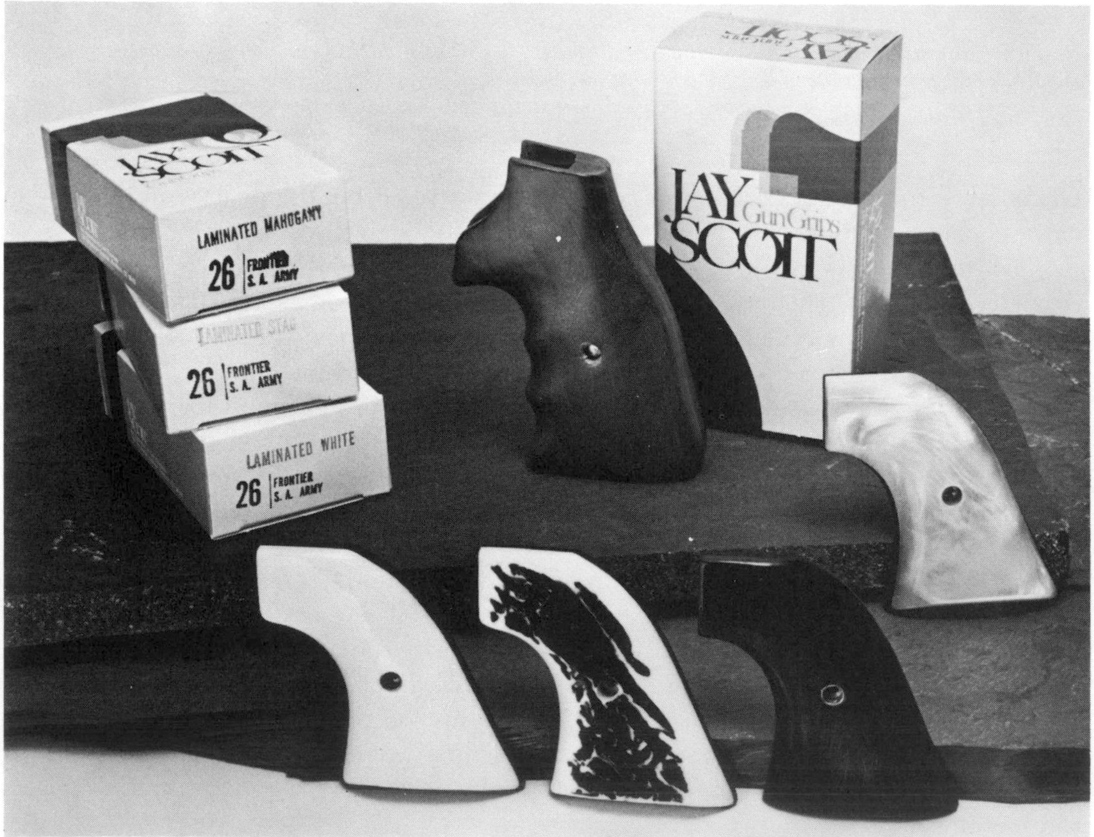

Like everyone else, their "rubber" grips, called the Rangefield, fit the average hand with comfort. Shown here on a Model 19, these neoprene handles will likely outlast the shooter. One other set deserves mention, especially for those of you who have extra large hands or shoot the thunderous Ruger .44 single action magnums. Called simply Model OGF, and available in fancy grained wood, these grips combined with finger grooves help dampen the recoil to a pleasurable degree.

Pachmayr, a name synonymous with quality workmanship since the early 1900's has cut a niche in the grip field since they introduced their neoprene Presentation (for revolvers) and Signature (for automatics) series a few years ago. Made in black only, they come in semi-flared, round butt and compact designs. Molded with a steel insert for stability, these grips can be cut, shaped or filed to fit your hand. Counting over a 101 styles and models to fit any handgun (including the Contender), the Pachmayr group is indeed worthy of your consideration.

The Jay Scott operation of Colt Firearms is another one of those old line companies where fit and finish is paramount. Their Armarc grouping is not only a one-of-a-kind series among the stock makers, but they actually defy destruction. Made from a polyester laminate, these tough grips are impervious to sweat, animal blood or gun solvent. Really handsome on single action western-style guns in white or black pearl, they also are offered in ivory, stag, mahogany and zebra wood outside finishes.

In wood, the Gunfighter (with fingergrips), the Trophy (without thumbrest), and Expert (with thumbrest) come in walnut or zebra wood, and rough, smooth, and checkered final finishes. The rough series is interesting, as they are fully inletted but not final-finished, as to allow the do-it-yourselfer to do his thing. In all, with over fifteen different styles to fit over 498 combinations of handguns, one should not be at any loss to fit a set to his handgun.

Sile Grips of New York makes a lot of the standard factory grips you see on today's American handguns. Acting as a stock department for many of the firearm makers, Sile turns out a good and dependable product line. One in particular really caught my attention; their Model 77-0, made to fit my Colt Python. For those of you who may shoot a Python in wadcutter matches, look into this model. They fit the hand well and, incorporat-

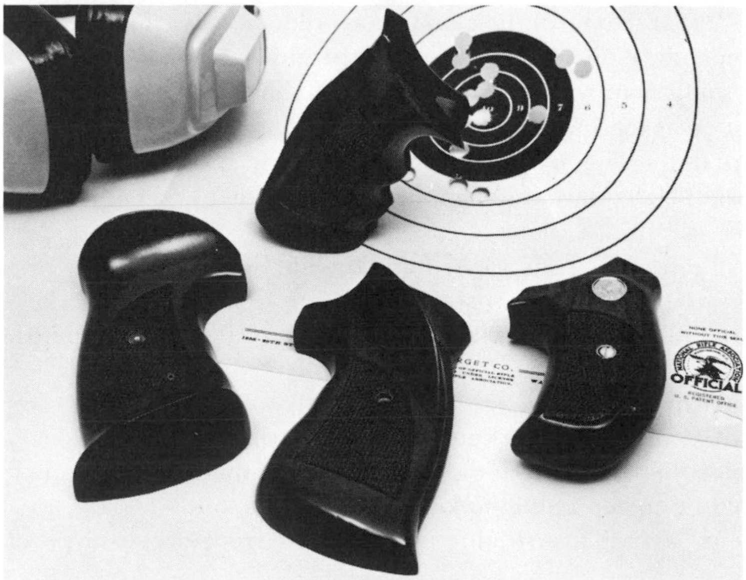

As a stocking company for some American firearm makers, Sile also offers models to fit the Ruger, Colt Python Target, and S&W J-frame lines.

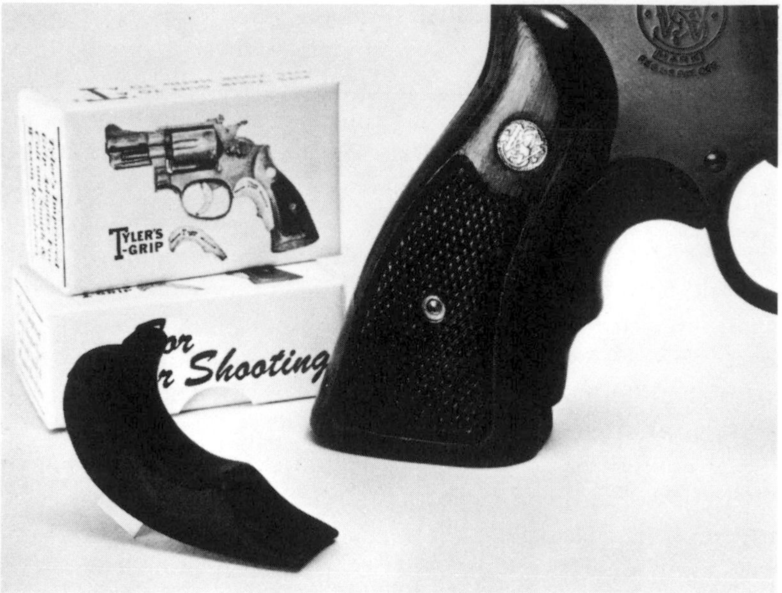

For handgunners who like the feel of the S&W small magna-grip, Tyler makes a "T" grip to help fill the void behind the trigger guard for more control.

ing a thumbrest and modest finger grooves, and aid in putting all those bullets in a nice tight group downrange.

Melvin Tyler has been making a handly little grip adapter for years for people who, because of the very nature of their jobs or hands, buy and use guns with small (magna) grips. This little insert gives more area to the gripping surface, yet does not add unnecessary bulk.

Materials used in the production of grips should play an important role in your decision. Walnut is a popular choice because it wears well and looks good. Neoprene gives a firm grip feeling to the gun with no chance of warping even in damp or humid climates. Plastic checkered grips come standard on some factory models (i.e., S&W's Model 59) but lack the warmth of wood or the flexibility of the neoprene/rubber combination. Plastic is durable however, and where the thickness of the gun frame must be compensated for the thinness of the grips, plastic is the choice.

In most cases, grip finishes tend to be of the glossy (polyurethene or varnish) or dull (oil) surface manufacture. Depending on your preference, the glossy finishes combined with figured wood make for some snappy looking presentation panels on display or engraved firearms. Oil-based products tend to go on work or target guns when the gun is to be subjected to unusual or hard times. Touch up is easy: The distressed spot should be first lightly sanded, then a light coat of boiled linseed oil applied for continued wood protection and appearance.

Checkering is cut after the final finish is applied and dryed. Most patterns are of a simple nature, and need not be extra fancy on such a small piece of wood. Coarse checkering is preferred by the majority of shooters, as the finer cuts tend to be of no help with heavy recoiling.

As for maintenance, wax should be used and applied lightly to glossy grips to keep the sheen; oil should be added as needed to perk up work-worn grips. One drop goes a long way. Too much will render the wood soft and punky in a short time. For additional protection, the inletting should be coated lightly to keep any moisture out.

A little bit of care on your part will insure a lifetime of service from any set of pistol grips on the market today.

HANDGUN GRIPS Factory Fancy Wood

Available from Colt's Custom Shop, Smith & Wesson, and Dan Wesson Arms.

The factory grips that come with all production guns are in all likelihood a standard run of grained American walnut. Now mind you there is nothing wrong with American walnut, but on the other hand there is a group of fellows out yonder (myself included) who craves nicely figured pistol grips on their guns. And to accommodate their wishes, the major companies offer fancy grained wood in a number of patterns and designs.

Of the three offering special grips in their literature, the Colt Custom Shop perhaps has the broadest selection. Included in their listings are such exotic numbers as genuine ivory (when available) and a material called Whaleen. This is a man-made substance similiar to ivory, but it wears hard and longer. Continuing on, we find that the old favorites of rosewood, mother-of-pearl, cocobolo and pewter are also sold through the Custom Shop.

Smith & Wesson offers a South American wood called Goncalo Alves, and the samples I've seen on engraved or special editions are simply striking.

Dan Wesson, besides offering three or four different styles, cuts some of their target grips in zebra wood. Colored black and yellow, this wood makes a fine finishing touch to any one of their handguns.

For factory fancy grips, one can turn to Colt's Custom Shop for a long list of different materials which include birdseye maple, rosewood, or even real ivory for the discriminating user.

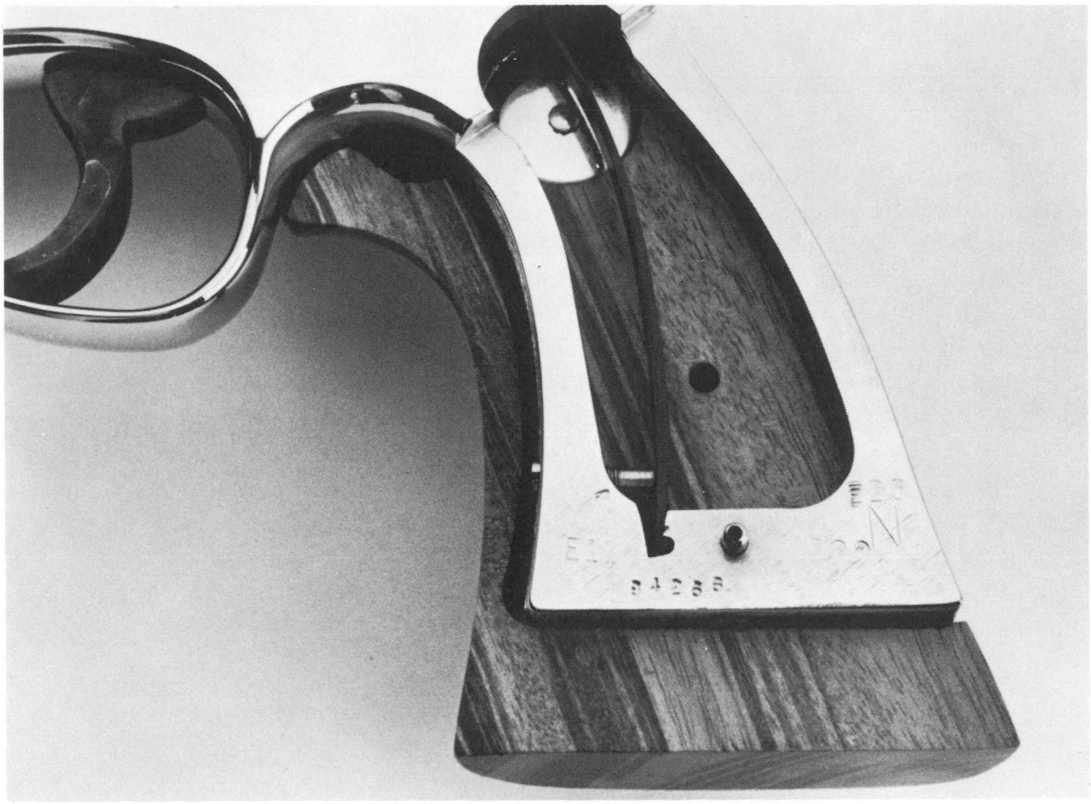

Handfilling target grips, like this S&W N-frame example, serve the needs of many shooters who like fancy wood and good workmanship.

Fancy grained Goncalo Alves wood is available from S&W to fit all their models, including both semiautomatics and revolvers.

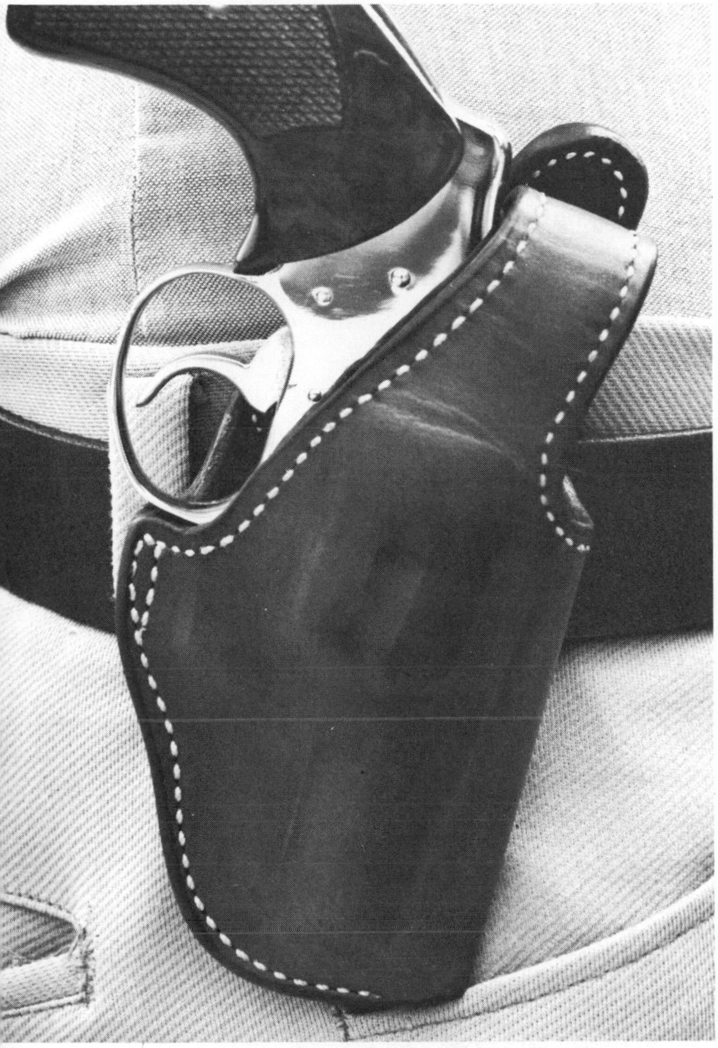

Made from premium saddle leather, this Bianchi Model 5 BHL also incorporates a sight channel for easy drawing and a $1^3/_4$- to $2^1/_4$-inch belt slot depending on the model and barrel length of the gun. It is shown here with the Colt Detective Special.

One of the most popular of all holsters in the Bianchi line is this Sportsman's Model with a plain Ranger Belt.

LEATHER PRODUCTS Holsters and Related Gear

Available from Bianchi, Brauer Brothers, Bucheimer, Chace, Don Hume, Jackass Leather, Pancake Leather, Safariland, Smith & Wesson, and Thompson/Center.

Strolling into any sporting goods store one is amazed at the amount of leather products on the market today. Counting all the major leather makers, smaller independents and one-man shops across the country, I totalled up just under seventy-five in my research. Add to that figure the number of different models, colors and designs, and your choice borders on the infinite.

Leather products are big business. Some of the larger companies do roughly four to six million dollars per annum on their leather goods and accessories. In all probability, this accounts for perhaps the biggest share of the accessory market.

Why? Well for instance, take the holster segment. Most gun retailers agree that when a fellow comes in to purchase a handgun, in most cases he walks out with a holster as well. I say "most cases" because the other small percentage buy target guns which rarely see the inside of a holster. The leather industry is big on craftsmanship, with the human element considered in design and production. Although machines do the heavy cutting, buffing and sewing, each holster is made on pretty much an individual basis. Top quality hides have to be inspected for color and perfection. As with most quality consumer goods in this country, good hides are on the decrease, mainly because of the law of supply and demand. As the demand increases, the supply tends to remain pretty well constant. Any leather worker worth his salt is always on the alert for good quality leather with minumum scratch and fence cut markings.

After a holster design is considered, a prototype is made. This first copy must pass all the check points necessary before the rig goes into production. Does it have appeal, and is it practical? Is there room enough for the grips, with possibly a little extra for custom wood?

Carrying long-barreled guns in the field is made easier by the use of a good quality shoulder rig. The Bianchi X2100 Phantom is made for both semiautomatics and revolvers and can be ordered with a fancy suede lining.

By incorporating a friction screw, Brauer Brothers can do away with the traditional over the top safety strap. Shown here is the inside belt model for snub-nosed revolvers.

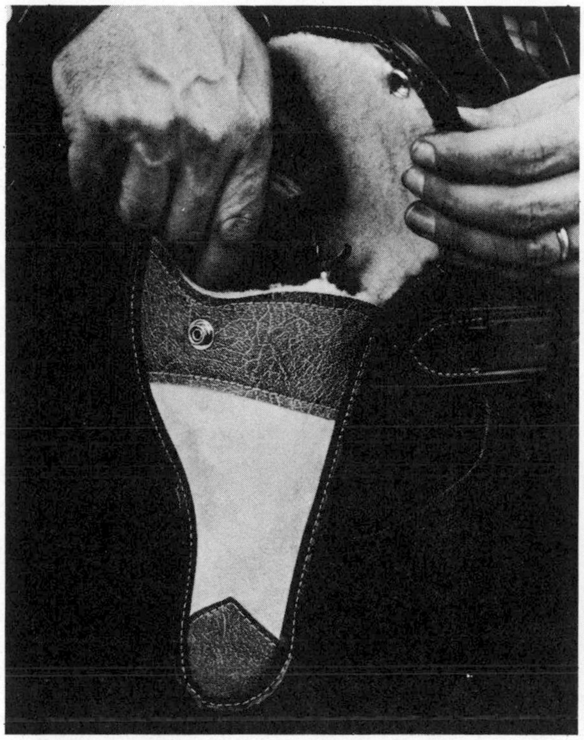

For storage and carrying, the Brauer Brothers Bark Tanned Shearling lined holster is said to repel moisture for extended periods of time.

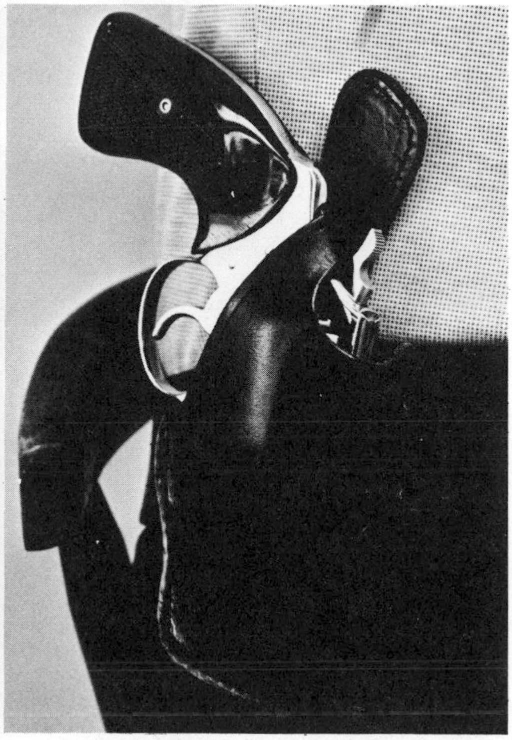

Holsters like this Bucheimer Hi-Ride are just the thing for the desk-bound officer or the detective on the go.

Western purists are not forgotten, as this quality example from Chace Leathergoods illustrates.

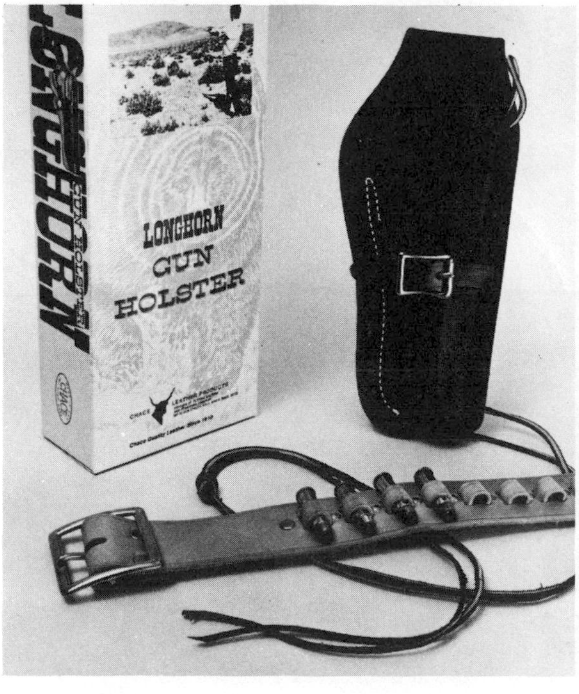

Canted for smooth draw, and reinforced with a metal insert, Don Hume's Jordan style holster is a rugged product desired by many shooters. Combined with a wide River Belt, it's a good choice for both police and sportsmen alike.

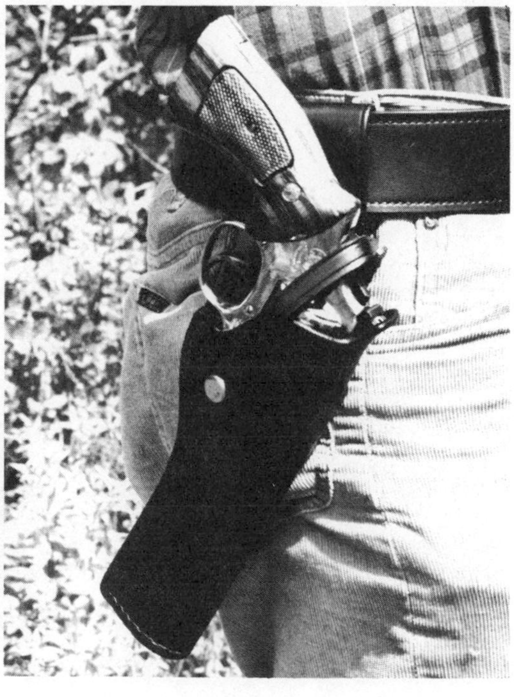

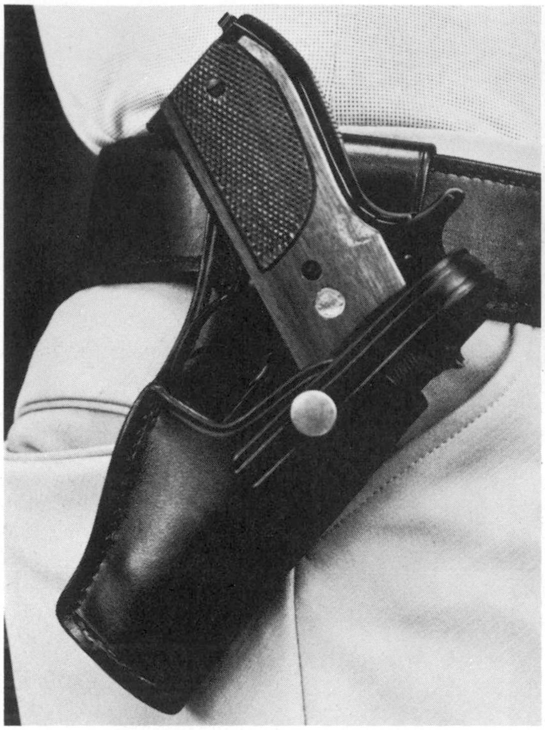

Here is a variation of the Jordan rig; this time for a S&W Model 39 automatic.

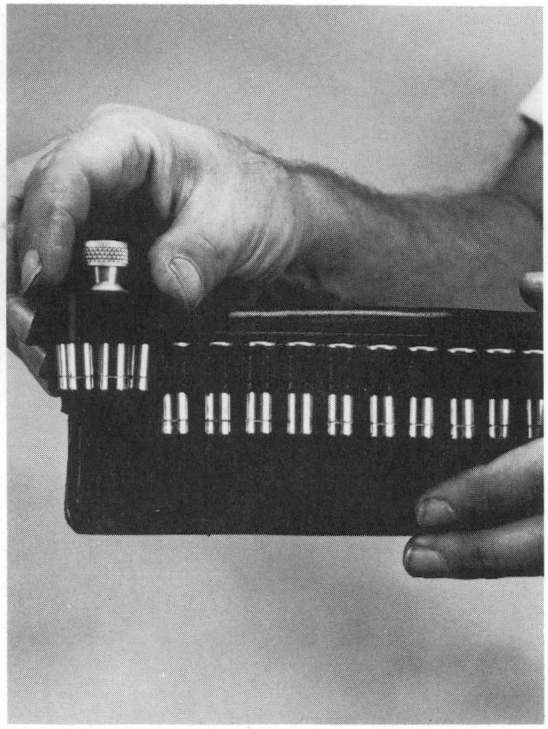

Many PPC-class shooters carry their speedloaders and extra rounds in a handy leather product Don Hume calls a "Matchmaker."

By using a full-welt construction, Jackass Leather has added strength to their series of flat holsters.

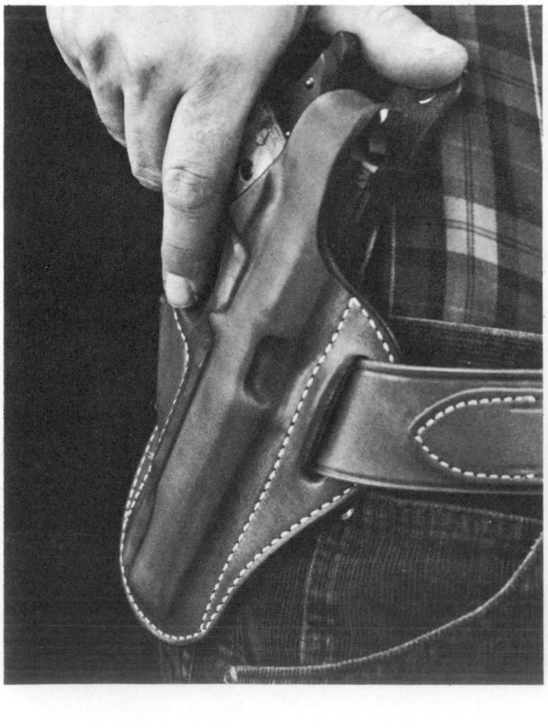

Shoulders rigs should fit the shooter snugly to ensure a quick draw under tense encounters. Before using this .45 for serious social work however, the front sight must be ramped or rounded off to prevent any exit problems.

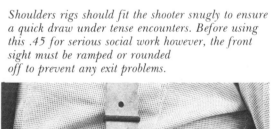

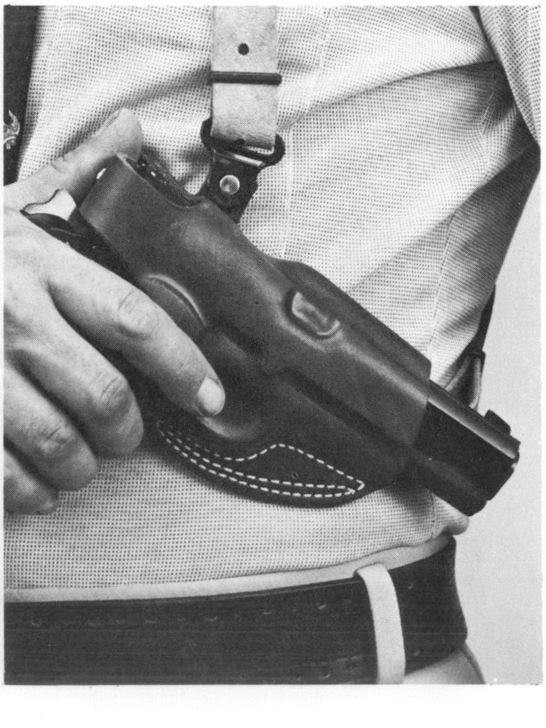

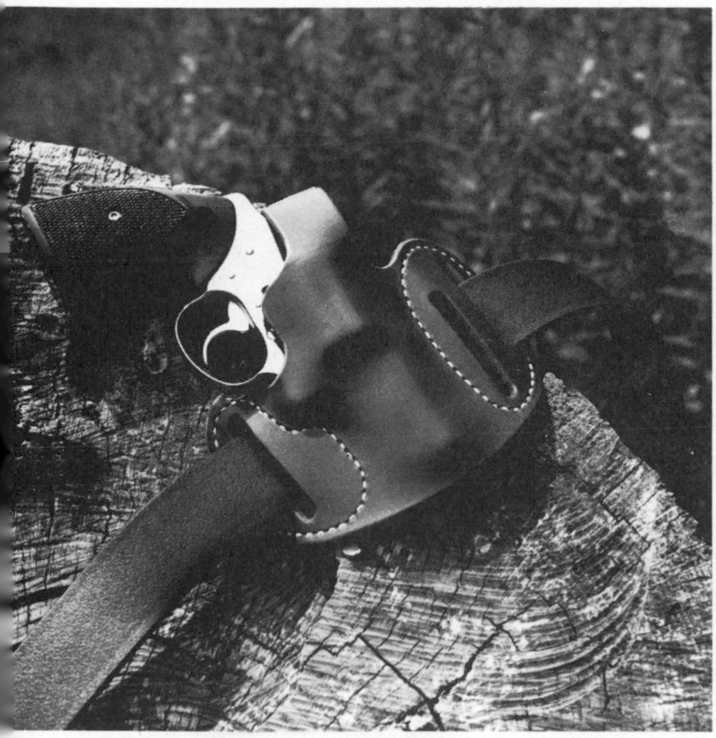

Roy's Original "Pancake" design is noted for flatness and concealability. Cut from two plys of 7/8-ounce leather, these holsters are available for most models of American handguns.

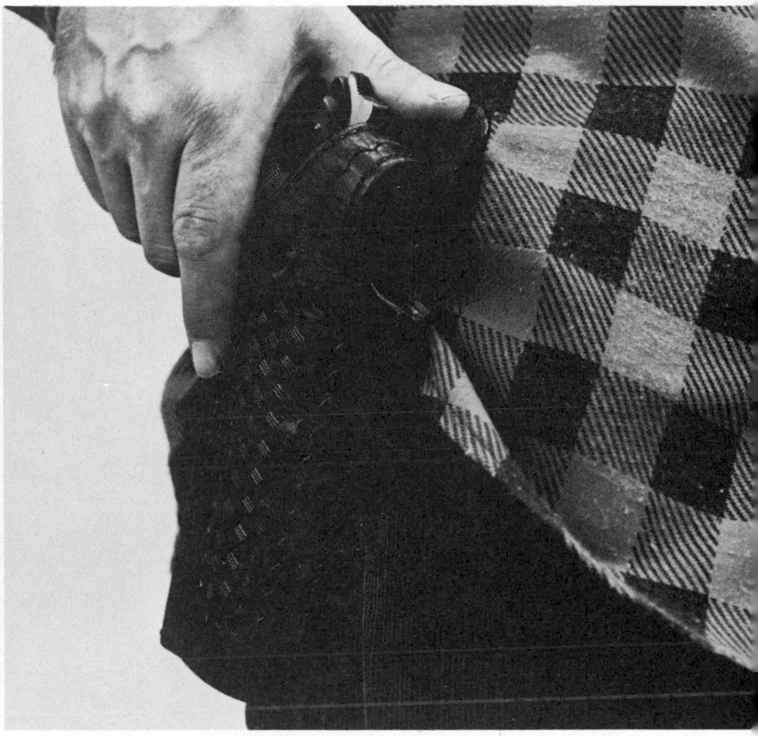

One of the author's favorite .45 holsters is this Safariland Model 254 Border Patrol. It has a jacket slot, basketweave finish, and is lined with suede for minimum wear on the pistol.

Like many holster makers, Safariland offers their version of the high-ride model. Called the Model 28 "Low Silhouette," their design makes use of a new hidden belt loop that eliminates a lot of the bulge associated with this type of leather product.

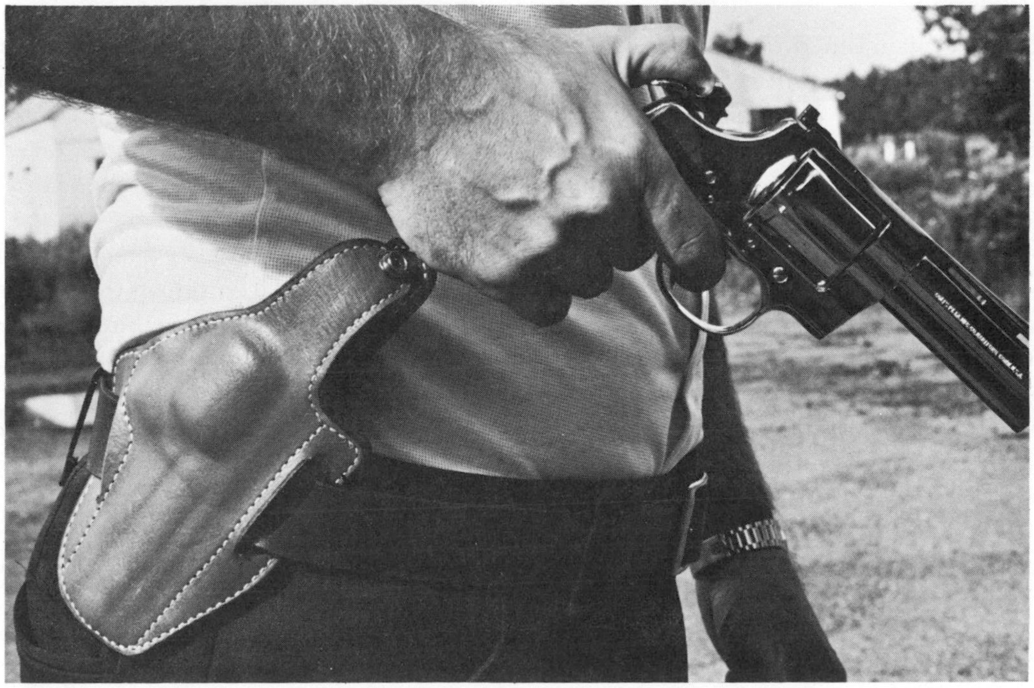

Excellent workmanship and attention to detail are traits for which Smith & Wesson is known in handguns, and now in leather products. This lined shoulder holster is a prime example of their work and is molded for the big N-frame guns.

Will it be plain, lined or carry basketweave exterior design? These and numerous other questions have to be answered before the holster in question is turned loose on the buying public. Then and only then, are the cutting and shaping molds made for this model. Attention is paid to the grain and texture of the leather, as well as the thickness it takes to assure a lifetime of service and durability. The holster is then folded in half or made in two pieces, depending on the model, then stitched together.

Every company has its own way of doing things, so there is variety even in stitching. Bianchi uses numerous waxed-lined type threads together to hold its products tight. Safariland uses plain strong nylon on theirs. Either way both must be doing something right as I have never seen a good holster come apart except by misuse.

As for styles, there are four basic categories of handgun holsters: right-hand from the hip; left-hand from the hip; crossdraw, on the opposite side from the shooting hand; and the shoulder holster. Your preferences and requirements will dictate the proper holster or leather accessory.

Because there are a couple of hundred different and distinctive models, sizes, shapes, and colors to choose from, I am only going to mention the most important considerations. Leather gear, like handgun grips, is a highly personal item and a matter of personal preference. I'll let the photographs do the talking in this section, but by your use of the check list below, you should be able to secure a holster consistent with your needs.

Twelve Points To Consider When Choosing A Handgun Holster

1. Material. Do you want the natural feel and look of leather or do your job requirements require the use of a man made synthetic like Clarino or Wessonhide? The above two products require little care, tolerate a lot of abuse, and are easily cleaned with a damp cloth. Leather is more traditional and for those who take exceptional pride in their weapons, it the only choice. In any case, weigh all the prospects and possibilities, then make your decision.

2. Purpose. Will it be used for hunting, backpacking, fishing, defense, or law enforcement? Each has its special needs, so a well thought-out decision is important.

3. Personal Requirements. Do you want (or need) a belt holster, high ride, drop loop, inside pants, crossdraw, or special competition rig?

4. Mounting. Depending on the use, should the holster belt loop be rigid or attached via a swivel mechanism?

5. Safety Strap. If there is no expressed need for a super quick draw, a safety strap covering part of the gun and hammer is adequate. However, men in police work favor a thumb break as it allows the gun to be drawn and put into immediate use with less movement on the part of the officer. It covers the hammer spur, holds the gun in place effectively, yet allows for a quick and dependable draw.

6. Shoulder Rig. This is a tough personal decision which can only be made by the wearer. Hunters prefer this rig above others, mainly because the gun is out of the way, yet can be

This close-up photograph illustrates the concealed thumb break feature on the S&W Model B06-36 police holster.

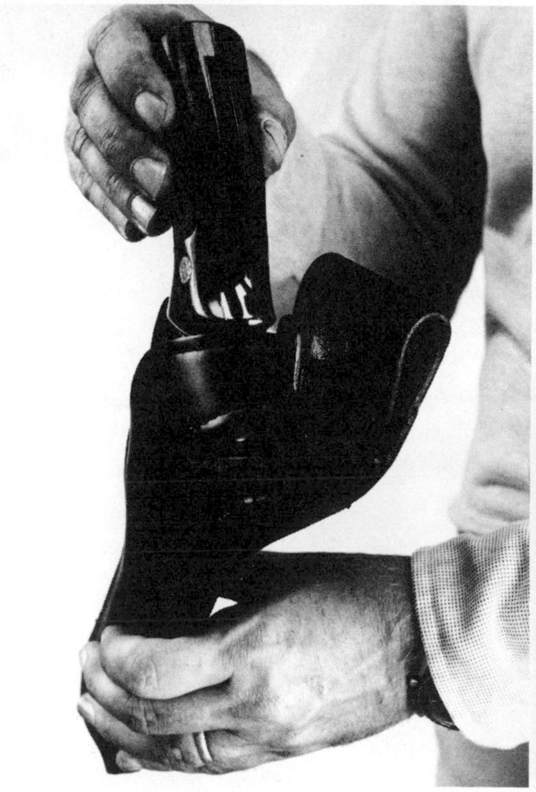

Although not actually in the leather business, Thompson/Center does offer some leather goods for its Contender single shot pistols. Shown here is a shoulder holster that can double as a belt model if the shooter desires.

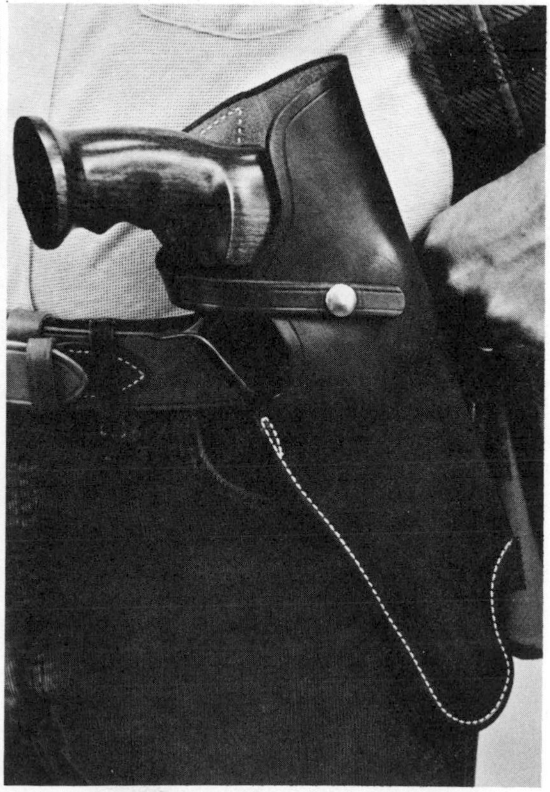

grabbed easily if the need arises. The reasons for selecting this style are obvious in police work, especially in undercover operations.

7. Gun Fit. A must requirement for all holsters. When purchasing a new holster, take the gun along. Options like wide hammers or triggers can interfere with the gun being able to sit correctly in the holster. Always be sure of what you are buying; if in doubt, check the manufacturer's catalog of specifications.

8. Safety. Slide the gun in the holster and buckle it up. Shake the whole thing up, down and sideways as violently as you can. I have seen snaps that did not snap very tightly. This in turn can give you trouble in the field, especially if the footing gets rough and you slip or fall. Holsters with friction devices, such as those made for combat shoots, must display good holding quality. In this case it is best to check the holster in the store rather than face an embarrassing disqualification at the match.

9. Accessibility. Can you reach the gun easily? Consideration should be made for long-barreled handguns. A Colt Buntline has no place on the hip, for by the time the barrel clears the leather, you'd be so bent out of shape that quick sight alignment would be difficult. Belt, high ride or shoulder holster—no matter what, it must fit your style of shooting.

10. Color, etc. Black, brown, natural, roughout or basketweave, the frills are up to you.

11. Options. The catalogs are full of them. Sight guards, sight tracks, hammer guards, suede linings, open bottoms, closed bottoms etc., etc. Again, only you can decide what is applicable for your purposes. Choose wisely. Holsters, like cars, do the job well even if they have only the basic features.

12. Quality. The final checkpoint. Look for full-welted seams, recessed snaps, double stitching in places of stress, thickness of material, and a rich final finish.

Good holsters will outlast the owner with the proper care and treatment. Know your requirements, shop wisely, and you will never be disappointed with the fine products offered by the American leather industry.

MAGAZINES Spares

Available from AMT, Bauer, Colt, Crown City Arms, Safari Arms, Sile, and Smith & Wesson.

Spare magazines are silent partners that really don't get much fanfare in the shooting press as a glamorous accessory, but they should always be there when you need them. Years ago, most semiautomatic pistols came with two, now because of rising costs and inflation, that small luxury is gone. In any event, always keep a spare or two for any one auto. And for Pete's sake, try them! I personally know one fellow who kept his spares nice and neat and brand new, but never used them. One day at a match . . . well you know the rest. Both failed to function properly. For the match shooter, spare clips are cheap insurance indeed.

MAGAZINE RUBBER PADS

Available from H&D Products and Safari Arms.

Made from neoprene rubber, this little accessory helps to seat the magazines fully during a hurried match or when oversized grips are used. Glued to the base of the magazine with epoxy cement, these pads also serve as a cushion when the clip hits the ground during a reloading stage.

The use of spare magazines enables the combat shooter to extend his shooting capabilities to meet all types of match requirements. Check them out for flawless feeding and ejection before using them in competition.

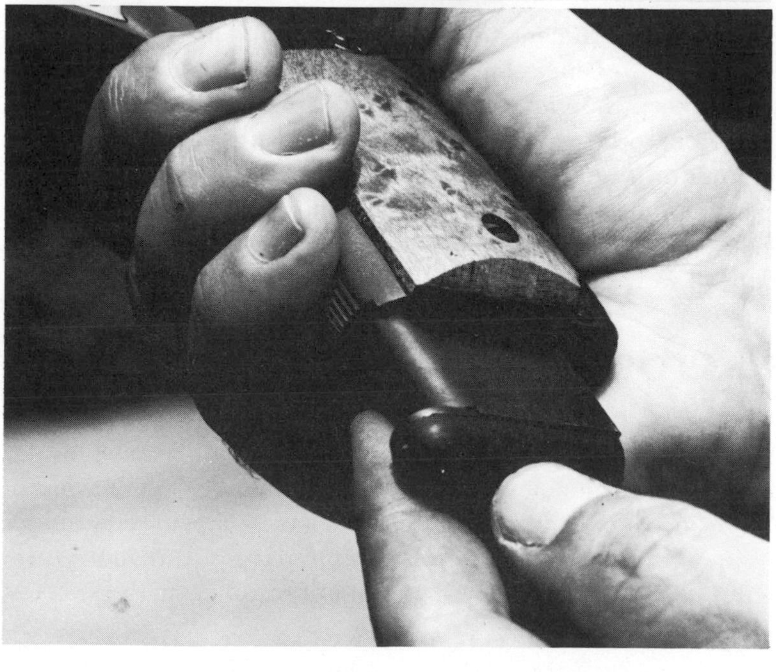

These thin rubber base pads aid in insertion, as well as protecting the clips from damage when they hit the ground.

Depending on your hand or shooting style, mainspring housings are made in either the arched (left) or flat models (right) from many sources.

MAINSPRING HOUSINGS

Available from Colt, Crown City Arms, and Pachmayr.

As standard issue on all Colt Government model .45's, the arched housing was introduced in the early 1900's as an aid to better shooting. It adds bulk to the bottom back of the pistol, and this tends to keep the gun pointing in an upward attitude. The flat housing is aimed at target shooters who have no need for this feature, because it may hinder some in keeping the gun down and on target. If your problem lies in either of these two areas, switch to the opposite housing and see if any improvement is noticed. In any case, once you are satisfied, stick with one or the other. Constant switching will only aggravate the problem, and lead to frustration and poor scores.

RECOIL COMPENSATORS

Available from Mag-Na-Port Arms and P.S.I. Company.

As an accessory item, recoil reduction devices find favor with many big-bore enthusiasts. Besides the ability to get on target faster with repeat shots, compensators reduce recoil by as much as 40 percent. Of course many variables enter into the picture in the form of caliber size (they work better on the larger calibers), weight of the gun, grip thickness or style, and even barrel length.

Of the two I investigated, Mag-Na-Port is the most popular and plentiful in a survey taken at a local ranges. For over a decade this product has made inroads into virtually all shooting sports encountered. Two slots are made in the barrel via the Electrical Discharge Machining (EDM) method. This in itself is a by-product of the space industry and will neatly cut thru your barrel without leaving any burrs or roughness and without even disturbing the finest bluing job.

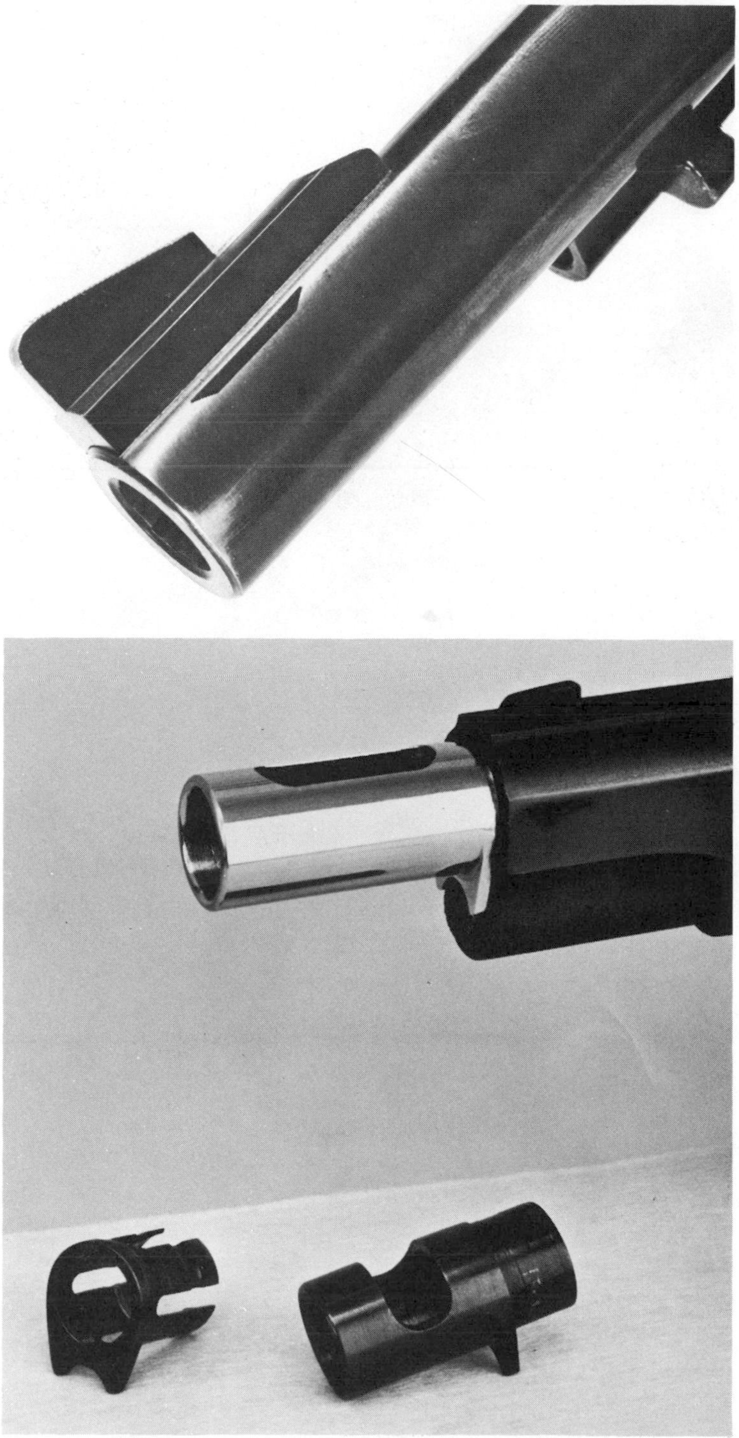

Depending on the weapon involved, recoil devices can either be cut into the barrel (Mag-Na-Port) or attached (PSI) as photographed on the .45 Auto.

Of the shooters questioned, most agreed the Mag-Na-Port compensator reduced felt recoil, especially in the larger magnums; all agreed that it reduced muzzle flip. Linear recoil (backward movement) was not affected that much, only because the vents are cut in such a way as to divert the gas in an upward fashion.

The P.S.I. device takes the place of the barrel bushing on .45 autos, hence is limited to that specific arm. It is about half the cost of Mag-Na-Port but then again it cannot be applied to revolvers or autoloaders not of the Colt .45 design. For the boys in combat shooting with open bottom holsters, it will make its mark. Once it is attached, the shooter will soon realize its value.

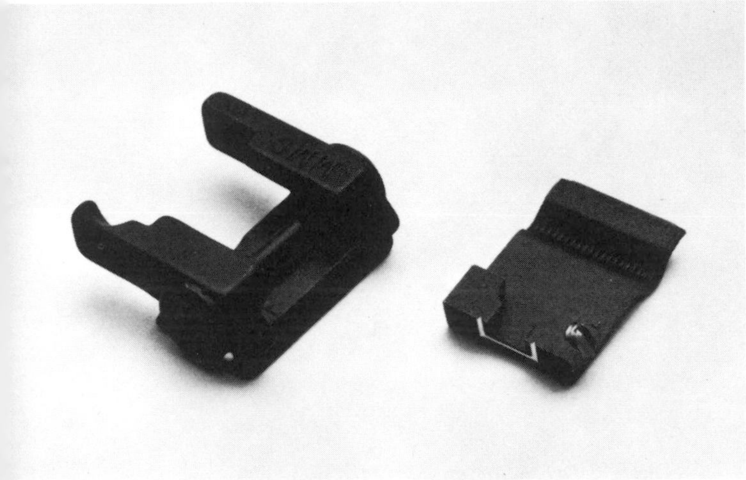

By using the standard front sight, the home gunsmith can add adjustable rear sights to his .45 automatic like these made by MMC.

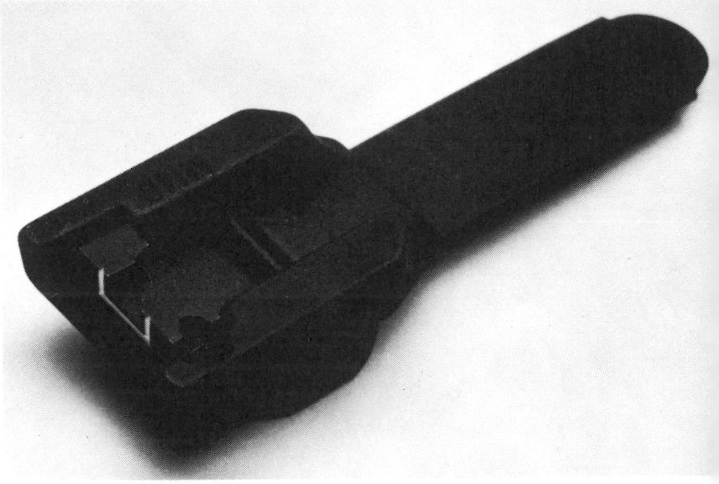

MMC rear adjustable sights for the Smith & Wesson Models 39/59 add the extra dimension of an elevation mode for serious combat shooters.

SIGHTS Metallic

Available from Bo-Mar, Colt (Elliason), Micro Sight, Miniature Machine, Omega, Poly Choke, and Smith & Wesson.

Handguns today are extremely accurate, thanks to recent innovations in firearm metallurgy, moderate barrel lengths, and metallic sights. The biggest gain recently has been in metallic sights. With the resurgence of shooting competitions across the country, specialized sighting equipment had to be designed and built.

Starting with the basics, any good rear sight has to be built with crisp windage and elevation adjustments. Click stops are preferred over friction movements, only because of their ability to hold any position better during heavy shooting and/or recoil.

On the average most hunting, police, and defense sights can be adjusted to within $\frac{3}{8}$-inch elevation at 50 yards. For windage, they move about $\frac{1}{4}$-inch for each click. On super-tuned target guns, the same figures apply but only at 25 yards!

When considering a replacement rear sight, look at all the options. First, order a rear sight blade with a white outline. This is probably the best advance in years to aid the shooter in picking up a good sight picture. Next, blade width and height must be considered. For target match shooting nothing beats an oversized blade for perfect alignment on the paper target. Target rear sight blades should also have a slight tip to the rear to minimize any reflections from indoor lights or a bright sun.

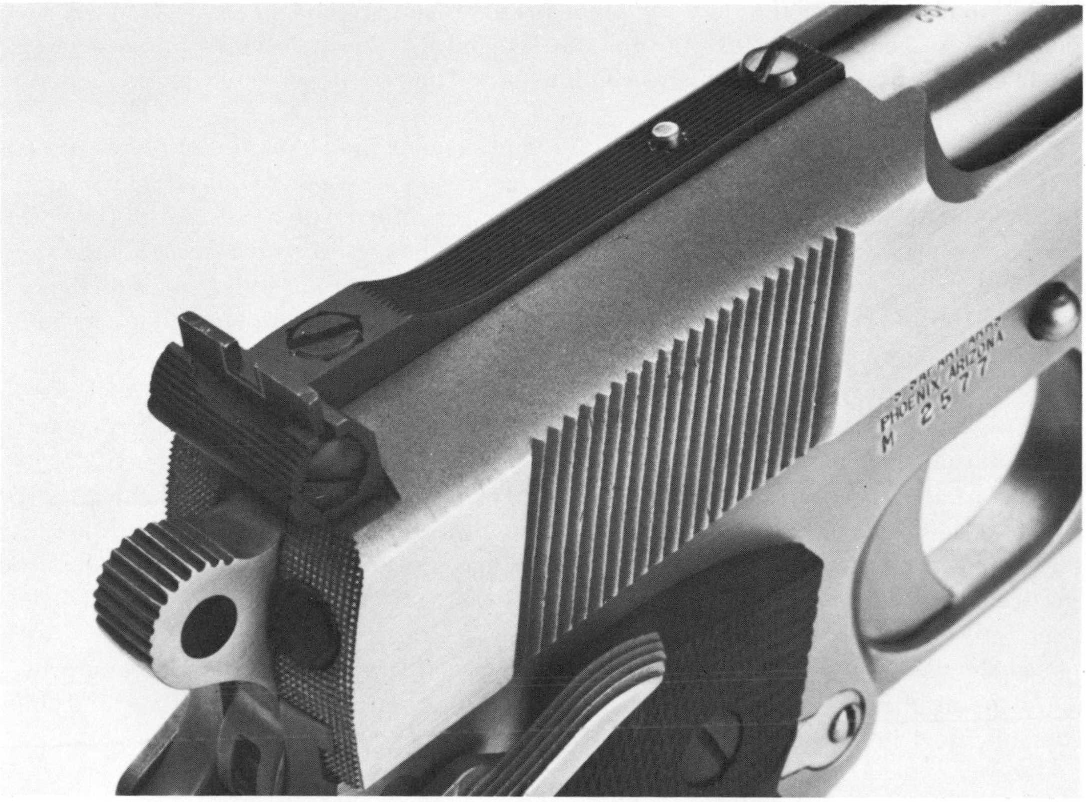

For overall improved shooter accuracy, some manufacturers' custom shops are adding the dependable and time-proven S&W Micrometer sights to their own line of guns. Illustrated here is the .45 manufactured by Safari Arms. Note the ambidextrous speed safety and checkering detail on the rear of the slide.

Dedicated target shooters insist on good clean sights, and in this photo Micro Sights installed on a tuned .45 go a long way to ensure solid hits on the X-ring.

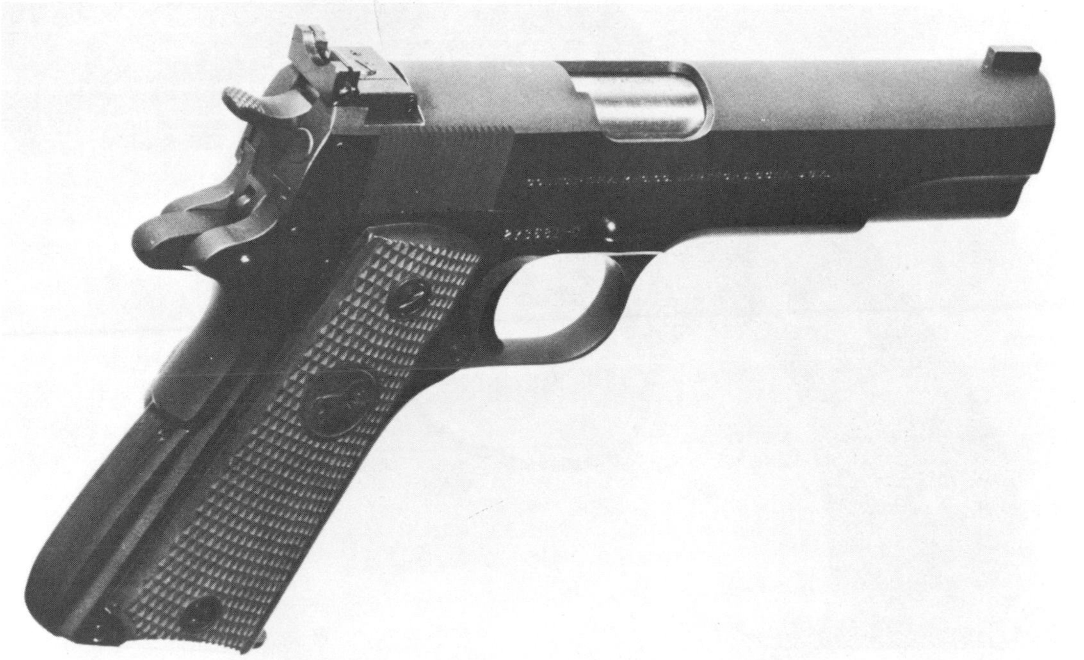

Finally, consider the duty requirements of these precision sights. PPC match men prefer a replacement sight like the Bo-Mar Winged Rib. Easily installed on most service revolvers, this rib has been on many winning guns. They are dependable and rugged, and this keeps them in demand.

Micro and Miniature Machine offer replacement sights for the .45 Government Model as well as the S&W Model 39/59. There has always been a lot of talk about the lack of full sight control on these guns. They come factory-equipped with a sight which is adjustable only for windage, and many feel this is a handicap. I have always felt this is not the case. If you're serious enough about shooting, you will zero your gun in with one load—the one that is the most accurate. Windage always seems to be more of a problem than elevation. Apparently Smith & Wesson felt the same way and elected to go this route.

If you're having problems, either replacement sight will fill the bill. And to offer you more of a choice, S&W markets their own replacement sight for the purists who demand a fully adjustable sight.

The above mentioned guns are examples of course. As they come straight from the box, rear sights on American handguns are generally excellent. I say generally only because there are certain models in any lineup, from all makers, which are at the lower end of the cost scale. The sights may not be as fancy as those on the premium models, but nevertheless quite useful and serviceable.

Metallic sights have come a long way in the last few years. Already, we see improvements in all lines in the matter of easy replacement, a stronger sight picture, and finer adjustments. I hope the trend continues.

Highly refined, easy to install, and a well-engineered system of adjustments are three of the reasons which make this Bo-Mar Winged add-on assembly very popular with match shooters.

A Contender pistol topped with a Redfield 4× scope and rings makes for a handy, accurate, and deadly varmint combination.

SIGHTS Optical

Available from Bushnell, Burris, Hutson, Leupold, Thompson/Center, Redfield, and Tasco.

Sooner or later the question will come up "Should I scope one of my handguns?" And the answer may be "Try it, you'll like it!"

Scoping a handgun today is an adventure in itself. The state of the art in the manufacturing of optical sights is at its highest point ever. Choice of optical power, for instance, is not limited to one or two selections, but to at least six different magnifications. In essence, the handgunner never had it so good.

In considering a scope for any handgun, the purchaser should always weigh the variables. Since mounting systems are covered in the following section, we will only review the physical characteristics of pistol scopes here.

Scopes, like cameras, have glass lenses, and, all the same principals apply. Good clear lenses, combined with a high relative brightness and flatness of field are points to consider with any scope.

Image contrast refers to the clear distinction of the dark areas from the light—the "snap" and brilliance of the image. If any scope blends everything into a neutral gray band, look at another brand. Along with image contrast goes resolution. This is the true ability of any optical product to decipher detail in images put in front of it. We are not talking about distortion now, but sharpness. Pick a spot about 100 yards out the window from your sporting goods store. Lay the scope on a flat surface and observe the clarity. At that distance you should be able to see every crack and mortar joint in a brick building. If not, again, look at another product.

Other points to consider when choosing the scope are freedom from aberration (the bending of light rays thru a scope can lead to poor image quality), tight manufacturing tolerances (good fit or finish), and a written statement from the maker that his scope is sealed against fogging.

The magnification or power of the scope should be determined by the accuracy range of your particular handgun and the load you use. For example, there is no reason why a modest power 1× or 1½× scope can't be used with a gun chambered for the .38 Special. However, a gun using the high-stepping .357 Magnum would require a scope falling in the 2× to 2½× range, while a T/C Contender in .357 Herrett would need a 4× scope.

Don't forget, and this is important, we are not trying to increase our range to the point of crippling animals, only to the point of increased accuracy over a given range or distance. To over-shoot any caliber while hunting would be disastrous to both the shooter and the animal.

Eye relief is long on pistol scopes because of the distance between the eye and the rear element of the scope. The scoped handgun in most cases is held at arm's length, contrary to rifle scopes, which are mounted near the action. Such small eye relief on handguns would result in some odd-looking shooters and positions.

The popular Duplex reticle as pictured here through a Leupold scope, gives the user an excellent sight picture as well as drawing his eye to the center of the optical sight.

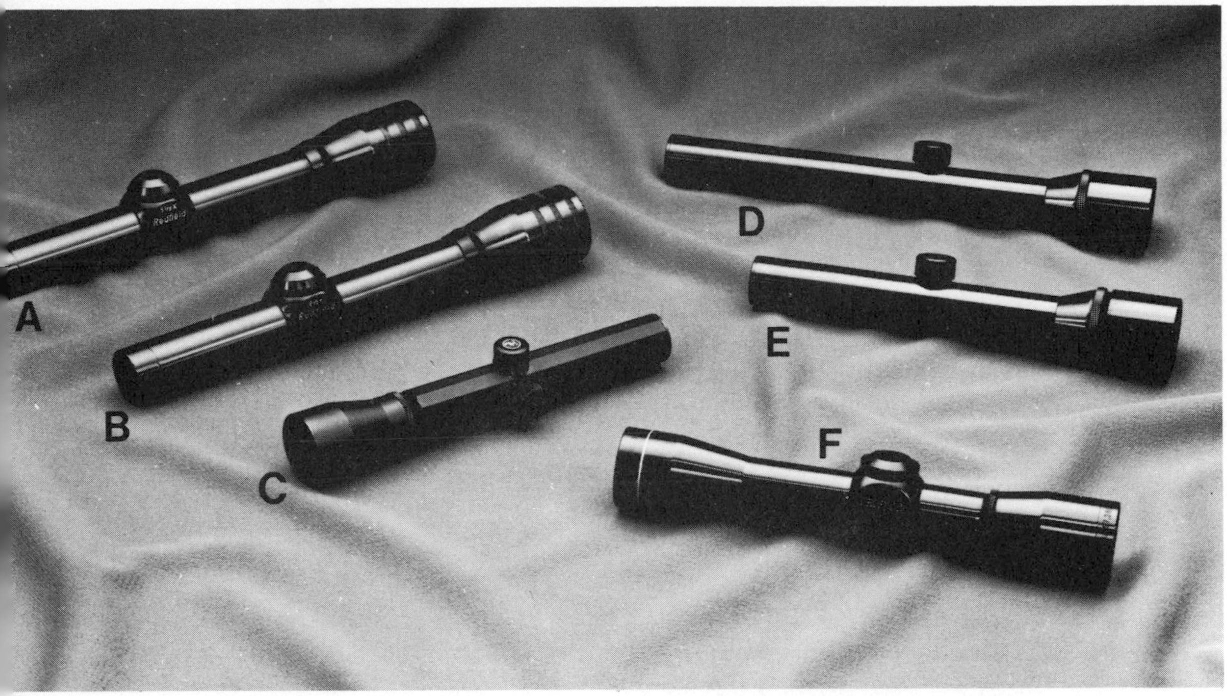

From Bushnell to Thompson/Center, scope choices abound. Examples shown are (A) Redfield 1½×, (B) Redfield 2½×, (C) Thompson/Center 1½×, (D) Bushnell 2½×, (E) Bushnell 1.3×, and (F) the Leupold M8-4× scopes.

The Remington XP-100 teamed with the high-stepping .221 Fireball cartridge and a Bushnell scope is an efficient hunter/varmint pistol.

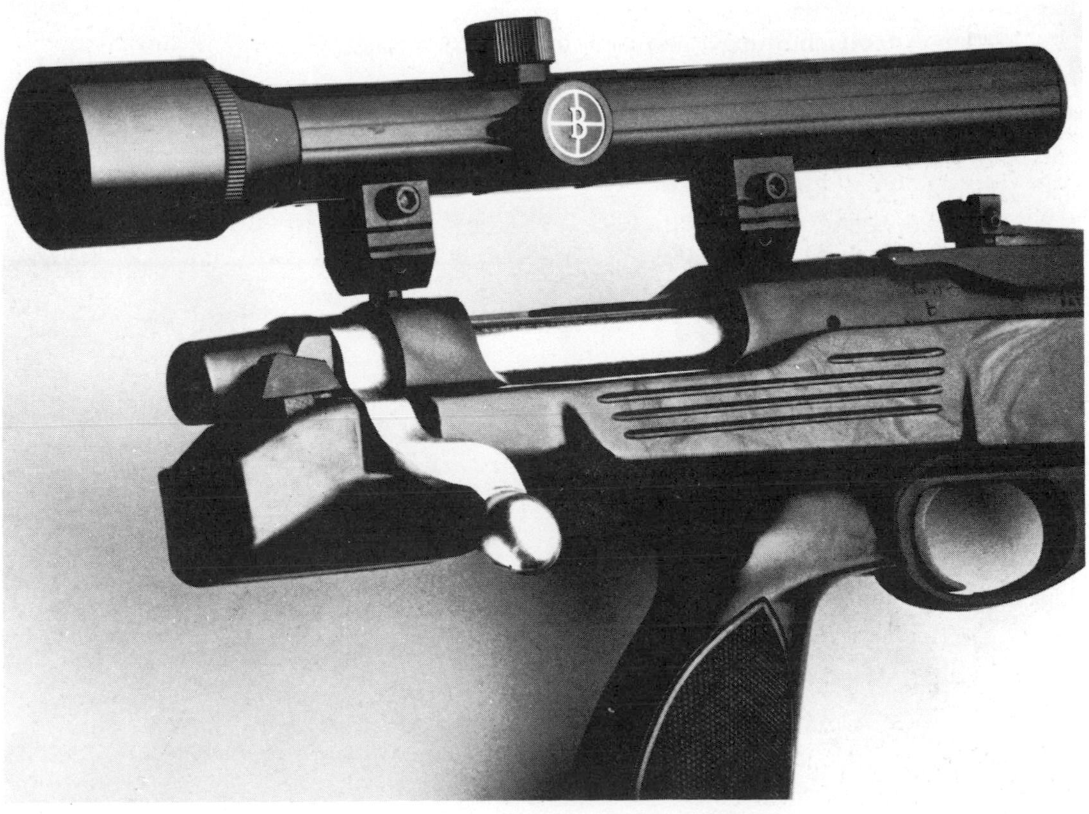

The weight of the scope should have a bearing on your decision. Holding a handgun out an arm's length for even a small period of time can give the strongest of us the shakes. Scope size is important. Length, the size of the objective and eye piece all add bulk to the scope. Before forking over that hard-earned cash, mount a mock set-up to your handgun to see if everything is okay.

Finally focus adjustments should be quick and precise with the reticle jumping in and out of focus as you turn that knob. For reticles, the choice is yours. Some prefer the popular duplex, others a straight crosshair.

Hunting or just plain plinking with a scoped handgun can lead to many additional hours of enjoyment. With the newly formed sport of Hunters Silhouette Matches, many find the clause which reads "any sight may be used" leading them right down the path of a new optically-equipped handgun.

SIGHTS (Optical) Scope Bases and Rings

Available from Buehler, Bushnell, Conetrol, Leupold, Thompson/Center, Redfield, Weaver, and Whitney.

Pistol scope mounting systems are as many and varied as the scopes themselves. Depending on the type of firearm they are to be mounted on, scope rings and bases come in all shapes, sizes, and styles.

Rings themselves are a Pandora's Box of variety. Cinching down the scope can be made from the top (Buehler), bottom, (Conetrol), side (Leupold and Redfield), or even on a modified rail arrangement (T/C or Bushnell). However done, and no matter how fancy they may be, scope rings perform an important task in holding the optical sight in perfect alignment shot after shot.

Scope-to-base mounting is accomplished several ways, by different means. Slotted or tapered dovetail, double dovetail and universal pin/stud mounts are all popular ways of assuring the scope will stay put when the forces of a magnum cartridge put the "Gs" to it.

Milled and machined from solid bar stock, scope bases are a vital link between any scope/gun combination. They must be made to withstand the constant pounding from heavy recoiling arms, yet keep their zero and remain intact. In automobile accidents, the experts often talk about that it is not the crash that hurts, it's that sudden stop: Well, in the world of scopes, it's the sudden start.

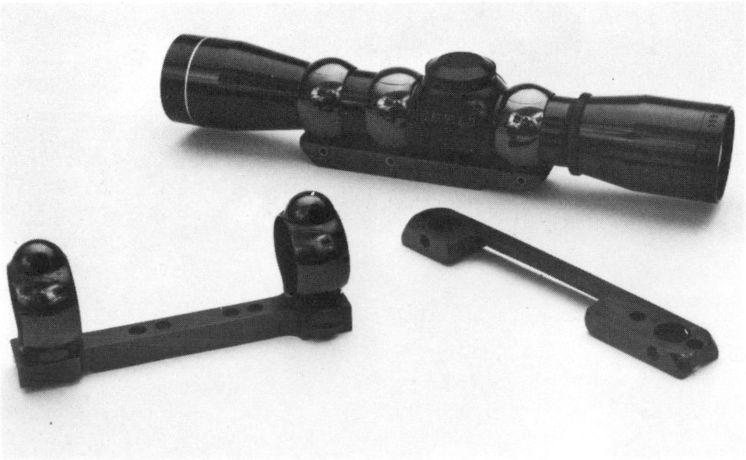

Perhaps the most important elements of a good scope/gun combo are the mounts and rings. Especially heavy calibers need the Conetrol 3-ring system (top) while moderate recoiling guns can employ the standard 2-ring Buehler or Conetrol systems.

The initial snap of the gun during heavy recoil can tear scope, rings and bases right off the gun. Proper installation is necessary to assure a low casualty rate between your gun and its fine optical equipment. Work carefully, clean all parts with solvent and use a slow curing epoxy cement between the base and the handgun frame or receiver. Some installations are complicated, so employ the services of a competent gunsmith when necessary.

All scope mount and ring makers have their own designs by which to attach a scope to any particular gun. Starting at the top left, Thompson/Center uses a modified rail, Redfield the conventional system, and Bushnell a universal base and pin arrangement.

Whitney has a .45 scope mount that attaches directly to the gun via the grip panels. No drilling or tapping is required which makes for a neat and simple installation.

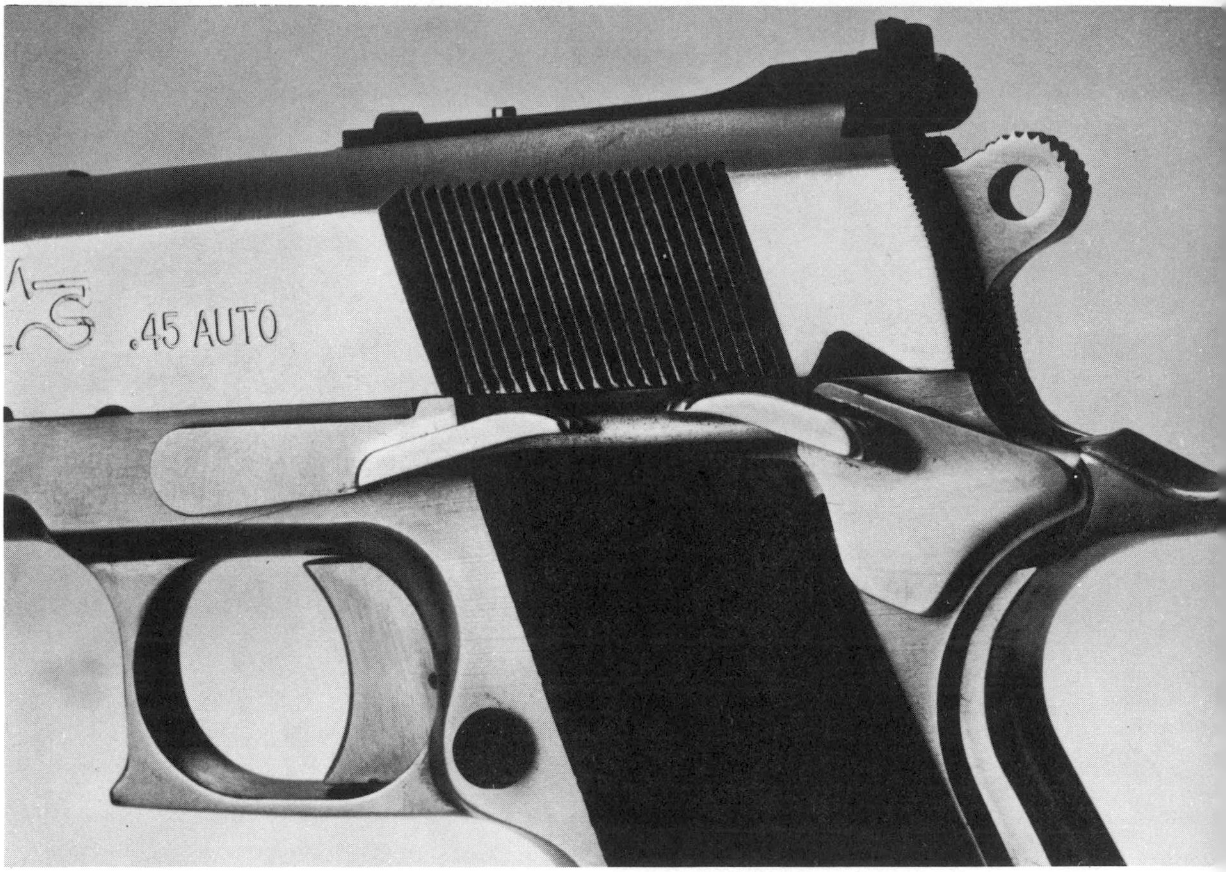

When speed is a prime requisite, extended slide releases and speed safeties are standard equipment on combat-modified handguns.

SPEED SAFETIES/SLIDE RELEASES

Available from Colt's Custom Shop, H&D Products, and Safari Arms.

Many combat shooters find that during the course of a match, the contestant is forced to use his weak hand in order to make it more challenging. And to make matters worse (as if firing a full-house .45 isn't bad enough from the weak hand) the shooter must at the same time retain complete control of his weapon with reference to closing the slide and/or flipping off the safety.

Designed primarily through the efforts of combat shooters and progressive companies, slide releases and ambidextrous safeties are as much as part of the gun as practical grips. Extended slide releases are made so to allow the shooter to close the slide without changing the position of the shooting hand. They are especially handy while running and reloading at the same time. Most are available from different concerns in a left-side only configuration. One company, Safari Arms, offers the release in a left/right or ambidextrous model. Some close fitting may be required, so if in doubt, consult your gunsmith.

Extended speed and ambidextrous safeties are designed for convenience. Shaped to lie directly under the thumb, such a unit is an important item on any competition arm. Again, they are available in either left-hand only or ambidextrous versions for the government .45, but users of the Smith & Wesson 39/59 should not feel left out. Safari Arms just

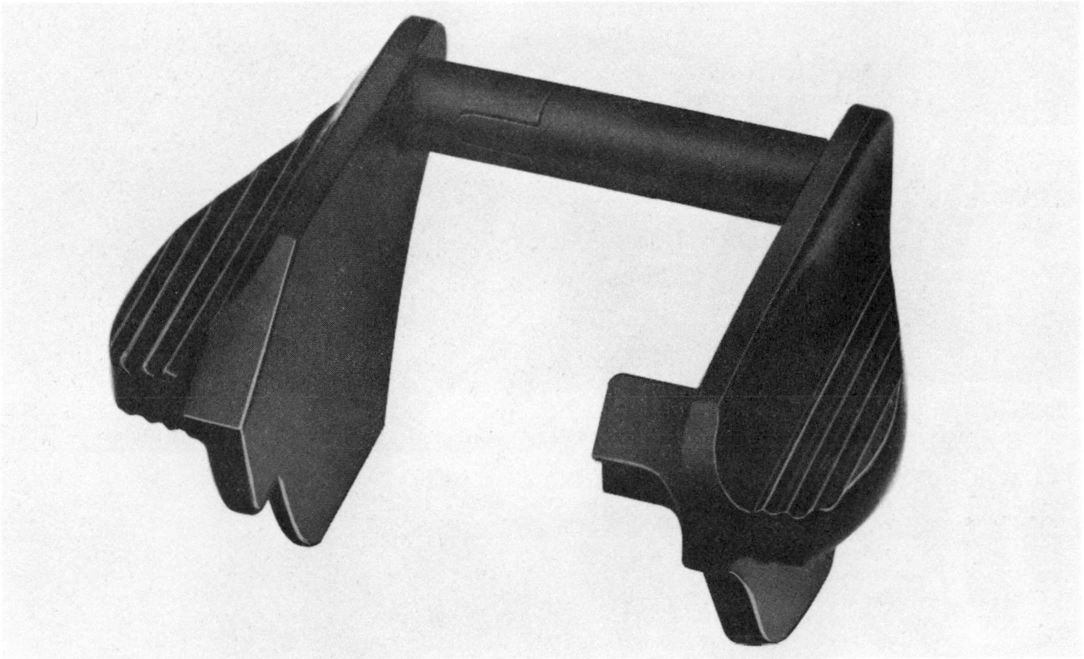

Colt's entry into the ambidextrous safety field is this neat package from its custom shop.

A fully equipped S/A combat handgun will include such items as the left-right safety, Commander-type hammer and a Beavertail grip safety. As an additional option, all Safari Arms .45s can be finished in a non-glare and maintenance-free Teflon coating.

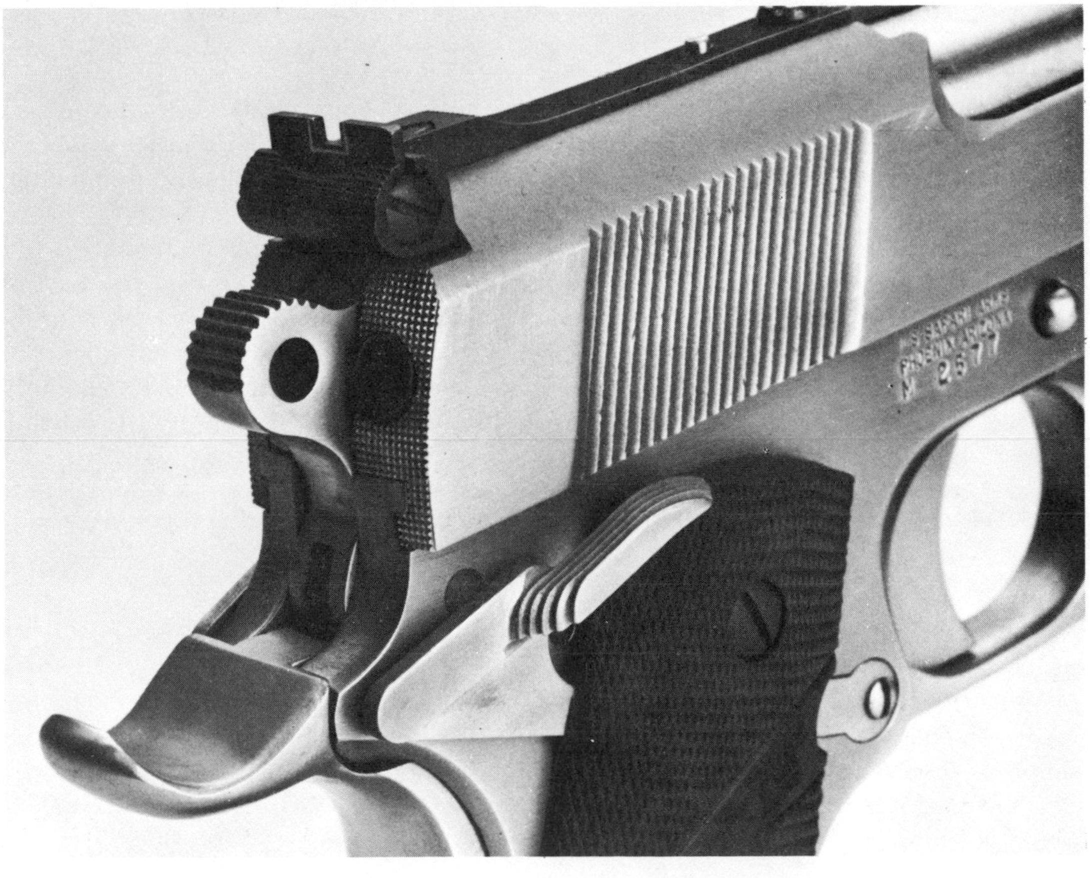

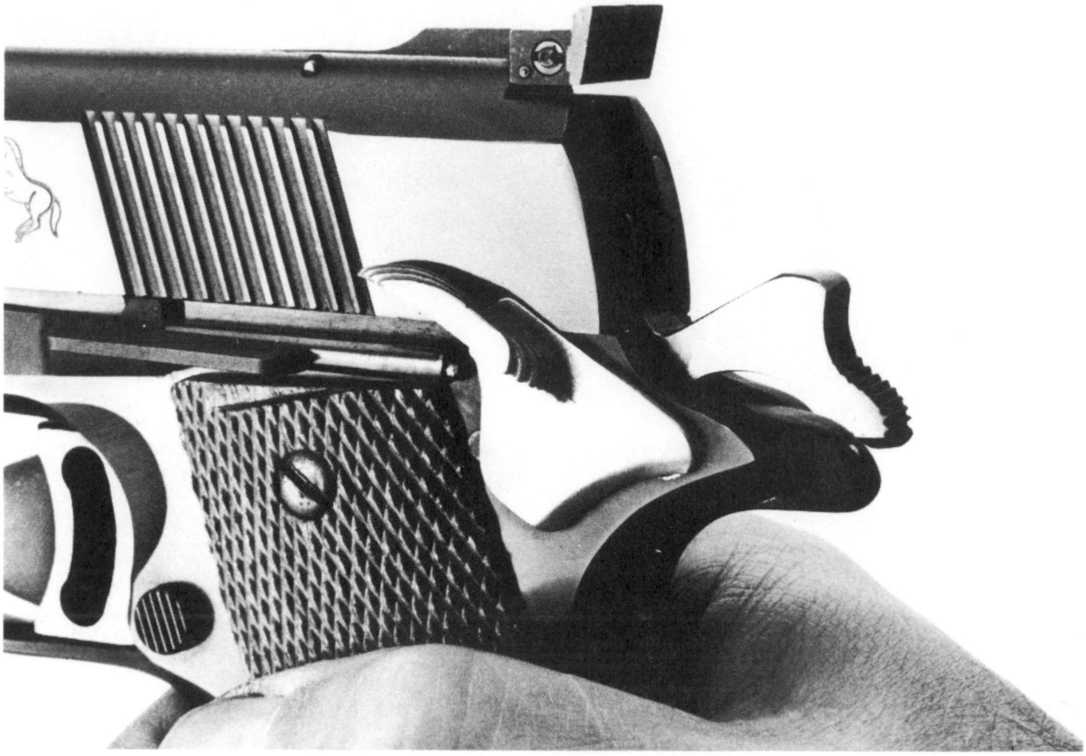

Small items can be important in any match, so H&D's extended slide release and Safari Arm's speed safety help to save valuable seconds by providing an edge to the user in ease of operation alone. Both can be user-installed with a minimum of effort and time.

recently introduced an ambidextrous model for these weapons. Besides being made to fit these two guns, it also fits the sleek Model 52 with ease. Part of the right grip must be cut away for proper functioning, however, so if your 52 is equipped with big hand-filling target grips, consider this before your purchase.

Installation requires care and concentration. Usually these items are furnished with excess metal which must be stoned to function properly. Using a vernier you have to compare both the factory and the custom models, then work the custom part down until it fits. Too much metal taken away will result in a safety that is not safe! Remember, the new safety must prevent the sear from moving far enough to disengage the pistol's hammer. If you feel squeamish about such jobs, see a pro. It will be better for both of us if you do!

SPEED LOADERS

Available from Bianchi, HKS, and Safariland.

Speed loaders are to revolvers what magazines are to automatics. They enable the match shooter or police officer to load his weapon in as little as three to six seconds from the time the last shot is fired. Cartridges are held in place by a central knob, which when turned about a ⅛ of a turn, drops the rounds into the chambers of the gun. The loaders are simplicity themselves and will last indefinitely with little or no care on the part of the owner. Leather products are available in the form of double or triple belt cases made in open or closed versions.

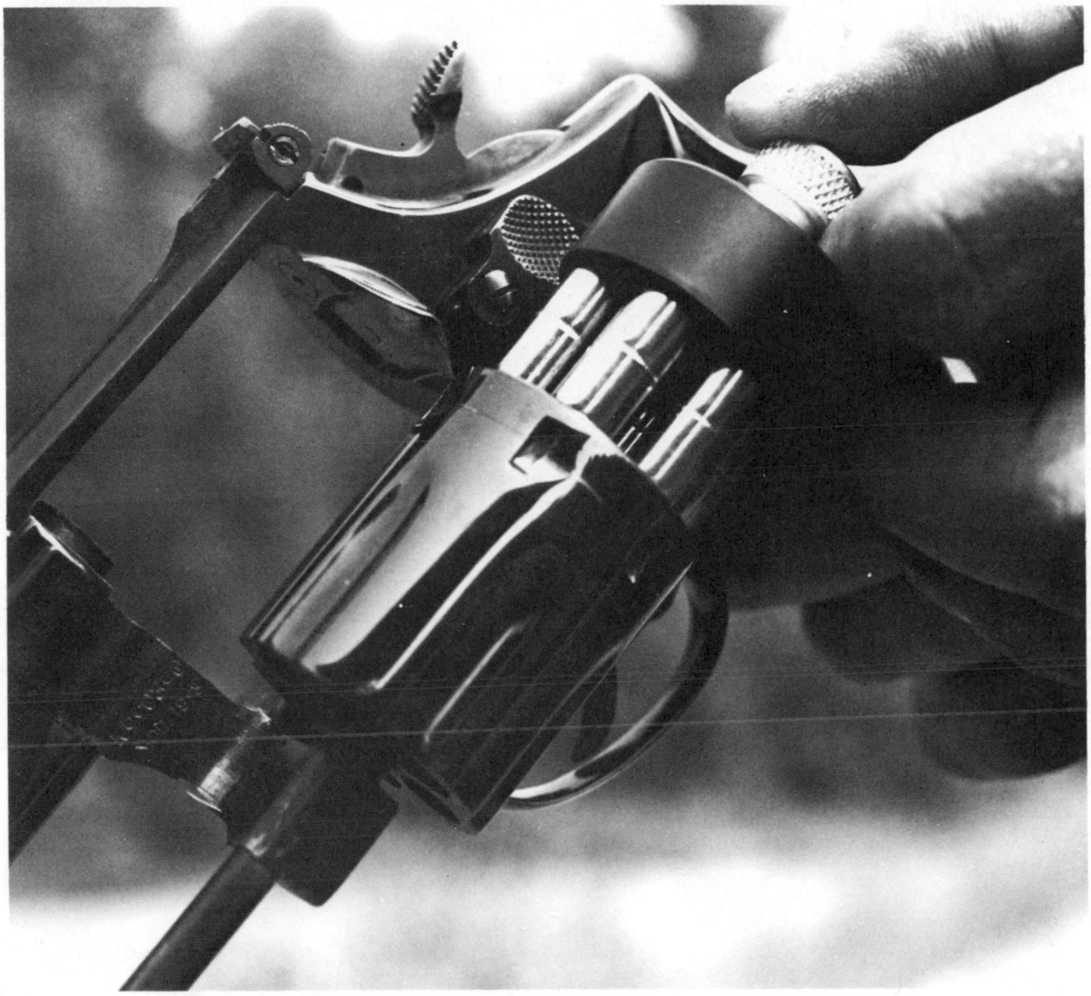

In police or match use, the six-shot speed loader pays for itself in terms of ease and convenience in a very short time.

DU PONT
HI-SKOR
HERCULES
H110
BRAND
DANGER
EXTREMELY FLAMMABLE
PRECAUTION ON BACK OF CAN
Hornady
Hornady
100
38 CAL. 158 GR.
.357 Hollow Point
HERCULES
SMOKELESS
2400
RIFLE
POWDER
Remington
Remington
100 Sierra Pistol Bullets
.38 CAL.
.357 Diameter
125 gr. Hollow Cavity
SPEER
HOLLOW POINT
.357 Magnum
Test Firearm: Colt Mk III Trooper
Barrel Length: 6" 1-14" Twist
Test Case: Speer/DWM
Test Primer: CCI-550
Bullet Dia.: .357"
Sierra Bullets

EIGHT

Handloading for Performance

Handloading is perhaps the most interesting aspect of the shooting sports, and it is certainly one of my favorite pastimes and hobbies. Aside from the enormous popularity of shooting in competition, handloading, or reloading of ammunition is the one facet of the shooting sports that gets more people interested and involved in more types of shooting than any of the other categories combined.

By using various combinations of bullets, powders, primers, cases, and different loadings, the handgunner can ensure the optimum performance for his purposes. The right choice of ingredients will help you hit the mark every time, whether that mark is a paper target, game, or someone with criminal intent. Naturally, shooter error can be a factor, but it is comforting to know that when the time comes, you have managed to stabilize all possible variables with the cartridges in your gun.

There are three reasons for handloading; accuracy, economy, and versatility. To be accurate, you must be consistent. Once a particular handloading combination has been found which best suits your purposes, stick with it. Use the same brand of cases, bullets and primers throughout. Measure powder charges with the utmost precision. These factors go a long way to ensure the shot-after-shot consistency you want and need. This applies to either handloaded or factory ammunition, which brings us to the second advantage of reloading; economy.

Economically speaking, reloading is the only way to go if you like to shoot a lot. To be competitive, you must shoot, shoot, and shoot some more, and in this day and age of rising prices the shooter must strive to keep the cost of practicing down so he can enjoy it more.

Factory ammunition currently costs approximately thirty-three cents per round. This is for the standard .357, 158-grain jacketed hollow- or softpoint ammo traveling at 1,235 feet per second.

Now if you want to be one of the boys who handloads his own ammo, here are some enlightning facts to ponder. Aside from the initial cost of equipment, which properly taken care of will last a lifetime, here is a cost breakdown. These figures are calculated on a per round basis and all items listed are cost per unit.

Reloaded .357 Round (per 50)

A.—Jacketed Bullet	$0.0787 each
—Powder	$0.0185 per charge
—Primer	$0.0113 per round
—Total Cost	$0.1085 or eleven cents per round
B.—50 Unprimed Cases	$0.1250 per case
—Total (A&B)	$0.2335 or twenty-three cents per round

As you can see reloaded ammunition is exactly one-third the cost of commercial fodder! The fifty cases will last roughly twelve to fifteen loadings and are computed accordingly. Please note that the above is for first class, high-performance premium hunting or defense ammo.

For strictly target shooting, we substitute lead bullets for jacketed, and powder charges are much smaller. In this case, our cost comes to a mere six cents per round as compared to about twenty-five cents for the factory-loaded rounds. If you want to go through the trouble of casting your own bullets, you can scrounge lead scraps such as wheel weights, linotype metal and various alloys to help cut costs even more drastically per round. Allowing for the investment in casting and sizing equipment, we can pare our costs to the bone, or to a mere one and a half cents, per round!

Now you can easily see that reloading your own ammunition is the answer in these days of rising inflation. There is one exception I'd like to make here. A lot of target men I know will practice with reloaded ammunition for the cost savings of course, but when it comes time to shoot for the loot, out comes the factory stuff. Since many a match is won by only a point or two, these fellows will not even trust themselves. Here the cost is justified. Rather than lose because of a missed powder charge or possibly an inverted primer, these dedicated shooters will spare no cost. Peace of mind has a great deal to do with winning.

The third reason for loading your own is versatility. You can match any bullet to any gun for any task you have. The combinations are staggering and if you don't believe me, grab the loading manuals by Sierra, Lyman, Speer, or Hornady and look at the array of loads listed for any one bullet or caliber. In short, you have the complete freedom of load choice for any activity you may choose, be it hunting, defense, target, or combat-style competition shooting.

A PLACE OF YOUR OWN

Before any reloading is to be started, one must have a place to set up shop. I was fortunate, because after laying out the rooms in the basement, I had an area about 8 × 12 feet left over. This was to become my gun/reloading room, and as you can see by the photograph, it turned out very well.

Your work space should be enclosed. It should not be, for instance in an open corner of the basement. Not that the science of reloading is dangerous, but it is best to keep young,

Top quality reloads start in a room where organization has top priority. A work flow should be established to ensure against costly mistakes.

prying hands and eyes out of harm's way. You will be using powder and primers, and safety must be the primary consideration.

After that is settled, build a bench, and I mean *build* a bench. Start out with 2 × 4's and go from there. Use braces and bolt it to the floor and wall studs. A compound press can generate a lot of force and the last thing you need is a table jumping around the room.

When the frame is up, consider now what to use for the top. A prefabricated formica top available in even lengths (4, 6, 8, or 10 feet) makes for a solid top. Two by fours or 2 × 6s picked for straightness, sanded down, and stained is a choice for a sturdy top. Figure your requirements and head for the lumber yard.

A final note here on setting up the room. The key to accurate and dependable ammunition comes from being totally organized. Know what you have to work with and where it is located. Keep powders and primers separated and don't pre-mix or bottle anything. You may forget what you have done and this could cause trouble later on.

BASIC TOOLS OF THE HANDLOADER

Shopping around for handloading equipment, you will find an array of products which seems to have no end. For those of you starting out, the following brief explanations of equipment will give you an idea of what's needed, but it is best to go to your local friendly neighborhood gun dealer for advice. Most dealers have a press or two set up so you can see the features and advantages of each.

The first time item up for discussion will be the loading press. The most common type on the market today is what everyone calls the "C" press. It is obviously shaped like a "C" and is available from just about every maker of reloading supplies. All presses are tapped for the standard ⅞ by 14 threads per inch, which is now your common reloading die size. Presses will be different in camming action, which is no more than the ability to size a case with the least amount of apparent pressure.

Another type that rates high in the popularity polls is the "O" press. This is for the fellows who comtemplate reloading rifle cartridges in the future. Being anchored at both ends, this press can withstand greater force to take on tough jobs like swaging and sizing long rifle cases at a later date.

Turret presses prove to be popular with target shooters. You can set up your dies for a special load you are testing or shooting and leave them on the turret. My Lyman has six threaded holes in the top, so using three of them for my wadcutter load, I still have three left for another load I may be producing at the same time. Lyman, Pacific, RCBS, C&H, Herters, Redding, and Bonanza are some of the firms marketing top quality presses.

Lyman's novel six station turret press enables the handloader to set up for two cartridges at the same time.

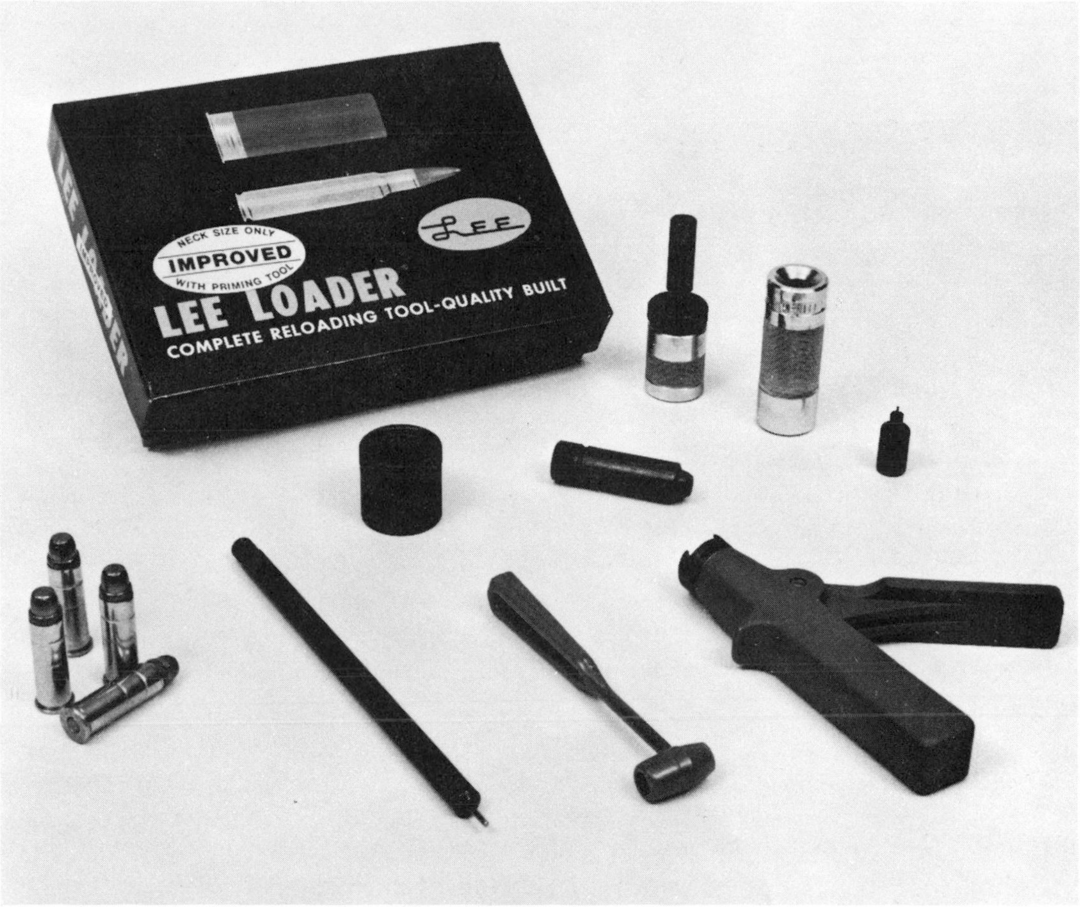

With a very small investment, the Lee Loaders can turn out good reloads for the infrequent shooter. For a budding nimrod these kits can teach the basics of reloading in a very short time.

Substitutes for a press are the hand loading tools marketed by Lee Loading and Lyman Gunsite. Only a minimum investment is required and regardless how slow the operation may be, you can turn out good, accurate ammo. For in-the-field use, these sets are hard to beat.

Loading Dies

Your next investment will be in a good set of reloading dies. Lyman, RCBS and Pacific are well-known makers of reloading dies and again your choice is basically what tickles your fancy. Some are chrome-plated, hard-plated or just machine shop finished to a smooth and durable finish.

Reloading dies for handgun cartridges are commonly purchased in sets of three and include a resizing, expanding and bullet-seating die. For the purist who likes to put extra effort in his handloads, a four-set die is available and includes the resizing, expanding, bullet-seating, and a separate crimping die. The crimping die is sold as a taper crimper for autoloader cartridges or a standard roll crimper for revolver rounds whose crimp can be made on the bullet cannelure.

As another option here, you may well consider a carbide resizing die. This ultra-hard metal allows you to resize without lubrication, therefore saving both time and energy

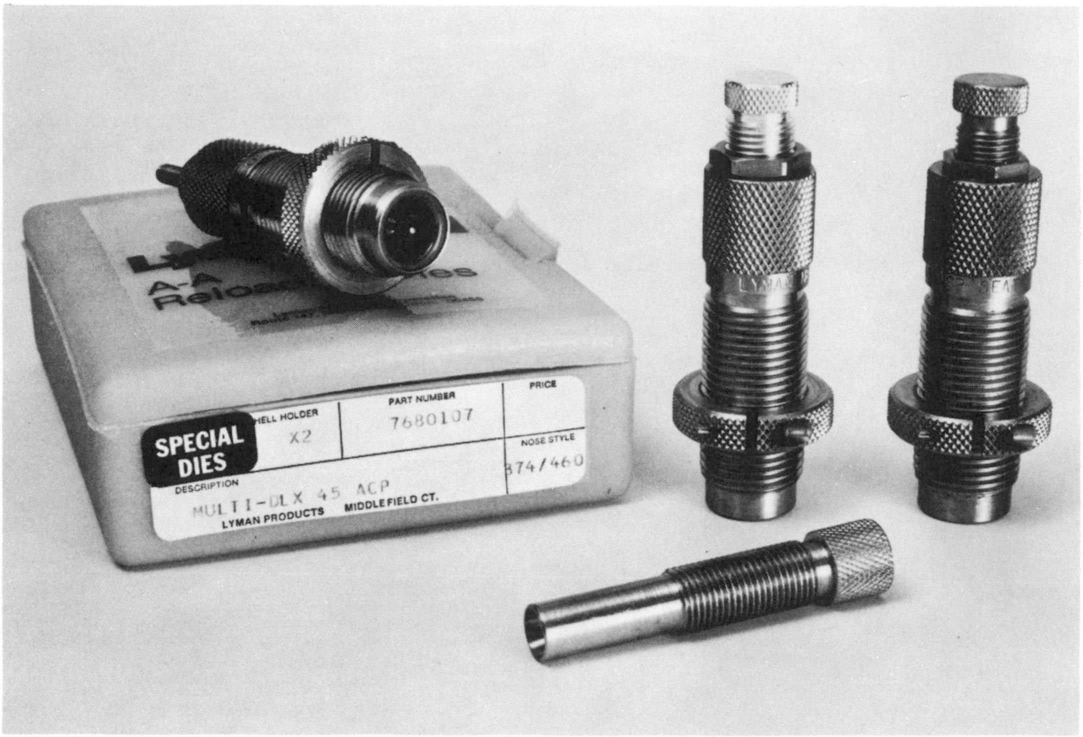

Designed for the advanced handloader, die sets like this Lyman set can turn out accurate reloads by the hundreds.

Powder measures with adjustable drums ensure accurate loads without weighing every charge.

cleaning cases. The carbides last a lifetime. If you shoot a lot of one cartridge it definitely pays to have one.

Shell Holder

The shell holder is simply a means of pulling the case back out of the dies. They come in various sizes for different calibers and there are either fixed or multi-caliber holders. As some will fit a number of cases, the need to buy one every time you purchase a set of dies should be carefully checked in the maker's catalog under general specifications.

Priming Equipment

Here you have a number of choices. You can prime your cases in your hand with a Lee Loader, on the press with a priming arm, or separately via a bench-type priming tool. I use the arm that comes with the press, because as the case is expanded (second die) and is drawn down out of the die, I automatically push the arm in to prime the case. Each one has its advantage, but as always, convenience should be one of your primary concerns.

Powder Scales And Measures

Variety seems to be the byword in this chapter and powder scales and measures are no exceptions. Depending upon your requirements, powder measures come in all shapes and sizes. Some are the fixed type, meaning they will only throw a set charge. For example, if

Powder scales (left) must be used in conjunction with powder measures (right) to ensure the accurate volume of propellant per pistol case.

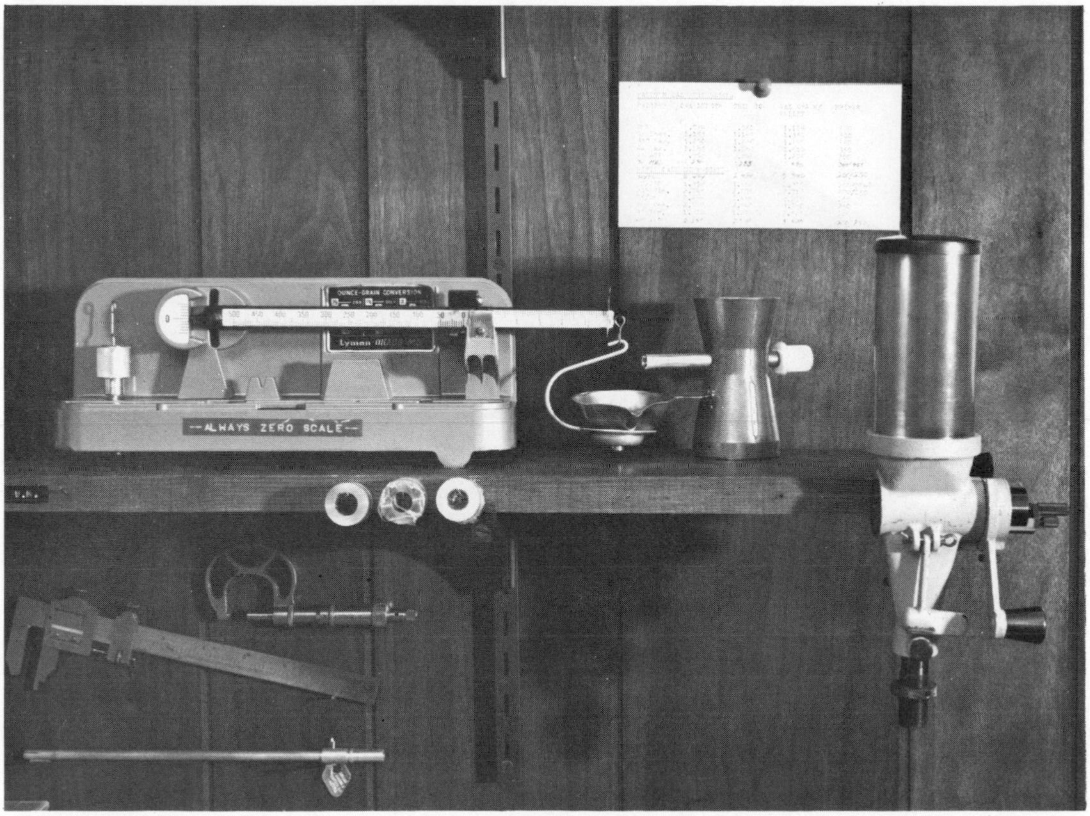

your practice load is 2.8 grains of Bullseye, you purchase the measure with a fixed rotor delivering 2.8 grains; it is that simple. Others have a rotary adjustable chamber which allows the individual to set the charge to the load being used.

Once you adjust the measure you need something to measure it on. Enter the powder scale. Made to measure in grains, the common types go from as little as a 1/10 of a grain to upward of 1,000 grains. You can put down as little as $10.00 or as much as $150.00 for a super scale. But regardless whether you measure powder in Lee powder scoops or a sophisticated measure, always check the charge by weighing it. Don't guess at anything. A double charge of a fast burner like Bullseye can damage a gun beyond repair or worse yet, *you*!

Case Trimmer

Gone are the days when a case trimmer was considered a luxury. Handgun cases do stretch beyond maximum limits and must be brought back to factory and SAAMI specs. This is especially true in autoloaders where the case's headspace on the case mouth. Too long a case will prevent the slide from returning to its original closed position, hence preventing the gun from being fired—not very nice in a dangerous encounter.

With the trimmer goes a little item called a pilot. The pilot slips into the case during trimming, thereby keeping it true and in-round during the operation. Hand trimmers are available with their own guides and should be considered if your budget is tight.

This wraps up the basic equipment needed to perform the reloading operations I will illustrate later on in the chapter. The following items are intended to make life a bit easier. They make swell little presents which the kids can give Dad on his birthday or Christmas.

Precision products such as case length gauges, deburring tools, and trimmers should be on every serious handloader's list of necessary tools.

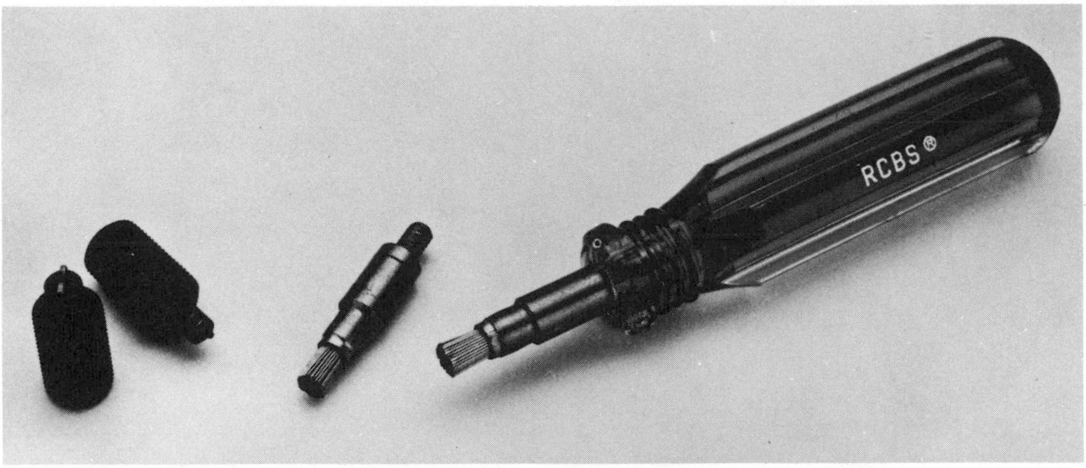

Clean primer pockets enable the complete seating of all primers. Special tools are available from Lee (left) and RCBS (right).

After all cases are trimmed to proper specifications the deburring tool is used to slightly chamfer the inner (A) and outer edges. One slight twist is sufficient. Overdoing it will lead to case-mouth splits.

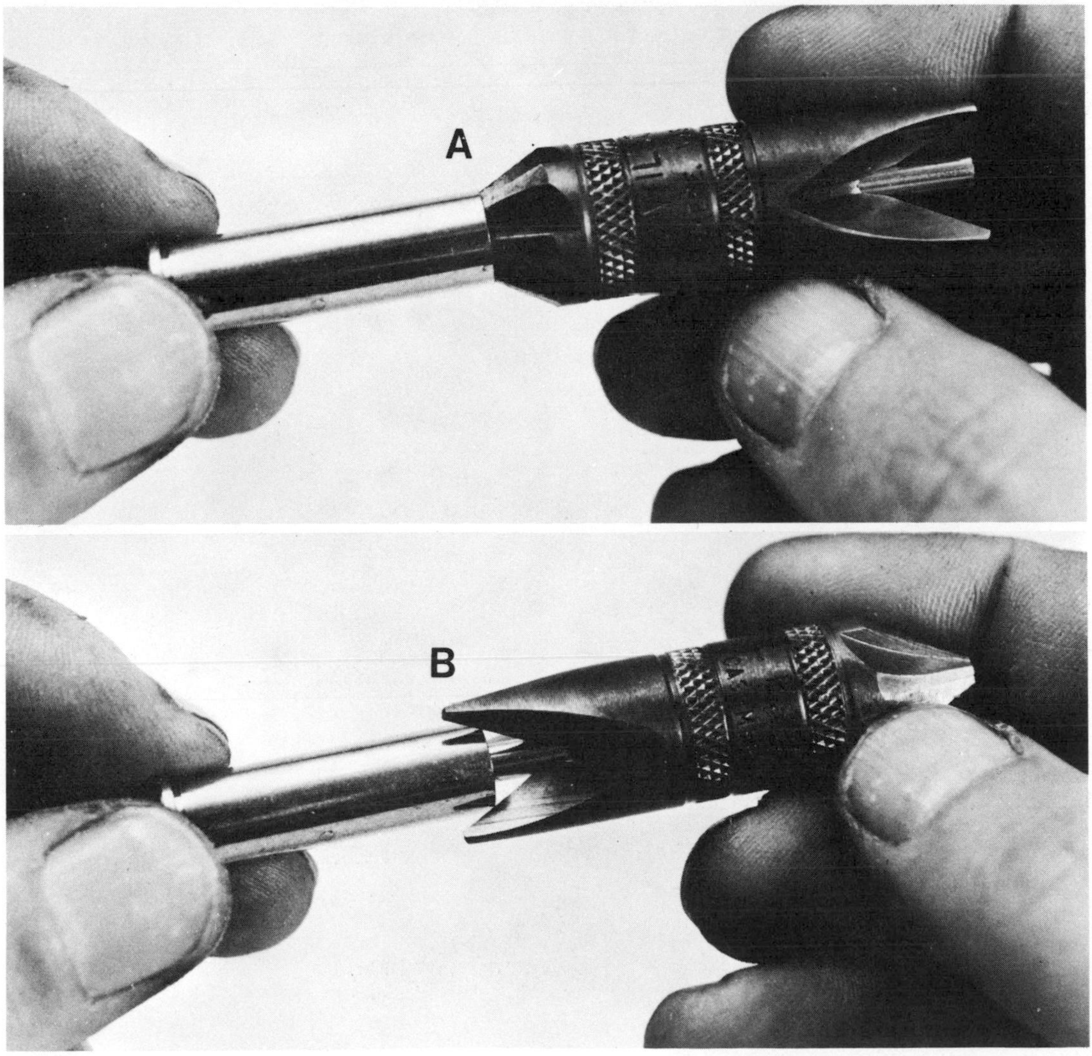

This bullet puller from Quinetic's makes fast work of parting the bullet from the case in the event there is a mistake in loading.

Any handloader worth his salt will have a precision set of calipers on his loading bench for accurate measurements on cases, bullet diameters, and overall cartridge lengths.

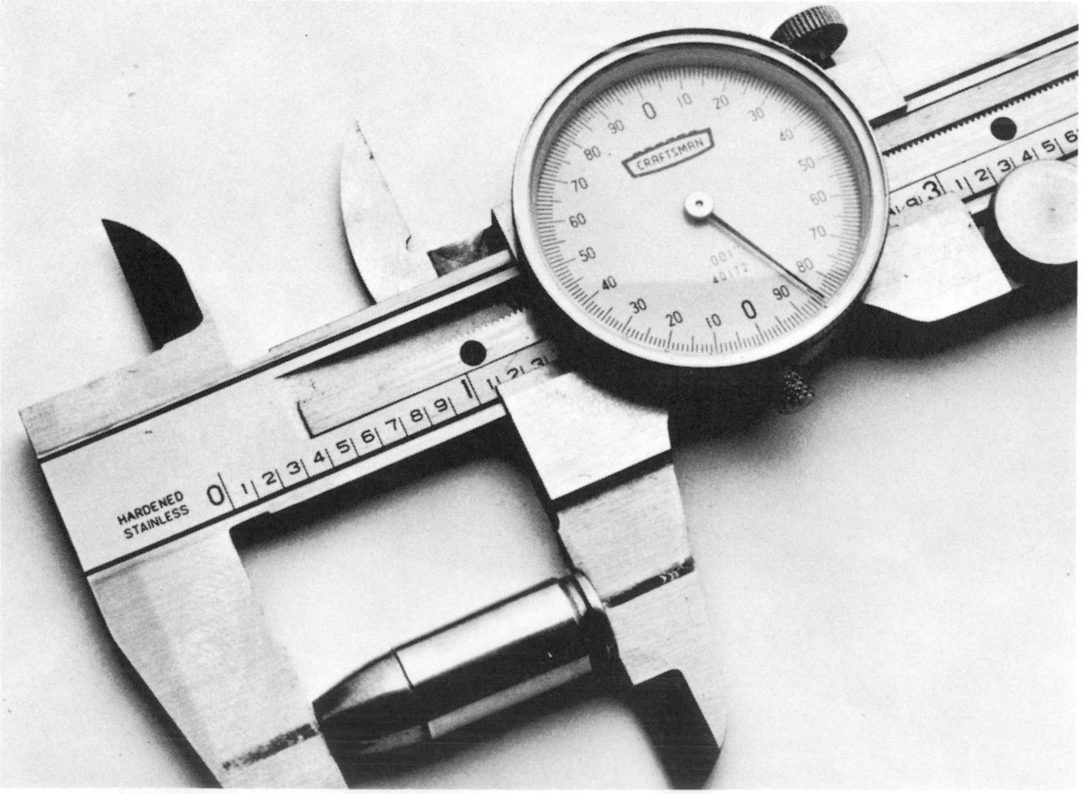

PRIMER POCKET CLEANER: A few twists cleans all primer pockets of unwanted residue. Comes in two sizes.

PRIMER FLIPPER: A handy gadget for flipping primers all one way, keeps oily fingers off sensitive primers.

DEBURRING TOOL: After case trimming, removes all burrs. For inside or outside of any case.

POWDER FUNNEL: For filling bigger cases and returning powder back to its container from powder measure.

LOADING BLOCKS: Made to accommodate fifty cases, it is indispensable in keeping charged cases from being tipped over. Easy to make yourself.

BULLET CONTAINERS: Similar to above, but made to hold fifty loaded rounds when going to the range or field. With cover.

STUCK CASE REMOVER: To remove an unlubed or damaged case from the resizing die without damaging the die.

BULLET PULLER: Used if you have made a mistake in loading, perhaps the wrong powder charge, or for extracting bullets from military surplus ammo.

CALIPERS: Extremely useful in measuring all cases during and after trimming, and needed for final confirmation of overall length. Should measure in thousandths of an inch.

POWDER TRICKLER: The trickler is used in concert with a powder scale, for those demanding the utmost in precision of measured powder loads.

BERDAN DECAPPING TOOL: For depriming non-Boxer primed cases.

PRIMER POCKET SWAGER: A quick way to remove the primer crimp on military cases.

USING THE MANUALS

Commonly referred to as the "Bibles" of reloading, the various manuals put forth by Sierra, Hornady, Speer, Lyman, Hodgdon, and Dupont should be taken as gospel most of the time. There are those times, however, when a given load shows signs of extreme pressure in your particular gun and reload combinations. No two guns are alike and since rifling tools wear, manufacturing tolerances tend to widen a bit. These manuals are your best bet in finding that just right performer.

Before any reloading is attempted, I strongly advise the purchase of one or two of these manuals. They contain a wealth of knowledge and information, much more than I can compact into a single chapter. All calibers are indexed according to size, volume and the powders best suited for optimum performance.

Other sections in these books will outline powder selection and choice, bullet specifications, trajectory tables, exterior ballistics and much, much more. I can't stress enough the importance of these reloading manuals.

CARTRIDGE COMPONENTS

Before we get into the actual reloading of centerfire cartridges for repeated use, we are going to take a look at the actual components needed to turn out top flight handgun ammunition. All the components are from commercial sources, except for hand-cast lead bullets, and are available through your local gun dealers.

Cases

The mainstay of the whole reloading game is the cartridge case. Formed from brass, the case must retain the ability to stretch or flow with the high pressures generated in any handgun. Steel cases are available from some surplus suppliers, but my advice is to shun such bargains. When resized, steel cases often will not stay within proper tolerances. For example, a typical problem encountered in loading the .45 ACP with these steel cases is that after resizing, they exhibit no tension whatsoever in the neck area to grasp the bullet. Inserting a bullet is hopeless, for it just slides down inside the case making any sort of taper crimping impossible.

Your best bet then is to invest in good, fresh, factory unprimed cases, available in rimmed (.38 Special, .357, .41 and .44 Magnums) or rimless (9mm, .38 Super, .45 ACP). All ammo makers turn out millions of cases for handloaders.

All new cases should be run through the resizing die before any reloading is done. This is not to say the factory is giving us out-of-round or eccentric cases (heaven forbid!) but a resizing die helps to bring everything in line, therefore helping us in our quest for accurate loads.

One other factor deserves mentioning. Sooner or later your dealer may be out of your favorite brand of unprimed cases, so, perhaps forced by the pressure of an upcoming match, you switch to another brand. Fine so far. But you should make some tests to make sure all is well with your load before going to your match. Upon returning however, it is a good idea after resizing and inspection to segregate all cases by make and/or headstamp. There are two important reasons for this.

First, separating all cases will insure equal inside case volume when it comes to powder space. No target shooter worth his salt will ever shoot a match using perhaps two or three cases of different makes. Differing case volumes will have an effect on the burning rate of any powder and will affect accuracy, point of impact, and in some highly-tuned automatics, proper functioning of the piece.

Second, no two case manufacturers use the same formula or method of drawing their products. Hence, neck tension can and will be different in terms of holding the bullet snug against the forces of recoil. A prime example is the rimless case where little or no crimp is allowed because of the way it headspaces in the chamber of automatic weapons.

In conclusion then, don't be "penny wise and pound foolish." Stay away from bargains or military surplus handgun brass, and you will increase your chances for some excellent results.

The Right Bullet

If you think you had trouble selecting a handgun for your own particular needs, wait until you try to select the right bullet. Bullets come copper jacketed, lead swaged and are cast in all weights, sizes, diameters, and internal and external configurations. And to give you Excedrin headache number 12, they will come packaged as flat nose, round nose, wad-cutters, semi-wadcutters and hollow or soft points. And to further vex the reloader, there is a little number appropriately named "jacketed hollow cavity."

In practice though, things are really not that bad. To put it into perspective, let's look at an example. A layman's first glance at the controls and instruments of a space age jet cockpit will fill him with confusion. Yet to the trained pilot, all the instruments are there for his visual contact, yet he only looks at one at a time, If, for instance he needs to know engine temperature, his eyes pick up that gauge, engine rpm another, cabin heat still another. On and on. . . .

So the same with the choice of bullets on the market. You will decide what your individual needs are, and consequently you will zero in on the right bullet tailored for the job at hand. Since all bullets are a personal choice depending on their use (target, hunting, or defense) I will only briefly discuss a random sampling of popular types and styles in five different calibers. The final decision is, of course, yours.

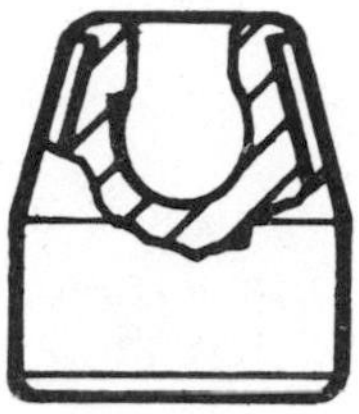

Sierra 90-grain
jacketed hollow cavity

Hornady 100-grain
full metal jacket

9mm Luger. Since 95 percent of all guns chambered for the 9mm Luger fall into the semiautomatic type, proper bullet design with reference to easy feeding without hangups or problems is therefore the prime concern of all bullet makers. Every effort must be made by the handloader to keep all rounds within proper overall length limits to insure complete and flawless operation of his automatic pistol. Not really known as a popular hunting round, the 9mm can be lethal against any opponent if the right bullet type is chosen and proper reloading techniques are used.

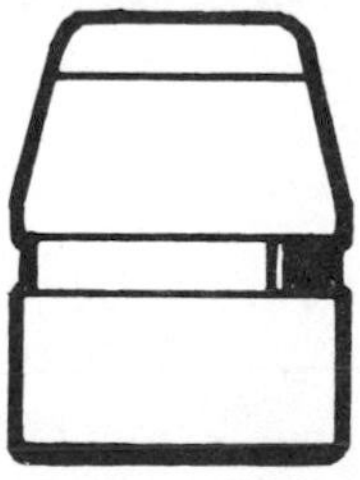

Sierra 125-grain
jacketed soft point

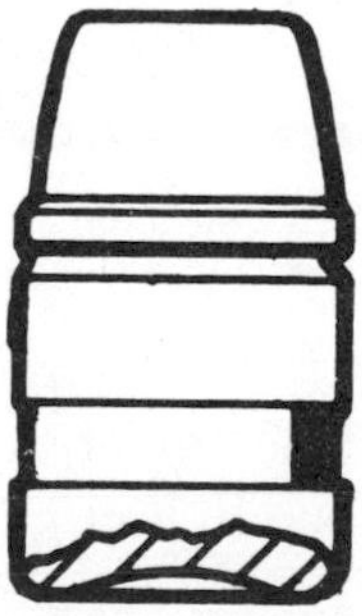

Speer 158-grain
lead swaged
Keith type bullet

Hornady 148-grain
lead hollow base
target wadcutter

.38 Special/.357 Magnum. As we get into larger caliber bullets, construction starts to vary, depending on the projectile. In the .38 Special loading (lower velocity), bullet choice runs the gamut from lead to copper jackets hunting type bullets. For target shooters, the ever popular hollow base wadcutter is noted for excellent accuracy with minimum loadings, and its ability to cut clean, sharp-edged holes in any paper target stock. Magnum loadings dictate the use of jacketed bullets (hollow or soft points) at high velocity to take full advantage of proper expansion characteristics and taut string trajectories, while at the same time avoiding the problems associated with bore leading.

Sierra 170-grain
jacketed hollow cavity

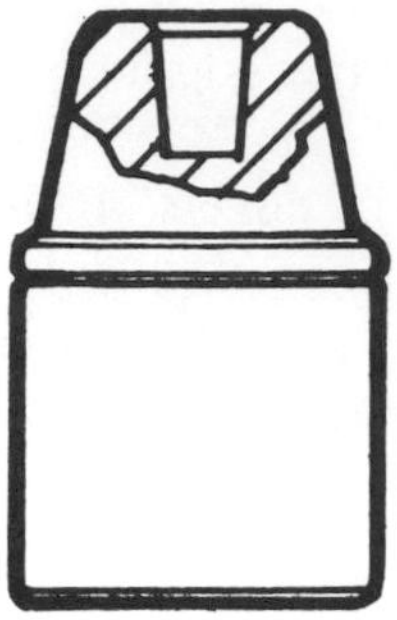

Speer 200-grain
jacketed hollow point

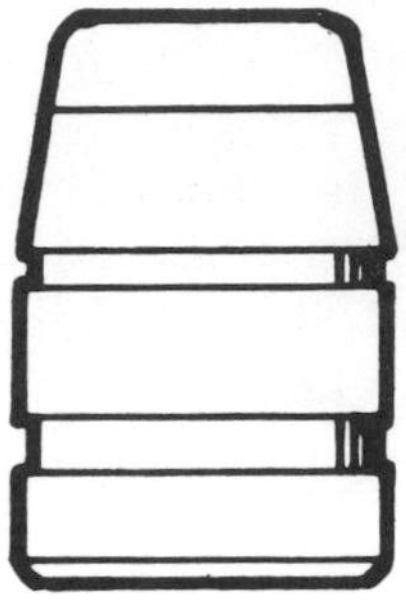

Remington 210-grain
jacketed soft point

.41 Magnum. A big bore handgun by anybody's standards, the .41 Magnum takes the back seat to very few when it comes to power, speed and penetration. Though limited in the number of styles available, the modern handloader has more than enough choices in hard-hitting jacketed projectiles. I have had excellent accuracy with the Remington 210-grain soft point driven to 1,200 feet per second. Bullet-casters should cast their lead bullets hard to prevent leading when driven to higher velocities.

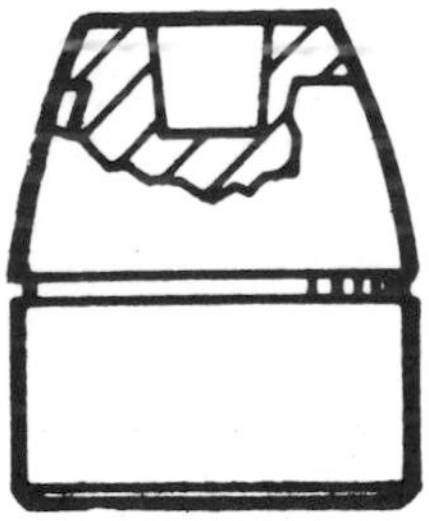

Speer 200-grain
jacketed hollow point

Sierra 240-grain
jacketed hollow cavity

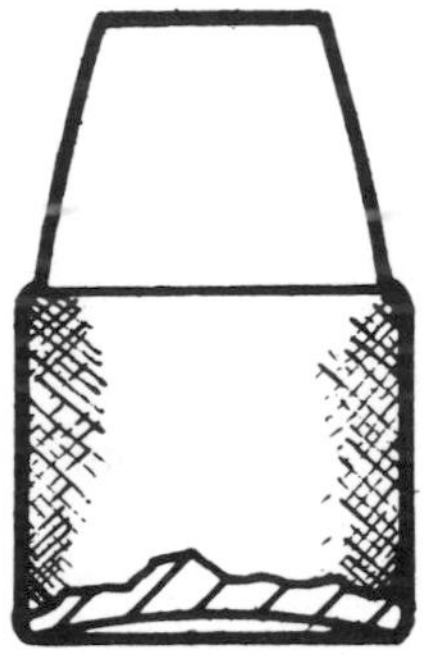

Hornady 240-grain
lead swaged
semi-wadcutter bullet

.44 Magnum. Designed with the big game hunter in mind, most of these .429 bullets are made with extremely tough, heavy jackets to insure adequate penetration. Bullet types of every conceivable configuration and design are available to the hand loader. A heavy crimp, slow powder, and the right choice of bullet go a long way to make any big game hunt successful. Lead bullets can be used, but my advice is to keep velocities on the mild side to keep barrel leading to a bare minimum. As common with most calibers, some of the bullets available to handloaders are available in factory loadings.

Speer 200-grain jacketed hollow point

Hornady 230-grain full metal jacket (flat nose)

Hornady 230-grain full metal jacket (round nose)

.45 ACP. The mere mention of a .45 Automatic years ago brought only one bullet design to mind—the infamous 230-grain round nose, or "hardball" as it is known. Today the picture has changed radically. Yes, the hardball ammo and bullets are still here, and ever-popular I might add, but so is a host of other styles. Hollow points are now being made by more than a couple of manufacturers, as hunting with "ol' slabside" is on the increase. As with the 9mm, bullet selection is important relative to smooth and uninterrupted feeding in any sidearm. As this cartridge headspaces on the mouth, a mild taper crimp is preferred over a roll crimp for good ignition. Lead swaged bullets are available, and for the target shooter one can hardly beat Speer's 200-grain semi-wadcutter in any 2700 competition match.

POWDER CHOICE

For most handgun loadings, powder choice is dictated by the recommendations found in all loading manuals. A basic handgun powder selection table is included below for convenience and ease of sorting through the maze of combinations listed in these manuals. The table was drawn up as a guide to show the prospective handloader just what powder is best for any one particular caliber. Remember this is only a guide; proper testing and evaluation on your part will actually decide the best powder for your needs and handguns.

Basic Handgun Powder Selection Table

Calibers	Bullseye	231	Unique	H-110	2400
.380 ACP	X	X	X		
9mm Luger	X	X	X		
.38 Super	X	X	X		
.38 Special	X	X	X	X[1](H.P.)	X[1](H.P.)
.357 Magnum			X	X	X
.41 Magnum			X	X	X
.44 Magnum			X	X	X
.45 ACP	X	X	X		
.45 Colt	X[2]		X[3]		X[3]

Note: For the proper amount of powder to be used, for any given caliber, bullet and primer combination, please consult a late edition of any reputable loading manual.

(1) H.P.—High Performance loads, Plus-P and equivalent
(2) Colt handguns and replicas
(3) Ruger and T/C Contenders only

I am also including a simplified list of current popular handgun powders to assist in any selection if one powder or brand is not available and an alternate is needed. The powders are listed according to their burning rates and characteristics. Indoor or target loads use a fast powder (Bullseye, 231), small game loads go the medium route (Unique, HS 6 or 7), and high performance or magnum loads will require slower burning powders (2400, H-110).

Smokeless powder, canister lots, from fastest to slowest burning

(fast) 1. Hercules Bullseye
2. Olin (W-W) 231
3. Hodgdon HP 38
4. Hercules Red Dot
5. Dupont Hi-Skor 700X
6. Hercules Green Dot
7. Dupont SR 4756
8. Hodgdon HS 5
9. Hercules Unique
10. Hodgdon HS 6
11. Hodgdon HS 7
12. Hercules Herco
13. Hercules Blue Dot
14. Olin (W-W) 630
15. Hercules 2400
16. Hodgdon H-110
17. Olin (W-W) 296
18. Dupont 4227
19. Olin (W-W) 680
(slow) 20. Dupont 4198

WARNING

When approaching maximum loads in any manual, please start at least 5 per cent below any red line or maximum listings, watch for pressure signs (tight extraction, primer cratering) and work up ever so slowly. Remember, these manuals, like the charts, are meant to be a practical approach. Common sense, continued visual checks of components and/or equipment are the best insurance to safe and accurate handloading.

Powder should be stored in a cool dry place away from primers or other combustibles. Never mix powders to experiment, and do not buy powder in unmarked containers. Keep all containers marked and legible and out of the reach of children. Additional consumer and storage information can be obtained through the Sporting Arms and Ammunition Manufacturers Institute (SAAMI), 420 Lexington Avenue, New York, NY 10017.

PRIMERS

Often termed the "spark plug" of the reloading components, primers are indeed the heart of the ignition system. Extremely simple in construction, the primers of today consist of nothing more than an explosive mix contained neatly in a cup which is inserted into the cartridge case under minimal force. When struck by the firing pin, the mixture explodes, starts the powder burning which in turn forms a gas and pushes the bullet out of the barrel. All this happens in less time than the human mind can even comprehend.

Modern primers used in this country are called "Boxer" primers, named after the British Army officer Edward Boxer who designed them. There is a second type called the Berdan, but its use is limited from a handloader's point of view. Instead of one centrally located hole, the Berdan has two or three holes off center, making decapping a very difficult and time-consuming project. Although rare, you can still find Berdan primed military surplus ammunition on some dealers' shelves. My advice is to stay away from

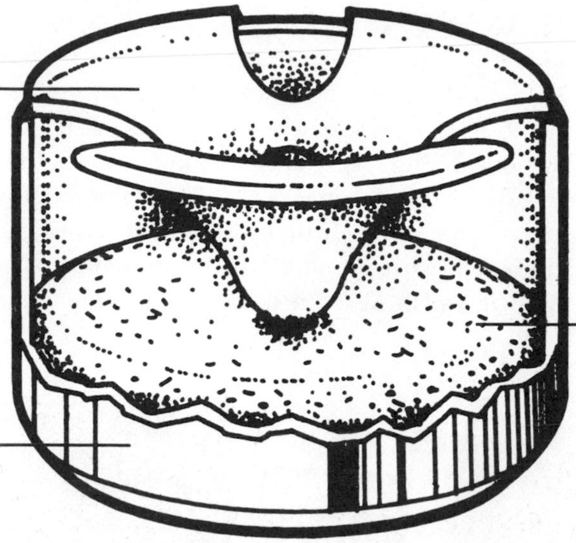

Berdan-primed ammo and always start with fresh American-made, Boxer-primed ammo or components.

Listed in two distinct categories and in two diameters, primers are made to fit all of the handloader's requirements. Small pistol primers are .175 inches in diameter, with the large pistol primers coming in at .210 inches.

They are also available in either a regular or magnum labeling, which refers to the burning rate. Regular primers are for 85 percent of all the powders listed. For slower types like H-110 or 2400, magnum primers go a long way to insure good ignition and combustion due to a longer and hotter burning cycle for these particular primers.

For complete interchangeability between various manufacturers the following chart is offered:

U.S. Primer Listing (Boxer)

Primer	Remington	Winchester Western	CCI	Federal	ALCAN
Small Pistol	1½	1½-108	500	100	Small Pistol Max-Fire
Small Pistol Magnum	5½	1½M-108	550	—	—
Large Pistol	2½	7-111	300	150	Large Pistol Max-Fire
Large Pistol Magnum	—	7M-111F	350	—	—

For safety's sake, *never* store any primers out of their special container, such as in a closed jar. This will only add to confusion at a later date, not to mention the risk of a possible explosion of primers in a confined space. Your best bet is to place all primers in a cool dry place and again, away from all combustibles or powders.

"ROLLING YOUR OWN"

Generally speaking, the reloading of American centerfire metallic cartridges is broken down into ten basic and distinct operations. First up is the lubrication of the fired case, followed by resizing and decapping. Next is the cleaning of the newly resized cases and performing a visual check of the case for cracks or splits, primer residue and overall length. Next, trim the case if necessary, to keep them within factory specs. Next is the belling of the case to accept the bullet, with priming possibly done at the same time, depending on your equipment. We will finish up with powder charging, bullet seating, and bullet crimping.

To lube or not to lube! Newer tungsten-carbide dies cut resizing time in half by eliminating the use of resizing lubricant.

Lubrication

Since all reloading dies are made to close tolerances, proper lubrication is imperative not only to aid in smooth operation but to prevent the case from being stuck in the die. Only a thin film is needed, as excessive lubricant will only clog the die and dent the case. For those of you who reload many thousands of rounds each year, an investment in a tungsten-carbide die may prove to be a wise decision. Tungsten-carbide dies are extra hard, durable, and diamond smooth, and require no lubrication to resize cartridge cases.

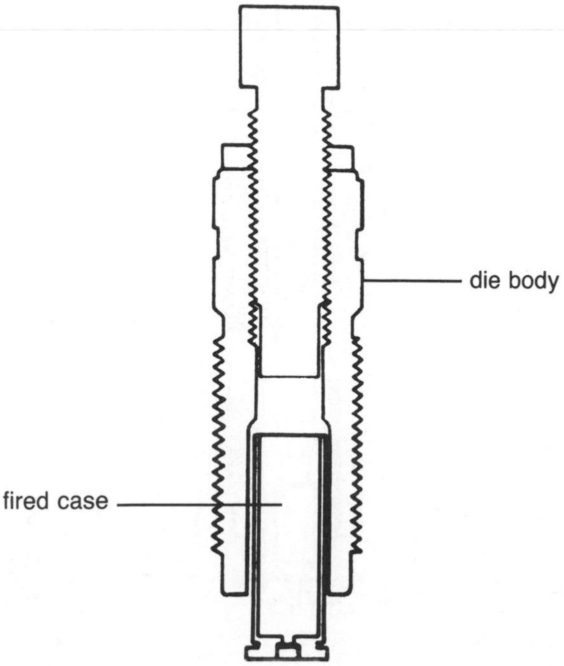

Full Length Resizing

Since the brass has expanded during firing, the case must be brought back to factory specs by resizing. Our first cutaway drawing illustrates the resizing die. This die is screwed down in the press until it touches the shell-holder. The lock ring is then set and tightened for die stability. In this operation the case completely enters the die, as all straight-walled cases must be full-length resized. This is to insure that after the reloading of the cartridge has been completed, it will chamber in any handgun made for that particular cartridge.

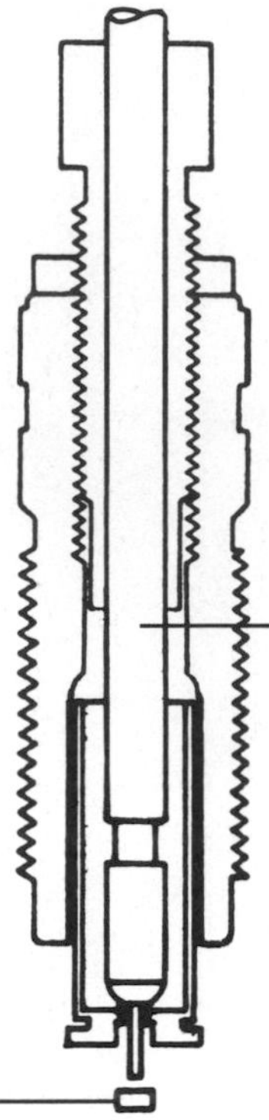

Decapping (or Depriming)

The decapping was not shown in the resizing illustration for a couple of reasons. For one, it sometimes adds to the confusion for a novice handloader, and not all companies make the decapping part of the resizing operation. In either case, whether you purchase dies with the resizing/decapping performed as one operation (Lyman), or decapping seperate (RCBS or Pacific), the expended primer must be removed as part of the total reloading cycle.

Cleaning and Inspection of All Cases

Cleaning is next and consists of nothing more than getting rid of greasy residue left by the case lubricant. Most anything around the house can be used as an agent; lighter or cleaning fluid sprinkled on an old towel would be sufficient. Cases are rolled back and forth in the towel or done individually. The latter method is preferred as it does a better job. You don't want any film left on the cases to contaminate either the primer or the powder.

All cases also should be inspected for cracks or mouth splits. Side-cracked cases should be thrown away, as well as some of the mouth-split hulls. The reason I say "some" is because cases like the .357 Magnum can be trimmed back to .38 Special specifications with no ill effects if the split is not too severe.

Primer pocket residue should be checked during each reloading. I clean mine before I reprime, but other shooters do their every second or third time. The amount of build-up will determine the frequency of cleaning.

Overall case length must be checked at least every other reloading on light loads and every time on magnum, fullhouse reloads. When the case is fired it does stretch or flow forward because of lack of resistance, and, if allowed to go unchecked, this will in time prevent the chambering of a cartridge in any handgun. This is especially true in semiautomatics where an overly long case will, in most instances, prevent the firearm from closing completely, thus preventing the firing of the next round. All case length charts are in the appendix of this book for easy reference.

Mouth-split .357 Magnum cases can be trimmed back to .38 Special but should be separated as illustrated by case number 1. Number 2 has possibilities, but number 3 should be discarded.

Primer residue should be cleaned out of the pocket to ensure complete and full seating of a new primer. At right is a Lee pocket primer cleaner.

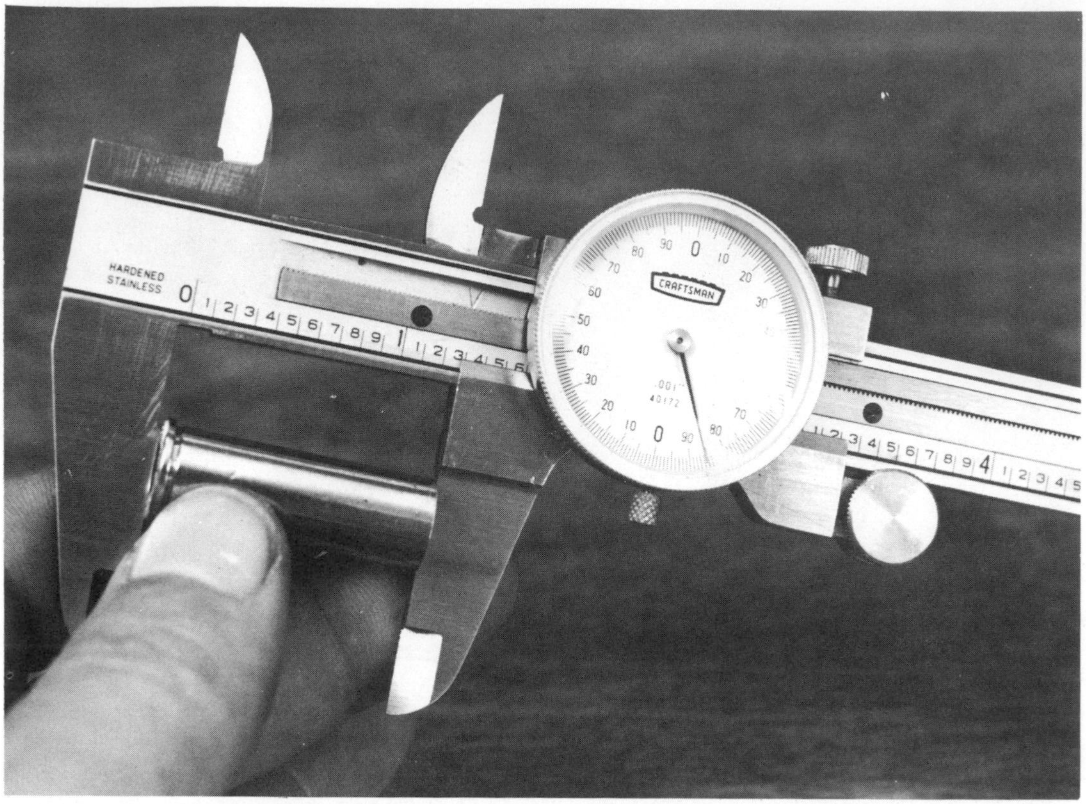

After sizing, the case length has to be checked to see if trimming is necessary. Overlength cases will have an effect on the crimp of the finished reload.

Stretched or overlength case problems can be solved by running them through a case trimmer. A few quick turns is all it takes to get all cases to one standard length.

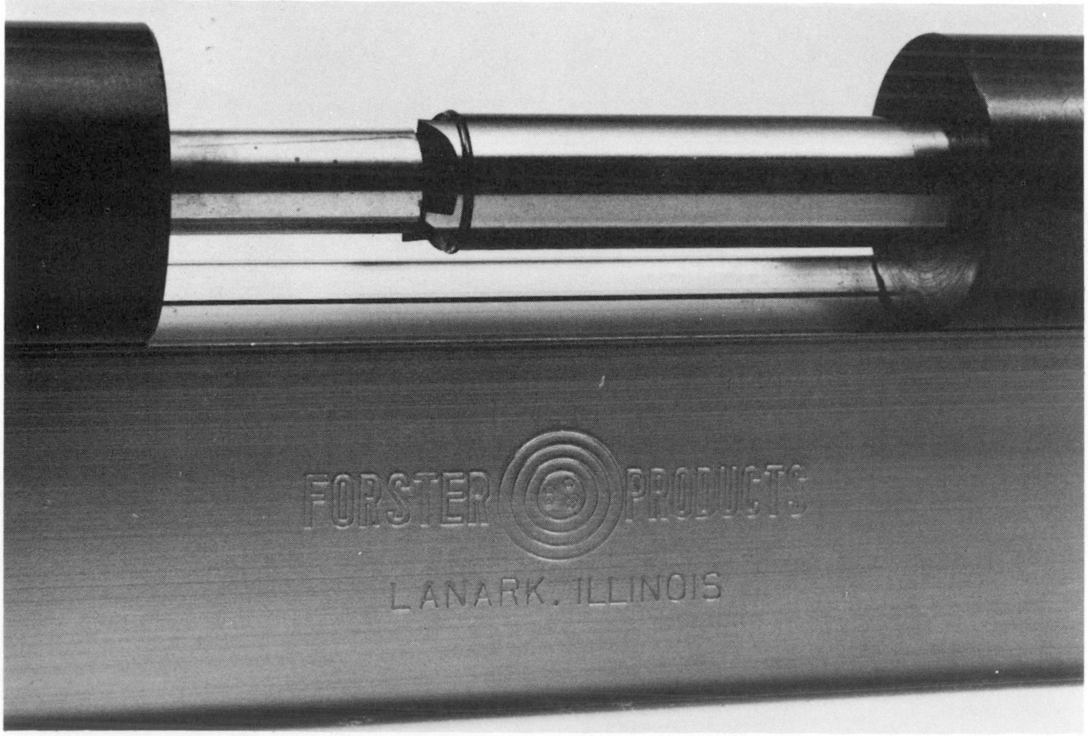

The Independents. Clockwise from top left: Detonics .45 Professional; Dan Wesson, .357 Magnum; Charter Arms Bulldog, .44 Special; Detonics .45 Master; The gun in the center is a Charter Arms Undercover, .38 Special.

The Single Shots. Clockwise from left: Remington XP-100 with scope; Jurras Howdah Pistol; Thompson/Center Contender standard model.

A wide array of accessories is available to help the serious shooter improve his accuracy and ensure his safety.

.357 Magnum

The .357 Magnum was developed and introduced in the mid-1930's as the world's most powerful handgun cartridge of that time. It was originally offered in the 8¾" barrel so as to exploit its high velocity to the greatest degree possible. Today, handguns chambered for the .357 are available with barrels as short as 2½" or as long as the 10" Thompson/Center Contender single-shot. Not surprisingly, the snubnosed .357's deliver a large amount of bark and muzzle blast when fired with full-power loads, and for that reason they are not particularly pleasant to fire.

As is noted in the discussion of the .38 Colt Super, two cartridges having different pressures and the same dimensions can ... one is fired in a handgun that was not designe... consideration prompted the designers of the ... as a high-performance version of the .3... .357 .135" longer than that of the ... from being fired in gun... dimensions are iden... .357 Magnum a...

...length
...m the
...When
...ve, or
...ovide
...rip and a
...lets forward.
...hed with caution and

Test Firearm: Colt Mk III Trooper
Barrel Length: 6" 1-14" Twist
Test Case: Speer/DWM
Test Primer: CCI-550
Bullet Dia.: .357"

Sierra Bullets

Accuracy, economy, versatility—three very good reasons for loading your own.

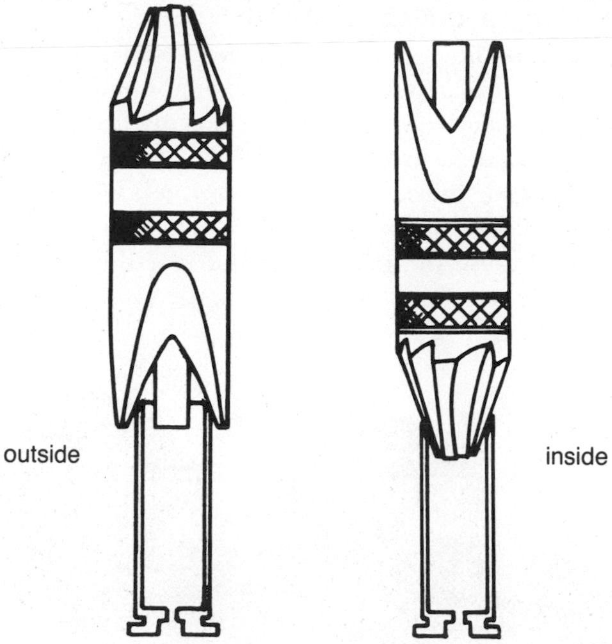

Case Trimming

If the case is over-length, trimming is the next step. All case trimmers on the market today are easy to use, but care must be taken not to over-trim the case because this could hinder the gun's operation and raise pressures inside the case because of reduced volume. Work slowly and measure carefully. After trimming, you should deburr the outside of the case ever so slightly for easy insertion into the cylinder of the gun. Next, deburr inside for easy bullet seating. Please remember that only a light touch is needed, as too much of chamfering will lead to mouth splitting at a later date.

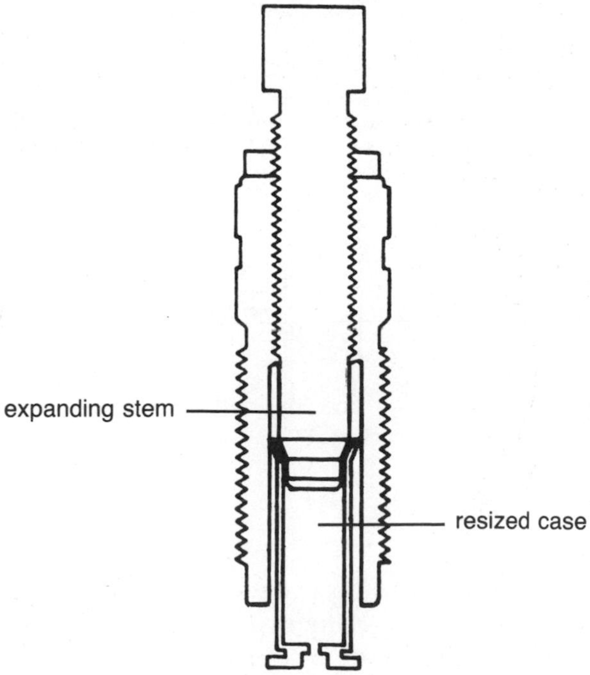

Expanding (or Belling) of the Case Mouth

Now that the preliminaries are finished, we now can get into the more interesting aspects of our reloading venture. The next step is to expand the mouth of the case so it accepts the bullet readily. After some practice you may find a little more belling is needed to start lead bullets than jacketed. The reason is that lead bullets are made slightly oversize to upset in the bore, and because of outside lubrication and the softness of the lead, it will be to your advantage to slightly overbell to compensate for this. Little or no belling when using outside lubricated lead bullets will cause the collapse of the case during final crimping. Only expand as the need arises as too much will only work the brass unnecessarily and lead to mouth splits.

Forty-Five denting, caused by ejection from some pistols, will resize easier if inserted into the belling/expanding die first, then returned to the resizing die for full length sizing.

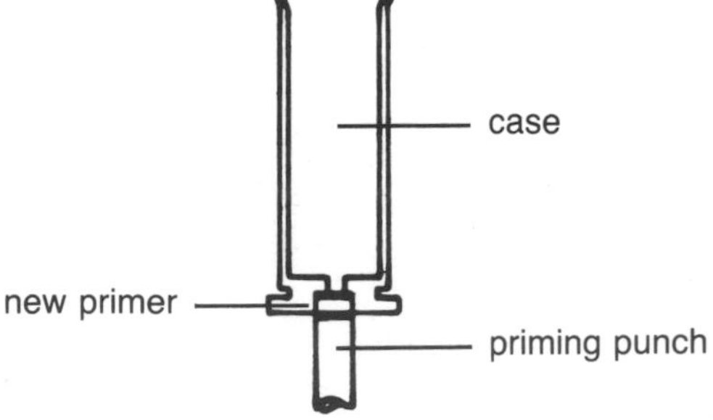

Priming

The priming stage can be done in one of three ways. First, depending on your die set, you may wish to prime on the downstroke of the expanding cycle. Another alternative is by hand using a Lee priming tool, which is sensitive enough to allow you to actually "feel" the seating of the primer, or third, as a totally separate operation on a bench-type priming tool like the RCBS automatic Priming Tool. In any case make sure the primer is seated flush with the bottom of the case rim and keep your oily fingers off them! By having the priming station this far behind the resizing cycle, you will alleviate the problem of getting the primers slicked up with grease. Once the primers are seated, they become tough little critters against moisture, but against the capillary action of oil and grease the resistance is nil. Choose the right primer for the job (small or large, regular or magnum), seat it correctly, pay strict attention to detail, and your rate or misfires will be reduced to zero.

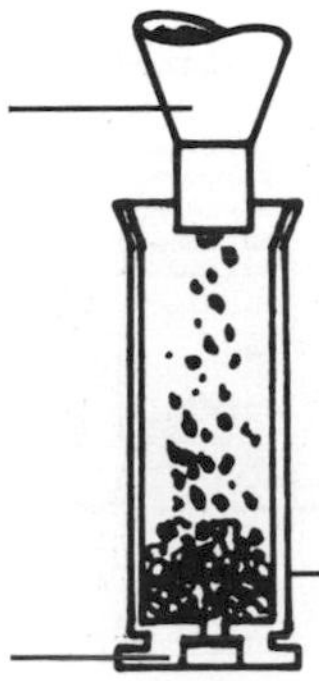

Powder Charging

Your full and undivided attention should be given to this operation. Most of the powders used in handguns are fast burning, but even the so-called "slow burners" do not take all of the space available in the case. So it is possible to *double charge* a case without much effort, which could lead to a complete disaster including a damaged gun or an injured person. Reloading in itself is not dangerous, but concentration and common sense must be exercised at all times. If the above seems like a warning, it is!

On with the charging. The very first thing to do is to zero your powder scale. Do this in a closed room away from drafts. Refer to the instructions packaged with the powder measure, then set the slide for the number of grains stated on the instruction sheet which comes the closest to your choice in the manual. This is only an approximation. The correct charge has a lot to do with your operation of the drop tube and the powder used. Set the scale to the weight you want, then weigh the charge. Adjust the powder measure if need be and weigh ten charges. All should be very close to the first one. If not, it could possibly be that the powder charge is too light. Some measures are made for medium to heavy charges, others are made to throw light or target loads.

When everything is ready, start filling the cases with the amount of powder you have chosen based on the manual. Check every tenth charge. Powder measures can and do change if only by vibration so it is wise to keep tabs on them. After fifty cases are done, take a small penlite and visually check all for consistent initial charges, therefore ruling out the possibility of troublesome extra-light, double, or over-charges.

Bullet Seating

With only two more steps to go to complete the entire operation, we began to see our reloaded cartridge taking shape. Taking the bullet seating die, screw it into the press, and back the bullet seating screw all the way out.

Now take one of the primed, charged, and belled cases and put it into the shell

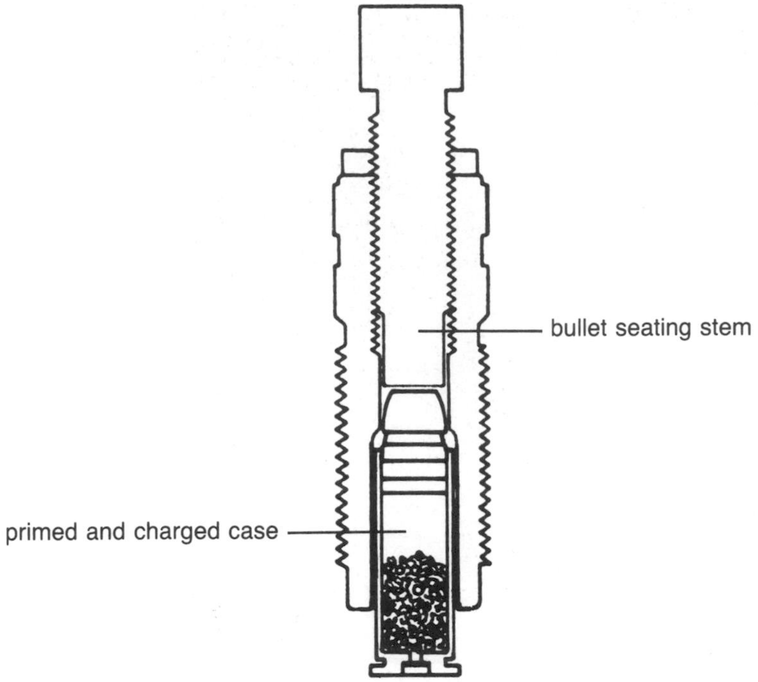

holder. Raise it to its highest point and leave it there. Screw the seating body down until it just touches the mouth of the case. Unscrew the body about a half a turn back and leave it—this is the uncrimped position.

Next, lower the case out of the die and place the bullet of your choice on top. Push the whole case (with bullet) up into the die again. turn the seating stem down slowly until it comes in contact with the bullet. By alternately raising and lowering the cartridge case and turning down the seating stem, the bullet will be pushed into the case. When it gets to the desired overall length (you will have to keep checking this with the calipers), stop! This is the end of the operation, and is the perfect ending for cartridges that require no heavy crimping such as the semiautomatic rounds of 9mm or .45 ACP, which headspace on the mouth of the case.

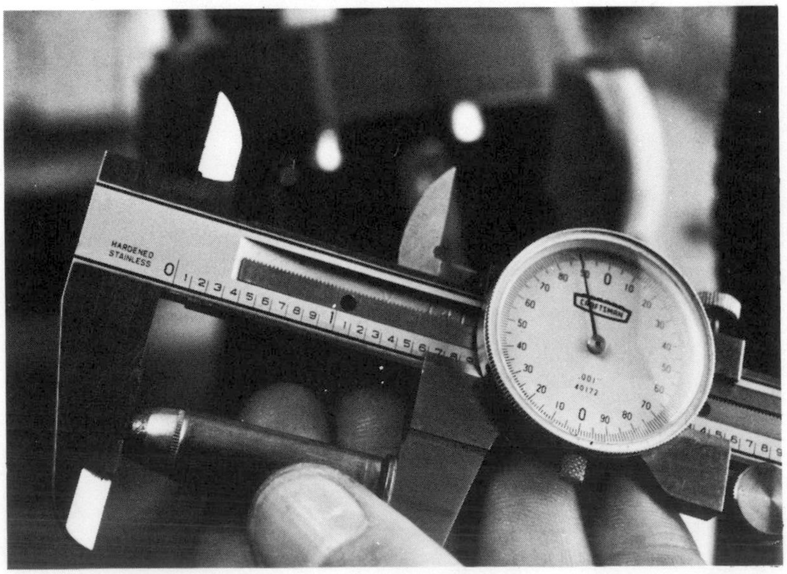

Perfection in reloading is attained by monitoring all steps carefully, including the checking of the cartridge's overall length (OVAL). This part is important as too long a cartridge will hamper the flawless operation of both automatics and revolvers.

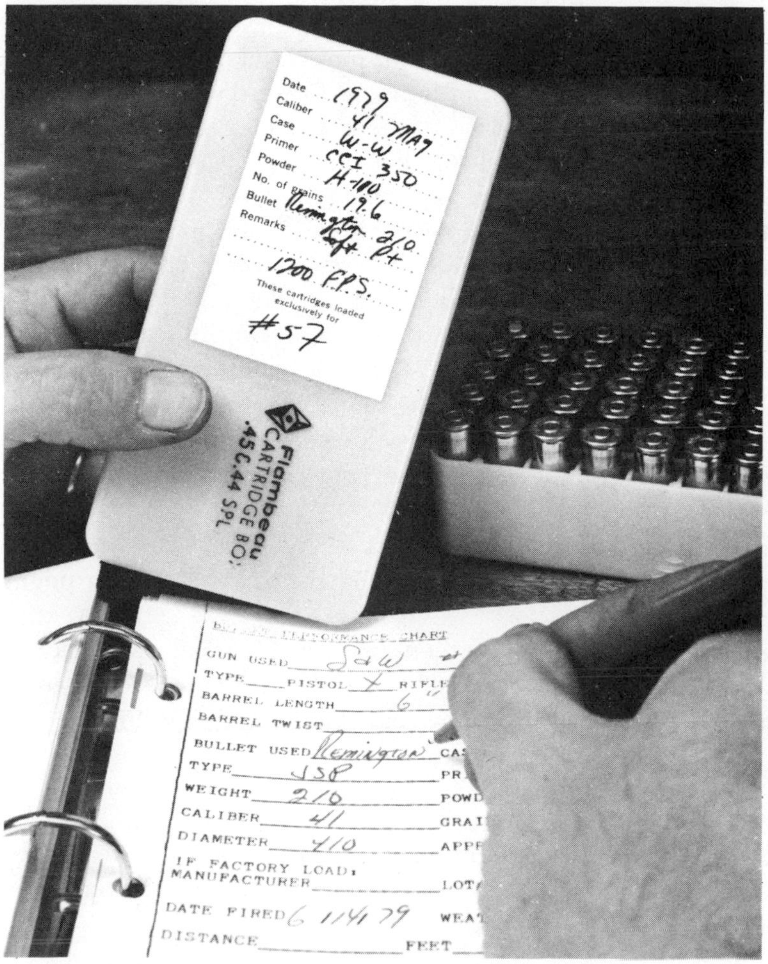

All handloads must be packaged, labeled, and logged in for future shooting or testing. Bullet type, powder, grains per charge, and other data should be written on both the cartridge box and kept on file in a three-ring notebook.

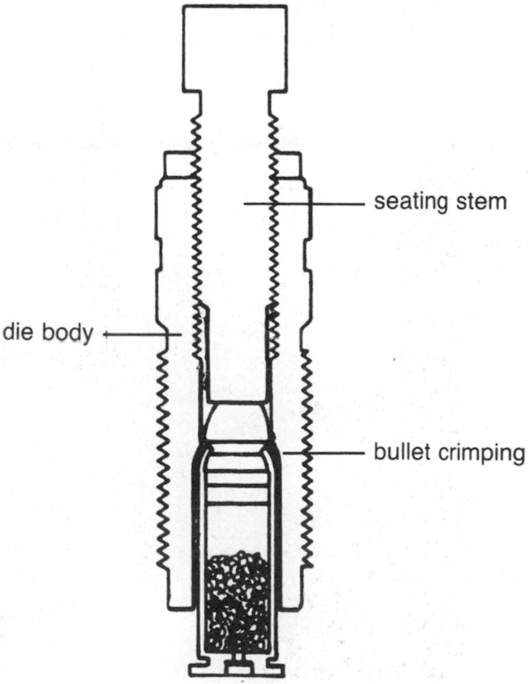

Bullet Crimping

Bullet crimping is required for all ammunition used in modern revolvers. The crimp serves a twofold purpose. For one, it keeps the bullet from jumping forward during recoil—by lodging itself against the outside of the frame or barrel—thereby rendering the gun totally useless. And two, it ensures complete combustion of slow-burning powders by actually holding the bullet in place a few milliseconds longer to perform this feat. Mind you, it does not slow down any movement of the bullet, it just allows the bullet to stay in place until the right pressure peak is reached. The crimping operation is a major contribution to the premium performance of any magnum load and should not be taken lightly.

The crimp is accomplished easily. Starting where we left off on the seating of our projectile, we will adjust the die so it touches the mouth of the case we are using. After that, seat the bullet to the desired overall length (lead) or to the cannelure (jacketed). Then back off on the seating screw one-fourth of a turn and tighten it down. Next turn the die body down three-fourths of a turn and tighten it. Run a sample through to see if all is well and continue to process the rest.

The amount of crimp (light, medium, or heavy) will have an effect on accuracy, so if you think you may be able to squeeze a little more out of any given cartridge, you might spend some time with crimp variations.

Finish up by checking all rounds, then place them in a suitable box or plastic case. Label the box and record all information for future reference after testing has been completed. Store all ammunition in a safe area, out of the reach of young, inquisitive hands.

FINAL TESTING AND EVALUATION

We have mastered the finer techniques of practical reloading, but the best is yet to come. Field testing of the reloaded ammunition will show graphically how various combinations

Range testing is an important ingredient in assessing any handload. Use a steady rest and establish a standard by which to judge other cartridges and handloads. Like many other shooters, the author uses a 25-yard distance for testing handgun loads.

of components, all working together, help to deliver the goods at any prescribed target and distance.

After you have gotten over the excitement of loading and shooting a few boxes of "home-grown fodder," go out and get a box of each of the various bullets in, say, the popular 158-grain weight. Now going to the manuals, pick out a powder or two in the velocity range you desire and load ten each of the Speer, Remington, Sierra, and Hornady bullets. You now have the basis for subjective, and most of all, practical testing.

Because handgun shooting is no more accurate than the shooter himself, all testing of loads, guns, and the shooter can only be held in very limited tolerances. A hand weapon with the popular 6-inch barrel and open sights is much more difficult to field test than a

When all the smoke has cleared, compare all targets. The group in the bottom left is what the dedicated handloader is looking for in both performance and accuracy.

For bullet expansion in game, tests can be made to roughly simulate results either in sand (pair at left) or by shooting through 3/4-inch pine boards for penetration and bone-smashing ability.

Pressure signs can be read by the condition of the primer after firing. On the left is a normal fired case, right illustrates a flattened primer. This is the first sign of pressure, and should be watched carefully.

Firing pin striking force can lead to problems concerning bullet grouping. Too light of a pin fall (left) can cause misfires, while too heavy (right) could have an effect on accuracy.

rifle with a 24-inch barrel equipped with a slick telescopic sight. Limits must be set by the shooter's ability to hold a group in a certain area, and these should never be over-stepped until his proficiency has earned him the right to do so.

All handgun testing should be done at 25 yards with the gun braced on a sand bag or other convenient rest. A good measurement to go by is a 2- to 2½-inch group at this distance, and for hunting you can well figure this group will open up to at least 10 inches at 100 yards. Any handgunner who cannot place all his shots in either group should never consider hunting until he improves.

Back to the bench. Set up your targets at 25 yards and get comfortable. I use sand bags for a practical rest. Rigid gun rests are fine, but don't kid yourself, you will never shoot as well as when your gun is in a vise-like grip, not even on one of your good days. Taking those ten of each we loaded before, shoot five of each at separate targets (to allow for errors) letting each shot break away as clean as humanly possible. Let the gun cool between groups of five shots and check the results.

If everything goes well, you should see a difference. The right combination of bullet, powder, and primer will show up as the smallest or tightest group. This, then, is the load for this particular gun and bullet weight. You have now tailored this loading to your gun and your style of shooting.

Satisfied with the results and keeping all the brass separate within the confines of their respective groups, one last item is left to check in detail. Since pressure is a big part of all cartridge ballistics, one easy way to keep tabs on it is to make a visual check of the primer. Normal pressure readings will show up as nothing more than our photograph of the .357 case illustrates: Almost as if nothing happened to the primer in question, except that it got smacked by the firing pin.

The .44 Magnum case illustrates the first sign of higher-than-normal pressure factors —a flattered primer. If extraction of the case from the firearm was easy, you may still be within safe limits. There is no need to go to extreme measures to get a few extra feet per second out of this cartridge as it would be of no value. Besides battering the weapon, in a short time, it could lead to a burst cylinder.

In conclusion, if you should desire more power or velocity than you are now getting out of a certain cartridge, just go up one. For instance, some shooters may feel that the popular .357 Magnum may be lacking in power for the next big game hunt. If this is the case, then move up to the .41 or .44 Magnum. Here you will find a new ballgame in bullets, powders, and guns in this ever challenging and interesting hobby of reloading ammunition.

In any sport or hobby involving firearms, safety should be a primary consideration. Following are some tips which may help you avoid a tragic accident.

- Exercise care and common sense in all phases of the reloading process—don't become distracted.
- Keep all powders cool and dry.
- Do not mix powders, and stay away from bargain buys on unmarked or aged propellents.
- Never smoke while handling powders or primers.
- Keep primers in their factory containers, properly labeled, and away from any powder.
- Do not under any circumstances go above the maximum loads listed in the reloading manuals.
- If in doubt, check all bullets with a micrometer before use. A .429 diameter bullet reloaded in a cartridge for use in a .41 Magnum hand gun (.410 diameter) can cause damage to the firearm and personal injury to the shooter.
- Check all cases for splits and cracks. Separate by maker, and properly resize to insure positive functioning in your guns.
- Watch for pressure signs mentioned in the text.
- Keep all components (bullets, primers, powders, and ammo) out of the reach of small children.
- Make sure you keep detailed records of reloaded cartridges and final results. Label all boxes.
- Set up a proven routine in all stages to avoid costly mistakes.

Nyclad
38 SPECIAL + P
CCI
Remington.
357 Magnum
41 REM. MAG.
FEDERAL
357 MAGNUM
HIGH VELOCITY
Dependable

NINE

American Centerfire Cartridges

PART ONE GENERAL INFORMATION AND COMPONENT LISTINGS

The handgunner in this country has never had a wider choice of versatile and efficient cartridges than he has now. Starting with the .25 Automatic and ranging upwards to the thunderous magnums, today's shooter has literally hundreds of options to choose from.

In general, all cartridges are broken down into two distinct categories; reloaded and factory loadings. Part One of this chapter will deal with the reloader and his hobby, while part two will discuss the factory offerings. For the benefit of the handloaders, I will group all components in an effort to provide a reference section for basic information for any particular caliber or cartridge.

For this reason, I have listed several specifications for handloading, some of which have never been put forth in a book of this nature. While some of these specifications will need a brief explanation for proper use and interpretation, others are self explanatory.

To begin with, the first item under "General Specifications" is the "Maximum Overall Length with Bullet." For our purposes, this is the outer limit of which one may seat a bullet in the case and still have reliable functioning of a handgun. Most all of the bullets I ran into had a factory cannelure built in, which provides for a ready made guide for bullet seating. But there are, and will be, exceptions. Machine tools may wear out or reamers may run short on one day or another. So after a particular bullet is seated, check it out by physically inserting the whole cartridge into the weapon. Here it's a good idea to make up a dummy round with no primer or powder to keep for future reference when loading this bullet/cartridge combo again.

"Grains of water" also needs a few words. This unit of measure is listed as a guide only and refers to case capacity. Under no circumstances should this comparison between case volumes be interpreted as a reference or standard by which to judge or load a cartridge case with that much powder. It is used more frequently in figuring the proper powder and velocity with a Powley Computer for rifle cartridges, and is included here only as a guide to those advanced reloaders who can put these figures to good use, perhaps in designing a new "wildcat" round built around similiar lines of some of the standard cases listed here.

The rest of the items explain themselves and are included as a reference source for any of the popular American centerfire cartridges. Any manufacturer listed will be found in the appendix of this book if any questions arise pertaining to the components they make. Write to them for technical help or advice when you can't find the answer in this book or your reloading/handloading manual. They are only to glad to help.

.22 REMINGTON JET

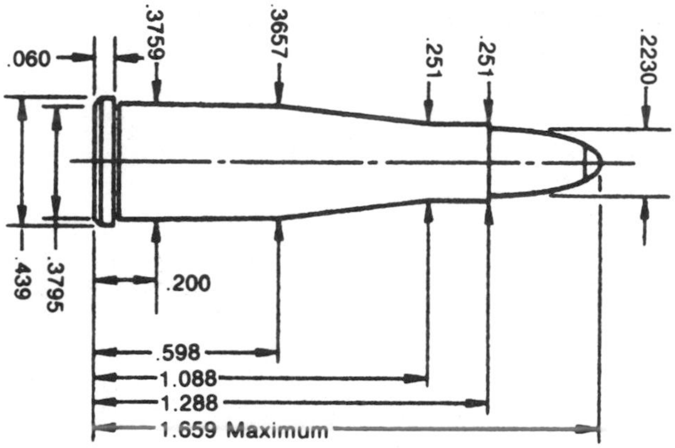

General Specifications

Maximum Overall Length with Bullet:	1.659 inches
Length Of Case Not To Exceed:	1.288 inches
Trim To Length:	1.283 inches
Grains Capacity In Water:	16.9
Primer Size:	Small Rifle

Factory Specifications:
2,100 fps @ 390 ft-lb with a 40-grain bullet
Factory ammunition available from Remington Arms.

For Reloading:

Unprimed cases from Remington Arms.
Jacketed and lead bullets from Hornady, Sierra, and Speer.

Comments And Suggestions:

Introduced in May of 1961, the .22 Jet was a joint effort between Smith & Wesson and Remington Arms. As soon as this new cartridge hit the field, reports of cylinder lockups began coming in. The problem was that if any oil or residue was allowed to build up in the chambers, the case would wedge itself up against the frame or recoil shield, and this would render the piece inoperative. Use of lighter fluid or solvent would remedy the situation and, if the user followed these instructions, he had no problems with either the gun or the cartridge.

The Model 53 could be special ordered with an extra cylinder for the .22 rimfire, thus S&W offered its first convertible handgun since the year 1893. To compensate for the two cartridges, S&W installed dual firing pins on the frame. One flick of the "switch" would allow the use of either of the two cartridges.

The .22 Jet is nothing more than a .357 Magnum case necked-down gradually to .22 caliber. Using .223 40-grain bullets, handloaders can realize velocities of around 1,900 fps.

Although discontinued in 1974, the .22 Jet still has a small but dedicated following, especially among the "dyed in the wool" varmint hunters. Those of you who desire to try this round now can try your luck with the Thompson/Center Single Shot Contender. With its closed breech design one can get velocities of 2,200 fps, plus!

Tie this cartridge in with a Contender, a scope and a pocketful of rounds, and you are in for an afternoon of fun and good shooting.

.221 REMINGTON FIREBALL

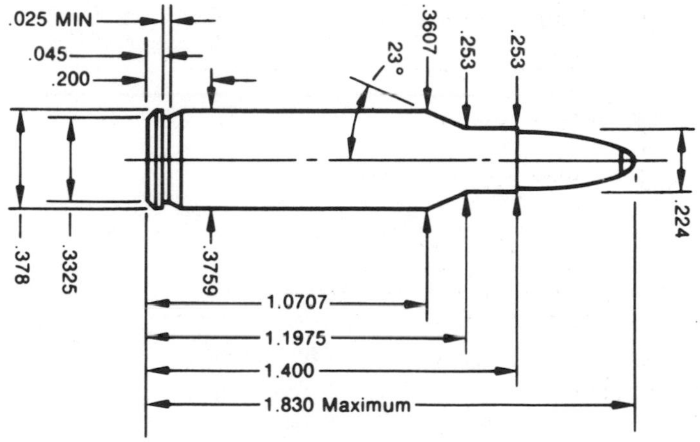

General Specifications

Maximum Overall Length with Bullet: 1.830 inches
Length Of Case Not To Exceed: 1.400 inches
Trim To Length: 1.395 inches
Grains Capacity In Water: 20.8
Primer Size: Small Rifle
Factory Specifications:
2,650 fps @ 780 ft-lb with a 50-grain bullet
Factory ammunition available from Remington Arms.

For Reloading:

Unprimed cases from Remington Arms.
Jacketed and lead bullets from Hornady, Remington, Sierra, and Speer.

Comments And Suggestions:

Mate this round to a Remington XP-100 and you have a pair that may shoot ½-inch groups at 100 meters. Rated as more of a rifle than a handgun by the purists, the XP-100 is more than a match for those willing to try it. Introduced to the public in 1962, the Fireball is still going strong, availability being one reason as Remington products are heavily distributed around the country. This gun and cartridge combo is a favorite of small game and varmint hunters nationwide.

Using a case that is nothing more than a .222 Remington shortened a bit, handloaders find this round easy on the hand and pocketbook. With various bullet weights and types available from all of the major firms, one can get lost in the myriad of possibilities available for this versatile round.

.30 CARBINE (PISTOL)

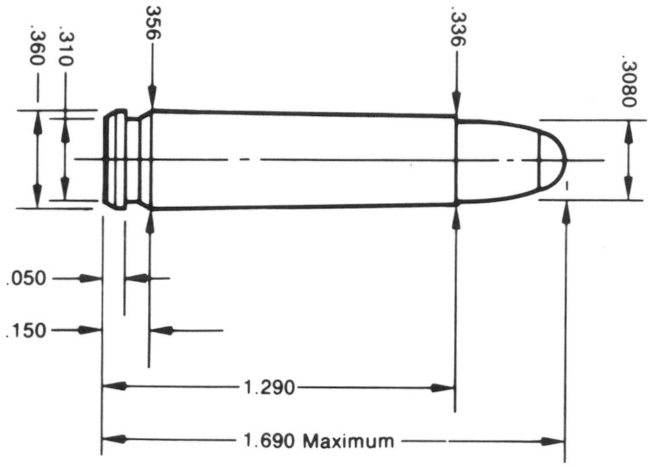

General Specifications

Maximum Overall Length with Bullet:	1.690 inches
Length Of Case Not To Exceed:	1.290 inches
Trim To Length:	1.285 inches
Grains Capacity In Water:	13.9
Primer Size:	Small Rifle

Factory Specifications:
1,990 fps @ 967 ft-lb with a 110-grain bullet
Factory ammunition available from Remington Arms and Winchester-Western.

For Reloading:

Unprimed cases from Remington Arms and military surplus.
Jacketed and lead bullets from Hornady, Remington, Sierra, and Speer.

Comments And Suggestions:

Although primarily a rifle round, the .30 Carbine has had limited success as a pistol round since the introduction of the Ruger Blackhawk in 1968, and later the Thompson/Center Contender.

Since the shooter/reloader is limited to a bullet weight of 110 grains, and a round nose at that, it is easy to see why this round is not in the top ten. High pressures and rough chambers can cause extraction problems in the field, and should be dealt with accordingly.

Small rifle primers are recommended for most of the powders, but the use of magnum primers with such slow burners as H-110 and 2400 will go a long way to ensure complete and consistent ignition.

.380 AUTOMATIC

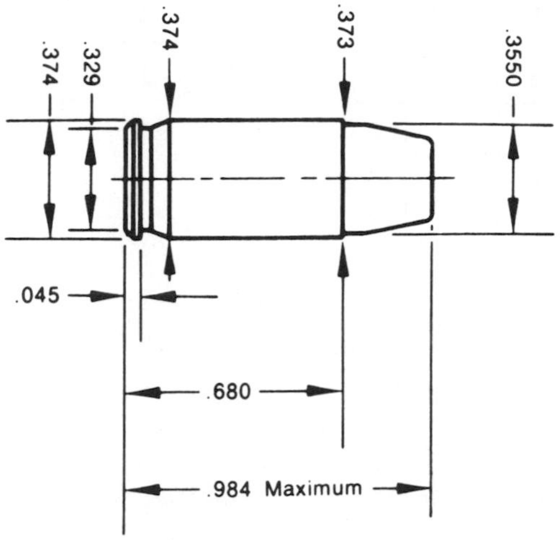

General Specifications

Maximum Overall Length with Bullet: .984 inches
Length Of Case Not To Exceed: .680 inches
Trim To Length: .677 inches
Grains Capacity In Water: 6.0
Primer Size: Small Pistol
Factory Specifications:
955 fps @ 192 ft-lb with a 95-grain bullet
Factory ammunition available from Federal, Frontier, Remington, Smith & Wesson, Speer, and Winchester-Western.

For Reloading:

Unprimed cases from Federal, Remington, Smith & Wesson, and Winchester-Western.
Jacketed and lead bullets from Hornady, Remington, Sierra, Smith & Wesson, and Speer.

Comments And Suggestions:

Using the same diameter bullets as the 9mm and the .38 Super (.355), the .380 Automatic is the lightest cartridge to be considered for a self-defense round. Although marginal at best, it is a round that can be chambered in a small "pocket" auto. It is easy to shoot and can be very effective at close range. Hence it is the perfect gun for the lady of the house to tuck away in a drawer or in her purse. In the same vein, many police officers carry a gun chambered for the .380 as a backup piece. Naturally, as with any gun used for defense purposes, tests should be performed to check complete reliability and feeding by firing at least a hundred rounds or more. Any handgun with a failure rate of 20 per cent would have to be ruled out, for this amounts to at least one malfunction per clip.

As with other automatic rounds, neck tension is important as this alone must hold the bullet because a roll crimp is not allowed. Using a 90-grain bullet, a fast powder and small pistol primers, velocities up to 1,100 fps can be reached with careful handloading. This is the redline and should be approached with caution.

9mm LUGER

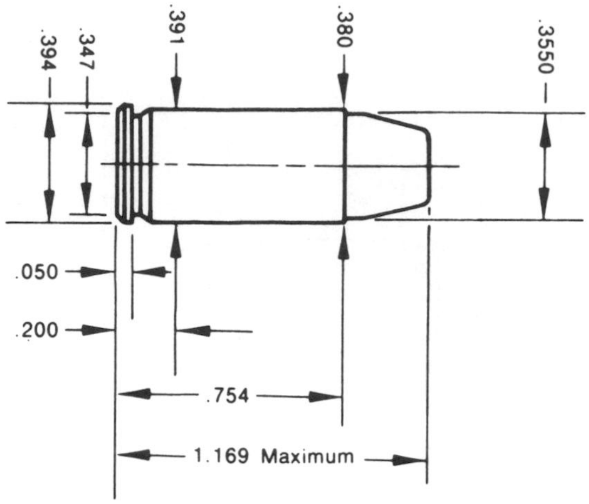

General Specifications

Maximum Overall Length with Bullet:	1.169 inches
Length Of Case Not To Exceed:	.754 inches
Trim To Length:	.751 inches
Grains Capacity In Water:	8.7
Primer Size:	Small Pistol

Factory Specifications:
1,155 fps @ 341 ft-lb with a 115-grain bullet
Factory ammunition available from Federal, Frontier, Remington, Smith & Wesson, Speer, and Winchester-Western.

For Reloading:

Unprimed cases from Federal, Remington, Smith & Wesson, Winchester-Western.
Jacketed and lead bullets from Hornady, Remington, Sierra, Smith & Wesson, and Speer.

Comments And Suggestions:

The 9mm Luger is an extremely popular round with today's shooter. Born in the year 1904, its popularity has grown slowly but steadily among knowledgeable handgunners. Chambered for a multitude of handguns, it is literally used around the world in semiautomatic pistols, machine pistols, and automatic weapons. Since the advent of more high performance loads, the 9mm Luger is finding itself more in favor with law enforcement departments than it did a few years ago.

You can reach the full potential of this round by handloading. Since there is a large supply of military brass floating around it is wise to check for both consistency in the neck area and the older type of Berdan primers. Since the European Berdan primers have two small holes rather than one (like our Boxer type), any attempt to decap these rounds will be futile without the proper hand tools. My advice is to buy fresh American-made 9mm empty cases and go from there.

Factory ballistics start at 1,155 fps for the 115-grain bullet, but velocities as high as 1,450 fps can be had using 90-grain bullets combined with the faster-burning powders like Bullseye, 700X, or Unique. Here it is essential to start about 10 per cent below maximum and work up to a load that is both comfortable for the shooter and easy on the gun.

.38 SUPER

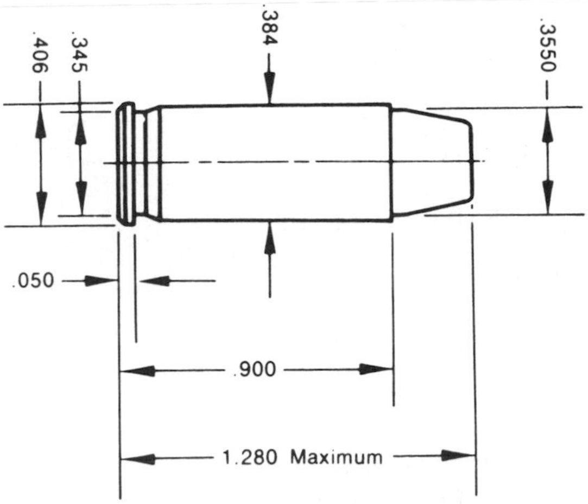

General Specifications

Maximum Overall Length with Bullet: 1.280 inches
Length Of Case Not To Exceed: .900 inches
Trim To Length: .895 inches
Grains Capacity In Water: 10.7
Primer Size: Small Pistol
Factory Specifications:
1,280 fps @ 475 ft-lb with a 130-grain bullet
Factory ammunition available from Remington and Winchester-Western.

For Reloading:

Unprimed cases from Remington and Winchester-Western.
Jacketed and lead bullets from Hornady, Remington, Sierra, Smith & Wesson, and Speer.

Comments And Suggestions:

Since the only American handguns chambered for the .38 Super are Colt's Government and Commander models, the shooter is limited in his choice of firearms. Ditto for factory ammunition, but you may find your favorite load with either Remington or Winchester. With the Remington, you have but one choice—a 130-grain full metal jacketed round. Winchester has stepped ahead with a 125-grain JHP and a 130 FMJ at velocities of 1,040 and 1,280 feet per second respectively. The first and third loadings are considered in the Plus-P category and should be used only in arms of current manufacture.

For reloading, make sure your dyes are set to insure good neck tension on all bullets. Bullet weights of 90, 100, 110, 115, and 125 grains will give the experimenter plenty of leeway. Here priorities should be given to consistent feeding in any semiautomatic weapon and the avoidance of soft-tipped bullets if at all possible. Using 125-grain bullets, reloading buffs can come pretty close to factory specs by using Blue Dot, Herco or Unique powders. As for muzzle flash, Unique produced the brightest with lighter bullets; AL-5, AL-7 and Bullseye the least.

.38 SPECIAL

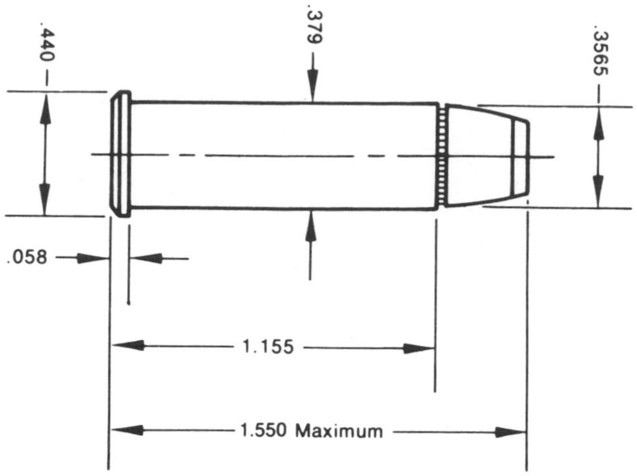

General Specifications

Maximum Overall Length with Bullet: 1.550 inches
Length Of Case Not To Exceed: 1.155 inches
Trim To Length: 1.150 inches
Grains Capacity In Water: 11.7
Primer Size: Small Pistol
Factory Specifications:
755 fps @ 200 ft-lb with a 158-grain bullet
Factory ammunition available from Federal, Frontier, Remington, Smith & Wesson, Speer (ammo and shotshells), and Winchester-Western.

For Reloading:

Unprimed cases from Federal, Remington, Smith & Wesson, and Winchester-Western.
Jacketed and lead bullets from Hornady, Remington, Sierra, Smith & Wesson, and Speer.

Comments And Suggestions:

This round has the honorable title of being the most widely used and reloaded centerfire cartridge of all times. To go into every possible load, bullet and primer combination would take more space than I am allowed here. Every major firearms maker chambers his guns for this round. With bullet weights from 95 to 200 grains, in both jacketed and lead styles, the handloader can spend a lifetime just trying various loads for his handguns.

As a police load it is often put down. This is due in part because a majority of police departments have chosen either the 158- or 200-grain lead roundnose bullets for the men on the force. Case studies have shown these loads ineffective to cope with the types of criminals walking around these days. In light of this, the major ammunition companies have responded with loads designated Plus-P. By using these in guns of current manufacture, using semi-jacketed and jacketed bullets, and boosting the velocities upward 200 to 250 fps, the police now have a more efficient weapon. Although no cure-all, it does instill more confidence in the ranks of all law enforcement personnel.

Except for target rounds, the .38 Special is used in revolvers and must be crimped to prevent the bullets from moving forward during recoil, which would render the gun useless. A finer round cannot be found for the aspiring shooter/reloader.

.357 MAGNUM

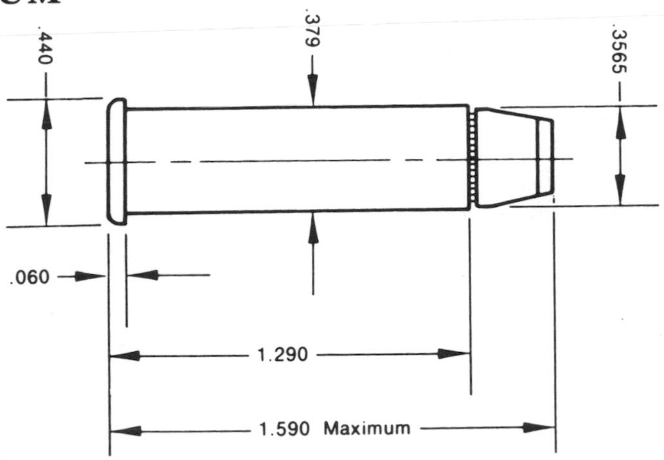

General Specifications

Maximum Overall Length with Bullet: 1.590 inches
Length Of Case Not To Exceed: 1.290 inches
Trim To Length: 1.285 inches
Grains Capacity In Water: 15.2
Primer Size: Small Pistol
Factory Specifications:
1,235 fps @ 535 ft-lb with a 158-grain bullet
Factory ammunition available from Federal, Frontier, Remington, Smith & Wesson, Speer, and Winchester-Western.

For Reloading:

Unprimed cases from Federal, Remington, Smith & Wesson, and Winchester-Western.
Jacketed and lead bullets from Hornady, Remington, Sierra, Smith & Wesson, and Speer.

Comments And Suggestions:

The .357 was the cartridge that started the magnum era for handgunners. Born in 1935, it remained "King of the Hill" in power for some twenty years until the .44 Magnum marched in. The .357 case is approximately .135 inches longer than the .38 Special to prevent the higher performance loads from being fired in guns of questionable quality or age. If you are looking for a .38 Special, it is wise to consider purchasing the .357 model, for even if there is a slight price difference, it will be offset by the fact that you can fire both rounds in the same gun. Please note that the reverse is not possible: i.e., you cannot fire a .357 in a gun chambered for the .38.

Carrying its share of excessive muzzle blast, the .357 generates about twice the velocity and three times the energy as its .38 Special brother. Hunters and sportsman seem to choose this caliber because of the availability of a medium frame gun averaging around 35 ounces, which is a joy to carry around all day in the field. With plenty of power for deer-size game within reasonable range, the .357 is both accurate and deadly.

For reloaders, the list of components is endless. Using the same bullet diameter as the .38's, favorite loads can be worked up with little or no effort. Jacketed bullets, slow burning powders, and magnum primers will insure top quality handloads for any occasion.

If you don't care to reload, factory ammunition is available in every useful bullet weight imaginable.

.41 MAGNUM

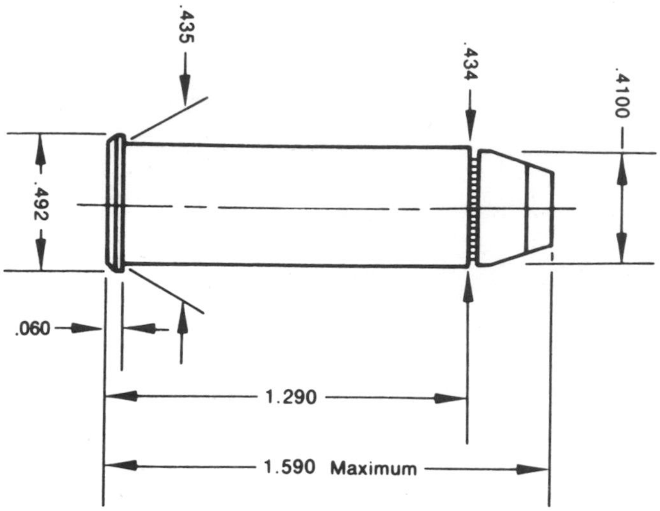

General Specifications

Maximum Overall Length with Bullet:	1.590 inches
Length Of Case Not To Exceed:	1.290 inches
Trim To Length:	1.285 inches
Grains Capacity In Water:	21.0
Primer Size:	Large Pistol

Factory Specifications:
1,300 fps @ 788 ft-lb with a 210-grain bullet
Factory ammunition available from Remington and Winchester-Western

For Reloading:

Unprimed cases from Remington and Winchester-Western.
Jacketed and lead bullets from Hornady, Remington, Sierra, and Speer.

Comments And Suggestions:

The .41 Magnum was introduced in 1964, which qualifies this round as the "new kid on the block." It was born with the assumption that a major portion of the police departments around the country would pick it up, but this never happened. It seemed too powerful for many of the officers to handle. It's really too bad because here is a smooth Smith & Wesson handgun, the Model 57, chambered for a superior round with good knockdown power and moderate recoil. Of course to do all this, S&W had to put this cartridge into one of their bigger N-framed guns, which is probably another reason for the thumbs-down reaction of the police.

From a hunter's standpoint, it's a delight. It can be carried in a hip or shoulder holster, and loaded with either a 170- or 210-grain bullet. From a reloader's point of view, the .41 is easy and fun to load. Again because of its huge case, plenty of slowing-burning powder is called for here as is a magnum-type primer. With my Model 57 and Remington Soft Points, 2-inch groups or less at 25 yards are all too common. The .41 Magnum is a good round and deserves more acceptance than it now gets.

.44 SPECIAL

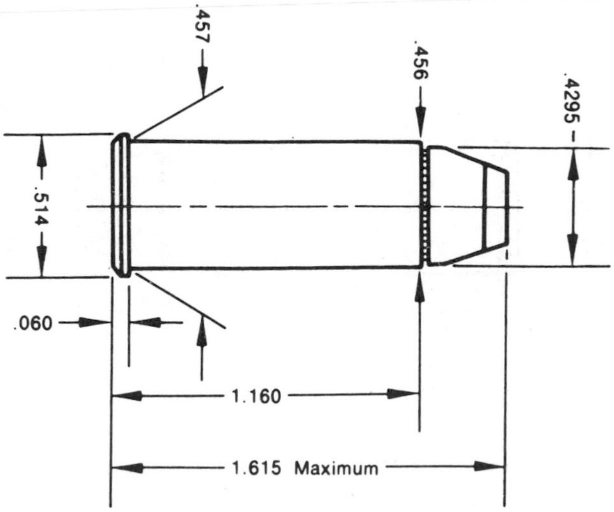

General Specifications

Maximum Overall Length with Bullet: 1.615 inches
Length Of Case Not To Exceed: 1.160 inches
Trim To Length: 1.155 inches
Grains Capacity In Water: 20.5
Primer Size: Large Pistol
Factory Specifications:
755 fps @ 731 ft-lb with a 246-grain bullet
Factory ammunition available from Remington and Winchester-Western

For Reloading:

Unprimed cases from Remington and Winchester-Western.
Jacketed and lead bullets from Hornady, Remington, Sierra, and Speer.

Comments And Suggestions:

If any round deserves consideration by any police department in the country, aside from the .45 ACP, it is the .44 Special. The .44 Special uses the same bullets as the .44 Magnum, and can be used in all guns chambered for the big .44. This round has gone through the same changes as its smaller cousin, the .38 Special. Just as the .357 is nothing more than a hyped-up .38 Special, the .44 Magnum is a hyped-up .44 Special.

The .44 Special is a very accurate round, and can be loaded with either jacketed or lead bullets from 180 to 240 grains with velocities at around 1,100 fps for the 180-grainer. Charter Arms is the only maker that chambers this round for a double action handgun, Colt offers its SAA, however both Ruger and Smith & Wesson .44 Magnums can shoot this round with ease.

It is an excellent round for the Sunday plinker and small game hunter. Although overshadowed by its bigger brothers, one could not go wrong by favoring the .44 Special.

.44 MAGNUM

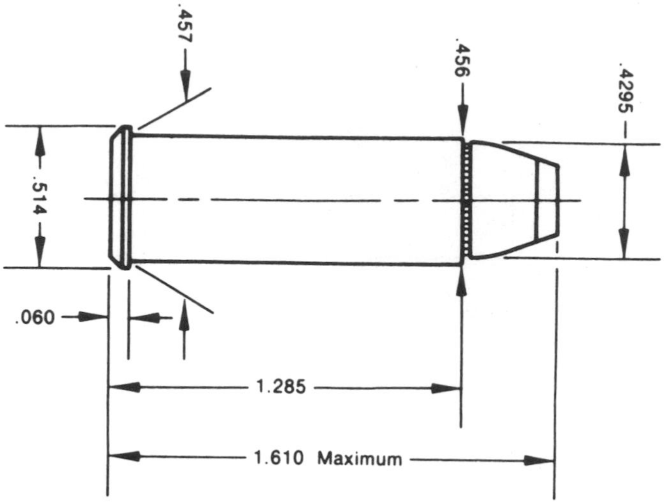

General Specifications

Maximum Overall Length with Bullet:	1.610 inches
Length Of Case Not To Exceed:	1.285 inches
Trim To Length:	1.280 inches
Grains Capacity In Water:	25.2
Primer Size:	Large Pistol

Factory Specifications:
1.180 fps @ 741 ft-lb with a 240-grain bullet
Factory ammunition available from Federal, Frontier, Remington, Smith & Wesson, Speer (ammo and shotshells), and Winchester-Western.

For Reloading:

Unprimed cases from Federal, Remington, Smith & Wesson, and Winchester-Western.
Jacketed and lead bullets from Hornady, Remington, Sierra, Smith & Wesson, and Speer.

Comments And Suggestions:

The .44 Magnum has to rank in the shooter's Hall of Fame as the number one cartridge for knockdown power and recoil. It has more than enough of both to satisfy most anyone.

Introduced in the year 1956 as a joint venture of Remington and Smith & Wesson, the .44 has been chambered in more guns than I can list here. In fact, because of the great demand of this caliber in guns made by S&W, the asking price (black market) for their Model 29 has, in recent months, risen up to the $450 level for their popular 6-inch version.

Jacketed and lead bullets are available in every make and design for the serious handloader. Cases are plentiful which helps maintain the popularity of this round. Holding up to 25.2 grains of water, the big .44 gets its velocity from heaps of slow-burning powders like H-110 and 2400. Magnum primers and a heavy roll crimp are necessary to ensure good ignition no matter the weather or temperature.

If the shooter does not reload, there is enough factory ammunition available to keep him occupied for some time. Factory loads are distributed around the world and range from the high-stepping 180-grain soft points to the slower moving and heavier 240-grainer.

This is truly a handgunner's cartridge and worthy of your consideration.

.44 AUTO-MAG

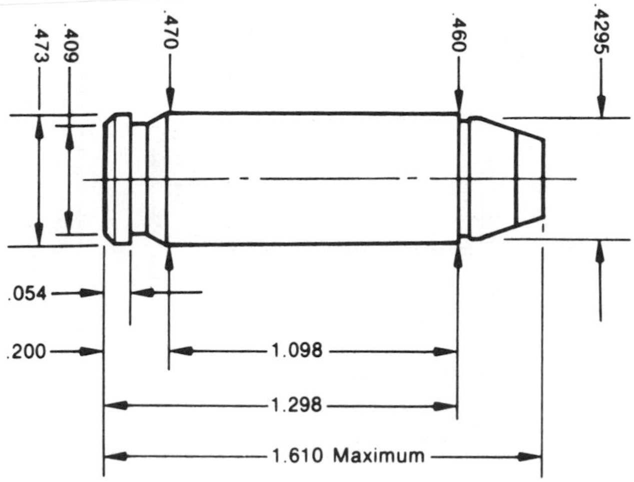

General Specifications

Maximum Overall Length with Bullet:	1.610 inches
Length Of Case Not To Exceed:	1.298 inches
Trim To Length:	1.296-98 inches
Grains Capacity In Water:	26.2
Primer Size:	Large Pistol

Factory Specifications: N/A

Factory ammunition available from your local dealer as supply varies from year to year.

For Reloading:

Unprimed cases must be made from .30-06, .308, or .243 rifle brass.

Jacketed and lead bullets from Hornady, Remington, Sierra, Smith & Wesson, and Speer.

Comments And Suggestions:

The Auto-Mag pistol was put into production in 1971. It is a stainless steel, semiautomatic; a heavy and powerful handgun. Production has been sporadic over the years and when they are being made, cost per pistol has been as high as $1,000.00.

Strictly a reloader's cartridge, the Auto-Mag round is made from .30-06, .308 or .243 brass cut to approximately 1.300 inches. Then you have to ream the inside neck area out until you get a wall thickness of .015 inches. Finally you trim the case to 1.296 to 1.298 inches for final loading.

Aside from the difficulty in making the cases (RCBS makes it a bit easier by making the dies), the rest of the components are available anywhere. All bullets are the same as those used in the .44 Special/Magnum series. Magnum pistol primers are standard fare, and as with the .44 Magnum, mountains of slow-burning powder are needed to get the velocities quoted in the reloading manuals. It is possible to get velocities to exceed 1,550 fps with careful handloading.

For practical purposes, one should favor the .44 Magnum over the Auto-Mag for availability of guns and brass. The .44 Auto-Mag is a cartridge for the experimenter and dedicated gun buff.

.45 AUTO RIM

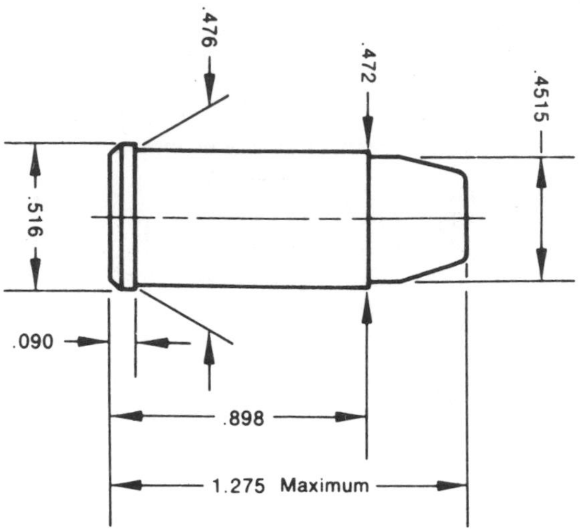

General Specifications

Maximum Overall Length with Bullet:	1.275 inches
Length Of Case Not To Exceed:	.898 inches
Trim To Length:	.895 inches
Grains Capacity In Water:	13.3
Primer Size:	Large Pistol

Factory Specifications:
810 fps @ 335 ft-lb with a 230-grain bullet
Factory ammunition available from Remington Arms.

For Reloading:

Unprimed cases from Remington Arms.
Jacketed and lead bullets from Hornady, Remington, Sierra, and Speer.

Comments And Suggestions:

Since there are no guns presently manufactured in this country for the .45 Auto Rim, one must turn to guns of World War I vintage in order to continue the use of this cartridge. If one can find a Smith & Wesson Model 1917 Military in good condition he is in luck! Being both accurate, easy to load and carry, there are some possibilities for its use in the field. Not many, but some.

The .45 Auto Rim is nothing more than a rimmed version of the .45 ACP. It was made for revolvers and can be used in them without the use of the half-moon clips. Use of these clips is dictated only when the user is firing .45 ACP cartridges in a gun chambered for the .45 Auto Rim.

So similiar to the .45 ACP, it is hardly worth the effort to pursue this cartridge. The .45 AR uses the same bullets, primers and quick burning powders as the .45 ACP, and has the same case measurements as its distant cousin.

For one to shoot and reload this cartridge would be agony in this writer's opinion. There are better things to do with one's time.

.45 ACP

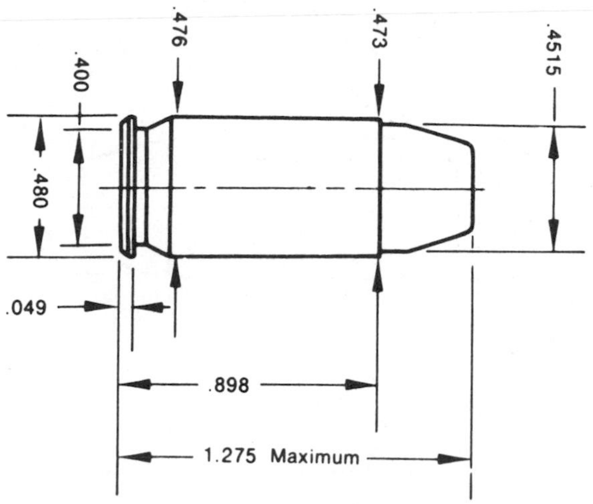

General Specifications

Maximum Overall Length with Bullet: 1.275 inches
Length Of Case Not To Exceed: .898 inches
Trim To Length: .895 inches
Grains Capacity In Water: 13.9
Primer Size: Large Pistol
Factory Specifications:
810 fps @ 335 ft-lb with a 230-grain bullet
Factory ammunition available from Federal, Frontier, Remington, Smith & Wesson, Speer, and Winchester-Western.

For Reloading:

Unprimed cases from Federal, Remington, Winchester-Western, and military surplus.
Jacketed and lead bullets from Hornady, Remington, Sierra, and Speer.

Comments And Suggestions:

One of the most popular cartridges in the United States over the past few years is the .45 ACP. Known to its makers as the Automatic Colt Pistol round, this cartridge has a large following of shooters across the land.

But only recently has the .45 Auto become popular. It was grossly underestimated by reloaders and factories alike until the advent of high-speed, light bullets in the 185-grain area. With these bullets, factory velocities jumped to around 940 fps, developing 363 foot pounds of energy. Handloaders (myself included) have gotten speeds of 1,000 fps plus, but only be careful and extensive testing. For close-range work on bear or boar, this round with a 185-grain hollow point cannot be beat.

Combat shooters have had a great influence on this round and semiautomatic pistols of the Colt/Browning design have sprung up in all variations including the ever-popular stainless steel models.

The .45 ACP is a true rimless design. The case mouth must seat itself against a lip at the front of the chamber, so constant attention must be paid to detail when reloading and trimming. Since little or no crimp is allowed, I find a taper crimp is the way to go. Extensive use of taper-crimped rounds in my combat-tuned Gold Cup has yet to produce a misfire or ejection malfunction. For flawless feeding, a jacketed "Hardball" round is recommended.

.45 COLT

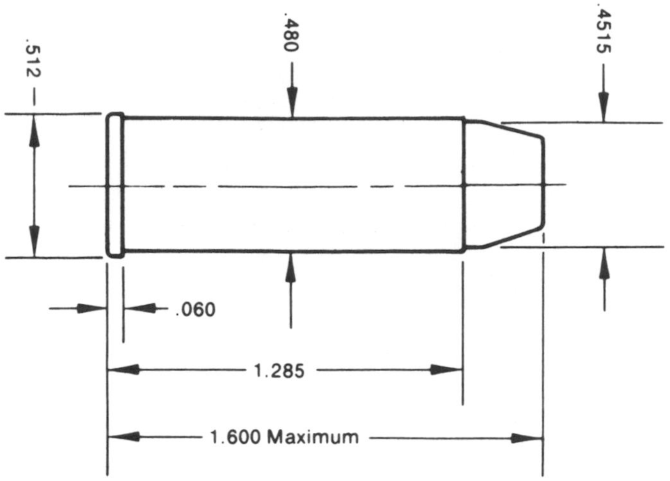

General Specifications

Maximum Overall Length with Bullet: 1.600 inches
Length Of Case Not To Exceed: 1.285 inches
Trim To Length: 1.280 inches
Grains Capacity In Water: 30.3
Primer Size: Large Pistol
Factory Specifications:
860 fps @ 410 ft-lb with a 250-grain bullet
Factory ammunition available from Federal, Remington, and Winchester-Western.

For Reloading:

Unprimed cases from Remington and Winchester-Western.
Jacketed and lead bullets from Hornady, Remington, Sierra, and Speer.

Comments And Suggestions:

This cartridge goes back a long time (1873) and was originally brought out for the black powder version of Colonel Colt's famed "Peacemaker."

When purchasing a Colt Single Action revolver, it's best to check groove diameter. Pre-war Colts run about .454 inches and bullets of today tend to give mediocre accuracy. Post-war Colts have a groove diameter of .451 to .452 and with proper bullets and powders will give excellent accuracy.

For reloaders, it may be well to note that most reloading manuals carry data under two categories. The first one is for all older black powder Colts and replicas; loads here tend to be on the moderate side. This is as it should be, for these guns cannot take the strain and pressures the newer models can.

The second section is for modern guns of strong design, namely the Ruger and T/C Contender handguns. It is here that the handloader can get the most out of his guns. Since factory loads tend to be on the mild side (because of the older guns), reloading is the only way to upgrade this cartridge. I want to state here, there is no need to "magnumize" this great cartridge; go to the .41 or .44 mags instead. The joy of shooting this round is in its mild recoil and easy report.

As always, maximum loads in any caliber from any reloading manual should be approached with care and caution.

.30 HERRETT (CONTENDER)

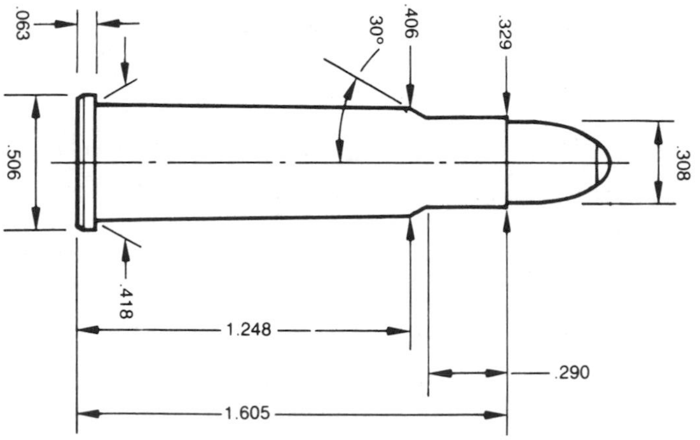

General Specifications

Maximum Overall Length with Bullet:	Variable
Length Of Case Not To Exceed:	1.605 inches
Trim To Length:	1.600-1.605 inches
Grains Capacity In Water:	29.5
Primer Size:	Large Rifle

Factory Specifications:
None available—handloaded only
Factory ammunition not available.

For Reloading:

Unprimed cases for Wildcat round formed from .30-30 brass.
Jacketed and lead bullets from Hornady, Remington, Sierra, and Speer.

Comments And Suggestions:

The .30 Herrett chambered in the Contender Single-Shot pistol was a three part effort brought to life in 1973. Available from Thompson/Center, it is an extremely high-stepping round designed for use on deer and plains antelope.

It was designed and developed by Steve Herrett and Bob Milek, though Thompson/Center is the only manufacturer currently chambering this cartridge in an American firearm. The .30 Herrett is made for use in a 10-inch barrel length and in a new model called the "Super 14." This is merely a 14-inch bull barrel and uses a larger and extended forearm. This barrel combined with the extra weight and heft, and topped off with a good 2× to 4× scope is a excellent varmint rig in open farm country.

Strictly a reloader's cartridge, the .30 Herrett is formed from .30-30 Winchester brass trimmed back to 1.605 inches, then lightly fire-formed to acquire the proper shoulder angle and chamber fit.

Hodgdon's or Dupont IMR 4227 seem to be the powders to use, as well as large rifle primers to insure complete ignition. Overall length will range from 2.070 to 2.200 depending on what bullet is used. For the best detailed analysis of this cartridge, it is wise to purchase a copy of the second edition of Sierra's reloading manual. Here the reloader will find all the information, specs, and comments on reloading he will need.

.35 REMINGTON (CONTENDER)

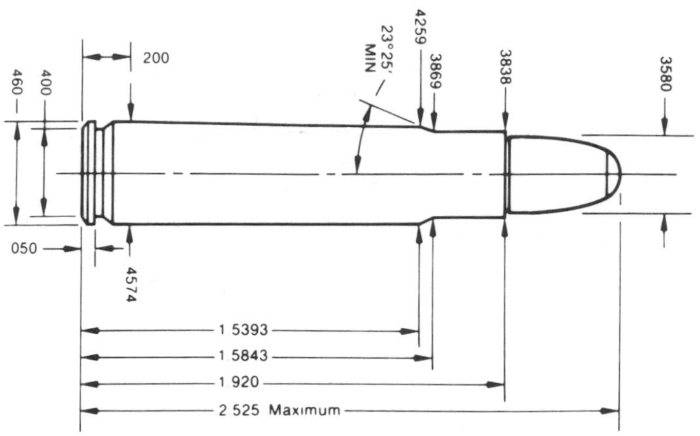

General Specifications

Maximum Overall Length with Bullet: 2.525 inches
Length Of Case Not To Exceed: 1.920 inches
Trim To Length: 1.915 inches
Grains Capacity In Water: 37.0
Primer Size: Large Rifle
Factory Specifications:
2,080 fps @ 1,921 ft-lb with a 200-grain bullet (when fired from a rifle)
Factory ammunition available from Remington and Winchester-Western

For Reloading:

Unprimed cases from Remington and Winchester-Western.
Jacketed and lead bullets from Hornady, Remington, Sierra, and Speer.

Comments And Suggestions:

Bowing to the pressure of the silhouette shooters, T/C decided to chamber their Contender for this easily available factory round in 1977. This was done to help those fellows who desired a .35 caliber gun, but who didn't have the time to reload a wildcat cartridge like the .357 Herrett.

Factory specifications of 2,080 fps and developing 1,921 ft-lb satisfy most shooters in the silhouette game. By using a 200-grain bullet, downrange ballistics drop to around 1,080 fps at 300 yards. By handloading, and using everything at the redline, you may gain an additional 160 fps—hardly worth the effort, considering the pressures generated on both the shooter and the firearm. If you are going to go that far, it's best to switch over to the .357 Herrett where the pressures will be more stable and accuracy much improved.

Everything considered, the .35 Remington in a Contender matched with a shoulder holster (with or without a scope) makes for a handy rig for the deer hunter. Many fellows still carry a .30-30 or .35 Remington carbine through the woods, and since the ranges are short, carrying a handgun for this purpose makes a lot of sense and leaves both hands free for walking or climbing. For smaller game, 158-grain .357 bullets can be loaded, as well as the newer 170 full metal jacketed additions. These will prevent damage to the hide and meat of the animal.

.357 HERRETT (CONTENDER)

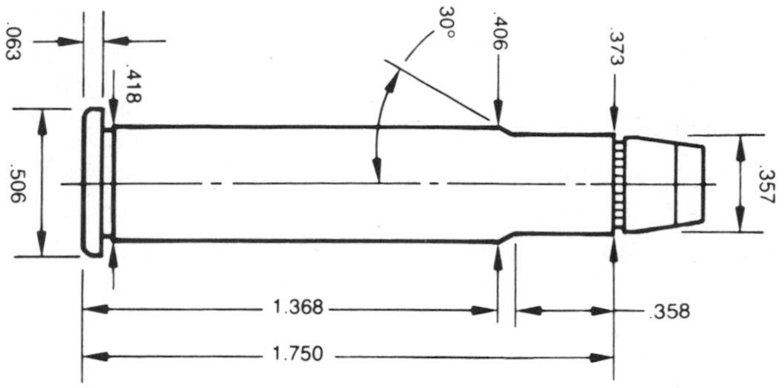

General Specifications

Maximum Overall Length with Bullet:	Variable
Length Of Case Not To Exceed:	1.750 inches
Trim To Length:	1.745-1.750 inches
Grains Capacity In Water:	32.0 (Est.)
Primer Size:	Large Rifle

Factory Specifications:
None available—Handloaded only
Factory ammunition not available.

For Reloading:

Unprimed cases for wildcat round formed from .30-30 brass.
Jacketed and lead bullets from Hornady, Remington, Sierra, and Speer.

Comments And Suggestions:

The .357 Herrett was introduced after the .30 Herrett and is designed for bigger game animals. Using a bullet of .357 diameter, the .357 Herrett can be loaded up to suit the requirements of most hunters in the field. I am not saying that this round is a cure-all for everything that walks, but for the handgun hunter that wants a challenge in the wilds against larger game, and can get close enough by patient stalking, this may be his cup of tea.

Again since this is a handloaded round, one is wise to consult the Sierra manual. As with the .30 Herrett, 4227 powder and large rifle primers should be used for best results.

One must form his own cases through the use of dies. To complete the task, you have to fire-form the cases in the gun to get the correct shoulder angle, and to ensure snugness in the chamber. This along with making sure the case headspaces on the shoulder and not on the rim is extra insurance for long case life in this cartridge.

PART TWO
FACTORY LOADED AMMUNITION AND SPECIFICATIONS

The availability and choice of commercial factory loadings in the United States has grown at a phenomenal rate in recent years. This is due in part to the heavy dependence of most law enforcement agencies on this type of ammo. Nevertheless the American handgunner does buy factory loadings for his personal use as the need arises, perhaps because he can't purchase the necessary components to assemble that one special combination he'll need on his next hunt. Another reason might be the uncanny faith that some target shooters put into factory target rounds to help score extra points and bring home the gold.

But whatever the reasons, the major munitions makers continue to grind out ammunition at a rate unthinkable a decade ago. It's because of this mass production that we are blessed with factory loads which are easily obtainable in most any part of the country. Even in the thickets of Maine, I have yet to encounter the smallest general store without at least two to three boxes of .38 Specials on the shelf. In short, it's there when and if you need it.

When it comes to selection, the choice is simply mind boggling! The six major producers of factory loadings produce 277 different loads in all calibers, and that is not counting some of the smaller operations in the country, which I am sure would jump that total up by at least 20 or 25 per cent.

It goes without saying that anything that your little heart may desire is available through the major manufacturers. From the smallest .25 Automatic round, rising in scale and power to the bigger calibers, the variety is there.

In addition, the popular .38 and .357s have more than enough loads and combinations to keep a hearty gun buff testing rounds for many moons to come. To illustrate our point, you can purchase over the counter factory ammo in the following bullet weights. Starting at the lower end, the 95-grain Semi-Jacketed Hollow Point is available in a Plus-P configuration. From here, the only way is up, so we continue with the 110, 125, 140, 148, 150, 158, and 200-grain projectiles. For more fun at the range, mix in jacketed hollow and soft points, lead swaged and wadcutter bullets, Plus-P and regular pressure loadings, plus a sprinkling of .38 shot shells, and you just have to wonder who stays up at night thinking up these combos.

We should give credit to the "Big Boys" for being the first to respond to the shooter's needs and desires by producing all (or most all) of the components needed to make good handloads. They deserve much credit for their attention to detail with reference to close tolerances on both brass and bullets. They should also be congratulated for introducing new and exciting cartridges to work with.

It was Remington, in close cooperation with Smith & Wesson, who brought us the .357, .41 and .44 Magnums. Now Winchester-Western, working with the Wildey Corporation, is bringing us the 9mm and .45 Winchester Magnums. These are high pressure rounds to be used only in the new Wildey Automatic Pistol or the T/C Contender.

Another development worth noting, is Smith & Wesson's Nyclad ammunition which, according to recent lab tests, reduces the airborne lead contaminates for those of us who, because of weather or other problems, must confine our shooting practice to indoor ranges. Frontier has recently introduced a 9mm and .45 ACP round loaded with their newely designed flat nose (hardball loading) bullet. The list goes on.

Lead swaged bullets loaded with mild charges are in the factory catalogs. In the opinion of many, you just can't beat some of the factory lots for bullet consistency and uniformity. From target wadcutters to semi-wadcutters to round nose bullets, you would be hard pressed to find anything better.

One additional point should be mentioned before we get into the various manufacturers and their wares—pressure. Only the larger factories have the facilities, time, and money to pour into research regarding pressure. They have come up with a common sense method of measuring both pressure and velocity which the layman can understand easily. Years ago, every measurement for testing magnum loadings was recorded in a "closed breech test barrel" roughly 8½ inches in length. Naturally, velocities were high, the result of barrels that were longer than the average handgunner had in his possession. In addition, they lacked one important ingredient: a cylinder gap. This is where you lose pressure, hence your velocity drops, putting gray hairs in the heads of many who just couldn't figure out what was really going on.

Now, the factories are using vented test barrels which help to put all of the testing results in a better prospective. If I may quote from a Remington catalog:

> The key elements of the Vented Test Barrel procedure will include:
> 1. Powder orientation: laid horizontally in the case for firing.
> 2. Cylinder gap controlled at .008 inches.
> 3. Barrel length held to a constant 4 inches.
>
> Each of these factors affect velocity, a critical element of on target effect. The Vented Test Barrel method of measuring bullet performance now permits the shooter to "predict" bullet performance in barrels of any length.

That says it all, and I congratulate all member companies of SAAMI on this move toward a better understanding of their products. Believe me, it's appreciated!

Since most of the groundwork has been covered regarding factory ammunition, we can now delve a little deeper into detail and explore the offerings now available for six of the country's biggest producers of commercial factory ammunition. The companies are listed in alphabetical order.

Since single shot pistols lack restrictions (revolving cylinder/headspace problems), specialized factory ammunition can be made with greater freedom, as shown here by the large shotshell capacity of the T/C "Hot-Shots."

At 10 feet, the shotshell pattern is fairly even and devastating. The large hole over the 9 is from the plastic shot cup.

Round-to-round consistency is remarkable even in factory loaded cartridges. The Winchester-Western .357 Magnum series proved not only powerful but extremely accurate also.

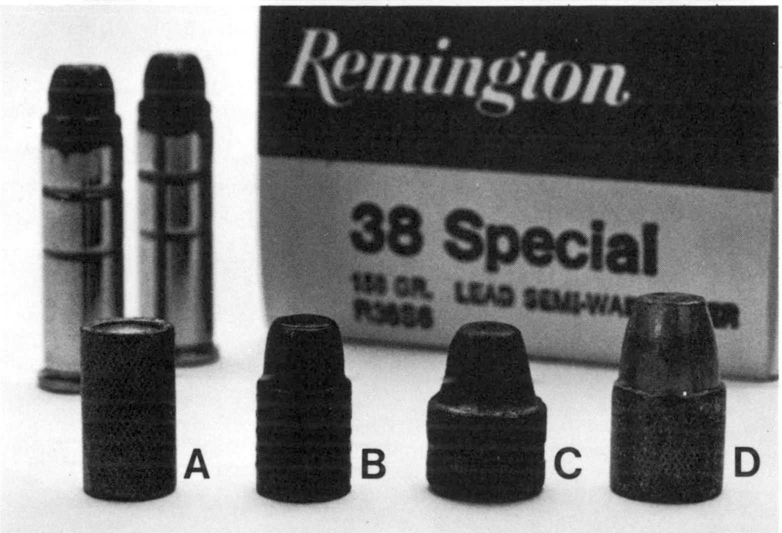

For just about every lead bullet, there is a factory load. Hard alloys and proper lubrication have kept barrel leading to a minimum. The Hornady 148-grain hollow base wadcutter is shown in .38 caliber (A). Remington's 58-grain semi-wadcutter (B) is also in .38. Speer's 200-grain semi-wadcutter (C) appears in .45 ACP caliber. In .44 Magnum is the Hornady 240-grain semi-wadcutter (D).

Federal's series of .45 Colt ammunition proved to be one of the most accurate of all loads and/or cartridges tested. The gun is Colt's New Frontier Single Action Army with adjustable sights.

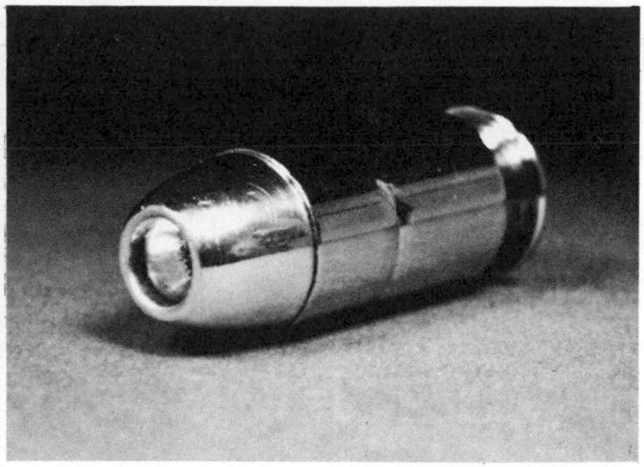

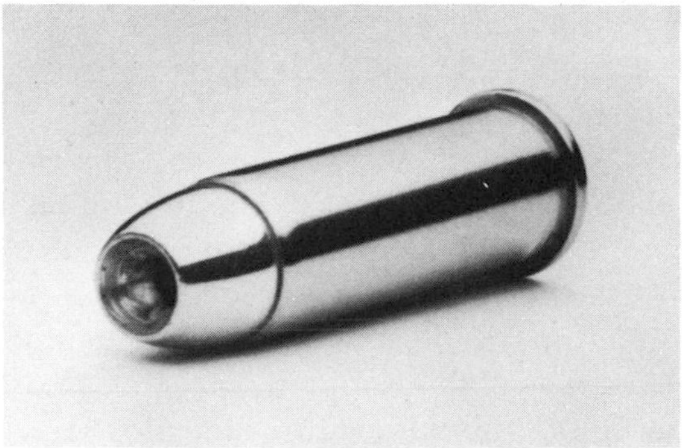

cal. 38 spl. (95 gr.) sthp

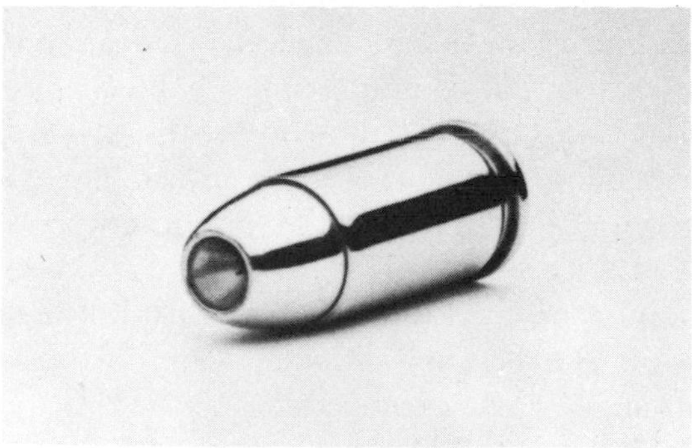

cal. 32 auto (60 gr.) sthp

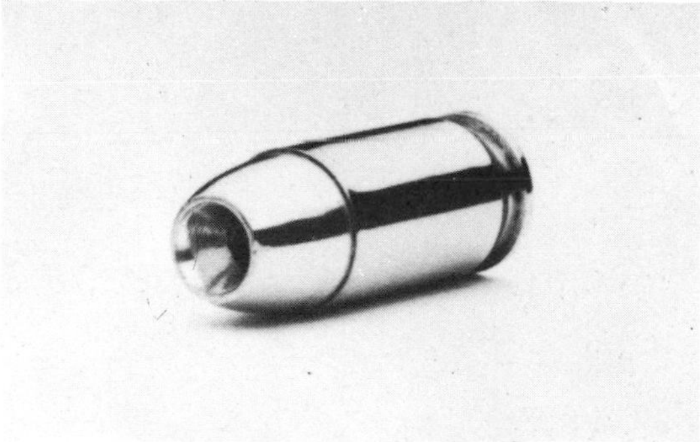

cal. 380 auto (85 gr.) sthp

Innovations keep rising from the American ammo makers. W-W's new line of Silvertip ammunition was made to upset very quickly. Tests substantiated those claims.

CCI

CCI LAWMAN AMMUNITION

CCI Lawman Ammunition, until recently packaged under the Speer label, is still part of the CCI/Speer/RCBS conglomerate. Using Speer bullets in all of its twenty-three loadings, CCI engineers compute and use the precise powder which matches the performance ratio they desire. This company, like all of the others mentioned in this chapter, has a broad selection of choices across the board.

First up is the .380 Automatic. CCI loads this one with a Speer 88-grain bullet traveling at 1,050 feet per second at the muzzle. In the jacketed hollow point configuration, this loading is good for personal defense at close distances, such as in the home.

Next up is the 9mm. As of now CCI lists two loadings. One is the 100-grain hollow point, the other a jacketed soft point tipping the scales at an even 125 grains. Caution is advised when using the latter for self protection. Because of the soft point, it may hang up in some semiautomatics that have not been polished or throated well. Some pistols just simply refuse to digest any lead-tipped bullet of any make. There have always been problems with soft point/auto combinations. If you want to use this round in your gun, please fire off at least a box or two before committing yourself to this load for defense use.

In the .38 Special, CCI provides ten different choices. Bullet weights go from the light 110-grain jacketed hollow points on up to the popular 158-grain bullets. Plus-P loads are available in six out of the ten mentioned, and again, please check your weapon to establish its capacity to handle these hotter than normal rounds. Some of the smaller, light-framed guns may hang up after extensive use, so if in doubt, contact the firearms company concerning the use of this specialized ammo.

CCI also offers the American shooter seven listings in the .357 Magnum series, two in the .44 Magnum, and one in the famous .45 ACP caliber.

This company's lineup would not be complete without the mention of its shotshells tailored especially for two calibers—.38 Special and .44 Magnum—all filled with the precise amount of No. 9 shot to make decent patterns at reasonable distances.

FEDERAL® AMMUNITION

FEDERAL AMMUNITION

The Federal Cartridge Company of Minneapolis, Minnesota has fifty years experience under its belt manufacturing all types of ammunition. Long a leader in shotshell and rifle ammunition, Federal is now making a name for itself in the handgun field.

By sticking to a no-nonsense selection of popular cartridges, Federal can devote its time to constant improvement of the total line. Using Sierra bullets in the majority of its loadings, Federal has tapped a supplier that is known for quality control and accuracy. Cases are drawn and formed to extremely close tolerances, then passed by quality control only after close visual inspection.

For semiautomatic enthusiasts, Federal now markets nine different loadings in five different calibers. The smallest is on .25 caliber with a 50-grain bullet. Next is the .32 Auto. Traveling at 810 and 905 fps respectively, these are as small as you should go for home or backup use. The .380 ACP is next, offered in two versions, followed by the 9mm Luger, again in two bullet choices. The 9mm shoots either a 115-grain jacketed hollow point at 1,160 fps or a military type 123-grain metal-cased "Hardball" load. The pride of the auto line is undoubtably the .45 ACP, which Federal lists in three loadings; the 185 JHP, 185-grain metal case semi-wadcutter, and the standard 230-grain metal case round.

In the revolver section, there are nine listings for the .38 Special, four of which are available for police use. Federal load number 38B is a lead round nose blasting out of the standard 4-inch barrel at 755 fps. Next is a lead semi-wadcutter round, number 38C which gives a slight edge in stopping power. Catalog number 38D is a Plus-P load, which should be used only in modern guns with medium-sized frames because of its velocity of 915 fps and 294 foot-pounds of energy.

The best load of the bunch for all modern police departments to consider is Federal's number 38E. The combination of a Plus-P power rating, and a 125-grain JHP bullet with 248 foot-pounds, makes for a highly accurate, easily shootable, low-recoiling round.

Federal, like the rest of the independents, does not market any loading in the .41 Magnum. It's really a shame too, because this round could be used with some imaginative loadings to make it more popular in the eyes of many.

Federal also offers a .44 Remington Magnum in two bullet weights, 180 and 240 grains. The 180-grain bullet is a popular round for hunting. With a velocity of 1,610 fps and 1,045 foot-pounds, this load combines good power with a straight line trajectory for exceptional accuracy at moderate ranges.

One of the most accurate loads I tested was the .45 Colt. Fired in a Colt New Frontier .45, this load delivered 1 to 1¼-inch groups consistently at 25 yards. For the man willing to tolerate the hard trigger break and long hammer throw of the Colt, this is a good combination for target shooting and hunting.

Components are available from Federal in the form of cases and primers. Handloaders can rest assured that all cartridge cases made by Federal meet the requirements for long life and durability.

FRONTIER CARTRIDGES

FRONTIER/HORNADY AMMUNITION

Frontier cartridges are offered to the American handgunner in six calibers and twenty-seven loadings. Since Frontier is a subsidiary of Hornady, all use Hornady bullets, are packaged in fifty-round boxes, except for some .44 and .45 loadings, and are, as the company slogan reads, "accurate, deadly, and dependable."

Starting out with .380 Automatic, Frontier offers two choices; a 90-grain JHP for semi-defense use, followed by a 100-grain FMJ. I say semi-defense, because I believe that any round below the 9mm level is marginal in all but ideal conditions. Be that as it may, the 9mm Luger 90 and 115 JHP are logical selections for home defense where quarters are tight and neighbors are close. Many state or local police agencies use the "Big 9," which is overwhelming in terms of firepower. Also available in the full metal jacketed variety are loadings carrying 100- and 124-grain bullets.

The 124-grain selection includes the new Hornady FMJ/Flat Point bullet. Designed by Hornady and the Air Force ballistics unit, this bullet has proven itself in performance and flawless feeding. A while back, many shooters and law enforcement personnel complained of malfunctions in their Smith and Wesson Model 59s. Some bullet designs just did not function or feed in this weapon. My tests conclude that this factory loading goes through this gun like greased lightning. I've had no problems whatsoever with Frontier rounds fired in a M59, and years of tests in the field have borne this out conclusively.

The .38 Special No. 8, which includes Plus-P loading and jacketed and lead bullets, is an alternative which will please any shooting buff. Starting in at 110 grains, Frontier rounds are made in ascending weights of 125-grain JHP or JSP, 148-grain wadcutters, and the popular 158-grain bullet in JHP, JFP, and LRN (lead round nose) and SWC (semi-wadcutter) styles.

Next on the agenda, the .357 Magnum marches in with five loadings in two bullets weights; 125 and 158. It would really be a blessing for the silhouette boys if Frontier/Hornady would bring out their 160-grain FMJ bullet loaded high and safe enough for good knockdown power for those "way out yonder" metal targets.

The .44 Magnum is catalogued with two jacketed and one lead choice. Combining good bullet mass and expansion properties these .44 rounds are a favorite with hunters in the field.

Coming into the stretch, the .45 ACP, like its cousin the 9mm, shares the same FMJ flat nose bullet design. As mentioned before, for ease of functioning and accuracy these loads can't be beat, especially if your involvement in a combat match dictates a load you can put full confidence in. Other choices include a high-powered 185-grain JHP round, a 185-grain match SWC, a 200-grain SWC, and the standard military .230 round nose hardball equivalent.

As with most of the other companies involved in factory-loaded ammo, Frontier offers all of the bullets used in these loadings separately for those of you who like the performance of a particular design, but, because of the higher cost of commercial ammo, enjoy handloading your own.

Remington.

REMINGTON ARMS

With the honor of being the oldest arms and ammunition company in continuous production (since 1816), Remington Arms today continues in the spirit of its founder to provide the American shooter with high quality rifles, shotguns, handguns, and factory-loaded ammunition.

Remington is one of those vibrant companies, who with the help of its parent Dupont, keeps pouring millions of dollars into research and development projects not only to better its own products, but to share those findings and ideas with the public. Before introducing a new product to the general public, they take it to shooting matches, offer it to gun writers, and talk to plain ol' shooters like us to get feedback.

They also work in conjunction with other companies. For example, Remington and Smith & Wesson collaborated on the production of three famous magnum cartridges; the .357, .41, and .44. Smith & Wesson would design and build the gun, and Remington then would calculate all the necessary figures to come up with a round to match the designer's ideas. Both companies worked very closely together, and when something wasn't right, it was duly noted and corrected.

When the .44 Magnum was being considered as a production cartridge, Remington produced the fullhouse loads for the gun while it was still in the pre-production stages. After some testing it was noted that possibly a slight improvement could be made in the gun to better tolerate the heavy recoil. Smith complied and increased the barrel and frame from 39½ to 47 ounces. It made all the difference in the world, thanks to both companies working together to produce a superior product.

By and large though, Remington is the top producer of factory loadings by virtue of total listings. The present catalog has fifty different and varied loadings in twenty-three calibers, plus three blanks for stage or starting gun use.

For varmint hunters, Remington starts with the .22 Remington Jet and .221 Fireball, for which their XP-100 pistol is chambered. Progressing further we see the .25, .30 Luger, .32 S&W and .32 S&W Long, .32 Short and Long Colt, and finishing up with the .32 (7.65mm) Auto.

Looking at the .357 lineup we find Remington has obliged us with seven different loads. From 110-grain semi-jacketed hollow points to 158-grain lead and jacketed bullets, Remington pretty well covers this field.

Next come the 9mm, .380, .38 ACP, .38 Super, and .38 S&W varieties. The .38 Special has eleven listings to suit everyone from target shooters to small game hunters and law enforcement personnel.

Remington is one of two companies, the other being Winchester, to produce and market the .41 Remington Magnum. The .41 is a great cartridge, one that deserves more recognition. Since police departments seem to have little or no interest in it any more, my opinion is that Remington (or Winchester-Western) should now pick up the ball by developing new combinations and bullets for the handgun hunters in the field. Recent tests by myself indicate that a 170-grain jacketed bullet traveling at 1,450 fps-plus, makes for a highly accurate and dependable round. Now sixteen years old, the .41 perhaps needs a little shot in the arm to get it going again. Enough editorializing.

For those of you who must have the extra power the .44 "maggie" gives, Remington offers five versions starting with a super-zapping 180-grain semi-jacketed round buzzing around at 1,610 fps with 1,036 foot pounds under its belt. The others are of the 240-grain weight in lead and jacketed forms, plus a mild, medium velocity addition for the boys who must "plink" with a .44.

Rounding out the field, additional performers include the .44 Special, .45 Colt, .45 ACP with four loadings in two bullet weights, the .45 Auto Rim, and three blanks in three calibers.

In speaking of all these cartridges we tend to forget the components. Remington sells cases, bullets and primers for all cartridges produced by them. As expected, all are top quality, close-tolerance products.

SMITH & WESSON AMMUNITION

When one thinks in terms of quality in domestic handguns, one thinks of Smith & Wesson. Sticking with the most popular calibers, the Smith & Wesson Ammunition Company is offering the American handgunner a choice of 37 different cartridge loadings. This, according to our list at the beginning of the chapter, puts S&W ammo in third place if you go by numbers alone.

The .380 is first up with two choices; jacketed hollow pointed or full metal cased projectiles. As mentioned before, the .380 is not regarded as the optimum round for home defense or personal protection.

The 9mm is next and S&W gives us five selections, one of those with Nyclad covered bullets. Smith follows the pack with conventional offerings in the 9mm, that of jacketed bullets in the usual designs.

Since Smith & Wesson supplies the majority of handguns for police use, it comes as no surprise that they expend a great deal of time and energy to supply ammunition for those weapons. They produce no fewer than sixteen .38 Special loads of which six are Nyclad, and most are Plus-P or the equivalent. Only one other company, Winchester-Western comes close to that figure, and they too, are known for working closely with the men in blue.

The same holds true for the .357 caliber. Smith lists eleven factory loadings, more than even the two largest munitions firms, Remington and Winchester. Smith & Wesson also loads two .45 ACP rounds suitable for defense and target shooting. For the hunter, the S&W .44 Magnum is topped off with the industry standard 240-grain bullet.

Perhaps the biggest news to come out of any company in ages is the new covered bullets Smith & Wesson calls Nyclad. Nothing more than lead swaged bullets covered with a super tough nylon coating, these bullets are a boon to police departments who have to shoot most of the time on indoor ranges. These special rounds reduce bore leading to almost nothing, and moreover, they reduce the airborne lead and smoke pollutants by 89 per cent! To any range officer who spends hours qualifying the troops, Nyclad can mean the difference between staying healthy or getting lead poisoning.

Pulled bullets from Nyclad rounds show consistent charges and uniformity in the coating process. Micrometer readings on bullets sized and coated are all within .38 caliber specifications. Since the demand for Nyclad ammunition at present outstrips the supply, S&W currently does not offer the bullets separately for the handloader. We'll just have to wait our turn. Nevertheless, there will be additional loadings coming out in 9mm, .38 Special and .357 Magnum. In testing now, prototypes are being readied for the big bores, including the .45 ACP, and the hefty .44 Magnum. Smith & Wesson should be given a big pat on the back for this bold step in ammunition technology.

WINCHESTER-Western.

WINCHESTER-WESTERN

Ever since its beginnings, around 1866, Winchester Arms has been highly attuned to the needs of American shooters. First with smokeless powder in metallic cartridges, Winchester brought out this innovative discovery when it launched the famed Model 94 lever action rifle.

The Winchester-Western Company was not always known as such. Winchester, by itself, was a producer of quality long arms. When the Great Depression struck, Winchester, like many companies, had financial troubles. The Western Cartridge Company came to the rescue and the two merged. With expert guidance and advice from the Western Company, Winchester Arms survived those lean years to grow into the stable, energetic, and diversified arms maker it is today.

By glancing at the recent W-W catalog its easy to see how this company holds a good spot on the total market. Winchester-Western not only makes handgun ammo, but rimfire, centerfire rifle bullets, shotshells, shotguns, and rifles. The famous "94" has sold a couple of million copies, while the popular Model 70 is now sold in sixteen calibers. This, plus constant upgrading and improvements in desired features, helps the Winchester group remain popular with the shooting public.

W-W markets forty-nine different handgun loads in twenty cartridges. Like many others in the field W-W starts the lineup with the .25 Automatic. Progressing up the power scale we see the .256 Winchester Magnum, .30 Luger, .32 Auto, the S&W rounds (.32 Short and Long) and the .357 Magnum selections.

It's interesting to note that in the six listings of the .357, one round is really different than any other offered on the market by anyone. The one I am referring to is code X3572P; metal piercing. Also available in the .38 Special as a Plus-P loading, this round is obviously aimed at the law enforcement segment.

The 9mm is next, and W-W lists four loads currently being made. The 9mm Winchester Magnum, along with its sister round, the .45 Winchester Magnum, is this company's recent contribution to the field of commercialized "wildcat" cartridges. It is manufactured to be chambered in the new Wildey Automatic pistol, and Thompson/Center will offer barrels in one or both of these rounds for its Contender line soon.

The .38 Special enjoys heavy support at Winchester with twelve loads. From the 95-grain "Silvertip" hollow point to bullet weights of 110, 125, 148, 150, 158 and 200 grains, W-W blankets the market with a well-rounded group of entries.

Like Remington, this firm markets two rounds in the .41 Magnum, only two in the big .44, one in the .45 Colt and three in the .45 Automatic. An extensive listing, worthy of

CENTERFIRE PISTOL and

CALIBER	BULLET WT. GRS.	BULLET TYPE	SYMBOL	PRIMER
25 Automatic (6.35mm)	50	FMC	X25AP	1½-108
256 Winchester Magnum Super-X	60	OPE(HP)	X2561P	6½-116
30 Luger (7.65mm)	93	FMC	X30LP	1½-108
32 Automatic	71	FMC	X32AP	1½-108
32 Automatic	60	STHP	X32ASHP	1½-108
32 Smith & Wesson (inside lubricated)	85	Lead	X32SWP	1½-108
32 Smith & Wesson Long (inside lubricated)	98	Lead	X32SWLP	1½-108
32 Short Colt (greased)	80	Lead	X32SCP	1½-108
32 Long Colt (inside lubricated)	82	Lead	X32LCP	1½-108
357 Magnum Jacketed Hollow Point Super-X	110	JHP	X3573P	1½-108
357 Magnum Jacketed Hollow Point Super-X	125	JHP	X3576P	1½-108
357 Magnum Super-X (inside lubricated)	158	Lead	X3571P	1½-108
357 Magnum Jacketed Hollow Point Super-X	158	JHP	X3574P	1½-108
357 Magnum Jacketed Soft Point Super-X	158	JSP	X3575P	1½-108
357 Magnum Metal Piercing Super-X (inside lubricated, lead bearing)	158	Met. Pierc.	X3572P	1½-108
9 mm Luger (Parabellum)	95	JSP	X9MMJSP	1½-108
9 mm Luger (Parabellum)	100	JHP	X9MMJHP	1½-108
9 mm Luger (Parabellum)	115	FMC	X9LP	1½-108
9 mm Luger (Parabellum)	115	STHP	X9MMSHP	1½-108
9 mm Winchester Magnum	115	FMC	X9MMWM	1½-108
38 Smith & Wesson (inside lubricated)	145	Lead	X38SWP	1½-108
38 Special (inside lubricated)	158	Lead	X38S1P	1½-108
38 Special Metal Point (inside lubricated, lead bearing)	158	Met. Pt.	X38S2P	1½-108
38 Special Super Police (inside lubricated)	200	Lead	X38S3P	1½-108
38 Special Super-X Jacketed Hollow Point + P	110	JHP	X38S6PH	1½-108
38 Special Super-X Jacketed Hollow Point + P	125	JHP	X38S7PH	1½-108
38 Special Super-X + P	95	STHP	X38SSHP	1½-108
38 Special Super-X (inside lubricated) + P	150	Lead	X38S4P	1½-108
38 Special Metal Piercing Super-X (inside lubricated, lead bearing) + P	150	Met. Pierc.	X38S5P	1½-108
38 Special Super-X (inside lubricated) + P	158	Lead-HP	X38SPD	1½-108
38 Special Super-X Semi-Wad Cutter (inside lubricated) + P	158	Lead-SWC	X38WCP	1½-108
38 Special Super-Match and Match Mid-Range Clean Cutting (inside lubricated)	148	Lead-WC	X38SMRP	1½-108
38 Special Super Match (inside lubricated)	158	Lead	X38SMP	1½-108
38 Short Colt (greased)	130	Lead	X38SCP	1½-108
38 Long Colt (inside lubricated)	150	Lead	X38LCP	1½-108
38 Automatic Super-X (For use only in 38 Colt Super and Colt Commander Automatic Pistols)	125	JHP	X38A3P	1½-108
38 Automatic Super-X + P (For use only in 38 Colt Super and Colt Commander Automatic Pistols)	130	FMC	X38A1P	1½-108
38 Automatic (For all 38 Colt Automatic Pistols)	130	FMC	X38A2P	1½-108
380 Automatic	95	FMC	X380AP	1½-108
380 Automatic	85	STHP	X380ASHP	1½-108
41 Remington Magnum Super-X (inside lubricated)	210	Lead	X41MP	7-111F
41 Remington Magnum Super-X Jacketed Soft Point	210	JSP	X41MJSP	7-111F
44 Smith & Wesson Special (inside lubricated)	246	Lead	X44SP	7-111
44 Remington Magnum Super-X (Gas Check) (inside lubricated)	240	Lead	X44MP	7-111F
45 Colt (inside lubricated)	255	Lead	X45CP	7-111
45 Automatic	185	STHP	X45ASHP	7-111
45 Automatic	230	FMC	X45A1P	7-111
45 Automatic Super-Match Clean Cutting	185	FMC-WC	X45AWCP	7-111
45 Winchester Magnum	230	FMC	X45WM	7-111

Met. Pierc.-Metal Piercing FMC-Full Metal Case SP-Soft Point JHP-Jacketed Hollow Point JSP-Jacketed Soft Point Met. Pt.-Metal Point
OPE-Open Point Expanding HP-Hollow Point PP-Power Point WC-Wad Cutter SWC-Semi Wad Cutter STHP-Silvertip Hollow Point
Specifications are nominal. Test barrels are used to determine ballistics figures. Individual firearms may differ from these test barrel statistics.

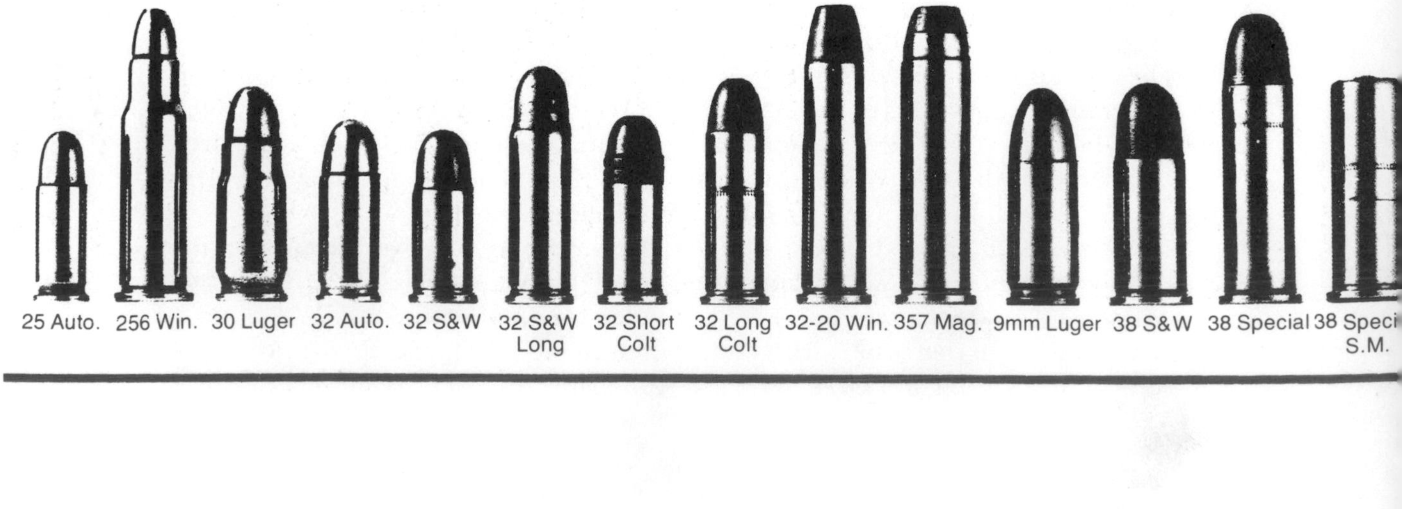

25 Auto. 256 Win. 30 Luger 32 Auto. 32 S&W 32 S&W Long 32 Short Colt 32 Long Colt 32-20 Win. 357 Mag. 9mm Luger 38 S&W 38 Special 38 Speci S.M.

REVOLVER CARTRIDGES

VELOCITY-FPS			ENERGY FT-LBS.			MID RANGE TRAJECTORY INCHES		BARREL LENGTH INCHES
MUZZLE	50 YDS.	100 YDS.	MUZZLE	50 YDS.	100 YDS.	50 YDS.	100 YDS.	
810	755	700	73	63	54	1.8	7.7	2
2350	2030	1760	735	550	415	0.3	1.1	8½
1220	1110	1040	305	255	225	0.9	3.5	4½
905	855	810	129	115	97	1.4	5.8	4
970	895	835	125	107	93	1.3	5.4	4
680	645	610	90	81	73	2.5	10.5	3
705	670	635	115	98	88	2.3	10.5	4
745	665	590	100	79	62	2.2	9.9	4
755	715	675	100	93	83	2.0	8.7	4
1295	1094	975	410	292	232	0.8	3.5	4V
1450	1240	1090	583	427	330	0.6	2.8	4V
1235	1104	1015	535	428	361	0.8	3.5	4V
1235	1104	1015	535	428	361	0.8	3.5	4V
1235	1104	1015	535	428	361	0.8	3.5	4V
1235	1104	1015	535	428	361	0.8	3.5	4V
1355	1140	1008	387	274	214	0.7	3.3	4
1320	1114	991	387	275	218	0.7	3.4	4
1155	1047	971	341	280	241	0.9	3.9	4
1225	1095	1007	383	306	259	0.8	3.6	4
1475	1264	1109	556	408	314	0.6	2.7	5
685	650	620	150	135	125	2.4	10.0	4
755	723	693	200	183	168	2.0	8.3	4V
755	723	693	200	183	168	2.0	8.3	4V
635	614	594	179	168	157	2.8	11.5	4V
1020	945	887	254	218	192	1.1	4.8	4V
945	898	858	248	224	204	1.3	5.4	4V
1100	1002	932	255	212	183	1.0	4.3	4V
910	870	835	276	252	232	1.4	5.7	4V
910	870	835	276	252	232	1.4	5.7	4V
915	878	844	294	270	250	1.4	5.6	4V
915	878	844	294	270	250	1.4	5.6	4V
710	634	566	166	132	105	2.4	10.8	4V
755	723	693	200	183	168	2.0	8.3	4V
730	685	645	150	130	115	2.2	9.4	6
730	700	670	175	165	150	2.1	8.8	6
1245	1105	1010	430	340	285	0.8	3.6	5
1280	1140	1050	475	375	320	0.8	3.4	5
1040	980	925	310	275	245	1.0	4.7	4½
955	865	785	190	160	130	1.4	5.9	3¾
1000	921	860	189	160	140	1.2	5.1	3¾
965	898	842	434	376	331	1.3	5.4	4V
1300	1162	1062	788	630	526	0.7	3.2	4V
755	725	695	310	285	265	2.0	8.3	6½
1350	1186	1069	971	749	608	0.7	3.1	4V
860	820	780	420	380	345	1.5	6.1	5½
1000	938	888	411	362	324	1.2	4.9	5
810	776	745	335	308	284	1.7	7.2	5
770	707	650	244	205	174	2.0	8.7	5
1400	1232	1107	1001	775	636	0.6	2.8	5

+P Ammunition with (+P) on the case head stamp is loaded to higher pressure. Use only in firearms designated for this cartridge and so recommended by the gun manufacturer.

V-Data is based on velocity obtained from 4″ vented barrels for revolver cartridges (38 Special, 357 Magnum, 41 Rem. Mag. and 44 Rem. Mag.) and unvented (solid) test barrels of the length specified for 9mm and 45 auto pistols.

38 Short Colt | 38 Long Colt | 38 Auto. | 380 Auto. | 38-40 Win. | 41 Rem. Mag. | 44 S&W Special | 44 Rem Mag. | 44-40 Win. | 45 Colt | 45 Auto. | 45 Auto S.T.H.P.

Courtesy: WINCHESTER-WESTERN

your consideration when you are thinking of factory ammo.

Further enhancing its place in the hearts of all shooters, Winchester has introduced their now successful "Silvertip" bullet mentioned before. Tremendous upset and expansion properties, and smooth functioning in automatic pistols are the major advantages of these projectiles, but for the present time these are available only in commercial loadings. For those of you wishing to experiment with these, availability is limited to the .38 Special (Plus-P), .45 Automatic, 9mm Luger, .380 and .32 Auto calibers. Complete specs are included here for your convenience.

The Silvertip bullets, like the S&W Nyclads, are improvements in the basic lead-swaged and jacketed bullets. Either one is a definite contribution to the field of ballistics and should be noted as such. These new designs are part of an era, a new generation of ideas, helping to keep the entire industry eager to investigate, design, and generate new products that will benefit all involved.

Ballistics Data
Winchester Silvertip Hollow Point vs. Conventional JHP Cartridges

Caliber	Bullet Wt.-Grs.	Bullet Style	Velocity Feet per Second Muzzle	Velocity Feet per Second 50 Yds.	Velocity Feet per Second 100 Yds.	Energy-Foot Pounds Muzzle	Energy-Foot Pounds 50 Yds.	Energy-Foot Pounds 100 Yds.	Mid-Range Trajectory 50 Yds.	Mid-Range Trajectory 100 Yds.
9mm Luger	115	STHP	1,225	1,095	1,007	383	306	259	0.8″	3.6″
9mm Luger	115	JHP	1,155	1,047	971	341	280	241	0.9″	3.9″
.45 Auto	185	STHP	1,000	938	888	411	362	324	1.2″	4.9″
.45 Auto	185	JHP	940	890	846	363	325	294	1.3″	5.5″

Specifications are nominal. Test barrels are used to determine ballistics figures. Individual firearms may differ from these test barrel statistics.

Ballistics Data
Winchester Western Silvertip Hollow Point Cartridges

Caliber	Bullet Wt.-Grs.	Bullet Style	Velocity Feet per Second Muzzle	Velocity Feet per Second 50 Yds.	Velocity Feet per Second 100 Yds.	Energy-Foot Pounds Muzzle	Energy-Foot Pounds 50 Yds.	Energy-Foot Pounds 100 Yds.	Mid-Range Trajectory 50 Yds.	Mid-Range Trajectory 100 Yds.
.38 Special*	95	STHP	1,100	1,002	932	255	212	183	1.0″	4.3″
.380 Auto**	85	STHP	1,000	921	860	189	160	140	1.2″	5.1″
.32 Auto**	60	STHP	970	895	835	125	107	93	1.3″	5.4″

*Data based on velocity from 4″ vented barrel.

**Specifications are nominal. Test barrels are used to determine ballistics figures. Individual firearms may differ from these test barrel statistics.

HOPPE'S
TRADE
NITRO
POWDER
NO.9
MARK
REG. U.S.
DANGER

TEN

Maintenance

GENERAL MAINTENANCE

The maintenance and care of a handgun should begin the very first day you bring it home. From that point on, your efforts will be the determining factor in keeping that piece in good repair and in working order. Since handguns rarely wear out with normal useage, the purchase of any fine gun at today's prices constitutes a sizable investment and it should be treated as such.

If any one of your guns is being used above the norm (for instance for target or combat shooting), that much extra care and effort must be given to compensate for the extra duty the gun is doing for you. I have competition guns today that are no worse off for wear just because of the added attention they receive. The bluing and grips will wear of course, but mechanically they are all in top-notch condition.

Although your new handgun is not plagued by the use of corrosive primers or old fashioned black powder, proper cleaning procedures must be used to ensure dependability in any given weapon no matter the weather, conditions or even the odds.

Like every job, we must have the right tools, equipment, and supplies. Your basic maintenance kit should include the following:

1. Pistol cleaning rod
2. Proper size patches
3. Brass bore brushes
4. Clean rags
5. Toothbrush
6. Gunsmith screwdrivers

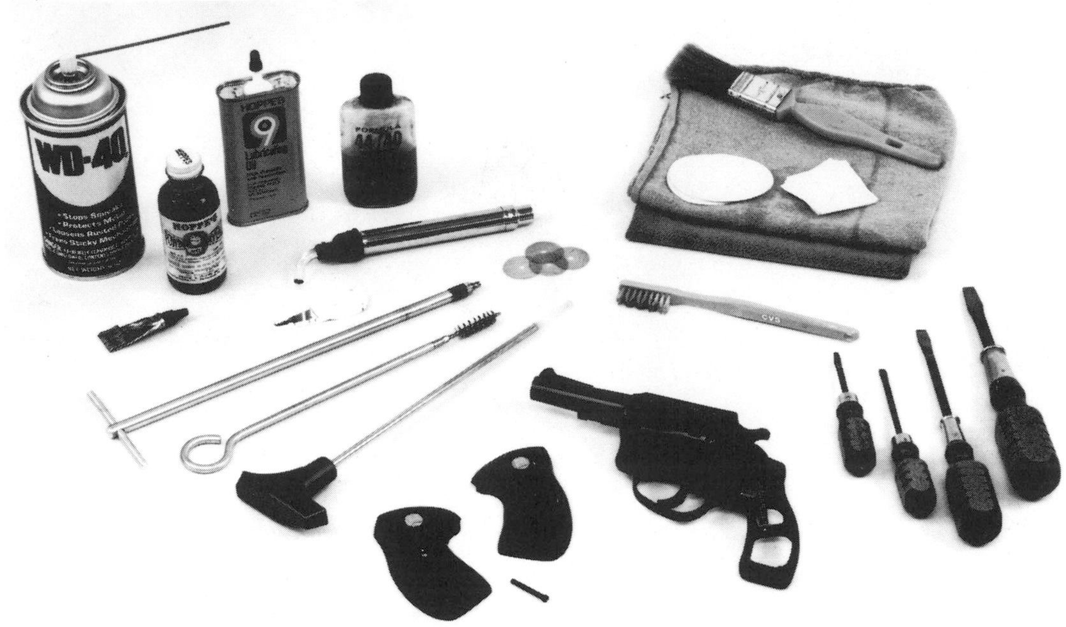

Maintenance supplies shown here are available at local gun dealers or hardware stores.

7. Lewis Lead Remover
8. Bore light or mirror
9. Hoppe's No. 9 (or similiar powder solvent)
10. Bore oil
11. WD-40 (or other appropriate lubricant)
12. Bottle of bluing solution (for touch-ups)

The above may seem like a long list, but if you purchase one of the gun cleaning kits on the market today, items 1, 2, 3, 9, and 10 will come with it. The clean rags and a toothbrush are easily found around the house. Probably the biggest outlay of cash will be for a good set of gunsmith screwdrivers. A set of eight different sizes runs about $20.00 and they are specially ground to fit just about every screwhead on handguns, rifles, and shotguns. They are worth the cost because ordinary household screwdrivers are not made for square edged screws, and they often slip out and mar the screwheads, or worse yet, the finish.

The bore light will enable you to check the rifling for powder or lead deposits and the Lewis Lead Remover will make the job easier to get rid of both.

Upon arriving home with your handgun, the first item to get rid of is the coating of factory grease or preservative. After removing the wood grips, brush the weapon down with a good solvent such as Perchlorate Ethylene (Perc) which is both fast drying and grease cutting. This will get most of the grease off and will enable you to check for nicks, scratches and other items that may warrant a trip back to the factory under the guarantee.

If everything is okay in that department, loosen the cylinder yoke, or crane, screw and remove the cylinder. Next, loosen and remove the sideplate screws, assuming the gun has a sideplate. To get at the innards, the flush-mounted side plate will have to come off. But wait! Do not pry it off by placing a screwdriver under it and wedging it against the frame. What you *must* do is tap the opposite side of the frame with a soft mallet or wooden

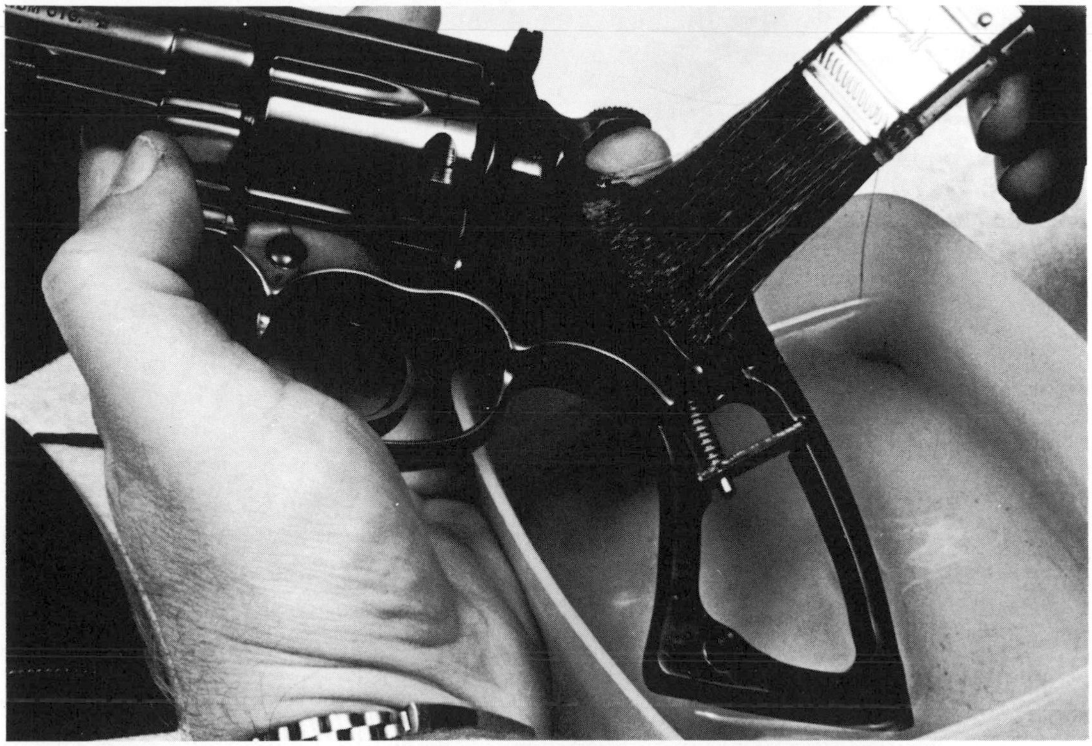

Upon arriving home with your new handgun, your first step should be a good top-to-bottom cleaning in solvent to get rid of the factory grease.

Never pry off the sideplate on any revolver. Gently tap the opposite side of the gun with a plastic or rubber hammer to dislodge the tightly fitting part.

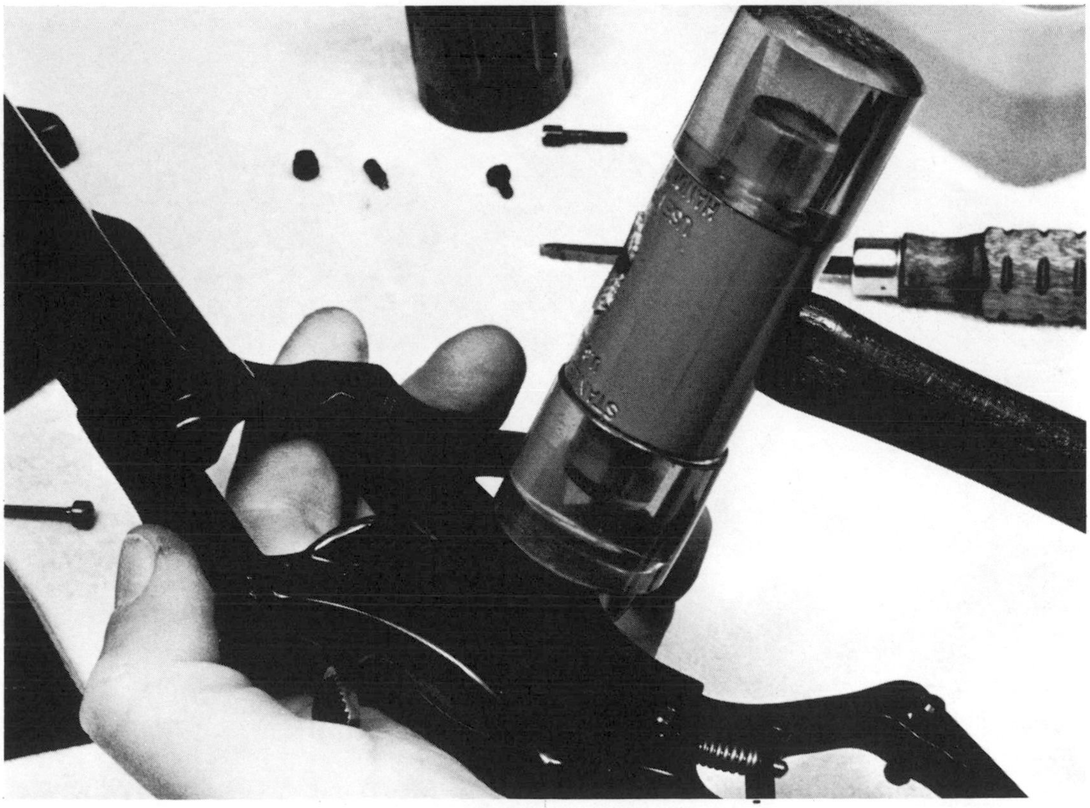

screwdriver handle. By tapping it gingerly, and with patience, the plate will drop from its hairline fitting and come off. This in turn will reveal the heart of the action, our next objective.

After a through flushing with the solvent, an inspection of all parts is in order. Checking for burrs and metal filings is my top priority. Looking closely, I check around the hammer, trigger, rebound slide, and spring. This examination may reveal particles under or close to the bolt. If not caught now, these minute flakes can cause damage later on. Since some of the internal parts are case hardened, wearing can accelerate once the skin of that surface is broken.

Next examine all pivot points for even contact and freedom of movement on the frame. If by chance you are mechanically inclined or can take the major parts out of the piece, so much the better. If you had rather not fool with that, a good brisk flushing as mentioned earlier should get all the factory residue out of the internal system.

Satisfied with that, take a drop of oil on a rag and go over all the parts you can get to. That one drop of oil on the cloth should last through the whole internal action. All you are trying to do is put some preservative into the pores of the metal. The less the better, you don't need a build-up inside to gum up everything. For myself, I like a gun on the dry side, to me they seem to function better and pick up less powder fouling or dust.

To finish up, take a toothpick and apply a small drop of oil on all pivot points, trigger/hammer contacts, and via capillary action, under the rebound slide and bolt. Fit the side plate back on, making sure the hammer block and associated parts are all in their proper places. Tap the plate on, tighten down all screws and check for smoothness of operation.

After cleaning the inside of the gun, a drop or two of oil at key pivot points will make for a smoother action. Don't overdo it!

The field stripping of an automatic is all that is necessary for routine maintenance and cleaning.

For single action revolvers, many of the same procedures apply. However since their lockwork cannot be exposed as readily as on a double action model, it is best to fill a bigger container with solvent and slosh the whole gun around in it. After a through drying, check for rough spots and burrs especially in the trigger, hammer, cylinder latch, and pawl areas. Additional inspection of the ejector assembly as a whole may show particles of grit or grease in the spring.

For semiautomatics, generally the same operations apply. After field-stripping the piece down as far as the factory instructions indicate, flush as before. Most semiautomatics break down to the slide, barrel, frame, recoil spring, and related parts. Magazines are a separate item and should be treated as such.

Check for burrs in the slide frame area and especially in the magazine well. Grit in this part of the frame will raise havoc later as tolerances here are close. Taking a toothpick or sharp object, test the interia firing pin to insure its proper function when the hammer falls. If need be, and it really doesn't hurt, push the firing pin in, drop the firing pin stop, and remove the pin for cleaning and inspection. No oil is wanted or needed here, as in cold weather oil will get gummy and slow the action of the firing pin down to a crawl.

A

B

C

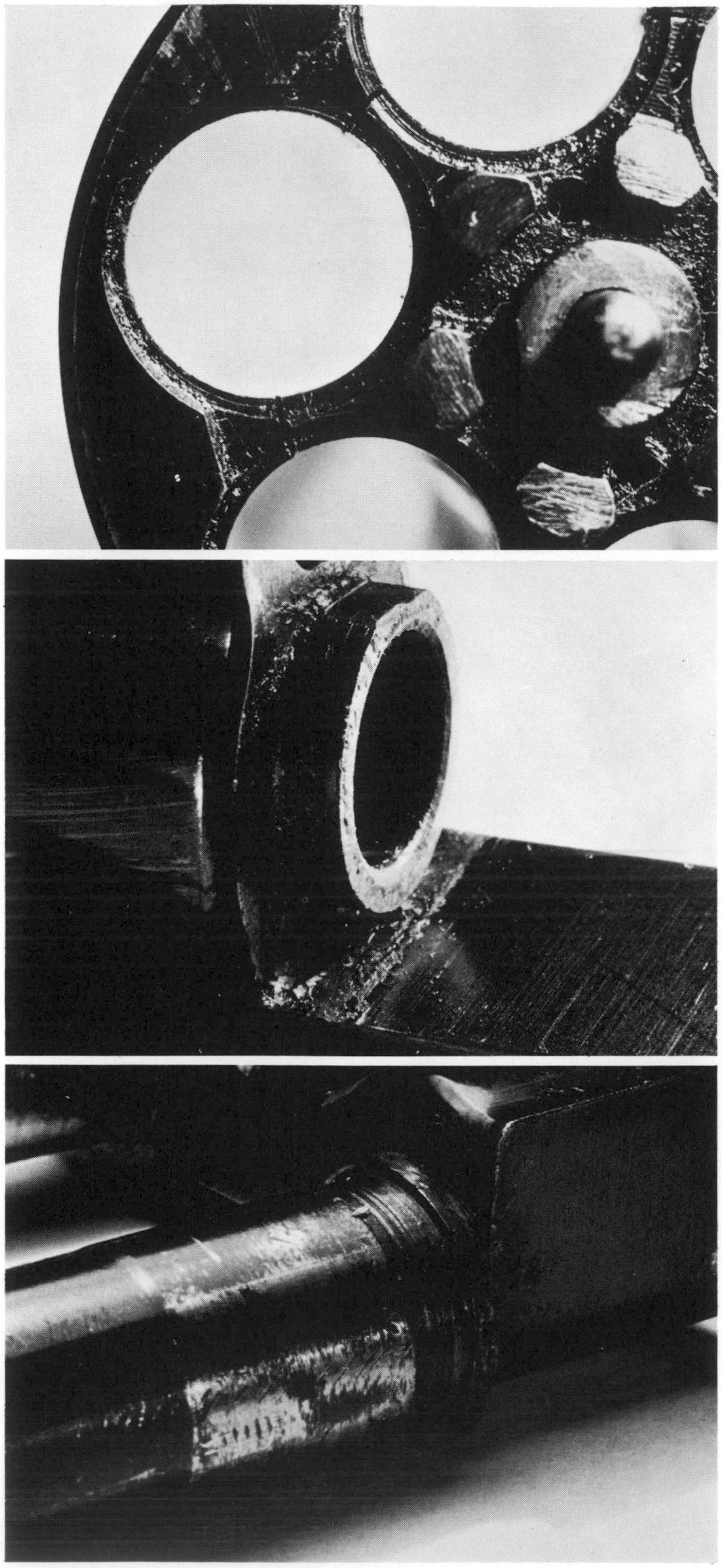

Extensive use of lead bullets can lead to the buildup of residue on major parts of a revolver. The rear of the cylinder (A), breech end (B), and cylinder crane (C) are all points that must be checked to ensure trouble-free service.

Sparingly coat the internal parts with a drop or two of good gun oil and reassemble. I always find the key to lubrication is in the user himself. The use of the gun will determine how much or how little to lubricate.

In any case, highly machined and polished areas like the bore and cylinder chambers must be protected between trips to the range. I find that if the piece is going to be used frequently, as in the case of the competition shooter, a patch with WD-40 down the bore and cylinders will suffice. It's easy to get out before firing and will protect enough without getting messy. For longer periods, over the winter for example, a light gun/bore oil is the best medicine.

Please remember though, if you go the oil route, make sure you clean it out before firing and after an extended storage period. Not only does oil thicken with age, it can raise pressures, possibly to a critical point.

Your first shooting and sighting-in session at the range will enable you to experience what high-powered modern ammunition can do to your nice shiny gun. Powder and lead fouling accounts for about 80 per cent of the debris around the cylinder, top strap, and crane; bullet fouling will take good care of the bore and chambers. However, routine cleaning will be less extensive than what we did before, on the then new handgun.

Strip the grips off and generously apply Hoppe's No. 9 all over the piece. If by chance you were out shooting lead bullets, now is the time to attack the bore and cylinders. Using the Lewis Lead Remover on a *dry bore* is the easiest method. Swabing the bore with a powder solvent only hinders the operation since the brass screened patches have a tendency

Whenever possible, barrels should be cleaned from the breech end to prevent the damage to lands and grooves on the muzzle end.

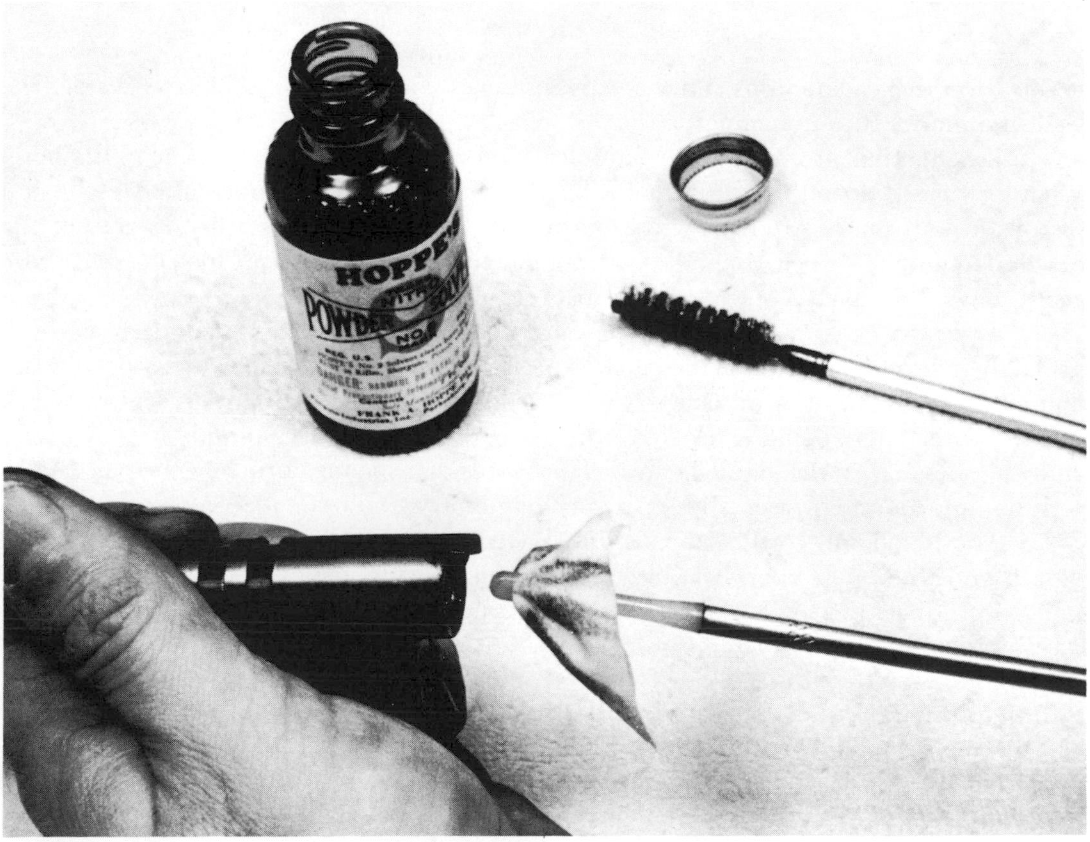

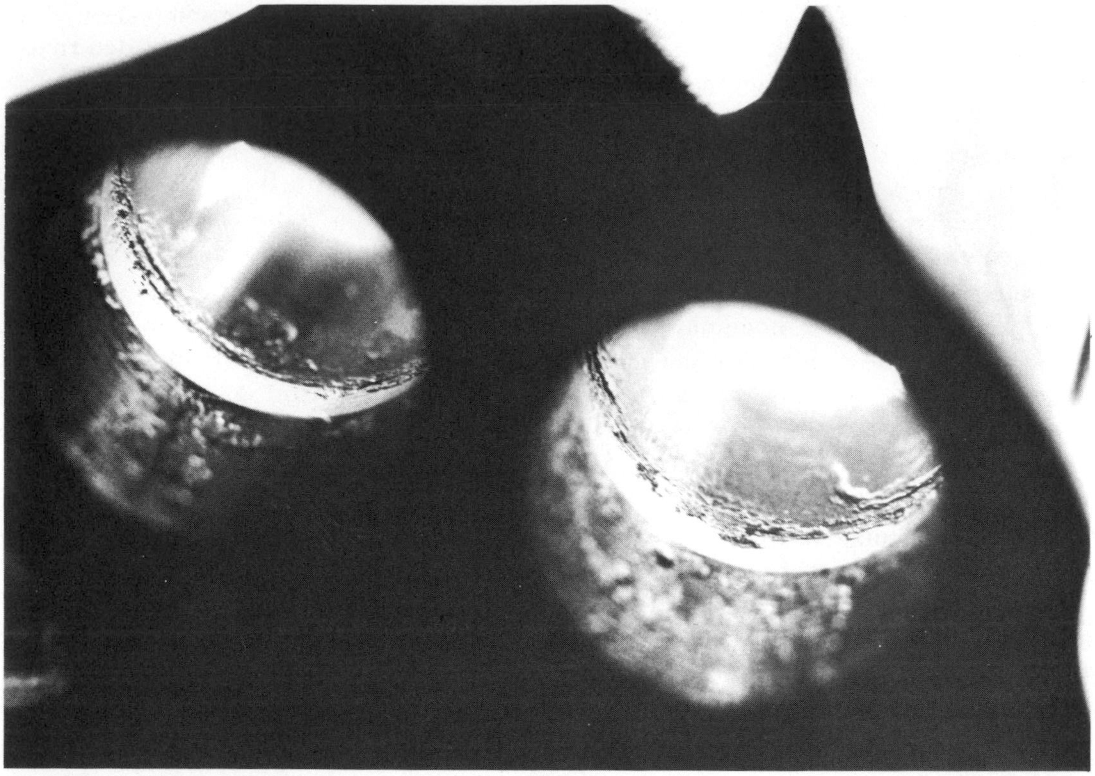

"Ringing" can be avoided in most cases by using .357 brass for .38 Special loads, .44 Magnum for .44 Specials, etc. This will lessen the gap the bullet has to jump, hence less chance of canting before beginning its trip down the barrel.

to skim over the lead deposits. A dry bore is best; in essence the brass patches will "grab" the lead in a more efficient manner.

Jacketed bullets on the other hand leave only a minute copper residue in the bore. What I generally do in this case is wet the bore and cylinders with Hoppe's, then let the gun sit for an hour or so. After the wait, go after the bore with a brass brush to get out the powder fouling and such, and follow with a patch or two to put clean solvent in the bore again. Lay all the pieces down for at least twenty-four hours.

The next day run a wet patch through the bore and cylinder chambers. You will probably note a green color on the patch. This is good; it means the solvent is working and doing its job. Follow up with some dry patches until the lands are bright and shiny. Lubricate the bore, and depending on where you are in the country (dry, humid, or wet climate) and what finish is on the gun (blue, nickel, or stainless), wipe the outside of the piece down with the appropriate preservative and put the gun away in a safe place.

Another point worth noting is this; you should always clean the barrel from the breech end when possible. This will be easy on all semiautomatics (barrel removed), Dan Wesson products and single shot pistols. When cleaning from the muzzle end, be extremely careful not to damage the lands or the crown of the muzzle. If need be, a false muzzle can be fashioned from a rifle case (for example a .30-06 case with the bottom cut off) but even with that, the first ¼-inch of the barrel will have to be cleaned separately. Either way, it's best to take your time and do the job right.

Another tip that will help to alleviate the tedious task of cleaning lead from cylinders is to use magnum cases when shooting lead bullets in revolvers so designated. To illustrate the point, one should use .357 cases instead of .38 Specials, .44 Magnums in place of .44 Specials. This will prevent a ring of lead (often called "ringing") from building up in front of the cases in the cylinders. Granted you may have to increase your powder charges by about 10 percent to compensate for differences in case volume, but you'll never have any trouble loading .38 or .44 Special jacketed loads in your revolver because of a lead or residue buildup.

Sights are easy to maintain. Just brush them off during regular maintenance to get rid of any powder residue that may turn those sharp black sights to a dull gray. No special lube is necessary; enough will seep in here and there to keep them in working condition. I have found though, on those sights that use a drift pin as a pivot on the front end (Colt Elliason and Ruger Micro Sights for example) that in most cases the pin should be removed, cleaned of foreign matter and both the hole and drift coated with LocTite before re-insertion. This will help it stay put.

Magazines are next. All should be completely submerged in a solvent before the initial firing and about once a year thereafter. Naturally, usage will determine cleaning frequency. S&W magazines are easy to take apart, Colt's a little harder. Unless there is a definite problem with the spring, there is little or no need to break them down for routine cleaning. I like my magazines to jump right out of the gun. Proper cleaning ensures that all the guiding surfaces inside the frame are clean. To test mine, I put an *unloaded* magazine in the gun, and holding it at a 45-degree angle, press the slide release. If everything is clean, and the spring tension is good, the magazine will literally "fly" out of the auto.

Care of the wood grips on any gun is probably the easiest of all. After checking for any cracks that eventually may split the grips under heavy recoil, all I do is apply a liberal coat of wax (on high-gloss grips) or boiled linseed oil on the oil-finished ones. This need not be done after every shooting session, but often enough to keep them looking good even after continued hard use.

TUNING

The word "tuning" has come into the handgunner's vocabulary more and more in recent years out of the fear that handgun manufacturers are putting less time into each gun because of customer demand and production schedules. This is partially true. One of the reasons is that highly sophisticated, tape-run machines are taking the place of the average worker. You must consider the days of the gunsmith apprentice are over, and with growing pay scales, machines produce more, at closer tolerances, and much quicker than do their human counterparts.

To tune a revolver or semiautomatic just for the sake of tuning is sometimes not justified. For one reason, once you start filing away at parts, you automatically void the guarantee, and two, you may loose the proper functioning of the piece in question. In all my evaluations of American guns, I have found that a good cleaning, removal of all burrs and a replacement trigger or main spring is more than enough for the average home gunsmith to tackle.

If you insist on having a tuned gun, or if your target gun could have a better pull, do one of two things. Write to some of the qualified men who advertise in the monthly gun journals, or if need be, call him and talk to him about your problem and ask what he can do to correct it. Ask for the names of others who have used his services in your part of the country. Call them, and then when you are satisfied, send your handgun to the gunsmith. He has the tools and specialized parts to do the tuning the right way to ensure consistent and reliable ignition everytime.

On factory premium target guns like the Smith & Wesson Model 52 and the Colt Gold Cup, contact the factory if all is not right. In most cases they can advise you of the proper trigger tolerances; then check them out on a good trigger gauge. Should anything be not to your satisfaction, ask to return the gun for factory work under the warranty.

Over the years, firearms have always been a source of pride and delight to their owners. To hold one, examine its clean lines, balance, and finish is a distinct pleasure. The fine art of cleaning a gun should never become a chore, for it is here that one gets to know his guns inside and out.

As far as cash outlays go, care, cleaning, and preventative maintenance are the least expensive of all gun-related activities. In the long run, considering the investment in tools and supplies, proper maintenance will prove to be one of the most profitable of all ventures encountered in the shooting sports.

Appendix

Metal Finishes for American Handguns

	Resistance to Corrosion	Resistance to Wear	How Applied	Available from
Bluing	Poor to Fair	Poor	Hot or Cold	Factory/ Gunsmiths
Nickel Plate	Good	Good	Cold	Factory or Gun Platers
Armoloy	Excellent	Good to Excellent	Cold	Armoloy, Inc.
Stainless Steel	Excellent	Excellent	Commercial metal, not a surface finish	Factory Stainless Guns
Hard Chrome	Excellent	Good to Excellent	Cold	Gun Platers

Basic Groove Diameters for Handguns

Caliber	Groove Diameter
9mm Luger	.354
.38 Special (Model 52)	.354
.38 Special/.357 Magnum	.357
.41 S&W Magnum	.410
.44 Special/.44 Magnum	.429
.45 ACP	.451
.45 Auto Rim	.451
.45 Colt (after 1945)	.451

Rifling Twist for American Handguns

9mm Luger	1 in 10″ S&W 1 in 16″ Colt
.38 Special	1 in 14″ Colt 1 in 17″ Charter Arms 1 in 18¾″ S&W
.38 Super	1 in 16″ Colt
.357 Magnum	1 in 14″ Colt 1 in 16″ Ruger 1 in 18″ Thompson/Center 1 in 18¾″ S&W
.41 Magnum	1 in 18¾″ S&W 1 in 20″ Ruger
.44 Magnum	1 in 20″ S&W and Ruger 1 in 22″ Thompson/Center
.45 Auto	1 in 16″ Colt
.45 Colt	1 in 16″ Colt

Shell Holder Chart (Handguns)

	Bonanza	**Lyman**	**Pacific**	**RCBS**
.22 Remington Jet	3	1	6	6
.221 Fireball	6	26	16	10
.30 Carbine	5	19	22	17
9mm Luger	18	12	8	16
.380 Auto	6	26	16	10
.38 Super	10	12	8	1
.38 Special	3	1	6	6
.357 Magnum	3	1	6	6
.41 Magnum	4	30	29	30
.44 Special	9	7	30	18
.44 Magnum	9	7	30	18
.44 Auto Mag	1	2	1	3
.45 Auto Rim	—	14A	31	8
.45 ACP	1	2	1	3
.45 Colt	21	11	32	20

Handgun Cartridge Interchangeability Chart

Cartridges in groups below will interchange

.25 Automatic
.25 Auto Colt (ACP)
.25 (6136) Auto Pistol
6.35mm Browning

.32 Colt Auto
.32 Auto Colt (ACP)
.32 (7.65mm) Auto
7.65 Auto Pistol

.32 S&W in .32 S&W Long, but never conversely

.32 S&W Long
.32 Colt New Police
.32 Colt Police Positive

.38 S&W
.38 Colt New Police
.38 Webley

.38 Colt Special
.38 S&W
.38 Special
.38 Special (Plus-P)
.38-44 Special (Plus-P)

.38 Special in .357 Magnum revolvers, but never conversely

.380 Automatic
9mm Browning Short (Corto Kurz)

9mm Luger
9mm Parabellum

.44 S&W Special or .44 Russian in a .44 Magnum, but never conversely

AMERICAN HANDGUN DIRECTORY

Accessories

Art Jewel Enterprises, Box 819, Berkeley, IL 60163
Bar-Sto Precision Machine, 633 S. Victory Blvd. Burbank, CA 91502
B-Square Co., Box 11281, Ft. Worth, TX 76109
J. M. Bucheimer Co., Box 280 Airport Road, Frederick, MD 21701
C'Arco, Box 2043, San Bernardino, CA 92406
Essex Arms Corp., Box 345 Island Pond, VT 05846
H & D Products, 8523 Canoga Ave., Canoga Park, CA 91304
Gil Hebard Guns, Box 1, Knoxville, IL 61448
Lee Custom Engineering Inc., Rt. 2, Hartford, WI 53027
Mag-Na-Port Arms, 30016 S. River Rd., Mt. Clemens, MI 48043
MTM, 5680 Webster Street, Dayton, OH 45414
Pachmayr, 1220 S. Grand Ave., Los Angeles, CA 90015
Pacific Tool Co., Drawer 2048 Ordnance Plant Rd., Grand Island, NE 68801
Pelson Inc., 13918 Equitable Rd. Cerritos, CA 90701
Safariland, 1914 S. Walker Ave., Monrovia, CA 91016
Williams Gun Sight Co., 7389 Lapeer Road, Davison, MI 48423

Ammunition (Commercial)

Federal Cartridge Co., 2700 Foshay Tower, Minneapolis, MN 55402
Frontier Cartridge Co., Inc., Box 1848, Grand Island, NE 68801
Lee E. Jurras & Assoc., Drawer F. Hagerman, NM 88232
Omark-CCI/Speer Inc., Box 856, Lewiston, ID 83501
Remington Arms Co., Bridgeport, CT 06602
Smith & Wesson Ammunition Co., 2399 Forman Road, Rock Creek, OH 44084
Winchester-Western, East Alton, IL 62024

Ammunition Components

Dupont Explosives Dept., Wilmington, DE 19898
Federal Cartridge Co., 2700 Foshay Tower, Minneapolis, MN 55402
Godfrey Reloading Supply, R.R. 1, Box 688, Brighton, IL 62012
Hercules Powder Co., 910 Market Street, Wilmington, DE 19899
Herter's Inc., Waseca, MN 56093
Hodgdon Powder Co., Inc., 7710 W. 50 Hwy., Shawnee Mission, KS 66202
Hornady Mfg., Co., Box 1848, Grand Island, NE 68801
Lyman Gun Sight Products, Middlefield, CT 06455
Markell Inc., 4115 Judah Street, San Francisco, CA 94112
Omark-CCI/Speer, Inc., Box 856, Lewiston, ID 83501
Remington-Peters, Bridgeport, CT 06602
Sierra Bullets, Inc., 10532 Painter Ave., Santa Fe Springs, CA 90670
Smith & Wesson Ammunition Co., 2399 Forman Rd., Rock Creek, OH 44084
Texas Contenders Firearms, 4127 Weslow Street, Houston, TX 77087
Thompson/Center Arms Corp., RFD 4, Box 2426, Rochester NH 03867
Winchester-Western, 275 Winchester Ave., New Haven, CT 06504

Centerfire Handguns

Arcadia Machine & Tool, 11666 McBean Drive, El Monte, CA 91732
Bauer Firearms, 34750 Klein Ave., Fraser, MI 48026
Charter Arms Corp., 430 Sniffens Lane, Stratford, CT 06497
Clerke Recreation Products, 2219 Main Street, Santa Monica, CA 90405
Colt, 150 Huyshope Ave., Hartford, CT 06102
Crown City Arms, Box 1126, Cortland, NY 13045
Harrington & Richardson, Industrial Rowe, Gardner, MA 01440
High Standard Sporting Firearms, 31 Prestige Park Circle, East Hartford, CT 06108
Interarms, 10 Prince Street, Alexandria, VA 22313
L. E. S., 3640 W. Dempster Street, Skokie, IL 60076
Merrill Co. Inc., Box 187, Rockwell City, IA 50579
Mikkenger Arms Co. Inc., 13509A Branch View, Farmers Branch, TX 75234
O. F. Mossberg & Sons Inc., Box 497, 7 Grasso Ave., North Haven, CT 06473
North American Arms Co. Box 158, Freedom, WY 83120
Pacific International Merchandising Corp., Box 8022, Sacramento, CA 95818
Remington Arms Co., 939 Barnum Ave., Bridgeport, CT 06602
Smith & Wesson, 2100 Roosevelt Ave., Springfield, MA 01101
Sterling Arms Corp., Box 385, 211 Grand Street, Lockport, NY 14094
Sturm, Ruger & Co. Inc., 63 Lacey Pl., Southport, CT 06490
Thompson/Center Arms, Rochester, NH 03867
United Sporting Arms Inc., 35 Gilpin Ave., Hauppauge, NY 11787
Dan Wesson Arms Inc., 293 Main Street, Monson, MA 01057
Western Arms Corp., 1107 Pen Rd., Santa Fe, NM 87501
Wichita Engineering & Supply Inc., 333 Lulu, Wichita, KS 67211

Cleaning Supplies

Armoloy, 204 E. Daggett Street, Ft. Worth, TX 76104
Brownell's Inc., Rt. 2, Box 1, Montezuma, IA 50171
Browning Arms, Rt. 4, Box 624-B, Arnold, MO 63010
Dri-Slide, Inc., Industrial Park, Fremont, MI 49412
Frank C. Hoppe Div., P.O. Box 97, Parkesburg, PA 19365
Jet-Aer Corp., 100 Sixth Ave., Paterson, NJ 07524
Numrich Arms Co., West Hurley, N.Y. 12491
Outers Laboratories, Box 37, Onalaska, WI 54650
Rig Products Co., Box 279, Oregon, IL 61061
Rocket Chemical Co. Inc., 5390 Napa Street, San Diego, CA 92110
WD-40 Co., 1061 Cudahy Pl., San Diego, CA 92110

Handgun Grips

Art Jewel Enterprises, Box 819, Berkeley, IL 60163
Beckelhymer's, Hidalgo & San Bernardo, Laredo, TX 78040
Fitz, Box 49697, Los Angeles, CA 90049
Franzite Grips Sports Inc., Box 683, Park Ridge, IL 60068
Fuzzy Farrant, 1235 W. Vine Ave., West Covina, CA 91790
J. L. Galef & Sons Inc., 85 Chambers Street, New York, NY 10007
Herrett's Stocks Inc., Box 741, Twin Falls, ID 83301
Hogue Combat Grips, Box 480, Morro Bay, CA 93442

Mershon Co., 1230 S. Grand Ave., Los Angeles, Ca 90015
Mustang Pistol Grips, Box 214, 28030 Del Rio Road, Temecula, CA 92390
Pachmayr, 1220 S. Grand Ave., Los Angeles, CA 90015
Schiermeier, Box 704, Twin Falls, ID 83301
Jay Scott Grips, 35 Market Street, Elmwood Park, NJ 07074
Sile Distributors, 7 Centre Market Pl., New York, NY 10013

Hearing Protectors

AO Safety Products, Div. of American Optical Corp., 14 Mechanic Street, Southbridge, Ma 01550
David Clark Co., 360 Franklin Street, Worcester, MA 01604
Sigma Eng. Co., 11320 Burbank Blvd., No. Hollywood, CA 91601
Safety Direct, P.O. Box 8907, Reno, NV 89507
Willson Safety Products Div., P.O. Box 622, Reading, PA 19603

Leather Goods

American Sales & Mfg. Co., Box 677, Laredo, TX 78040
Belt Slide Inc., Drawer 15303, Austin, TX 78761
Bianchi, 100 Calle Cortez, Temecula, CA 92390
Brauer Bros. Mfg. Co., 817 N. 17th, St. Louis, MO 63106
Browning, Rt. 1, Morgan, UT 84050
J. M. Bucheimer Co., Box 280, Airport Rd., Frederick, MD 21701
Chace Leather Products, 507 Alden Street, Fall River, MA 02722
Charter Arms Corp., 430 Sniffens Ln., Stratford, CT 06497
Don Hume, Box 351, Miami, OK 74354
The Hunter Co., 3300 W. 71st Ave., Westminister, CO 80030
Jackass Leather Co., 920 Waukegan Rd., Glenview, IL 60025
Kolpin Mfg., Co., Berlin, WI 54923
Lawman Leather Goods, Box 447, Katy, TX 77450
George Lawrence Co., 306 SW First Ave., Portland, OR 97204
S. D. Myres Leather Products, Box 357, Millis, MA 02054
Old West Quality Leathercraft Co., 2244-2 Main Street, Chula Vista, CA 92011
Ranger Leather Products Inc., Box 3198, East Camden, AR 71701
Rogers Holsters, Box 8028, Jacksonville, FL 32211
Roy's Custom Leather, Box G, Highway 132, Magnolia, AR 71753
Safariland, 1941 S. Walker Ave., Monrovia, CA 91016
Smith & Wesson Leather Co., 2100 Roosevelt Ave., Springfield, MA 01101
Thompson/Center Arms, Rochester, NH 03867
Triple K Mfg. Co., 568 Sixth Ave., San Diego, CA 92101
Whitco, Drawer 1712, Brownsville, TX 78520

Pistolsmiths

Bain & Davis, 559 W. Las Tunas Dr., San Gabriel, CA 91776
F. Bob Chow, 3185 Mission, San Francisco, CA 94110
Christy Gun Works, 875 57th Street, Sacramento, CA 95819
J. E. Clark, Rt. 2, Box 22A, Keithville, LA 71047
Giles .45 Shop, Rt. 1, Box 847, Odessa, FL 33556
Gil Hebard Guns, Box 1, Knoxville, IL 61448

Lee E. Jurras & Assoc., Drawer F. Hagerman, NM 88232
King's Gun Works, 1837 W. Glenoaks Blvd., Glendale, CA 91201
Mag-Na-Port Arms, 30016 S. River Rd., Mt. Clemens, MI 48043
Miniature Machine Co., 210 E. Popular, Deming, NM 88030
Pachmayr, 1220 S. Grand Ave., Los Angeles, CA 90015
Ron Power, Box 1604, Independence, MD 64055
Rupert's Gun Shop, Rt. 2, 8936 Amsden Road, Fenwick, MI 48834
L. W. Seecamp Co., Box 255, New Haven, CT 06502
Snapp's Gunshop, 6911 E. Washington Road, Clare, MI 48617
A. D. Swanson's, Box 606, Fallbrook, CA 92028
"300" Gunsmith Service, 4655 Washington Street, Denver, CO 80216
Trapper Gun Inc., 28019 Harper, St. Clair Shores, MI 48081
Walker Arms Co. Inc., Rt. 2, Box 73, Selma, AL 36701
Wilson's Gun Shop, 101-103 Public Sq., Berryville, AR 72616

Reloading Equipment

B-Square Eng. Co., Box 11281, Ft. Worth, TX 76110
Bonanza Sports, Inc., 412 Western Ave., Faribault, MN 55021
C-H Tool & Die Corp., Box L, Owen, WI 54460
Camdex, Inc., 23880 Hoover Road, Warren, MI 48089
Clymer Mfg. Co., 14241 W. 11 Mile Road, Oak Park, MI 48237
D. R. Corbin, Box 758, Phoenix, OR 97535
Fitz, Box 49697, Los Angeles, CA 90049
Flambeau Plastics, 801 Lynn, Baraboo, WI 53913
Forster Products, Inc., 82 E. Lanark Ave., Lanark, IL 61046
Gopher Shooter's Supply, Box 278, Faribault, MN 55021
Hensley & Gibbs, Box 10, Murphy, OR 97533
Herters, Inc. RR1, Waseca, Minn. 56093
B. E. Hodgdon, Inc., 7710 W. 50 Hwy., Shawnee Mission, KS 66202
Hornady (see Pacific)
Hulme Firearm Serv., Box 83, Millbrae, CA 94030
Lee Custom Engineering, 46 E. Jackson, Hartford, WI 53027
Lyman Gun Sight Products, Middlefield, CT 06455
MTM Molded Prod., 5680 Webster St., Dayton, OH 45414
Ohaus Scale Corp., 29 Hanover Road, Florham Park, NJ 07932
Omark-RCBS Operations, Box 1919, Oroville, CA 95965
Omark-CCI/Speer, Inc. Box 856, Lewiston, ID 83501
Pacific Tool Co., P. O. Drawer 2048, Ordnance Plant Road, Grand Island, NE 68801
Marian Powley, 19 Sugarplum Road, Levitown, PA 10956
Quinetics Corp., Box 13237, San Antonio, TX 78213
RCBS, Inc. (see Omark)
Redding Inc., 114 Starr Road, Cortland, NY 13045
Remco, 1404 Whitesboro Street, Utica, NY 13502
Rochester Lead Works, Rochester, NY 14608
SEACO Rel. Inc., P. O. Box 778, Carpinteria, CA 93013
Sandia Die & Cartridge Co., Rte. 5, Box 5400, Albuquerque, NM 87123
Remington Arms Co., Bridgeport, CN 06602
Sierra Bullets Inc., 10532 Painter Ave., Santa Fe Springs, CA 90670

Smith & Wesson Ammunition Co. Inc., 2399 Forman Road, Rock Creek, OH 44084
Star Machine, Inc., 418 10th Ave., San Diego, CA 92101
Texan Reloaders, Inc. P. O. Box 5355, Dallas TX 75222
L. E. Wilson, Inc., P. O. Box 324, 404 Pioneer Ave., Cashmere, WI 98815

Sights, Metallic and Optical

Bo-Mar Tool & Mfg. Co., Box 168, Carthage, TX 75633
B-Square Co., Box 11281, Ft. Worth, TX 76109
Maynard P. Buehler, Inc., 17 Orinda Highway, Orinda, CA 94563
Bushnell Optical Co., 2828 E. Foothill Blvd., Pasadena, CA 91107
Christy Gun Works, 875 57 Street, Sacramento, CA 95819
Conetrol, Highway 123 South, Seguin, TX 78155
Herter's Inc., Waseca, MN 56093
Hutson Corp., Box 1127, Arlington, TX 76010
King's Gun Works, 1837 Glenoaks Blvd., Glendale, CA 91201
Leupold & Stevens Inc., Box 688, Beaverton, OR 97005
Lyman Gun Sight Products, Middlefield, CT 06455
Micro Sight Co., 242 Harbor Blvd., Belmont, CA 94002
Miniature Machine Co., 210 E. Poplar, Deming, NM 88030
Poly-Choke, Box 296, Hartford, CT 06101
Redfield, 5800 E. Jewell Ave., Denver, CO 80224
Tasco, 1075 NW 71st Street, Miami, FL 33138
Thompson/Center Arms, Rochester, NH 03867
Williams Gun Sight Co., 6810 Lapeer Road, Davison, MI 48423

Special Products

Armoloy, 204 E. Daggett Street, Ft. Worth, TX 76104
Bonanza Sports Mfg., 412 Western Ave., Faribault, MN 55021
Brownell's, Main & Third, Montezuma, IA 50171
The Chapman Mfg. Co., Rt. 17, Durham, CT 06422
Eagle Sight Co., Box A-961 Palmdale, CA 93550
Gun Specialties, Box 31, College Park, GA 30337
H. K. S. Tool Products, 132 Fifth St., Dayton, KY 41074
Interarms, 10 Prince Street, Alexandria, VA 22313
Jet-Aer Corp., 100 Sixth Ave., Paterson, NJ 07524
Kart Sporting Arms Corp., Rt. 2, Box 929, Broad Avenue, Riverhead, NY 11901
Mag-Na-Port Arms, 30016 S. River Road, Mt. Clemens, MI 48043
Safariland, 1941 S. Walker Ave., Monrovia, CA 91016
Trapper Gun Inc., 28019 Harper, St. Clair Shores, MI 48081
Whitney Sales Inc., 6742 Tampa Ave., Reseda, CA 91336
David Woodruff, Box 5, Bear, DE 19701

Index